Fodor's

MONTRÉAL &
QUÉBEC CITY

WELCOME TO MONTRÉAL AND QUÉBEC CITY

France's old-world charm lives on in Montréal and Québec City, two enchanting Canadian cities with rich pasts. Their French heritage is ever-present, from the language to wonderful food to pockets of cobblestoned streets. Cosmopolitan Montréal rocks with lively cultural and shopping scenes; smaller Québec City is jam-packed with history. Visits are lovely year-round: summer brings festivals galore; spring and fall are perfect for city strolls and countryside jaunts; and winter, despite the cold, heats up with Winter Carnival, hot chocolate, and snow sports.

TOP REASONS TO GO

★ **French food:** *Haute* to hearty—including *poutine*, fries with cheese curds and gravy.

★ **Shopping:** Fashion-forward local designers, top-notch cold-weather wear, Inuit art.

★ **Festivals:** From Winter Carnival to Jazz Fest, Quebecers throw great parties all year.

★ **History:** Museums, monuments, and ancient fortifications bring the past to life.

★ **Hockey:** Tickets for Habs games are hard to get, but catch a game on TV at a local bar.

★ **Fun in the snow:** Winter brings ice-skating, tobogganing, skiing, and snowshoeing.

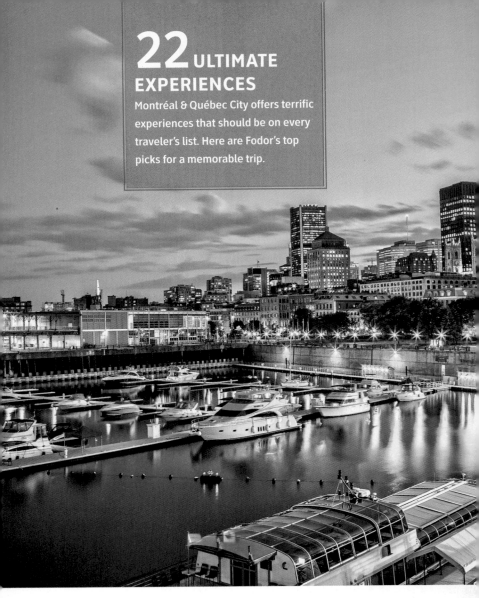

22 ULTIMATE EXPERIENCES

Montréal & Québec City offers terrific experiences that should be on every traveler's list. Here are Fodor's top picks for a memorable trip.

1 Exploring the Old Port

One of the city's most popular parks, Montréal's Old Port is the place to gallery-hop, cycle, stroll, take a jet boat ride on the Lachine Rapids, or just explore the waterfront at your leisure. *(Ch. 2)*

2 Strolling Rue du Petit-Champlain

Take the funicular down to explore Québec City's lamp-lit (and car-free!) Rue du Petit-Champlain—North America's oldest commercial street, and its surrounding lanes lined with centuries-old town houses, bistros, and unique boutiques. *(Ch. 10)*

3 Embracing Winter at Carnaval de Québec

One of the world's biggest—and oldest—winter celebrations, this festive midwinter fête encompasses scores of activities that are bound to make you forget it's below zero. *(Ch. 10)*

4 The Citadel

Québec City's La Citadelle is home to Canada's Royal 22nd Regiment, who turn out in bearskin caps and scarlet tunics for the daily changing of the guard. *(Ch. 10)*

5 Montmorency Falls

Ride an aerial cable car to admire the chute from above, or—if you're really daring—cross the suspension bridge above the Côte-de-Beaupré's breathtaking falls. *(Ch. 11)*

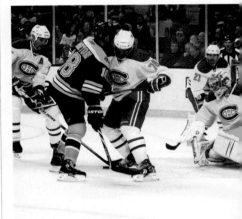

6 Île d'Orléans

This so-called Garden of Québec is a bucolic wonderland of centuries-old summer cottages, ancient churches, wineries, cider mills, culinary artisans, and produce stands. *(Ch. 11)*

7 Cheering the Habs

Nothing is more Canadian than hockey, and the fan energy and enthusiasm at a Montréal Canadiens (aka "Habs") game provides sport for even the most reluctant sports fan. *(Ch. 8)*

8 The Basilique Notre-Dame-de-Montréal

Everything about this magnificent Roman Catholic basilica is grand, from the 228-foot twin steeples to the 7,000-pipe organ to the 24-carat gold stars on the ceiling. *(Ch. 2)*

9 Dufferin Terrace

The long boardwalk in front of the Château Frontenac is one of Québec City's most romantic— and photogenic—spots. *(Ch. 10)*

10 The Gay Village

Once a tiny nook carved out of downtown Montréal, The Village is great for shopping, strolling, people watching, and partying. *(Ch. 2)*

11 Ferrying to Lévis

Treat yourself to views of a lifetime by taking the quick (and inexpensive) 20-minute trip aboard the commuter ferry from Québec City to the town of Lévis. *(Ch. 10)*

12 Climbing Parc du Mont Royal

Snowshoe, ski, or hike a network of trails leading through the dense wooded areas of this hill overlooking downtown Montréal. *(Ch. 2)*

13 Eating Poutine

Québec City has some of the best spots to sample poutine (fries drenched in gravy and cheese curds) including the Chez Ashton chain and Snack Bar St-Jean. *(Ch. 10)*

14 Musée des Beaux-Arts de Montréal

One of Canada's oldest museums has an exceptional collection of art including works by Rembrandt, Renoir, and Picasso, all housed in a former church. *(Ch. 2)*

15 Marché du Vieux-Port

At this foodies' haven in Québec City you'll be tempted by maple syrup products, chocolates, iced cider, and other local specialties. *(Ch. 10)*

16 Plains of Abraham

Filled with Québec City's runners, picnickers, and cyclists, it's hard to imagine the fierce battles between Empires that unfolded on this very spot in the 18th century. *(Ch. 10)*

17 Taking in Old Montréal

Shops and restaurants are touristy in this part of town, so your time is best spent winding through the old lamp-lit streets and marvelling at the architecture. *(Ch. 2)*

18 Jean Talon Market

As well flowers, fruits, and vegetables, Montréal's European style open market has food stands with crêpes, samosas, Turkish pastries and more. *(Ch. 2)*

19 Skiing Mont-Tremblant

With 662 acres of skiable terrain, this towering peak of the Laurentian Mountains, northwest of Montréal, is one of North America's top ski resorts. *(Ch. 9)*

20 Jazz Fest

Montréal's annual International Jazz Festival is the largest in the world, attracting millions of fans for more than 400 (mostly free!) concerts every summer. *(Ch. 1)*

21 Oratoire Saint-Joseph

One of Montréal's most visited sites, the world's largest shrine to St. Joseph literally brings visitors to their knees to climb the 99 steps to its front door. *(Ch. 2)*

22 Old Québec

A UNESCO World Heritage site, the enchanting Old City (Vieux Québec) features charming cobblestone streets lined with cafés, shops, galleries, and elaborate cathedrals. *(Ch. 10)*

Fodor's MONTRÉAL & QUÉBEC CITY

Editorial: Douglas Stallings, *Editorial Director*; Margaret Kelly, Jacinta O'Halloran, *Senior Editors*; Kayla Becker, Alexis Kelly, and Amanda Sadlowski, *Editors*; Teddy Minford, *Content Editor*; Rachael Roth, *Content Manager*

Design: Tina Malaney, *Design and Production Director*; Jessica Gonzalez, *Production Designer*

Photography: Jennifer Arnow, *Senior Photo Editor*

Maps: Rebecca Baer, *Senior Map Editor*; Mark Stroud and David Lindroth, *Cartographers*

Production: Jennifer DePrima, *Editorial Production Manager*; Carrie Parker, *Senior Production Editor*; Elyse Rozelle, *Production Editor*

Business & Operations: Chuck Hoover, *Chief Marketing Officer*; Joy Lai, *Vice President and General Manager*; Stephen Horowitz, *Director of Business Development and Revenue Operations*; Tara McCrillis, *Director of Publishing Operations*; Eliza D. Aceves, *Content Operations Manager and Strategist*

Public Relations and Marketing: Joe Ewaskiw, *Manager*; Esther Su, *Marketing Manager*

Writers: Chris Barry, Rémy Charest, Joanne Latimer, Marie-Eve Vallieres, Elizabeth Warkentin

Editor: Jacinta O'Halloran

Production Editor: Jennifer DePrima

Production Design: Liliana Guia

29th Edition

ISBN 978-1-64097-024-3

ISSN 1525–5867

All details in this book are based on information supplied to us at press time. Always confirm information when it matters, especially if you're making a detour to visit a specific place. Fodor's expressly disclaims any liability, loss, or risk, personal or otherwise, that is incurred as a consequence of the use of any of the contents of this book.

SPECIAL SALES

This book is available at special discounts for bulk purchases for sales promotions or premiums. For more information, e-mail SpecialMarkets@fodors.com.

PRINTED IN THE UNITED STATES OF AMERICA

10 9 8 7 6 5 4 3 2 1

CONTENTS

CONTENTS

MAPS

ABOUT
THIS GUIDE

Fodor's Recommendations

Everything in this guide is worth doing—we don't cover what isn't—but exceptional sights, hotels, and restaurants are recognized with additional accolades. Fodor'sChoice★ indicates our top recommendations. Care to nominate a new place? Visit Fodors.com/contact-us.

Trip Costs

We list prices wherever possible to help you budget well. Hotel and restaurant price categories from $ to $$$$ are noted alongside each recommendation. For hotels, we include the lowest cost of a standard double room in high season. For restaurants, we cite the average price of a main course at dinner or, if dinner isn't served, at lunch. For attractions, we always list adult admission fees; discounts are usually available for children, students, and senior citizens.

Hotels

Our local writers vet every hotel to recommend the best overnights in each price category, from budget to expensive. Unless otherwise specified, you can expect private bath, phone, and TV in your room. For expanded hotel reviews, facilities, and deals, visit Fodors.com.

Top Picks	Hotels &
★ Fodor'sChoice	Restaurants
	⊞ Hotel
Listings	↗ Number of
✉ Address	rooms
✉ Branch address	⑩ Meal plans
☎ Telephone	✕ Restaurant
🖶 Fax	⬥ Reservations
⊕ Website	🏛 Dress code
✉ E-mail	🗖 No credit cards
✉ Admission fee	$ Price
⊙ Open/closed	
times	**Other**
Ⓜ Subway	⇨ See also
✛ Directions or	☞ Take note
Map coordinates	🏌 Golf facilities

Restaurants

Unless we state otherwise, restaurants are open for lunch and dinner daily. We mention dress code only when there's a specific requirement and reservations only when they're essential or not accepted.

Credit Cards

The hotels and restaurants in this guide typically accept credit cards. If not, we'll say so.

EUGENE FODOR

Hungarian-born Eugene Fodor (1905–91) began his travel career as an interpreter on a French cruise ship. The experience inspired him to write *On the Continent* (1936), the first guidebook to receive annual updates and discuss a country's way of life as well as its sights. Fodor later joined the U.S. Army and worked for the OSS in World War II. After the war, he kept up his intelligence work while expanding his guidebook series. During the Cold War, many guides were written by fellow agents who understood the value of insider information. Today's guides continue Fodor's legacy by providing travelers with timely coverage, insider tips, and cultural context.

EXPERIENCE
MONTRÉAL AND
QUÉBEC CITY

1

MONTRÉAL & QUÉBEC CITY TODAY

Ask Quebecois what they think of their city, and they'll rattle off tons of things to improve: potholes, bureaucratic corruption, construction strikes, parking meters—the list goes on. Then ask them if they would move anywhere else in the world, and the answer is always a confident no. Any indication that the cold weather is gone, and Quebecois will head to an outdoor terrace, or *terrasse,* pronounced terr-ASS by Anglo Quebecois.

There's Music in the Air

With the massive success of home-grown band Arcade Fire, international record labels are paying more and more attention to the city. The emerging Montréal music scene is comparable to Seattle's Indie music explosion of the 1990s. Bands such as Milk and Bone, Half Moon Run, Grimes, and Chromeo are making Montréal concert halls the place to be.

Political Progress

Quebecois went to the polling stations in April 2014, and the result surprised not just locals but all Canadians; the incumbent separatist party, the Parti-Québécois, lost by a majority vote to the Liberal Party. With the Liberals currently in power, talk of provincial separation has ceased—at least until the next provincial election. The economy, particularly in Montréal, has been on an upswing and the "Pastagate" nonsense—in which the French-language police, responsible for the preservation of the language, wanted to ban the word "pasta" from an Italian restaurant menu—has ended.

On the municipal level, Montrealers were surprised with the unexpected win, in November 2017, of Valérie Plante, the first woman ever to be elected mayor of Montréal with a cheeky ad campaign touting her as "the best man for the job." Young (43), feisty, and affable, Plante campaigned on a promise to massively expand the subway system, make the city greener and more pedestrian and bike-friendly, and to invest in social housing. She also campaigned on a promise to ease traffic woes and put an end to calèches (horse-drawn carriages). Watch this space.

The Arts Make a Splash

Things are looking up, too, in Montréal's Downtown arts district, the Quartier des Spectacles, as it continues to expand and grow. It's also the only place in the world with year-round artistic projections on building facades and windows. Enjoy

WHAT WE'RE TALKING ABOUT

Montréal's municipal flag was updated in late 2017 to demonstrate the importance of indigenous peoples to the history and culture of the city. The white pine, a First Nations symbol of peace and harmony, was added to the center of the flag joining the fleur-de-lys, which represents Montréal's French history, the rose of the House of Lancaster symbolizing the city's British heritage, a clover for Irish descendants, and a thistle for Scottish descendants. Also in the spirit of reconciliation, City Hall says it will change the name of Amherst Street as it honored an 18th-century British general, Lord Jeffrey Amherst, who advocated the use of small-pox-infected blankets as a weapon against indigenous people. Suggestions include renaming the street after a First Nations chief.

the views, but watch your step—water fountains shoot up beneath many of its concrete walkways.

As for Québec City, it's emerging as a premier stop for summer concerts and festivals. On the Plains of Abraham, outdoor performances accommodate more than 250,000 spectators, and people come from all over to watch under the stars. Past performers including Madonna, Céline Dion, Paul McCartney, Rush, and Lady Gaga have helped put Québec City on the entertainment map.

Sports Fans in High Places

Montréal's soccer team, The Impact, began competing in Major League Soccer in 2012, which helped solidify its fan base. The addition of popular heavyweights such as Argentinian midfielder Ignacio Piatti, whose contract was extended in late 2017, means it is continuing to grow as a spectator sport and local attraction.

Not wanting to feel left out, Québec City's mayor, Regis Labeaume, decided that one of his priorities was to get an NHL team back in town. He built a C$400 million stadium, which opened in September 2015, and has been prospected as a potential venue for a new NHL team in the city.

Pedal Power

Montréal has come a long way since its 2009 introduction of Bixi, a bike-sharing scheme similar to those in New York City, London, Chicago, and many other cities. Using the system, you pay to take a bicycle from a rental station and then leave it at a station near your destination. Every year more bike paths are added to city streets (there are at least 500 km [300 miles] of them now), much to the chagrin of some drivers. In 2014, Bixi declared bankruptcy, but City Hall stepped in to defend the viability of the controversial scheme. In 2017, Bixi solidified its network (there are now 6,250 bikes and 540 stations) and the scheme enjoyed a record-breaking year, with more than 258,000 people taking a grand total of 4.8 million trips. Local fans—and visitors—are keeping their fingers crossed that Bixi is here to stay.

Food trucks are here to stay! There are 43 official food trucks in 31 fixed locations throughout the city, and we're not talking hot dog carts. Montréal's food trucks represent the cream of the city's culinary crop, with pulled-pork sandwiches, gourmet grilled cheese, oysters, dim sum, and other artisanal treats. You can check them out in one location on the first Friday of every month (May through October) when they all congregate at the Olympic Stadium Park. Come hungry.

Locals and visitors who love fast cars, loud engines, and a wild party weekend, will be happy to hear that the Grand Prix of Montréal has been renewed until at least 2024. Earplugs not included.

WHAT'S WHERE

1 Montréal. Both Montréal and the island on which it stands take their name from Mont-Royal, a stubby plug of tree-covered igneous rock that rises high above the surrounding cityscape. This is a bustling, multiethnic city of neighborhoods, from the historic Old City to the hip Plateau.

2 The Laurentians. The Laurentians (les Laurentides) encompass thousands of miles of forests, mountains, and lakes, but for many people the draw is Mont-Tremblant and its world-class ski slopes. At just 1½ hours' drive from Montréal, the area has also become a favorite weekend golf destination.

3 The Eastern Townships. Called les Cantons de l'Est in French, the Eastern Townships region has quaint architecture and rolling hills that might remind you of New England. Atop imposing Mont-Mégantic, you're 3,150 feet closer to the heavens. Far from city lights, the sky here is ideal for stargazing.

4 The Outaouais. Bordering the Ottawa River, the Outaouais is known for its many lakes, majestic views, hiking trails, and interesting wildlife, as well as the imposing Château Montebello, often called the world's largest log cabin.

5 Québec City. The capital of the province of Québec is the most French city in North America. Québec's Old City (Vieux Québec) is split into two tiers, separated by steep rock against which are more than 25 *escaliers* (staircases) and a funicular. The surrounding cluster of small, low-rise neighborhoods all have their own charm and flavor.

6 Île d'Orléans. Famed for its wine and cider as well as its strawberry crop and other local produce, the Île d'Orléans is often called the "Garden of Québec." Made up of six small villages, this charming island has several bed-and-breakfasts and fabulous farm stands.

7 Côte-de-Beaupré. The coast hugged by the St. Lawrence River embraces the thundering Montmorency Falls and the impressive Ste-Anne-de-Beaupré shrine. It leads to Mont-Sainte-Anne, famous for its skiing, golfing, and mountain biking.

8 Charlevoix. The big bang of an ancient meteor created picturesque valleys, cliffs, and mountains that brush the St. Lawrence River. This Canadian Switzerland has inspired painters, poets, and musicians for generations.

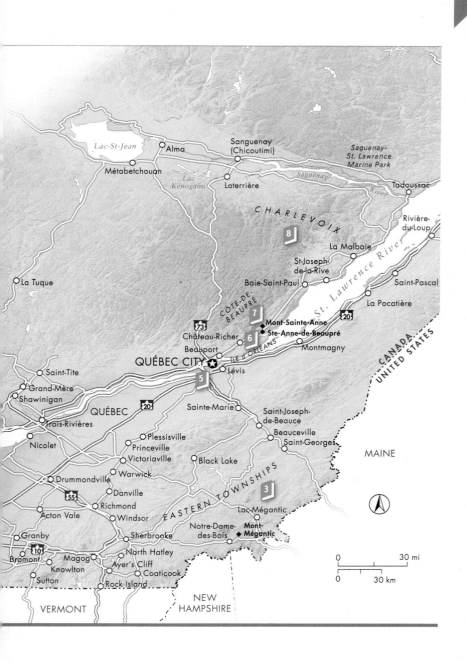

Lac-St-Jean
Alma
Métabetchouan
Sanguenay (Chicoutimi)
Saguenay-St. Lawrence Marine Park
Lac Kénogami
Laterrière
Saguenay River
Tadoussac
CHARLEVOIX
8
Rivière-du-Loup
La Malbaie
St-Joseph-de-la-Rive
La Tuque
Baie-Saint-Paul
St. Lawrence River
Saint-Pascal
CÔTE-DE-BEAUPRÉ
7
La Pocatière
73
Mont-Sainte-Anne
Château-Richer
6
Ste-Anne-de-Beaupré
20
Beauport
ÎLE d'ORLÉANS
Montmagny
QUÉBEC CITY
5
Lévis
CANADA
UNITED STATES
Saint-Tite
Grand-Mère
Shawinigan
QUÉBEC
20
Sainte-Marie
Saint-Joseph-de-Beauce
Trois-Rivières
Beauceville
Saint-Georges
Nicolet
Plessisville
Princeville
Victoriaville
Black Lake
MAINE
Drummondville
Warwick
Danville
55
Richmond
EASTERN TOWNSHIPS
3
Acton Vale
Windsor
Lac-Mégantic
Granby
Sherbrooke
Notre-Dame-des-Bois
Mont-Mégantic
10
North Hatley
Bromont
Magog
Knowlton
Ayer's Cliff
Coaticook
Sutton
Rock Island
NEW HAMPSHIRE
VERMONT

0   30 mi
0   30 km

GREAT ITINERARIES

Montréal and Québec City are perfect for long weekend trips, although if you'd like to see both areas, you could easily spend a week.

Essential Montréal in a Day

Start with a stroll to the peak of Mont-Royal, the city's most enduring natural symbol. Afterward, wander south on avenue du Parc and through McGill University's leafy campus to Downtown. The Musée des Beaux-Arts de Montréal, on rue Sherbrooke, was once the bastion of the Anglo-Canadian establishment, and is worth a visit.

For a Francophone perspective, head from Mont-Royal (the mountain) along rue Mont-Royal (the street) to rue St-Denis, home to funky boutiques and a boisterous strip of bars near the Université du Québec à Montréal.

In the late afternoon, head down to Old Montréal and pop into the Basilique Notre-Dame-de-Montréal before getting in some nightlife, as in the summer months the Old City is one of the most popular places to party. There are dozens of restaurants to choose from, as well as clubs and bars.

Day Trips and Overnights from Montréal

If you have only a couple of days for a visit and you need to concentrate on one area, the Laurentians are a good choice. Less than an hour's drive from Downtown Montréal, this resort area has recreational options (depending on the season) that include golf, hiking, and superb skiing, both Alpine and cross-country.

Pick a resort town to stay in and use that as a base for visiting some of the surrounding towns. Each town has its own style and appeal: St-Sauveur-des-Monts is lively, Morin Heights is tranquil, and Ste-Adèle is a center of gastronomy. Mont-Tremblant,

a sophisticated ski and golf resort, is worth a trip, particularly for the picturesque gondola ride to the summit.

You can combine a taste of the Eastern Townships with a two-day visit to the Laurentians. After an overnight stay in the Laurentians, head back south of Montréal to the Townships, which extend to the east along the border with New England. Overnight in Granby or Bromont: Granby has a zoo, and Bromont is known for golf, skiing, and its water park.

The next day, you can shop in pretty Knowlton (look for signs to Lac Brome) and explore regional history in such towns as Valcourt. Spend a night or two in the appealing resort town of Magog, along Lac Memphrémagog, or in the quieter North Hatley, on Lac Massawippi. You'll have good dining in either. Save some time for outdoor activities, whether it's golfing, skiing, biking, or hiking.

Essential Québec City in a Day

It's inspiring to start your day in Québec's Lower Town, the earliest site of French civilization in North America. Stroll along the narrow streets of the Quartier Petit-Champlain, visit the Maison Chevalier, and browse the craft stores and boutiques. From there, head to Place Royale, making a stop at the Église Notre-Dame-des-Victoires, and continue on to Terrasse Dufferin. In the afternoon, when the crowds thin out, check out the Musée National des Beaux-Arts du Québec or the Musée Canadien de l'Histoire.

Catch a gorgeous sunset from the Plains of Abraham—site of the battle that ended France's colonial dreams in North America—and marked the beginning of British rule in Canada—before dining anywhere on rue St-Jean, one of the best streets in the city for restaurants and nightlife.

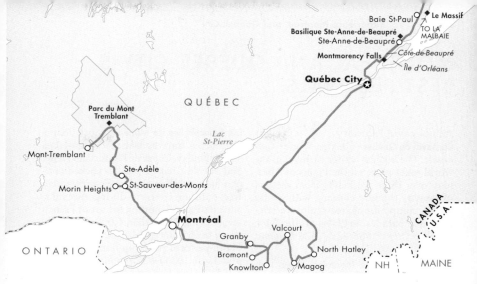

Day Trips and Overnights from Québec City

If you want to get out of Québec City for a day or two, take a 20-minute drive to Île d'Orléans, a picturesque island called the "garden of Québec." In summer, you can explore this idyllic island's boutiques, galleries, and food stands, then dine in a vineyard at Panache Mobile. Stay over in a cozy B&B, or continue on Route 138 northeast to Côte de Beaupré. Here you can visit the impressive Montmorency Falls and the ornate shrine at Ste-Anne-de-Beaupré. Don't miss the classic Québec cuisine of roast goose, *tourtière* (meat pie), and sugar pie at the historical Auberge Baker on Côte-de-Beaupré.

Another option is to take the Train du Massif de Charlevoix, which departs from the spectacular Parc de la Chute-Montmorency outside Québec City. It follows the St. Lawrence shore and the dramatic mountainous landscapes of Charlevoix. You'll visit the artistic community of Baie St-Paul, the impressive mountain Le Massif, and the cliff-top village of La Malbaie. You can do the two-segment rail trip in one day or stay overnight at the castlelike Fairmont Le Manoir Richelieu.

From La Malbaie, it's an hour by car to Tadoussac, at the confluence of the Saguenay and St. Lawrence rivers, where you can hop on a boat for a whale-watching excursion.

Montréal and Québec City over a Long Weekend

Looking for an ideal four-day getaway? It's possible to see the best of both cities without feeling rushed. Here's one expedient itinerary: Fly into Montréal's Trudeau International Airport on a Thursday evening, take a cab to your downtown hotel, put down your bags, and head out to grab a bite at a late-night bistro like L'Express. Spend Friday seeing the city's top sites, hit Old Montréal in the evening for dinner and nightlife, and enjoy a leisurely brunch on Saturday morning.

Rent a car from one of the many downtown rental agencies, then pack up and drive north to Québec City, which takes about three hours. Check into a B&B or boutique hotel in the Old City and spend the rest of the day exploring sites there. Spend Sunday morning in the Old City and dedicate the afternoon to the Fortifications, or take a day trip to the Côte-de-Beaupré or Île d'Orléans. On Monday, fly out of Québec City's Jean Lesage International Airport.

MONTRÉAL AND QUÉBEC CITY'S BEST FESTIVALS

January and February

Carnaval de Québec (*Québec Winter Carnival*). The biggest winter carnival in the world takes place on the Plains of Abraham over three weekends from the end of January to mid-February, with winter sports competitions, ice-sculpture contests, and parades. ⊠ *Plains of Abraham, Québec City* ☎ *866/422–7628* ⊕ *www.carnaval.qc.ca.*

Fête des Neiges de Montréal. Over four weekends from mid-January to mid-February, Montréal celebrates its winter festival at Parc Jean Drapeau across the Port from Old Montréal. Hockey games, tubing, skiing, dog sledding, and a Himalayan zip line are perfect activities to enjoy in the cold winter weather, but don't forget your toque. ⊠ *Montréal* ☎ *514/872–6120* ⊕ *www.parcjeandrapeau.com/events/fete-des-neiges-de-montreal* Ⓜ *Jean-Drapeau.*

Montréal en Lumière (*Montréal Highlights*). This festival brightens the bleak days of February with fabulous food and cultural activities. Leading chefs from around the world give demonstrations and take over the kitchens of top restaurants for special dinners. "Nuit Blanche," held on the last Saturday of this festival, lets you explore the city until the wee hours of the morning. Many of the events are free, and there are shuttle services to take you to the locations. Dress warmly. ☎ *514/288–9955, 855/864–3737* ⊕ *www.montrealenlumiere.com.*

June

Fringe Festival. Open to playwrights, acting troupes, dancers, comics, and musicians, the Fringe Festival, during the first three weeks of June, is run on a lottery system to determine which performers get on stage. ☎ *514/849–3378* ⊕ *www.montrealfringe.ca.*

Les FrancoFolies de Montréal. Such major Quebecois stars as Isabelle Boulay, Les soeurs Boulay, Coeur de Pirate, Paul Piché, and Nicola Ciccone play to packed concert halls, while lesser-known artists play free outdoor concerts during this mid-June festival celebrating the art of French songwriting. More than 1,000 musicians, many from France, Belgium, Senegal, and Haiti, perform rock, hip-hop, jazz, funk, and Latin. ☎ *514/876–8989, 855/372–6267* ⊕ *www.francofolies.com.*

Mondiale de la Bière. In Montréal, for five days every June, this beer festival transforms the exhibition hall of Palais de Congrès into a giant indoor beer garden serving some 600 ales, lagers, and ciders from nearly 100 microbreweries from Québec and around the world. Admission is free, tasting coupons are $1 each. ☎ *514/722–9640* ⊕ *www.festivalmondialbiere.qc.ca.*

July

Festival d'Été de Québec (*Québec City Summer Festival*). This exuberant 11-day music extravaganza in Québec City features rock, folk, hip-hop, and world-beat music. The main concerts rock nightly with 10 indoor and outdoor stages in early July in or near Old Québec, including one on the Plains of Abraham. ☎ *418/529–5200, 888/992–5200* ⊕ *www.infofestival.com.*

Festival International de Jazz de Montréal (*Montréal International Jazz Festival*). This major event attracts more than 1,000 musicians for more than 400 concerts held over a period of nearly two weeks from the end of June through the beginning of July. Past stars have included B.B. King, Ella Fitzgerald, Lauryn Hill, Wynton Marsalis, Chick Corea, Dave Brubeck, and Canada's most famed singer-pianist,

Diana Krall. You can also hear blues, Latin rhythms, gospel, Cajun, and world music. ☎ *514/871–1881, 855/299–3378* ⊕ *www.montrealjazzfest.com.*

Festival OFF. A sidekick of the Festival d'Été International de Québec, this music event takes to the stage in July at the same time as its big brother. Most of the shows are free and take place in offbeat spaces such as in front of Église St-Jean-Baptiste, Bar Le Sacrilège, and the Musée de l'Amérique Française, just to name a few. ☎ *418/529–5200, 888/992–5200* ⊕ *www.quebecoff.org.*

Juste pour Rire (*Just for Laughs*). Montréal's world-famous comedy festival hosts international comics, in French and English, from the second through third weeks of July. There are tons of shows to watch, from big concert halls to quaint bars. Walk around the Quartier des Spectacles during the festival and giggle your way from one outdoor act to another. The twins parade is not to be missed. ☎ *514/845–2322* ⊕ *www.hahaha.com.*

L'International des Feux Loto-Québec (*International Fireworks Competition*). Join the thousands heading to Montréal's Jacques Cartier Bridge or the Old Port to watch the free fireworks show most Wednesday and Saturday nights in late June and July. The launch site for this high-in-the-sky show, set off by competing international teams, is La Ronde, on Île Ste-Hélène. ☎ *514/397–2000* ⊕ *www.laronde.com/fr/ larondefr/linternational-des-feux/accueil.*

August

Festival International des Films du Monde (*World Film Festival*). For several days in Montréal from late August to early September, this festival presents about 400 films from all over the world, including feature films, documentaries, shorts,

animation, and student productions. During the festival, Cinema Under the Stars, in the Quartier des Spectacles, screens foreign films outdoors. Go early to grab a seat or bring your own blanket. ☎ *514/848–3883* ⊕ *www.ffm-montreal.org.*

Fêtes de la Nouvelle France (*New France Festival*). During this five-day festival, in early to mid-August, Québec City's centuries-old heritage comes alive. The streets of Lower Town are transported back in time, and events range from an old-time farmers' market to games and music—all done in period costume. ☎ *418/694–3311* ⊕ *www.nouvellefrance.qc.ca.*

St-Jean-sur-Richelieu's Hot-Air Balloon Festival. This colorful airborne event, the largest gathering of hot-air balloons in Canada, takes flight about 25 minutes' drive southeast of Montréal. The balloons are so vivid and plentiful that you can sometimes see them from Downtown. ☎ *450/346–6000* ⊕ *www.balloon-canada.com.*

October

Black and Blue Festival. Organized by the Bad Boy Club Montréal, this festival started more than 25 years ago as a gay community fundraiser for AIDS charities. It has grown to be a gay and gay-friendly week (in mid-October) of intense partying, featuring soirées like the Leather Ball, the Military Ball, and the Black and Blue Ball. ☎ *514/875–7026* ⊕ *www. bbcm.org.*

Festival of Colors. Farmers' markets, arts-and-crafts fairs, and weekend hikes are part of this festival, which celebrates the fall throughout Québec. If you head to a ski resort you can get a bird's-eye view of the splendid and vibrant red, orange, and yellow foliage from the chairlifts.

MONTRÉAL AND QUÉBEC CITY WITH KIDS

There's no shortage of fantastic activities in Montréal and Québec City for kids. Here's a sampling of what the little ones might enjoy during a visit.

MONTRÉAL WITH KIDS

Montréal's popular rent-a-bicycle system, **Bixi**, is a great way for families to see the city. The expanding network of car-free cycling paths now meanders around Parc du Mont-Royal and through Old Montréal, across Parc Jean-Drapeau on Île Notre-Dame, and along the Lachine Canal.

Kids who've had their fill of churches and museums can expend some pent-up energy at the adjacent **Old Port**, which has boats to pedal, a clock tower to climb, and a maze. There's also a waterfront beach, but alas, no swimming is allowed.

For culturally adventurous youngsters, there are outdoor dance and theater presentations at **Parc Lafontaine**. Kids can also explore the mysteries of bonsai trees and Chinese gardens at the **Jardin Botanique**.

What soccer is to Brazilians and baseball is to Americans, hockey is to Canadians. It's not a game, it's a religion! If you can score tickets (best to order in advance), catch a **Montréal Canadiens** game at the Centre Bell. A night with the "Habs" and their lively fans is a riveting family experience. Alternatively, take a one-hour tour (ages 5 and up) of the **Centre Bell**, which includes access to the Canadiens dressing room.

On hot summer days, spend some time at the Quartier des Spectacles, where the large fountains spread along the street will provide some fun and surely cool off your kids. You may even see some adults jumping in, too.

QUÉBEC CITY WITH KIDS

Ice-cream stands, street performers, and (in winter) a thrilling toboggan run make **Terrasse Dufferin** as entertaining for children as for adults, as do the **Plains of Abraham's** open spaces.

Place Royale in the Lower Town brings the 17th and 18th centuries to life for even the youngest children.

La Citadelle's changing-of-the-guard ceremony, complete with the Royal 22e Régiment's mascot, Batisse the Goat, has lots of kid appeal. The hands-on exhibits at the **Musée de la Civilisation** and the 19th-century jail cells preserved in the **Musée de Québec** are both must-see attractions.

And for a little animal fun, polar bears, seals, and walruses are the stars of the city's **Aquarium du Québec**.

OUTSIDE OF MONTRÉAL AND QUÉBEC CITY WITH KIDS

In the Laurentians, the gentle rides of the **Au Pays des Merveilles** and the **Village du Père Noël** (Santa's Village) are perfect for younger children. There are plenty of thrills at the **Water Parks** at Mont-St-Sauveur in the Laurentians and Bromont in the Eastern Townships.

Montmorency Falls, on the Côte-de-Beaupré, aren't as grand as Niagara, but they're higher, and crossing the suspension bridge above the spectacular chutes of water is a thrill. Farther along the St. Lawrence coast in **Tadoussac** you can take a boat ride for an up-close encounter with whales (be careful not to get saltwater in your camera or phone).

FREE AND CHEAP

There might be no such thing as a free lunch in Montréal or Québec City, but plenty of other things are free, or nearly so.

Art

Admission to the permanent collections of Montréal's Musée des Beaux-Arts (⊕ *www.mbam.qc.ca*) and Québec City's Musée National des Beaux-Arts ⊕ *www. mnbaq.org*) is always free. The Musée d'Art Contemporain (⊕ *www.macm.org*) is half price on Wednesday nights. Every summer the city of Montréal mounts an outdoor exhibit of art or photographs on the sidewalks of avenue McGill College between rues Ste-Catherine and Sherbrooke.

Concerts

Montréal's Christ Church Cathedral (*635 rue Ste-Catherine Ouest 514/843–6577*), a magnificent neo-Gothic treasure, and Oratoire St-Joseph (*3800 Chemin Queen-Mary*, ☎ *514/733–8211*) offer free organ recitals on Sunday afternoons at 3:30 pm and 4:30 pm throughout the year. And Les Petits Chanteurs du Mont-Royal, one of the finest boys' choirs in North America, sings the 11 am mass at the Oratoire every Sunday from March to December 24. They also perform several free concerts through the year.

Montréal's Festival Internationale de Jazz every June and Québec City's Festival d'Été in July have dozens of free, open-air concerts. These huge happenings bring thousands, and tens of thousands, of revelers to the streets.

Fireworks

From mid-June through July, the sky comes alive with light and color on most Wednesday and Saturday evenings when fireworks teams from around the world compete in the spectacular L'International des Feux Loto-Québec. You can pay for a seat at La Ronde amusement park, or join thousands of Montrealers in the Old Port, on the Jacques Cartier Bridge, and in Parc Champlain on the South Shore and watch for free.

Politics

Political junkies can join free guided tours of North America's only French-speaking legislature, the Assemblée Nationale du Québec (☎ *418/643–7239*). The parliamentary debates are on Tuesday to Thursday from August to November and February to May.

Science

McGill University's Redpath Museum (*859 rue Sherbrooke Ouest*, ☎ *514/398– 4086*) houses an eclectic collection of dinosaur skeletons, seashells, fossils, minerals, Egyptian mummies, and Stone Age tools in a beautiful 19th-century building. Watch for free lectures.

Sightseeing

For one of the best views of Québec City, take the C$3.35 ferry (*10 rue des Traversiers*, ☎ *418/643–8420*) for a mini-cruise across the St. Lawrence River to Lévis and back. Or for C$2.25, ride the Funiculaire du Vieux-Québec (*16 rue Petit-Champlain*, ☎ *418/692–1132*), the sharply vertical railway that creaks along the cliff from Lower Town to Upper Town.

A FOOD-LOVER'S TOUR OF MONTRÉAL

Many Montrealers are true gourmets, or at least enthusiastic food-lovers. And, indeed, the city has thousands of restaurants, markets, and food boutiques catering to just about every conceivable taste, from Portuguese barbecue to Tonkinese soup. Most menus are posted outside, so you can stroll around a neighborhood and leisurely choose whichever sounds most tantalizing.

Downtown

While you can't go wrong starting the day with a bowl of steaming café au lait at **Café Myriade** in Downtown, for something a little different head over to Chinatown for a dim sum breakfast at **Maison Kam Fung,** a neighborhood institution.

The Plateau

Fortified with filling dumpling dough, walk up through the streets of the Latin Quarter on rue St-Denis and you'll hit Square St-Louis.

Turn west, then north on boulevard St-Laurent and browse through dozens of ethnic food shops and delis, inhaling the aromas from the Caribbean, the Middle East, Asia, and Eastern Europe. If that reanimates your appetite, stop at the iconic **Schwartz's Delicatessen** and split one of the world's best smoked-meat sandwiches, served piled high on rye (it's best slathered with spicy deli mustard), with your walking companion.

Next, work up an appetite for lunch with a walk. Head east along avenue Duluth and take a stroll through Parc Lafontaine. There are two options for a bite to eat: exit the park on the southwest corner to rue Rachel and turn left for **La Banquise,** one of Montréal's top poutine spots (so popular you may have to wait in line to get in); or go northwest on rue de la Roche until you reach avenue Mont-Royal, a spirited stretch of terrasses, tattoo parlors, and thrift shops.

Stop for a bagel sandwich on a hot and sweet Montréal-style bagel at **St-Viateur Bagel & Café.** For a 100% vegan lunch or dinner with wine, head to **Invitation V** on rue Bernard on the Plateau/Mile End/Outremont border; even omnivores leave happy. In summer, stop for some ice cream at **Le Glacier Bilboquet,** on avenue Laurier Est, or try the Outremont location on rue Bernard.

Little Italy

Time to cheat. Hop on the métro at Laurier station and head north to the Jean-Talon stop for an afternoon visit to one of Canada's best markets, **Marché Jean-Talon.** You can spend hours browsing fish, sausage, and cheese shops and sampling everything from smoked buffalo to seasonal produce like heirloom tomatoes.

There's no leaving this area without stopping for dinner, so stroll over to boulevard St-Laurent and find a place to eat in Pétite-Italie (Little Italy). Two restaurants to try are **Inferno** and **Bottega Pizzeria.** Finish with a bracing espresso at **Café Italia,** where neighborhood men huddle around the TV to watch soccer.

From here, it's an easy walk back to the Jean-Talon métro stop for a ride back to Old Montréal or Downtown.

Highlights	A fat smoked-meat sandwich at Schwartz's Delicatessen; walking around the Marché Jean-Talon tasting vendors' samples.
Where to Start	Chinatown, located in Downtown, at the ornately decorated red gate on St-Laurent off boulevard René-Lévesque.
Length	About 5.5 km (3.5 miles) walking, plus the métro from Laurier to Marché Jean-Talon on the Orange Line.
Where to End	Little Italy. From here, you can walk back to the Orange Line that runs through Downtown.
Best Time to Go	Busy summer Saturday (the crowds are half the entertainment).
Worst Time to Go	Dull winter Monday.
Editor's Choices	Walking up boulevard St-Laurent, peeking in the delis and offbeat boutiques; the colorful streets of the Plateau; the maple ice cream at Le Glacier Bilboquet.

HOW TO SPEAK QUEBECOIS

FRANÇAIS, S'IL VOUS PLAÎT

Anytime you visit a foreign country, being familiar with the local language is sure to win you friends. Learn a few phrases, regardless of whether you pronounce them correctly, and the locals will appreciate it. More than 80% of Quebecois claim French as their mother tongue, and while many Quebecois are bilingual or know at least a little English, plenty more don't, especially outside Downtown Montréal and the less touristy areas of the province. Rest assured that you will come across more than a few unilingual Francophones.

As in France, accents and colloquialisms vary widely from region to region. Still, there are several commonly used, uniquely Quebecois words and expressions.

EVERYDAY TERMS

For starters, Montréal's impressive subway system is known as le Métro. If you go around asking French Canadians where the closest subway station is, you'll likely be greeted with a blank stare followed by a "Je m'excuse, mais je ne parle pas l'anglais" ("I'm sorry, but I don't speak any English"). Similarly, don't go looking for a "convenience store" when you need some last-minute item. Here, even Anglophones call them dépanneurs, or "deps" for short.

While here you'll probably spend a lot of time in centre-ville (Downtown) checking out splendid sights like the Palais de Justice (not a palace at all, but a courthouse). Except in order to do so you're likely going to need some l'argent (money), or better, un peu de cash, which is franglais (a curious yet distinct local hybrid of French and

English) for "a bit of money." And where will you be getting that money? Nowhere if you start asking people for the closest ATM. In Québec a bank machine is called a guichet (the gui pronounced like guitar, the chet like "shea").

DINING OUT

Of course, many things in Québec, like the menus in most restaurants, will be in both French and English, but you'll impress the waitstaff if you order a steak-frites avec un verre de vin rouge when you want steak with french fries and a glass of red wine. Later, when you ask for la facture or l'addition (your bill), and your waiter inquires if you've enjoyed your meal, tell him it was écoeurant (the literal translation is disgusting, or nauseating, but it's akin to saying something is "sick" for great) and you'll likely see a big amused grin come over his face. It's the rare tourist who's in the know when it comes to Quebecois slang and/or colloquialisms, so locals will certainly be impressed if they hear you coming out with the occasional mon char (my car) when talking about your wheels or, ma blonde, or ma copine (girlfriend), when introducing somebody to your female significant other. Conversely, if you're talking about a boyfriend, mon chum, or mon copain, is how the locals would say it.

HOLY SWEAR WORDS

Almost all Quebecois swear words—aka sacres—come courtesy of the Catholic Church, so while the literal translation of words like tabarnac (tabernacle) or câlice (chalice) might seem pretty tame or nonsensical in English, here they're the equivalent of the dreaded F-word.

EXPLORING
MONTRÉAL

WELCOME TO MONTRÉAL

TOP REASONS TO GO

★ **Browse public markets:** Amble through Marché Atwater, one of the city's oldest public markets, and the bustling Marché Jean-Talon, the largest open air market in North America.

★ **Check out the nightlife:** Enjoy famous nightlife spots that include rue Crescent, boulevard St-Laurent, and rue St-Denis, as well as Old Montréal and the Village, Montréal's gay epicenter.

★ **Get a dose of multiculturalism:** Explore ethnic neighborhoods and sample global cuisine.

★ **Celebrate Jazz Fest:** Montréal's biggest party, Jazz Fest, happens every year in late June and early July. Reserve early: hotels book up months in advance.

★ **Stroll Old Montréal:** Historic Vieux-Montréal has cobblestone streets, a great waterfront, fine restaurants and bed-and-breakfasts, and the Old Port, which buzzes with nightlife.

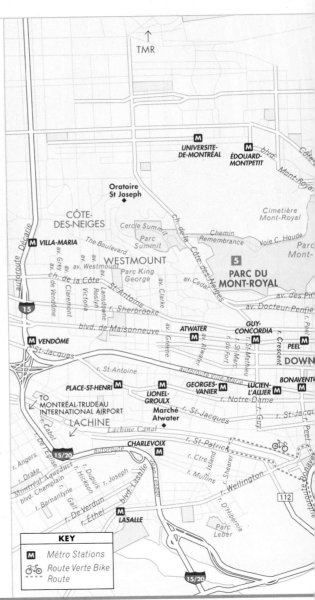

KEY

Ⓜ Métro Stations

🚲 Route Verte Bike Route

2

1 Old Montréal (Vieux-Montréal). The oldest part of the city is known for historical buildings, street performers, and charming restaurants.

2 Downtown and Chinatown. Shop on rue Ste-Catherine, walk over to Chinatown for lunch, and check out the museums.

3 The Latin Quarter and the Village. People-watching is the order of the day here. Have a drink on a terrace overlooking rue St-Denis.

4 The Plateau, Mile End, Little Italy, and Outremont. Come to these fashionable neighborhoods for Sunday brunch, upscale boutiques, and art galleries.

5 Parc du Mont-Royal. Where city dwellers seek refuge and enjoy some of the city's best world cuisine in adjoining Côte-des-Neiges.

6 Hochelaga-Maisonneuve. See the site of the 1976 Olympics, explore the universe in the planetarium, and take in great parks and gardens.

7 The Islands. Île Ste-Hélène and Île Notre-Dame make up Parc Jean-Drapeau, a vast playground with an amusement park, a casino, and the Grand Prix's Formula 1 race track.

Updated by
Elizabeth
Warkentin

Canada's most diverse metropolis, Montréal is an island city that favors style and elegance over order or even prosperity, a city where past and present intrude on each other daily. In some ways it resembles Vienna—well past its peak of power and glory, perhaps, yet still vibrant and grand.

But don't get the wrong idea. Montréal has always had a bit of an edge. During Prohibition, thirsty Americans headed north to the city on the St. Lawrence for booze, music, and a good time, and people still come for the same things. Summer festivals celebrate everything from comedy and French music and culture to beer and fireworks, and, of course, jazz. And on those rare weeks when there isn't a planned event, the party continues. Clubs and sidewalk cafés are abuzz from late afternoon to the early hours of the morning. And Montréal is a city that knows how to mix it up even when it's 20 below zero. Rue St-Denis is almost as lively on a Saturday night in January as it is in July, and the festival Montréal en Lumière, or Montréal Highlights, enlivens the dreary days of February with concerts, balls, and fine food.

Montréal takes its name from Parc du Mont-Royal, a stubby plug of tree-covered igneous rock that rises 764 feet above the surrounding cityscape. Although its height is unimpressive, "the Mountain" forms one of Canada's finest urban parks, and views from the Chalet du Mont-Royal atop the hill provide an excellent orientation to the city's layout and major landmarks.

Old Montréal is home to museums, the municipal government, and the magnificent Basilique Notre-Dame-de-Montréal within its network of narrow, cobblestone streets. Although Montréal's *centre-ville*, or Downtown, bustles like many other major cities on the surface, it's active below street level as well, in the so-called Underground City—the underground levels of shopping malls and food courts connected by pedestrian tunnels and the city's subway system, or *métro*. Residential Plateau Mont-Royal and trendy neighborhoods are abuzz with restaurants, nightclubs, art galleries, and cafés. The greener areas of town are composed of the Parc du Mont-Royal and the Jardin Botanique.

MONTRÉAL'S HISTORY

Montréal is the second-largest French-speaking city in the Western world, but it's not only Francophone culture that thrives here. About 14% of the 3.3 million people who call Montréal home claim English as their mother tongue.

Yet the two cultures are not as separate as they once were. Chatter in the bars and bistros of rue St-Denis east of boulevard St-Laurent still tends to be in French, and crowds in restaurants on rue Crescent in the Downtown core speak English. But the lines have blurred, with more conversations taking place in a Montréal mixture of the two languages.

Both linguistic groups have had to come to grips with no longer being the only player. So-called *allophones*—people whose mother tongue is neither French nor English—make up fully 19% of the city's population.

The first European settlement on Montréal island was Ville-Marie, founded in 1642 by 54 men and women under the leadership of Paul de Chomedey, Sieur de Maisonneuve, and Jeanne Mance, a French noblewoman, who hoped to create a new Christian society. The settlement's location near the confluence of the St. Lawrence and Ottawa rivers also meant a lucrative trade in beaver pelts, as the fur was a staple of European hat fashion for nearly a century.

The French regime in Canada ended with the Seven Years' War, also known as the French and Indian War. The Treaty of Paris ceded all of New France to Britain in 1763. American troops under generals Richard Montgomery and Benedict Arnold occupied the city during their 1775–76 campaign to conquer Canada, but their efforts failed and troops withdrew. Soon invaders of another kind—English and Scottish settlers—poured into Montréal. By 1832 the city became a colonial capital. But 1837 brought anti-British rebellions, and this led to Canada's becoming a self-governing dominion in 1867.

The city's ports continued to bustle until the St. Lawrence Seaway opened in 1957, allowing ships to sail from the Atlantic to the Great Lakes without having to stop in Montréal to transfer cargo.

The opening of the métro in 1966 changed the way Montrealers lived, and the next year the city hosted the World's Fair. But the rise of Québec separatism in the late 1960s under René Lévesque created political uncertainty, and many major businesses moved to Toronto. By the time Lévesque's separatist Parti Québécois won power in Québec in 1976—the same year the summer Olympics came to the city—Montréal was clearly Canada's No. 2 city.

Uncertainty continued through the 1980s and '90s, with the separatist Parti Québécois and the federalist Liberals alternating in power in Québec City. Since 1980 the city has endured two referenda on the future of Québec and Canada. In the cliff-hanger of 1995, just 50.58% of Quebecois voted to remain part of Canada. Montréal bucked the separatist trend and voted nearly 70% against independence.

PLANNING

GETTING HERE AND AROUND

AIR TRAVEL
Montréal's Trudeau International Airport (also often referred to by its previous name, Dorval) is about 24 km (15 miles) west of the city center.

GROUND TRANSPOR-TATION The easiest way to get in is to take a cab for a fixed fare of C$40 or a limousine for about C$55, unless your hotel provides transportation. The cheapest way to get into town is the 747 express bus, a 24-hour shuttle service from the airport to the main bus terminal with stops at the Lionel-Groulx métro station and several additional stops near Downtown hotels. The one-way fare is C$10 (accepted in coins only) —with 24 hours of unlimited bus and métro travel included in the price. Plan on it taking about a half hour outside rush hour to get to Downtown from the airport. Another alternative is the 204 bus, with a one way fare of C$3.25, taking you from the Dorval train terminal straight to the airport.

BICYCLE TRAVEL
An extensive network of bike paths and relatively flat terrain make Montréal ideal for bicycles. The Bixi (a contraction of "bicycle" and "taxi") system—with more than 3,000 sturdy aluminum-frame bikes at more than 300 credit-card operated stands throughout the city—makes two-wheel exploring easy. For just C$5 you can take as many bike trips as you like over a 24-hour period, or for C$12 you can extend that to 72 hours. A one-way trip is C$2.75. Pay attention to the time, though: the system is designed for short hops; keep any one bike for more than 30 minutes, and you'll be charged extra.

CAR TRAVEL
If you're driving in to the city, take I–91 or I–89 from Vermont, I–87 from New York, and Autoroute 20 (also known as Autoroute Jean-Lesage) from Québec City.

Having a car Downtown isn't ideal—garages are expensive and on-street parking can be a hassle. The city has a diligent tow-away and fine system for double-parking or sitting in no-stopping zones during rush hour, and ticket costs are steep. In residential neighborhoods, beware of alternate-side-of-the-street-parking rules and resident-only parking. In winter, street plows are ruthless in dealing with parked cars in their way. If they don't tow them, they'll bury them.

PUBLIC TRANSPORTATION
The Société de transport de Montréal (STM) operates both the métro (subway) and the bus system. The métro is clean and quiet (it runs on rubber tires), and will get you to most of the places you want to visit. For those few places that are more than a 15-minute walk from the nearest métro station, bus connections are available.

Métro hours on the Orange, Green, Blue, and Yellow lines are weekdays 5:30 am to 12:30 am and weekends 5:30 am to 12:30, 1, or 1:30 am (it varies by line). Trains run every three minutes or so on the most crowded lines—Orange and Green—at rush hours. The cash fare for a single ticket is C$3.25. One- and three-day unlimited-use cards are also available for C$10 and C$18.

MONEY-SAVING TIPS

There are several good ways to save money during your trip. If you'll be visiting three or more of the city's museums, consider buying a museum pass. It's available for C$75 for three days, but the better deal is the C$80 pass, which also includes unlimited access to Montréal's transportation system, including the métro and buses. ⊕ www.musees-montreal.org/en/passes/the-passes.

Tourist passes, which give you unlimited access to the transit system, also may be worth your while; one-day passes are C$10 while three-day passes will set you back C$18. Weekly passes cost C$25.75 but they're loaded electronically on a special Opus card that costs C$6.

Hitting the town earlier in the evening is a good way to save as well, by stopping into cafés and bars for food and drink specials offered during cinq-à-sept (5-to-7), Montréal's happy hour.

TAXI TRAVEL

Taxis in Montréal all run on the same rate: C$3.45 minimum and C$1.70 per kilometer (roughly ½ mile). They're usually easy to hail on the street, outside train stations, in shopping areas, and at major hotels. You can also call a dispatcher to send a driver to pick you up at no extra cost. A taxi is available if the white or orange plastic rooftop light is on.

⇨ *For more information on getting here and around, see Travel Smart.*

PLANNING YOUR TIME

Put Old Montréal and the Old Port at the top of your sightseeing list. Spend a full day walking around this area, head back to your hotel for a late-day break, and return for dinner. Aside from finding several of the city's top restaurants here, City Hall, Marché Bonsecours, and other charming buildings are illuminated at night. Also dedicate a full day to wandering around Downtown, rue Ste-Catherine, and Chinatown. Visit the Latin Quarter and the area around McGill University—both have a busy student life, but shouldn't be dismissed as places where only under-20s frequent. Even if you're too tired to go out on the town, take a nighttime walk down rue Crescent or rue St-Denis for a taste of the city's *joie de vivre.*

For browsing, shopping, and dining out, explore Outremont, Mile End, the Plateau, and Westmount. For kid-friendly activities, check out Hochelaga-Maisonneuve and the Islands for the Biôdôme, La Ronde, and the Jardin Botanique.

WHEN TO GO

To avoid crowds and below-freezing temperatures, Montréal's short spring, which typically starts in late April or early May but doesn't end until well into June, is ideal. Fall is gorgeous—and touristy—when the leaves change color, so expect traffic on weekends. Early September after Labor Day is another good time to visit.

OLD MONTRÉAL AND THE LACHINE CANAL

A walk through the cobblestone streets of Old Montréal (Vieux-Montréal is a lot more than a privileged stroll through history; it's also an encounter with a very lively present—especially in summer, when the restaurants and bistros spill out onto the sidewalks. Jugglers, musicians, and magicians jockey for performance space on the public squares and along the riverfront, and things get turned up a notch at the Old Port, one of the city's hottest spots for nightlife.

OLD MONTRÉAL (VIEUX-MONTRÉAL)

Fodor's Choice
★

Old Montréal, which was once enclosed by thick stone walls, is the oldest part of the city. It runs roughly from the waterfront in the south to ruelle des Fortifications in the north and from rue McGill in the west to rue Berri in the east. The churches and chapels here stand as testament to the religious fervor that inspired the French settlers who landed here in 1642 to build a "Christian commonwealth" under the leadership of Paul de Chomedey, Sieur de Maisonneuve, and the indomitable Jeanne Mance. Stone warehouses and residences are reminders of how quickly the fur trade commercialized that lofty ideal and made the city one of the most prosperous in 18th-century Nouvelle France. And finally, the financial houses along rue St-Jacques, bristling with Victorian ornamentation, recall the days when Montrealers controlled virtually all the wealth of the young Dominion of Canada.

History and good looks aside, however, Old Montréal still works for a living. Stockbrokers and shipping companies continue to operate out of the old financial district. The city's largest newspaper, *La Presse*, has its offices here. Lawyers in black gowns hurry through the streets to plead cases at the Palais de Justice or the Cour d'Appel, the City Council meets in the Second Empire City Hall on rue Notre-Dame, and local shoppers hunt for deals in the bargain clothing stores just off rue McGill.

GETTING HERE AND AROUND

The easiest way to get from Downtown to Old Montréal is aboard Bus 515, a shuttle that provides a quick direct link to several sites in the Old City and Old Port. It runs from 7 am to midnight. You can also take the métro Orange line to the Place-d'Armes and Square-Victoria stations, or you can walk, but the primary routes from Downtown go through some drab and somewhat seedy, although not especially dangerous, areas. If you feel like biking, it's better to rent a Bixi bicycle at a Downtown stand and drop it off at one in Old Montréal. Biking to Old Montréal is a breeze because it's all downhill, but the return trip to Downtown is a challenging workout.

Taxis can whisk you here from Downtown in about 10 minutes.

The best way to get around the Old City is on foot, but wear good shoes because the cobbles can be hard on the feet.

TIMING

Having enough time to see the sights, stroll around, and try some of the area's notable restaurants means dedicating at least one day. If it's your first time in the city and you're only here for an extended weekend, consider staying in one of Old Montréal's auberges or boutique hotels.

TOP ATTRACTIONS

Fodor's Choice   **Basilique Notre-Dame-de-Montréal** (*Our Lady of Montréal Basilica*). Few
★   churches in North America are as wow-inducing as Notre-Dame. Everything about the Gothic Revival–style church, which opened in 1829, seems designed to make you gasp—from the 228-foot twin towers out front to the tens of thousands of 24-karat gold stars that stud the soaring blue ceiling.

Nothing in a city renowned for churches matches Notre-Dame for sheer grandeur—or noise-making capacity: its 12-ton bass bell is the largest in North America, and its 7,000-pipe Casavant organ can make the walls tremble. The pulpit is a work of art in itself, with an intricately curving staircase and fierce figures of Ezekiel and Jeremiah crouching at its base. The whole place is so overwhelming it's easy to miss such lesser features as the stained-glass windows from Limoges and the side altars dedicated to St. Marguerite d'Youville, Canada's first native-born saint; St. Marguerite Bourgeoys, Canada's first schoolteacher; and a group of Sulpician priests martyred in Paris during the French Revolution.

For a peek at the magnificent baptistery, decorated with frescoes by Ozias Leduc, you'll have to tiptoe through the glassed-off prayer room in the northwest corner of the church. Every year dozens of brides—including Céline Dion, in 1994—march up the aisle of **Chapelle Notre-Dame-du-Sacré-Coeur** (Our Lady of the Sacred Heart Chapel), behind the main altar, to exchange vows with their grooms before a huge modern bronze sculpture that you either love or hate.

Notre-Dame is an active house of worship, so dress accordingly. The chapel can't be viewed weekdays during the 12:15 pm mass, and is often closed Saturday for weddings. ■TIP➜ **Don't miss the 40-minute multimedia spectacle ,"Aura," which celebrates the basilica's exquisite features through light and sound. See website for schedule** ⊕ *www.*

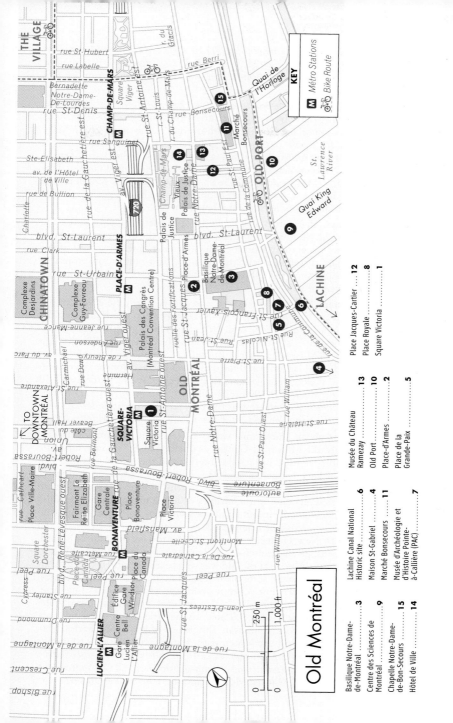

Old Montréal

Basilique Notre-Dame-de-Montréal 3
Centre des Sciences de Montréal 9
Chapelle Notre-Dame-de-Bon-Secours 15
Hôtel de Ville 14

Lachine Canal National Historic site 6
Maison St-Gabriel 4
Marché Bonsecours 11
Musée d'Archéologie et d'Histoire Pointe-à-Callière (PAC) 7

Musée du Château Ramezay 13
Old Port 10
Place-d'Armes 2
Place de la Grande-Paix 5

Place Jacques-Cartier 12
Place Royale 8
Square Victoria 1

KEY

M Métro Stations
      Bike Route

aurabasiliquenotredame.com/en ⊠ *110 rue Notre-Dame Ouest, Old Montréal* ☎ *514/842–2925, 866/842–2925* ⊕ *www.basiliquenddm. org* ⊒ *C$6 (with or without tour); multimedia show "Aura" C$25* Ⓜ *Place-d'Armes.*

Chapelle Notre-Dame-de-Bon-Secours (*Our Lady of Perpetual Help Chapel*). Mariners have been popping into Notre-Dame-de-Bon-Secours for centuries to kneel before a little 17th-century statue of the Virgin Mary and pray for a safe passage—or give thanks for one. Often, they've expressed their gratitude by leaving votive lamps in the shape of small ships, many of which still hang from the barrel-vaulted ceiling. This is why most Montrealers call the chapel the Église des Matelots (the Sailors' Church), and why many people still stop by to say a prayer and light a candle before leaving on a long trip.

These days, the statue of Our Lady of Perpetual Help guards the remains of St. Marguerite Bourgeoys, who had the original chapel built in 1657 and is entombed in the side altar next to the east wall of the chapel. The current chapel dates from 1771; a renovation project in 1998 revealed some beautiful 18th-century murals that had been hidden under layers of paint.

The 69-step climb to the top of the steeple is worth the effort for the glorious view of the harbor, as is the equally steep climb down to the archaeological excavations under the chapel for a glimpse into the history of the chapel and the neighborhood. The dig is accessible through the adjacent **Musée Marguerite Bourgeoys**, which also has exhibits on the life of St. Marguerite and the daily lives of the colonists she served. The chapel is closed mid-January through February except for the 10:30 am mass on Sunday. ⊠ *400 rue St-Paul Est, Old Montréal* ☎ *514/282–8670* ⊕ *www.marguerite-bourgeoys.com* ⊒ *Museum (includes archaeological site) and tower C$12; Chapel free* Ⓜ *Champ-de-Mars.*

OFF THE BEATEN PATH

Maison St-Gabriel. Thick stone walls, a steep roof, and mullioned windows mark the Maison St-Gabriel as one of Montréal's rare surviving 17th-century houses. But it's the interior and the furnishings that will sweep you back to the colonial days when St. Marguerite Bourgeoys and the religious order she founded used this house to train *les filles du roy* (king's daughters) in the niceties of home management. Les filles were young women without family or fortune but plenty of spunk who volunteered to cross the Atlantic in leaky boats to become the wives and mothers of New France. It wasn't an easy life, as the Maison's hard, narrow beds, primitive utensils, and drafty rooms attest—but it had its rewards, and the prize at the end was a respectable, settled life. St. Marguerite also had some state-of-the-art domestic equipment—the latest in looms and butter churns, labor-saving spit turners for roasting meat, and an ingenious granite sink with a drainage system that piped water straight out to the garden. Located on the little island of New France and deep in the working-class neighborhood of Pointe St-Charles, Maison St-Gabriel is off the beaten path, but it's well worth a 10-minute taxi ride from Old Montréal. ⊠ *2146 pl. Dublin, Pointe-St-Charles* ☎ *514/935–8136* ⊕ *www.maisonsaint-gabriel.qc.ca* ⊒ *C$15 weekdays; C$20 weekends* ☉ *Closed Mon.* Ⓜ *Square-Victoria, then Bus 61.*

Built on the actual foundations of the city, the impressive Pointe-à-Callière museum takes visitors back in time to 17th century Montréal.

Fodor'sChoice **Musée d'Archéologie et d'Histoire Pointe-à-Callière (PAC)** (*Pointe-à-Callière*
★ *Archaeology and History Museum*). The modern glass building is
impressive, and the audiovisual show is a breezy romp through Montréal's history from the Ice Age to the present. The museum presents
new local and international temporary exhibitions each year, but the
real reason to visit the city's most ambitious archaeological museum is
to take the elevator ride down to the 17th century.

It's dark down there, and just a little creepy thanks to the 350-year-
old tombstones teetering in the gloom, but it's worth the trip. This is
a serious archaeological dig that takes you to the very foundations of
the city. You begin on the banks of the long-vanished Rivière St-Pierre,
where the first settlers built their homes and traded with the First
Nations inhabitants. From there you climb up toward the present, past
the stone foundations of an 18th-century tavern and a 19th-century
insurance building. Along the way, filmed figures representing past
inhabitants appear on ghostly screens to chat to you about their life
and times.

A more lighthearted exhibit explores life and love in multicultural Montréal. For a spectacular view of the Old Port, the St. Lawrence River, and
the Islands, ride the elevator to the top of the tower, or stop for lunch
in the museum's glass-fronted café. In summer there are re-creations of
period fairs and festivals on the grounds near the museum.

In May 2017, the PAC unveiled a new pavilion and a refurbished stone
sewer to mark Montréal's 375th anniversary. The Fort Ville-Marie
pavilion showcases the remains of the forts and artifacts from the first
Montrealers. The 360-foot underground William collector sewer, built

in the 1830s and considered a masterpiece of civil engineering at that time, connects the original museum space with the new pavilion and features a sound-and-light show projected onto the walls of the collector sewer. ✉ *350 pl. Royale, Old Montréal* ☎ *514/872–9150* ⊕ *www. pacmuseum.qc.ca* 🎫 *C$20* Ⓜ *Place-d'Armes.*

Musée du Château Ramezay. Claude de Ramezay, the city's 11th governor, was probably daydreaming of home when he built his Montréal residence, which is on UNESCO's list of "1001 historic sites you must see before you die." Its thick stone walls, dormer windows, and steeply pitched roof make it look like a little bit of 18th-century Normandy dropped into the middle of North America—although the round, squat tower is a 19th-century addition. The extravagant mahogany paneling in the Salon de Nantes was installed when Louis XV was still king of France. The British used the château as headquarters after their conquest in 1760, and so did the American commanders Richard Montgomery and Benedict Arnold. Benjamin Franklin, who came north in a failed attempt to persuade the Quebecois to join the American Revolution, stayed here during that winter adventure.

Most of the château's exhibits are a little staid—guns, uniforms, and documents on the main floor and tableaux depicting colonial life in the cellars—but they include some unexpected little eccentricities that make it worth the visit. One of its prized possessions is a bright-red automobile the De Dion-Bouton Company produced at the turn of the 20th century for the city's first motorist.

Head outside, through the back door, and you'll enter gardens full of 18th-century tranquility. They are laid out just as formally as Mme. de Ramezay might have wished, with a *potager* for vegetables and a little *verger,* or orchard. You can sit on a bench in the sun, admire the flowers, and inhale the sage-scented air from the herb garden. ✉ *280 rue Notre-Dame Est, Old Montréal* ☎ *514/861–3708* ⊕ *www. chateauramezay.qc.ca* 🎫 *C$11* ⊘ *Closed Mon. late Oct. to late May* Ⓜ *Champ-de-Mars.*

FAMILY
Fodor's Choice
★

Old Port (*Vieux Port*). Montréal's favorite waterfront park is your ideal gateway to the St. Lawrence River. Rent a pedal boat, take a ferry to Île Ste-Hélène, sign up for a dinner cruise, or, if you're really adventurous, ride a raft or a jet boat through the turbulent Lachine Rapids. If you're determined to stay ashore, however, there's still plenty to do, including riding the Grande Roue, the tallest Ferris Wheel in Canada; soaking in the rays at the Clock Tower Beach (you can't swim, though); and enjoying street performances, sound-and-light shows, or art displays and exhibitions. Visiting warships from the Canadian navy and other countries often dock here and open their decks to the public. You can rent a bicycle or a pair of in-line skates at one of the shops along rue de la Commune and explore the waterfront at your leisure. If it's raining, the Centre des Sciences de Montréal on **King Edward Pier** will keep you dry and entertained, and if your lungs are in good shape you can climb the 192 steps to the top of the **Clock Tower** for a good view of the waterfront and the Islands; it was erected at the eastern end of the waterfront in memory of merchant mariners killed during World War I.

In winter, rent a pair of skates and glide around the outdoor rink. You can also, quite literally, lose the kids in **Shed 16's Labyrinthe,** a maze of alleys, surprises, and obstacles built inside an old waterfront warehouse. Every couple of years or so the **Cirque du Soleil** comes home to pitch its blue-and-yellow tent in the Old Port. But be warned: when the circus is in town, the tickets sell faster than water in a drought. ⊠ *Old Montréal* ☎ *514/496–7678, 800/971–7678* ⊕ *www.oldportofmontreal. com* Ⓜ *Place-d'Armes or Champ-de-Mars.*

FAMILY **Place Jacques-Cartier.** The cobbled square at the heart of Old Montréal is part carnival, part flower market, and part sheer fun. You can pause here to have your portrait painted or to buy an ice cream or to watch the street performers. If you have more time, try to get a table at one of the sidewalk cafés, order a beer or a glass of wine, and watch the passing parade. At Christmastime you can order a mulled wine in the market and warm up by one of the wood-burning stoves from your perch on an Adirondack chair. The 1809 monument honoring Lord Nelson's victory over Napoléon Bonaparte's French navy at Trafalgar angers some modern-day Québec nationalists. The campaign to raise money for it was led by the Sulpician priests, who were engaged in delicate land negotiations with the British government at the time and were eager to show what good subjects they were. ⊠ *Bordered by rues Notre-Dame Est and de la Commune, Old Montréal* Ⓜ *Champ-de-Mars.*

WORTH NOTING

FAMILY **Centre des Sciences de Montréal.** You—or more likely, your kids—can design an energy-efficient bike, create a television news report, explore the impact that manufacturing one T-shirt has on the environment, find out what it's like to ride a unicycle 20 feet above the ground, create an animated film, or just watch an IMAX movie on a giant screen at Montréal's interactive science center. A recent addition, Clic! The Zone for Curious Young Minds, is a colorful and fun area for four- to seven-year-olds. Games, puzzles, and hands-on experiments make it an ideal place for rainy days or even fair ones. The center also has a bistro serving lights meals, a coffee and pastry shop, and a food court. ⊠ *Quai King Edward, Old Montréal* ☎ *514/496–4724, 877/496–4724* ⊕ *www.centredessciencesdemontreal.com* ⊠ *C$15, IMAX C$12, special exhibits C$24–C$30* Ⓜ *Place-d'Armes.*

Hôtel de Ville (*City Hall*). President Charles de Gaulle of France marked Canada's centennial celebrations in 1967 by standing on the central balcony of Montréal's ornate city hall on July 24 and shouting "*Vive le Québec libre*" ("Long live free Québec"), much to the delight of the separatist movement and to the horror of the federal government that had invited him over in the first place. Perhaps he got carried away because he felt so at home: the Second Empire–style city hall, built in 1878, is modeled after the one in Tours, France. Free guided tours are available (reservations required). ⊠ *275 rue Notre-Dame Est, Old Montréal* ☎ *514/872–0077 for guided tours* ⊕ *www.ville. montreal.qc.ca* ⊠ *Free* Ⓜ *Champ-de-Mars.*

Marché Bonsecours (*Bonsecours Market*). You can't buy fruits and vegetables in the Marché Bonsecours anymore, but you can view an exhibit, shop for local fashions, crafts, and souvenirs in the row of upscale boutiques that fill its main hall, lunch in one of several restaurants, or grab a craft beer. But the Marché is best admired from the outside. Built in the 1840s as the city's main market, it is possibly the most beautifully proportioned neoclassical building in Montréal, with its six cast-iron Doric columns and two rows of meticulously even sashed windows, all topped with a silvery dome. Perhaps the Marché was too elegant to be just a farmers' market. ⊠ *350 rue St-Paul Est, Old Montréal* ☎ *514/872–7730* ⊕ *www.marchebonsecours. qc.ca* Ⓜ *Champ-de-Mars.*

Place-d'Armes. When Montréal was under attack, citizens and soldiers would rally at Place-d'Armes, but these days the only rallying is done by tourists, lunching office workers, calèche drivers, and flocks of voracious pigeons. The pigeons are particularly fond of the triumphant statue of Montréal's founder, Paul de Chomedey, with his lance upraised, perched above the fountain in the middle of the cobblestone square. Tunnels beneath the square protected the colonists from the winter weather and provided an escape route; unfortunately, they are too small and dangerous to visit. ⊠ *Bordered by rues Notre-Dame Ouest, St-Jacques, and St-Sulpice, Old Montréal* Ⓜ *Place-d'Armes.*

Place de la Grande-Paix. If you're looking for peace and quiet, the narrow strip of grass and trees on Place d'Youville just east of Place Royale is an appropriate place to find it. It was here, after all, that the French signed a major peace treaty with dozens of aboriginal nations in 1702. It was also here that the first French colonists to settle in Montréal landed their four boats on May 17, 1642. An obelisk records the settlers' names. ⊠ *Between pl. d'Youville and rue William, Old Montréal* Ⓜ *Place-d'Armes.*

Place Royale. The oldest public square in Montréal, dating to the 17th century, was a market during the French regime and later became a Victorian garden. ⊠ *Bordered by rues St-Paul Ouest and de la Commune, Old Montréal* Ⓜ *Place-d'Armes.*

Square Victoria. While Square Victoria officially lies within the recently created Quartier International, or International District, Montrealers consider it a part of Old Montréal. The square blends its French and English heritage with an 1872 statue of Queen Victoria on one side and an authentic Parisian métro entrance and a flower market on the other. Both are framed by a two-block stretch of trees, benches, and fountains that makes a pleasant place to relax and admire the handsome 1920's office buildings on the east side. The art nouveau métro entrance, incidentally, was a gift from the French capital's transit commission. ⊠ *Rue du Square Victoria, between rues Viger and St-Jacques, Old Montréal* Ⓜ *Square-Victoria.*

LACHINE

If you want to work up an appetite for lunch—or just get some exercise—rent a bike on rue de la Commune, in Old Montréal, and ride west along the 14-km (9-mile) Lachine Canal through what used to be Montréal's industrial heartland to the shores of Lac St-Louis. You could stop at the Marché Atwater to buy some cheese, bread, wine, and maybe a little pâté for a picnic in the lakefront park at the end of the trail. If paddling and pedaling sound too energetic, hop aboard an excursion boat and dine more formally in one of the century-old homes that line the waterfront in Lachine, the historic city borough at the western end of the canal that was once the staging point for the lucrative fur trade.

WORTH NOTING

FAMILY **Lachine Canal National Historic Site.** The canal is all about leisure—biking, rollerblading, strolls along the water and picnicking—but it wasn't always so. Built in 1825 to get boats and cargo around the treacherous Lachine Rapids, it quickly became a magnet for all sorts of industries. But when the St. Lawrence Seaway opened in 1959, allowing large cargo ships to sail straight from the Atlantic to the Great Lakes without stopping in Montréal, the canal closed to navigation and became an illicit dumping ground for old cars and the bodies of victims of underworld killings. The area around it degenerated into an industrial slum.

A federal agency rescued the site in 1978, planting lawns and trees along the old canal, transforming it into a long, narrow park, or *parc linéaire*. Some of the abandoned canneries, sugar refineries, and steelworks have since been converted into desirable residential and commercial condominiums. The bicycle path is the first link in the more than 97 km (60 miles) of bike trails that make up the **Pôle des Rapides** (*514/364–4490 www.poledesrapides.com*)

Two permanent exhibits at the **Lachine Canal Visitor Services Centre**, at the western end of the canal, explain its history and construction. The center also has a shop and lookout terrace. ⊠ *Lachine* ☎ *514/283–6054* ⊕ *www.pc.gc.ca* ⊠ *Free* Ⓜ *Angrignon, then bus 195.*

Fur Trade at Lachine National Historic Site. Located in the waterfront park at the end of the Lachine Canal, on the shores of Lac St. Louis, this 1803 stone warehouse has been converted into a museum that commemorates the industry that dominated Canada's early history. ⊠ *1255 boul. St-Joseph, Lachine* ☎ *888/773–8888, 514/283–6054* ⊕ *www.pc.gc.ca* ⊠ *C$4.*

Lachine Canal Nautical Centre. You can rent anything from a one-person kayak to a 13-passenger Voyageur canoe here and paddle along the canal. Electric boat rentals are also available. It's about 3½ km (2 miles) from Old Montréal. *Hours may change depending on weather, especially in May and September.* ⊠ *2985B rue St-Patrick, near Atwater Market, Verdun* ☎ ⊕ *www.h2oadventures.ca* Ⓜ *Lionel Groulx or Charlevoix.*

DOWNTOWN AND CHINATOWN

Rue Ste-Catherine—and the métro line that runs under it—
is the main cord that binds together the disparate, sprawling neighborhoods that comprise Montréal's Downtown, or
centre-ville, just north and west of Old Montréal.

DOWNTOWN

The heart of Downtown—with department stores, boutiques, bars,
restaurants, strip clubs, amusement arcades, theaters, cinemas, art galleries, bookstores, and even a few churches—runs from avenue Atwater to boulevard St-Denis. Ste-Catherine is also the main drag of the
Quartier des Spectacles, which runs west to east from rue Bleury to rue
St-Hubert. Inside this arts and entertainment district are the Place des
Arts and several other cultural venues; it also serves as the Downtown
home to most of Montréal's many summer festivals.

Walk farther north on rue Crescent to rue Sherbrooke and the lower
slopes of Mont-Royal and you come to what was once the most exclusive neighborhood in Canada—the **Golden Square Mile.** During the boom
years of the mid-1800s, baronial homes covered the mountain north of
rue Sherbrooke. Many are gone, replaced by high-rises or modern town
houses, but there are still plenty of architectural treasures to admire,
most of them now foreign consulates or university institutes.

And underneath it all—the entire Downtown area and then some—is
Montréal's **Underground City,** a vast network of more or less anything
you'd find on the street above.

GETTING HERE AND AROUND

Getting to and around Downtown is easy, thanks to the métro. There
are several stations along boulevard de Maisonneuve, which is a block
away from and runs parallel to rue Ste-Catherine. Many of them link
directly to the Underground City.

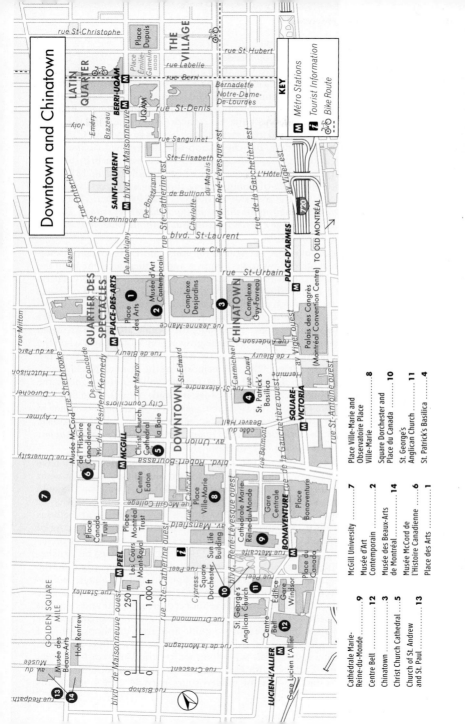

Downtown and Chinatown

TOP ATTRACTIONS

Cathédrale Marie-Reine-du-Monde (*Mary Queen of the World Cathedral*). The best reason to visit this cathedral is that it's a quarter-scale replica of St. Peter's Basilica in Rome—complete with a magnificent reproduction of Bernini's ornate baldachin (canopy) over the main altar and an ornately coffered ceiling. When Bishop Ignace Bourget (1799–1885) decided to build his cathedral in the heart of the city's Protestant-dominated commercial quarter, many fellow Catholics thought he was crazy. But the bishop was determined to assert the Church's authority—and its loyalty to Rome—in the British-ruled city. Bourget didn't live to see the cathedral dedicated in 1894, but his tomb holds place of honor among those of his successors in the burial chapel on the east side of the nave. ⊠ *1085 rue de la Cathédrale, (enter through main doors on boul. René-Lévesque), Downtown* ☎ *514/866–1661* ⊕ *www.cathedralecatholiquedemontreal.org* 🎫 *Free* Ⓜ *Bonaventure.*

Christ Church Cathedral. The seat of the Anglican (Episcopalian) bishop of Montréal offers downtown shoppers and strollers a respite from the hustle and bustle of rue Ste-Catherine, with free noontime concerts and organ recitals. Built in 1859, the cathedral is modeled on Snettisham Parish Church in Norfolk, England, with some distinctly Canadian touches. The steeple, for example, is made with aluminum plates molded to simulate stone, and inside, the Gothic arches are crowned with carvings of the types of foliage growing on Mont-Royal when the church was built. The stained-glass windows behind the main altar, installed in the early 1920s as a memorial to the dead of World War I, show scenes from the life of Christ. On the wall just above and to the left of the pulpit is the Coventry Cross; it's made of nails taken from the ruins of Britain's Coventry Cathedral, destroyed by German bombing in 1940. Free Saturday group tours can be arranged by calling the office. ⊠ *635 rue Ste-Catherine Ouest, Downtown* ☎ *514/843–6577* ⊕ *www.montrealcathedral.ca* 🎫 *Free* Ⓜ *McGill.*

Musée d'Art Contemporain (*Museum of Contemporary Art*). If you have a taste for pastoral landscapes and formal portraits, you might want to stick with the Musée des Beaux-Arts. But for a walk on the wild side of art, see what you can make of the jagged splashes of color that cover the canvases of the "Automatistes," as Québec's rebellious artists of the 1930s styled themselves. Their works form the core of this museum's collection of 5,000 pieces. One of the leaders of the movement, Jean-Paul Riopelle (1923–2002), often tossed his brushes and palette knives aside and just squeezed the paint directly onto the canvas—sometimes several tubes at a time. In 1948, Riopelle and his friends fired the first shot in Québec's Quiet Revolution by signing *Le Refus Global,* a manifesto that renounced the political and religious establishment of the day and revolutionized art in the province. The museum often has weekend programs and art workshops, some of which are geared toward children, and almost all are free. And for a little romance and music with your art, try the Vendredi Nocturnes (Nocturnal Fridays) with live music, bar service, and guided tours of the exhibits. Hours for guided tours vary. ■TIP➜ Admission is

The Musée des Beaux-Arts has one of Canada's largest permanent collections of Canadian art, as well as a gallery where you can buy paintings by local artists.

half-price Wednesdays after 5. ✉ *185 rue Ste-Catherine Ouest, Downtown* ☎ *514/847–6226* ⊕ *www.macm.org* 🎟 *C$19* ⊙ *Closed Mon.* Ⓜ *Place-des-Arts.*

Fodor's Choice ★ **Musée des Beaux-Arts de Montréal** (*Montréal Museum of Fine Arts*). Not surprisingly, Canada's oldest museum has one of the finest collections of Canadian art anywhere. The works of such luminaries as Paul Kane, the Group of Seven, Paul-Émile Borduas, and Marc-Aurèle Fortin are displayed here in a space built onto the back of the neoclassical Erskine and American United Church, one of the city's most historic Protestant churches. The nave has been preserved as a meeting place and exhibition hall and also displays the church's 18 Tiffany stained-glass windows, the biggest collection of Tiffany's work outside the United States. The rest of the gallery's permanent collection, which includes works by everyone from Rembrandt to Renoir, is housed in its two other pavilions: the neoclassical **Michal and Renata Hornstein Pavilion**, across Avenue du Musée from the church, and the glittering, glass-fronted **Jean-Noël-Desmarais Pavilion**, across rue Sherbrooke. All three are linked by tunnels. If you visit the museum in summer, spring or fall, you'll be greeted outside the main entrance by the Sun, Seattle sculptor Dale Chihuly's bright, twisted glass sculpture, now part of the MMFA's permanent collection thanks to an extensive fundraising campaign and generous donation from Montréal philanthropist Sebastian van Berkom. Unfortunately due to the city's brutal winters, the sculpture cannot be exhibited in the cold months. The museum also includes the Musée des Arts Décoratifs, where you can see some fanciful bentwood furniture designed by Frank Gehry, a marvelous collection of 18th-century English porcelain, and 3,000—count 'em—Japanese snuff boxes collected by, of all people, Georges Clemenceau, France's prime minister during World War I. ✉ *1380 rue Sherbrooke Ouest, Downtown* ☎ *514/285–2000* ⊕ *www.mmfa.qc.ca* ▣ *C$23; special exhibitions C$15* ⊘ *Closed Mon.* Ⓜ *Guy-Concordia.*

Musée McCord de l'Histoire Canadienne (*McCord Museum of Canadian History*). David Ross McCord (1844–1930) was a wealthy pack rat with a passion for anything that had to do with Montréal or Canadian history. His collection of paintings, costumes, toys, tools, drawings, and housewares provides a glimpse of what city life was like for all classes in the 19th century. If you're interested in the lifestyles of the elite, however, you'll love the photographs that William Notman (1826–91) took of the rich at play. One series portrays members of the posh Montréal Athletic Association posing in snowshoes on the slopes of Mont-Royal, all decked out in Hudson Bay coats and woolen hats. Each of the hundreds of portraits was shot individually in a studio and then painstakingly mounted on a picture of the snowy mountain to give the impression of a winter outing. There are guided tours (call for schedule), a reading room, a documentation center, a gift shop, a bookstore, and a café. ■TIP➔ **Admission is free Wednesday 5–9 pm.** ✉ *690 rue Sherbrooke Ouest, Downtown* ☎ *514/861–6701* ⊕ *www. mccord-museum.qc.ca* ▣ *C$20* Ⓜ *McGill.*

St. Patrick's Basilica. Built in 1847, this is one of the purest examples of the Gothic Revival style in Canada, with a high-vaulted ceiling glowing with green and gold mosaics. The tall, slender columns are actually pine logs lashed together and decorated to look like marble, so that if you stand in one of the back corners and look toward the altar you really do feel as if you're peering at the sacred through a grove of trees. St. Pat's—as most of its parishioners call it—is to Montréal's Anglophone Catholics what the Basilique Notre-Dame is to their French-speaking brethren—the mother church and a monument to faith and courage. One of the joys of visiting the place is that you'll probably be the only tourist there, so you'll have plenty of time to check out the old pulpit and the huge lamp decorated with six 2-meter- (6-foot-) tall angels hanging over the main altar. And if you're named after some relatively obscure saint like Scholastica or Aeden of Fleury, you can search for your namesake's portrait among the 170 painted panels on the walls of the nave.

For a solemn experience visit on the third Sunday of the month (September through to June) where the mass is sung completely in Latin. ✉ *454 boul. René-Lévesque Ouest, Downtown* ☎ *514/866–7379* ⊕ *www. stpatricksmtl.ca* ▣ *Free* ⊘ *Closed Sat. before Easter* Ⓜ *Square-Victoria.*

The Underground City (*La ville souterraine*). Place Ville-Marie, the cruciform skyscraper designed by I. M. Pei, was the tallest structure in the city when it opened in 1962. Located in the heart of downtown, it signaled the beginning of Montréal's subterranean city. Montrealers were skeptical that anyone would want to shop or even walk around in the new "down" town, but more than four decades later they can't live without it.

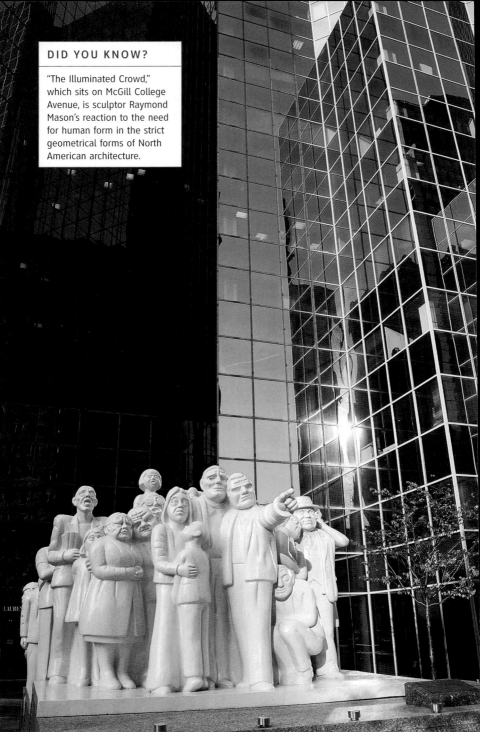

About half a million people use the 32-km (20-mile) Underground City, or *la ville souterraine*, daily. The tunnels link 10 métro stations, 7 hotels, 200 restaurants, 1,700 boutiques, and 60 office buildings—not to mention movie theaters, concert halls, convention complexes, the Centre Bell, two universities, and a college. In 2004 the Underground City was rebranded as the "RESO," a play on the word "réseau," which means network. You'll see the signs for it in the downtown area and can find a map of the network at ⊕ *montrealvisitorsguide.com/the-underground-city-map* ⊠ *Downtown.*

WORTH NOTING

Centre Bell. The Montréal Canadiens haven't won the Stanley Cup since 1993, and most of the team's fans can't remember the golden 1960s and '70s, when *Les Glorieux* virtually owned the trophy. The superstitious blame the team's fallen fortunes on its 1996 move from the hallowed Forum to the brown-brick Centre Bell arena. Still, Montréal is a hockey-mad city and the Habs, as locals call the team, are still demigods here, and there are even university courses based on this superstar team. (When they celebrated their 100th season in 2009–10, the city changed the name of the strip of rue de la Gauchetière in front of the Centre Bell to Avenue des Canadiens-de-Montréal.) The Bell Centre is also a concert venue for big name shows like Coldplay, Lady Gaga, and Jay-Z. ⊠ *1260 av. des Canadiens-de-Montréal, Downtown* ☎ *877/668–8269, 514/790–2525 for hockey tickets, 800/663–6786, 514/932–2582 for other events* ⊕ *www.centrebell.ca* Ⓜ *Bonaventure or Lucien-l'Allier.*

Church of St. Andrew and St. Paul. Montréal's largest Presbyterian church—sometimes affectionately called the A&P—is worth a visit, if only to see the glorious stained-glass window of the risen Christ that dominates the sanctuary behind the white-stone communion table. It's a memorial to members of the Royal Highland Regiment of Canada (the Black Watch) who were killed in World War I. ⊠ *3415 rue Redpath (main entrance on rue Sherbrooke), Downtown* ☎ *514/842–3431* ⊕ *www.standrewstpaul.com* ⚬ *Free* ☞ *For guided visit, phone in advance to make arrangements* Ⓜ *Guy-Concordia.*

McGill University. Merchant and fur trader James McGill would probably be horrified to know that the university that he helped found in 1828 has developed an international reputation as one of North America's best party schools. McGill also happens to be one of the two or three best universities in Canada, and certainly one of the prettiest. Its campus is an island of grass and trees in a sea of traffic and skyscrapers. If you take the time to stroll up the drive that leads from the Greek Revival Roddick Gates to the austere neoclassical Arts Building, keep an eye out to your right for the life-size statue of McGill himself, hurrying across campus clutching his tricorn hat. If you have an hour or so, drop into the templelike **Redpath Museum of Natural History** to browse its eclectic collection of dinosaur bones, old coins, African art, and shrunken heads. ⊠ *859 rue Sherbrooke Ouest, Downtown* ☎ *514/398–4455, 514/398–4086 museum* ⊕ *www. mcgill.ca; www.mcgill.ca/redpath (for museum)* ⚬ *Suggested donation: C$10* Ⓜ *McGill.*

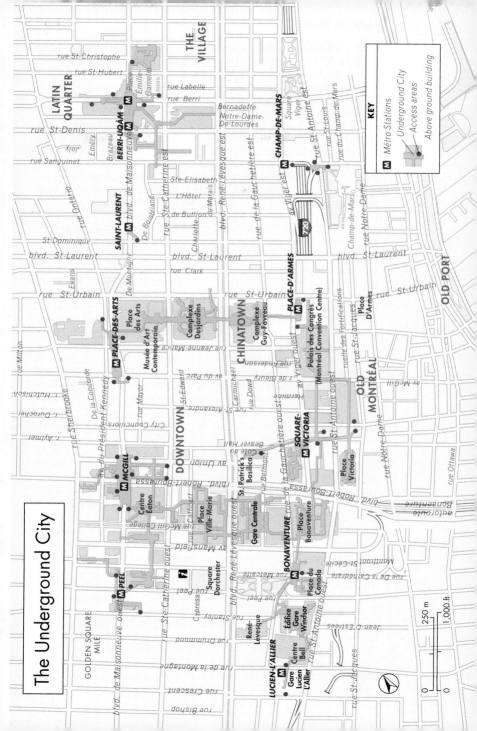

The Underground City

KEY

- M Métro Stations
- Underground City
- Access areas
- Above ground building

GOLDEN SQUARE MILE

THE VILLAGE

LATIN QUARTER

SAINT-LAURENT

PLACE-DES-ARTS

CHINATOWN

DOWNTOWN

CHAMP-DE-MARS

PLACE-D'ARMES

OLD MONTRÉAL

OLD PORT

SQUARE-VICTORIA

BONAVENTURE

LUCIEN-L'ALLIER

PEEL

McGILL

BERRI-UQAM

Streets and places:

rue St-Christophe
rue St-Hubert
Place Émilie-Gamelin
rue Labelle
rue Berri
Bernadette Notre-Dame-De-Lourdes
rue St-Denis
Square Viger
rue St-Antoine est
rue St-Tours
rue du Champ-de-Mars
Brazeau
Emery
rue Ste-Catherine est
blvd. de Maisonneuve
De Boisbriand
Ste-Elisabeth
L'Hôtel de Bullion
De Montigny
rue St-Urbain
rue St-Urbain
rue St-Urbain
Charlotte
rue de la Gauchetière est
av Viger est
Champ-de-Mars
blvd. St-Laurent
blvd. St-Laurent
blvd. St-Laurent
rue Clark
rue St-Edward
Place des Arts
Musée d'Art Contemporain
Complexe Desjardins
Complexe Guy-Favreau
Palais des Congrès (Montréal Convention Centre)
Place D'Armes
rue St-Jacques
ruelle des fortifications
rue Notre-Dame
De la Concorde
De la Montagne
av du Parc
rue Jeanne-Mance
av Anderson
l de Bleury
rue Hermine
rue Dowd
rue St-Alexandre
av Viger ouest
rue St-Antoine ouest
rue Notre-Dame
av McGill
rue Ottawa
rue Mentana
t. Durocher
t. Aylmer
rue Sherbrooke
City Councillors
av du Président Kennedy
Hutchison
Mayor
St-Urbain
Côte du Beaver Hall
Place Victoria
Centre Eaton
St-Patrick's Basilica
blvd. Robert-Bourassa
av Union
rue McGill College
Place Ville-Marie
Gare Centrale
Place Bonaventure
rue Metcalfe
blvd. René-Lévesque ouest
rue de la Gauchetière ouest
blvd. Robert-Bourassa
autoroute Bonaventure
rue Cathcart
rue Mansfield
rue Stanley
rue Drummond
Square Dorchester
Place du Canada
Montréal St-Cécile
rue De La Cathédrale
rue Crescent
rue Bishop
Square Peel
rue Peel
rue Peel
René-Lévesque
Édifice Windsor
Gare Windsor
Gare Lucien L'Allier
Centre Bell
rue Jean-D'Estrées
rue St-Antoine ouest
rue St-Jacques

250 m
1,000 ft

720

Place des Arts. Montréal's primary performing-arts complex has been undergoing a major renaissance. The center's main lobby was completely refurbished in 2010 and a new 2,000-seat concert hall for the Orchestre Symphonique de Montréal opened on the northeast corner of the site in the fall of 2011, fulfilling a decades-old dream of Montréal music lovers. Place des Arts is also the centerpiece of the city's **Quartier des Spectacles**, a square kilometer dedicated to arts and culture, with performance halls, dance studios, broadcasting facilities, and recording studios. The huge plaza in front of the complex is a favorite gathering place for locals and visitors—especially during the Jazz Festival and Just for Laughs, when it's packed with free concerts and entertainment. A C$34.2 million makeover to the arts center's esplanade is expected to be completed in 2018, with plans for it to function as a giant outdoor stage. ✉ *175 rue Ste-Catherine Ouest, Downtown* ☏ *514/842–2112 tickets, 514/285–4200 administration* ⊕ *www.placedesarts.com* Ⓜ *Place-des-Arts.*

Place Ville-Marie and Observatoire Place Ville-Marie. The cross-shape 1962 office tower was Montréal's first modern skyscraper; the mall complex underneath it was the first link in the Underground City. The wide expanse of the building's plaza, just upstairs from the mall, makes a good place to relax with coffee or a snack from the food court below. Benches, potted greenery, and fine views of Mont-Royal make it popular with walkers, tourists, and office workers. For $C19 you can take in 360-degree views of the city, by taking the elevator to the newly opened rooftop observation deck (⊕ www.ausommetpvm.com), where you'll also find a gourmet brasserie with a year-round terrace. ✉ *Bordered by boul. René-Lévesque and rues Mansfield, Cathcart, and University, Downtown* ☏ *514/866–6666* ⊕ *www.placevillemarie.com* ✎ *Observation Deck C$19* Ⓜ *McGill or Bonaventure.*

Square Dorchester and Place du Canada. On sunny summer days you can join the office workers, store clerks, and downtown shoppers who gather in these two green squares in the center of the city to eat lunch under the trees and perhaps listen to an open-air concert. If there are no vacant benches or picnic tables, you can still find a place to sit on the steps at the base of the dramatic monument to the dead of the Boer War. Other statues honor Scottish poet Robert Burns (1759–96); Sir Wilfrid Laurier (1841–1919), Canada's first French-speaking prime minister; and Sir John A. Macdonald (1815–91), Canada's first prime minister. ✉ *Bordered by boul. René-Lévesque and rues Peel, Metcalfe, and McTavish, Downtown* Ⓜ *Bonaventure or Peel.*

St. George's Anglican Church. This is possibly the prettiest Anglican (Episcopalian) church in Montréal. Step into its dim, candle-scented interior and you'll feel you've been transported to some prosperous market town in East Anglia (England). The double hammer-beam roof, the rich stained-glass windows, and the Lady Chapel on the east side of the main altar all add to the effect. It certainly seems a world away from Centre Bell, the modern temple to professional hockey that's across the street. ✉ *1101 rue Stanley, Downtown* ✛ *main entrance on rue de la Gauchetière* ☏ *514/866–7113* ⊕ *www.st-georges.org* ✎ *Free* Ⓜ *Bonaventure.*

CHINATOWN

Sandwiched between Downtown and the Old City is bustling **Chinatown.** The center of the action is at the intersection of rue Clark and rue de la Gauchetière, where part of the street is closed to traffic. On weekends, especially in summer, it's particularly busy, crowded with tourists as well as residents shopping in the Asian markets for fresh produce, meat and fish, and health supplements.

Chinese immigrants first came to Montréal in large numbers after 1880, following the construction of the transcontinental railroad, and there's been a steady influx of peoples from Asia and Southeast Asia—including the Vietnamese—since then. Now the city's Chinatown covers about an 18-block area between boulevard René-Lévesque and avenue Viger to the north and south, and near rue de Bleury and avenue Hôtel de Ville on the west and east.

GETTING HERE AND AROUND

The best way to enter Chinatown is through the ornate gates on boulevard St-Laurent—Place d'Armes is the closest métro station—then head for the hub at rue de la Gauchetière at the intersection of rue Clark.

THE LATIN QUARTER AND THE VILLAGE

Both the Latin Quarter and what's often known as the Gay Village have a steady energy during the day, busy with students heading to class and sitting hunched over laptops in cafés. Both neighborhoods get more fun in the evening, though, and generally the later, the better.

THE LATIN QUARTER

The **Latin Quarter** (Quartier Latin), just south of the Plateau, has been a center of student life since the 18th century, when Université de Montréal students gave the area its name (courses were given in Latin), and today it continues to infuse the city with youthful energy. When night falls, its streets are filled with multinational hordes—young and not so young, rich and poor, established and still studying.

The Université de Québec à Montréal (UQAM) spreads across the district, along with theaters, restaurants and bars, bookstores, and movie theaters. Some area businesses cater to a young clientele and their penchant for the loud and flashy, but the quarter is also home to some of the city's trendiest restaurants and nightspots. In summer, the streets of the Latin Quarter are busy with summer festival events, such as the Just for Laughs Festival in July.

GETTING HERE AND AROUND

The Latin Quarter is concentrated on boulevard de Maisonneuve and rue St-Denis. The busy Berri-UQAM métro station is the closest.

WORTH NOTING

Chapelle Notre-Dame-de-Lourdes (*Our Lady of Lourdes Chapel*). Artist and architect Napoléon Bourassa called his work here *l'oeuvre de mes amours*, or a labor of love—and it shows. He designed the little Byzantine-style building himself and set about decorating it with the exuberance of an eight-year-old making a Mother's Day card. He covered the walls with murals and encrusted the altar and pillars with gilt and ornamental carving. It's not Montréal's biggest monument to

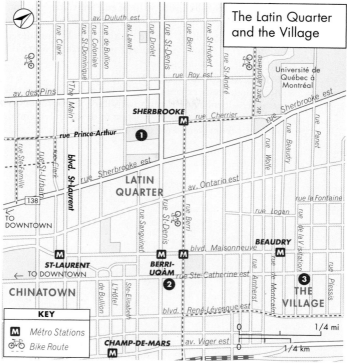

the Virgin Mary, but it's the most unabashedly sentimental. ✉ *430 rue Ste-Catherine Est, Latin Quarter* ☎ *514/845–8278* ⊕ *www.cndlm.org* ✉ *Free* Ⓜ *Berri-UQAM.*

Square St-Louis. The bourgeois families who built their homes around the fountain and trees here in the late 1870s would probably be dismayed to see the kind of people who congregate in their little park today. It's difficult to walk through the place without dodging a skateboarder or a panhandler. But they're generally a friendly bunch, and the square is still worth a visit just to see the elegant and colorful Second Empire–style homes that surround it. ✉ *Bordered by av. Laval and rue St-Denis between rue Sherbrooke Est and av. des Pins Est, Latin Quarter* Ⓜ *Sherbrooke.*

THE VILLAGE

Fodor's Choice ★ Often called the **Gay Village,** this area is the center of one of the most vibrant gay communities in the world, widely supported by residents of this proudly liberal, open-minded city. In recent years the municipal, federal, and provincial governments have taken it upon themselves to promote the Village and Montréal's gay-friendly climate as a reason for tourists to visit, but its restaurants, antiques shops (on rue Amherst), and bars make it a popular destination for visitors of all persuasions. The lively strip of rue Ste-Catherine running east of the Latin Quarter is the backbone of the Village.

In late July, the Village's Pride Parade, widely considered the biggest and most outrageous party of the year, attracts more than a million people.

GETTING HERE AND AROUND

The Village centers on the Beaudry métro station, which has its entrance adorned with rainbow pillars. Its borders are considered rue Ste-Catherine Est from Amherst to de Lorimier, and on the north–south axis from René-Lévesque to Sherbrooke.

2

THE PLATEAU, OUTREMONT, MILE END, AND LITTLE ITALY

Heading north and east of Downtown and the McGill campus will lead you to some of the most vibrant neighborhoods of Montréal, with a mix of ethnic communities, students, and young professionals. There aren't many traditional types of tourist attractions, but this is where you'll find exciting new restaurants, boutiques, and galleries are popping up, alongside long-established residential neighborhoods.

THE PLATEAU MONT-ROYAL

Plateau Mont-Royal—or simply the **Plateau** as it's more commonly called these days—is still home to a strong Portuguese community, but much of the housing originally built for factory workers has been bought and renovated by professionals, artists, performers, and academics eager to find a place to live close to all the action. The Plateau is always bustling, even in the dead of winter, but on sunny summer weekends it's packed with Montrealers who come here to shop, dine, and people-watch.

Many of the older residences in the Plateau and the nearby neighborhoods have the graceful wrought-iron balconies and twisting staircases that are typical of Montréal. The stairs and balconies, treacherous in winter, are often full of families and couples gossiping, picnicking, and partying come summer. If Montrealers tell you they spend the summer in Balconville, they mean they don't have the money or the time to leave town and won't get any farther than their balconies.

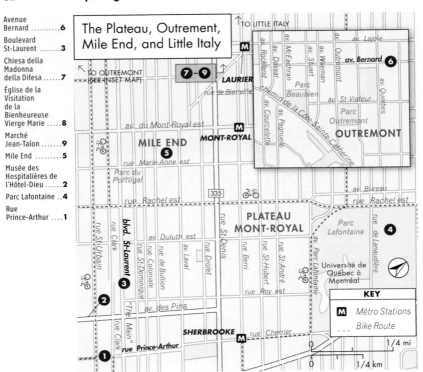

GETTING HERE AND AROUND

The Plateau's most convenient métro station is Mont-Royal on the Orange Line. It's a large district, but relatively flat and easy to walk around. If you want to cover more ground without resorting to a taxi, there are several Bixi bicycle stands in the area, and plenty of bike lanes.

TOP ATTRACTIONS

Boulevard St-Laurent. A walk here is like a walk through Montréal's cultural history. The shops and restaurants, synagogues and churches that line the 10-block stretch north of rue Sherbrooke reflect the various waves of immigrants that have called it home. Keep your eyes open and you'll see Jewish delis, Hungarian sausage shops, Chinese grocery stores, Italian coffee bars, Greek restaurants, Vietnamese sandwich shops, and Peruvian snack bars. You'll also spot some of the city's trendiest restaurants, cafés and galleries, as well as the dernier cri in skateboard fashion. The first immigrants to move into the area in the 1880s were Jews escaping pogroms in Eastern Europe. It was they who called the street "the Main," as in Main Street—a nickname that endures to this day. Even Francophone Montrealers sometimes call it "Le Main." ⊠ *The Plateau* Ⓜ *St-Laurent, Sherbrooke, or Mont-Royal.*

ART IN THE MÉTRO

Montréal was ahead of the curve in requiring all construction in the métro system to include an art component, resulting in such dramatic works as Frédéric Back's mural of the history of music in Place des Arts and the swirling stained-glass windows by Marcelle Ferron in Champs-de-Mars. The art nouveau entrance to the Square-Victoria station, a gift from the city of Paris, is the only original piece of Hector Guimard's architectural-design work outside the City of Light.

Operating since 1966, the métro is among the most architecturally distinctive subway systems in the world, with each of its 65 stations individually designed and decorated.

The newer stations along the Blue Line are all worth a visit as well, particularly Outremont, with a glass-block design from 1988. Even Place-d'Armes, one of the least visually remarkable stations in the system, includes a treasure: look for the small exhibit of archaeological artifacts representing each of Montréal's four historical eras (Aboriginal, French, English, and multicultural).

WORTH NOTING

Musée des Hospitalières de l'Hôtel-Dieu. The nuns of the Religieuses Hospitalières de St-Joseph ran Montréal's Hôpital Hôtel-Dieu for more than 300 years, until the province and the Université de Montréal took it over in the 1970s. The first sisters—girls of good families caught up in the religious fervor of the age—came to New France with Jeanne Mance in the mid-1600s to look after the poor, the sick, and the dying. The order's museum—tucked away in a corner of the hospital the nuns built but no longer run—captures the spirit of that age with a series of meticulously bilingual exhibits. Just reading the excerpts from the letters and diaries of those young women helps you to understand the zeal that drove them to abandon the comforts of home for the hardships of the colonies. The museum also traces the history of medicine and nursing in Montréal. *Guided tours are available for groups of 10 or more by reservation.* ⊠ *201 av. des Pins Ouest, The Plateau* ☎ *514/849–2919* ⊕ *www.museedeshospitalieres.qc.ca* ☞ *C$10 (cash only)* ☉ *Closed over Christmas and Easter holidays* Ⓜ *Sherbrooke, then Bus 144 or Place-des-Arts, then Bus 129 or 80.*

Parc Lafontaine. You could say that Parc Lafontaine is a microcosm of Montréal: the eastern half is French, with paths, gardens, and lawns laid out in geometric shapes; the western half is English, with meandering paths and irregularly shaped ponds that follow the natural contours of the land. In summer you can take advantage of bowling greens, tennis courts, an open-air theater (Théâtre de Verdure) where there are free events, and two artificial lakes with paddleboats. In winter one lake becomes a large skating rink. The park is named for Sir Louis-Hippolyte Lafontaine (1807–64), a pioneer of responsible government in Canada. His statue graces a plot on the park's southwestern edge. ⊠ *3933 av. Parc Lafontaine, The Plateau* ☎ *514/872–6381* ⊕ *www.montreal.com/parks* Ⓜ *Sherbrooke or Mont-Royal.*

ALL ABOARD THE EXPORAIL!

Exporail (*Canadian Railway Museum*). You can rattle around Canada's largest railroad museum in a vintage tram specially built in the 1950s for sightseeing tours in Montréal when the city still had a streetcar system. The museum has more than 120 train cars and locomotives, but if you're a steam buff, you won't want to miss CPR 5935, the largest steam locomotive built in Canada, and CNR 4100, the most powerful in the British Empire when it was built in 1924. To see how the rich and powerful traveled, take a look at Sir William Van Horne's luxurious private car. Of special interest to the kids will be the car that served as a mobile classroom. The museum is south of the city in the town of St-Constant. On the weekdays, the Agence metropolitaine de transport (www.amt. qc.ca) runs commuter trains from the Gare Lucien-l'Allier, next to the Centre Bell, to Candiac/St. Constant. Trains depart at 9:35 am and return at 1:27 pm. ✉ *110 rue St-Pierre, St-Constant* ☎ *450/632–2410* ⊕ *www.exporail.org* 🎟 *C$20.*

Rue Prince-Arthur. In the 1960s rue Prince-Arthur was the Haight-Ashbury of Montréal, full of shops selling leather vests, tie-dyed T-shirts, recycled clothes, and drug paraphernalia. It still retains a little of that raffish attitude, but it's much tamer and more commercial these days. The blocks between avenue Laval and boulevard St-Laurent are a pedestrian mall, and the hippie shops have metamorphosed into inexpensive Greek, Vietnamese, Italian, Polish, and Chinese restaurants and neighborhood bars. So grab a table, order a coffee or an *apéro*, and watch the passing parade. ✉ *The Plateau* Ⓜ *Sherbrooke.*

OUTREMONT

The gentrification of the Plateau has pushed up rents and driven students, immigrant families, and single young graduates farther north, following the main thoroughfares of boulevard St-Laurent as well as St-Denis. Above the Plateau and next to Parc du Mont-Royal, **Outremont** has long been Montréal's residential Francophone enclave (as opposed to Westmount, always stubbornly English right down to its neo-Gothic churches and lawn-bowling club). It has grand homes, tree-shaded streets, perfectly groomed parks, and two upscale shopping and dining strips along rue Laurier and avenue Bernard. The latter, with wide sidewalks and shady trees, is particularly attractive. The eastern fringes of Outremont are home to Montréal's thriving Hasidic community.

GETTING HERE AND AROUND

By métro, take the Blue Line to Outremont station. You can also get to Outremont from Downtown on Bus 55, which goes along St. Laurent Boulevard, or Bus 80, which goes through Mont-Royal Park along avenue du Parc. Both bus routes can be picked up outside the Place-des-Arts métro, and you need to get off at rue Laurier and walk west from there. (Outremont begins on the west side of Parc; the east side of Parc is Mile End.)

Alternately, you could stay on Bus 80 for a few more stops until you come to Bernard and then walk west. Both Laurier and Bernard avenues are Outremont's primary hubs for commercial activity. The Outremont métro stop lets you off on avenue Van Horne, another commercial hub but without the fun, interesting boutiques and restaurants of Laurier and Bernard. If you're coming from Downtown and feeling fit you could walk to Outremont in roughly 30–45 minutes, or, for that matter, just hop on a Bixi bicycle, taking the same route as Bus 80 and getting there in half the time.

TOP ATTRACTIONS

Avenue Bernard. If your taste runs to the chic and fashionable, then there is simply no better street than rue Bernard, west of Avenue Querbes, for people-watching. Its wide sidewalks and shady trees make it ideal for the kind of outdoor cafés and restaurants that attract the bright and the beautiful. ⊠ *Outremont* Ⓜ *Outremont.*

MILE END

In recent years **Mile End** has become one of the hippest neighborhoods in town, and it starts buzzing the moment restaurants open for brunch. Bordering Outremont, this funky area, historically home to Montréal's working-class Jewish community, is now full of inexpensive, often excellent restaurants and little shops selling handicrafts and secondhand clothes. Head east from Parc off streets like Bernard, St. Viateur, and Fairmount. By day it's a great place to take a stroll or sit on a café's *terrasse* (patio) to watch its residents—from artsy bohemians to Hasidic Jews—pass by.

GETTING HERE AND AROUND

To reach Mile End by public transit, take the métro's Orange Line to Laurier or Bus 55 from Place d'Armes métro station; get off at Fairmount or St. Viateur and walk west from there.

LITTLE ITALY

Farther north is **Little Italy,** which is still home base to Montréal's sizable Italian community of nearly a quarter of a million people, and though families of Italian descent now live all over the greater Montréal area, many come back here every week or so to shop, eat out, or visit family and friends, and the 30-odd blocks bounded by rues Jean-Talon, St-Zotique, Marconi, and Drolet remain its heart and soul. You'll know you've reached Little Italy when the gardens have tomato plants and grapevines, there are sausages and cans of olive oil in store windows, and the heady smell of espresso emanates from cafés.

GETTING HERE AND AROUND

You can take both the Orange and Blue lines to get to Little Italy: get off at Jean-Talon station and walk six short blocks to get to boulevard St-Laurent. Bus 55, which runs north along St-Laurent, will also get you here fairly quickly from Downtown, or you could just take a Bixi bike and get here in roughly 20 minutes. Once here, you can stop for produce and cheese at the Marché Jean-Talon, and you might just see a wedding party outside the Madonna della Difesa church.

TOP ATTRACTIONS

Chiesa della Madonna della Difesa. If you look up at the cupola behind the main altar of Little Italy's most famous church, you'll spot Montréal's most infamous piece of ecclesiastical portraiture. Yes, indeed, that lantern-jaw fellow on horseback who looks so pleased with himself is Benito Mussolini, the dictator who led Italy into World War II—on the wrong side.

The mural, by Guido Nincheri (1885–1973), was completed long before the war and commemorates the signing of the Lateran Pact with Pope Pius XI, one of Il Duce's few lasting achievements. The controversy shouldn't distract you from the beauties of the rest of the richly decorated church. ⊠ *6800 av. Henri-Julien, Little Italy* ☎ *514/277–6522* ◻ *Free* Ⓜ *Beaubien or Jean-Talon.*

OFF THE BEATEN PATH

Église de la Visitation de la Bienheureuse Vierge Marie. The oldest church on the island, the Church of the Visitation of the Blessed Virgin Mary had its stone walls raised in the 1750s, and the beautifully proportioned Palladian front was added in 1850. Decorating lasted from 1764 until 1837, with stunning results. The altar and the pulpit are as ornate as wedding cakes but still delicate. The church's most notable treasure is a rendering of the Visitation attributed to Pierre Mignard, a painter at the 17th-century court of Louis XIV. Parkland surrounds the church, and the nearby Îles de la Visitation (reachable by footbridge) make for a very good walk. You have to ride the métro to its northern terminus at the Henri-Bourassa station, and then walk for 15–20 minutes through some pretty ordinary neighborhoods to reach this church, but it's worth the trek. ⊠ *1847 boul. Gouin Est, Montréal North* ☎ *514/388–4050* ⊕ *www.eglisedelavisitation.org* ◻ *Free* Ⓜ *Henri-Bourassa.*

Fodor'sChoice ★ **Marché Jean-Talon.** If you're trying to stick to a diet, stay away: the smells of grilling sausages, roasting chestnuts, and fresh pastries will almost certainly crack your resolve. And if they don't, there are dozens of tiny shops full of Québec cheeses, Lebanese sweets, country pâtés, local wines, and handmade chocolates that will. Less threatening to the waistline are the huge mounds of peas, beans, apples, carrots, pears, garlic, and other produce on sale at the open-air stands. Visit on weekends during the warm summer months, and it will feel as if all of Montréal has come out to shop. ⊠ *7070 rue Henri-Julien, Little Italy* ☎ *514/277–1588* ⊕ *www.marchespublics-mtl.com* Ⓜ *Jean-Talon.*

PARC DU MONT-ROYAL

Fodor's Choice
★
In geological terms, Mont-Royal is just a bump of basaltlike rock worn down by several ice ages to a mere 760 feet. But in the affections of Montrealers it's a Matterhorn. Without a trace of irony, they call it simply *la Montagne* or "the Mountain," and it's easy to see why it's so well loved.

For Montrealers it's a refuge, a semitamed wilderness within the city. It's where you go to get away from it all. And even when you can't get away, you can see the mountain glimmering beyond the skyscrapers and the high-rises—green in summer, gray and white in winter, and gold and crimson in fall.

The nearly 500 acres of forests and meadows were laid out by Frederick Law Olmsted (1822–1903), the man responsible for New York City's Central Park. Olmsted believed that communion with nature could cure body and soul, so much of the park has been left as wild as possible, with narrow paths meandering through tall stands of maples and red oaks. In summer it's full of picnicking families; in winter cross-country skiers and snowshoers take over, while families skate at Lac aux Castors and ride sleds and inner tubes down groomed slopes. If you want to explore with minimum effort, you can hire the services of a horse-drawn carriage (or sleigh in winter).

GETTING HERE AND AROUND
If you're in good shape, you can walk, uphill all the way, from Downtown. Climb rue Peel to the entrance to Parc du Mont-Royal and then up the steep stairway to the top of the mountain. Or you can simply take the métro to the Mont-Royal station and catch Bus 11. If you have a car, there's good parking in Parc du Mont-Royal and at the Oratoire St-Joseph (the latter asks for a contribution of $5 per vehicle Monday to Saturday for anyone not attending a service or coming to pray). Biking up the mountain will test your endurance, but the park has an extensive network of scenic trails.

TOP ATTRACTIONS

Chalet du Mont-Royal. No trip to Montréal is complete without a visit to the terrace in front of the Chalet du Mont-Royal. It's not the only place to get an overview of the city, the river, and the countryside beyond, but it's the most spectacular. On clear days you can see not only the downtown skyscrapers, but also Mont-Royal's sister mountains—Monts St-Bruno, St-Hilaire, and St-Grégoire. These isolated peaks, called the Montérégies, or Mountains of the King, rise dramatically from the flat countryside. Be sure to take a look inside the chalet, especially at the murals depicting scenes from Canadian history. There's a snack bar in the back. ⊠ *Off voie Camillien-Houde, Parc du Mont-Royal* ⊕ *www.lemontroyal.qc.ca/en* ⌨ *Free* Ⓜ *Mont-Royal, then Bus 11 westbound.*

WORTH NOTING

Fodor'sChoice
★

Croix sur la Montagne (*Cross atop Mont-Royal*). Visible from up to 50 miles away on a clear day, the 98-foot-high steel cross at the top of Mont-Royal has been a city landmark since it was erected in 1924, largely with money raised through the efforts of 85,000 high-school students. Once upon a time, it took four hours and the labor of three to replace the 249 electric bulbs used to light the cross; today, the iconic cross is illuminated with a high-tech remote-control LED system. ⊠ *Parc du Mont-Royal* ⊕ *www.lemontroyal.qc.ca.*

FAMILY
Lac aux Castors (*Beaver Lake*). Mont-Royal's single body of water, actually a reclaimed bog, is a great place for kids (and parents) to float model boats or rent a rowboat in the summertime. In winter, the lake's frozen surface attracts whole families of skaters, and nearby there's a groomed slope where kids of all ages can ride inner tubes. The glass-fronted Beaver Lake Pavilion is a pleasant bistro that serves lunch and dinner. Skate and cross-country-ski rentals are available downstairs. ⊠ *Off chemin Remembrance, Parc du Mont-Royal* ⊕ *www.lemontroyal.qc.ca* Ⓜ *Mont-Royal, then Bus 11 westbound.*

Maison Smith. If you need a map of Mont-Royal's extensive hiking trails or want to know about the more than 180 kinds of birds here, the former park keeper's residence is the place to go. It's also a good spot for getting a snack, drink, or souvenir. The pretty little stone house—built in 1858—is the headquarters of Les Amis de la Montagne (The Friends of the Mountain), an organization that offers various guided walks—including moonlight snowshoe walks and cross-country ski lessons—on the mountain and in nearby areas. ⊠ *1260 chemin Remembrance, Parc du Mont-Royal* ☎ *514/843–8240* ⊕ *www.lemontroyal.qc.ca* Ⓜ *Mont-Royal, then bus 11 westbound.*

Observatoire de l'Est. If you're just driving across Mont-Royal, be sure to stop for a few moments at its eastern lookout for a view of the Stade Olympique and the east end of the city. Tourists enjoy the location as it's a great photo spot. ⊠ *Voie Camillien-Houde, Parc du Mont-Royal* Ⓜ *Mont-Royal.*

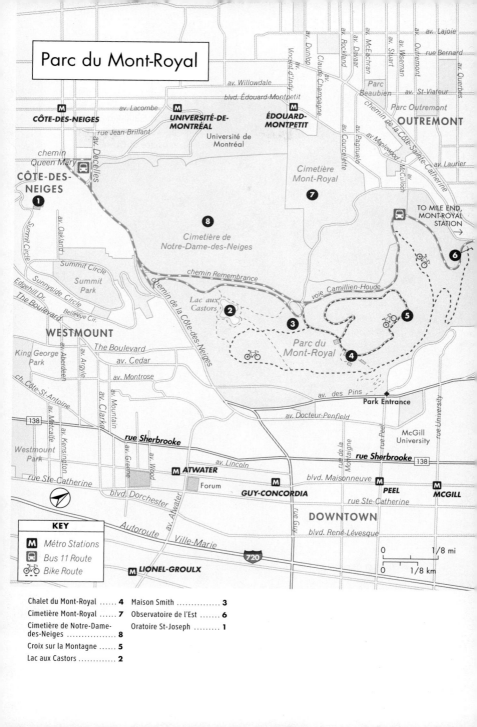

Parc du Mont-Royal

CÔTE-DES-NEIGES

av. Lacombe

UNIVERSITÉ-DE-MONTRÉAL

ÉDOUARD-MONTPETIT

av. Willowdale

blvd. Édouard-Montpetit

av. Lajoie

rue Bernard

Parc Beaubien

av. St-Viateur

Parc Outremont

OUTREMONT

Université de Montréal

rue Jean-Brillant

chemin Queen Mary

CÔTE-DES-NEIGES

Cimetière Mont-Royal

av. Laurier

TO MILE END, MONT-ROYAL STATION →

Cimetière de Notre-Dame-des-Neiges

Summit Circle

Summit Park

chemin Remembrance

voie Camillien-Houde

WESTMOUNT

Lac aux Castors

Parc du Mont-Royal

King George Park

The Boulevard

av. Cedar

av. Montrose

Park Entrance

av. des Pins

av. Docteur-Penfield

McGill University

rue Sherbrooke

Westmount Park

rue Sherbrooke

rue Ste-Catherine

av. Lincoln

ATWATER

Forum

blvd. Maisonneuve

PEEL

MCGILL

blvd. Dorchester

GUY-CONCORDIA

rue Ste-Catherine

DOWNTOWN

Autoroute Ville-Marie

blvd. René-Lévesque

720

LIONEL-GROULX

0   1/8 mi
0   1/8 km

KEY

- **M** Métro Stations
- Bus 11 Route
- Bike Route

2

CÔTE-DES-NEIGES

Not too many tourists venture north and east of Parc du Mont-Royal but the primarily residential neighborhoods of Côte-des-Neiges and the Town of Mount Royal (usually just called TMR) have much to offer.

One of Montréal's most-visited sites—the Oratoire St-Joseph (St. Joseph's Oratory)—sits atop the northern slope of Mont-Royal, dominating the surrounding neighborhood of Côte-des-Neiges. More than 2 million people of all faiths visit the shrine every year. The most devout pilgrims climb the staircase leading to the main door on their knees, pausing on each of its 99 steps to pray.

Even without the Oratoire (as well as the Cimetière de Notre-Dame-des-Neiges, another site worth seeing), Côte-des-Neiges is a district worth visiting. It's also an area where the dominant languages are neither English nor French.

It's largely working-class immigrants who live here—Filipino, Latin American, Southeast Asian, West Indian, Arab, Jewish, Chinese, and most recently people from Eastern Europe and Africa. It's also home to a sizable number of students, many of whom attend the Université de Montréal, as well as other smaller surrounding colleges and universities.

As a result, if you're looking for inexpensive, authentic world cuisine, there's no better place in Montréal to come to than Côte-des-Neiges. It's teeming with ethnic shops and restaurants—Thai, Russian, Korean, Indian, Peruvian, Filipino, and more.

GETTING HERE AND AROUND

Côte-des-Neiges is bordered by avenue Decelles to the north and the Cimetière de Notre-Dame-des-Neiges to the south. It's easy to get here by public transit, either the métro to the Côte-des-Neiges station or the 166 Bus from the Guy-Concordia métro station to chemin Queen-Mary. If you take a car—not a bad idea if you plan to visit the Parc du Mont-Royal as well—it's usually easy to get a parking space at the Oratoire St-Joseph (a contribution of $5 per vehicle is requested Monday to Saturday, except for those attending services or coming to the Oratoire to pray).

WHEN TO GO
Côte-des-Neiges bustles during the day, but is a little quieter at night.

TOP ATTRACTIONS

Fodor's Choice   **Oratoire St-Joseph** (*St. Joseph's Oratory*). Each year some 2 million peo-
★   ple from all over North America and beyond visit St. Joseph's Oratory.
The most devout Catholics climb the 99 steps to its front door on their
knees. It is the world's largest and most popular shrine dedicated to the
earthly father of Jesus (Canada's patron saint), and it's all the work of
a man named Brother André Besette (1845–1937).

By worldly standards Brother André didn't have much going for him,
but he had a deep devotion to St. Joseph and an iron will. In 1870 he
joined the Holy Cross religious order and was assigned to work as a
doorkeeper at the college the order operated just north of Mont-Royal.
In 1904 he began building a chapel on the mountainside across the road
to honor his favorite saint, and the rest is history. Thanks to reports
of miraculous cures attributed to St. Joseph's intercession, donations
started to pour in, and Brother André was able to start work replacing
his modest shrine with something more substantial. The result, which
wasn't completed until after his death, is one of the most triumphal
pieces of church architecture in North America.

The oratory and its gardens dominate Mont-Royal's northwestern
slope. Its copper dome—one of the largest in the world—can be seen
from miles away. The interior of the main church is equally grand,
although it's also quite austere. The best time to visit it is on Sunday
for the 11 am solemn mass, when the sanctuary is brightly lit and the
sweet voices of Les Petits Chanteurs de Mont-Royal—the city's best
boys' choir—fill the nave with music.

The crypt is shabbier than its big brother upstairs but more welcoming.
In a long, narrow room behind the crypt, 10,000 votive candles glitter
before a dozen carved murals extolling the virtues of St. Joseph; the
walls are hung with crutches discarded by those said to have been cured.
Just beyond is the simple tomb of Brother André, who was canonized a
saint in 2010. His preserved heart is displayed in a glass case in one of
several galleries between the crypt and the main church.

High on the mountain, east of the main church, is a garden commemorating the Passion of Christ, with life-size representations of the 14
stations of the cross. On the west side of the church is Brother André's
original chapel, with pressed-tin ceilings and plaster saints that is, in
many ways, more moving than the church that overshadows it. Note:
the oratoire operates a shuttle bus for visitors who aren't up to the
steep climb from the main parking lot to the entrance of the crypt
church. The main church is several stories above that, but escalators
and two elevators ease the ascent. ⊠ *3800 chemin Queen Mary, Côte-
des-Neiges* ☏ *514/733–8211, 877/672–8647* ⊕ *www.saint-joseph.org*
🖃 *Free. Parking: $5 per vehicle contribution requested (except for those
attending services or coming to pray)* Ⓜ *Côte-des-Neiges.*

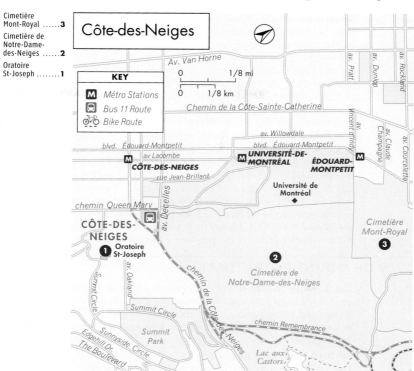

WORTH NOTING

Cimetière de Notre-Dame-des-Neiges (*Our Lady of the Snows Cemetery*). At 343 acres, Canada's largest cemetery is not much smaller than the neighboring **Parc du Mont-Royal,** and, as long as you just count the living, it's usually a lot less crowded. You don't have to be morbid to wander the graveyard's 55 km (34 miles) of tree-shaded paths and roadways past the tombs of hundreds of prominent artists, poets, intellectuals, politicians, and clerics. Among them is Calixa Lavallée (1842–91), who wrote "O Canada," the country's national anthem. The cemetery offers some guided tours in summer. Phone ahead for details. ⊠*4601 chemin de la Côte-des-Neiges, Côte-des-Neiges* ☎*514/735–1361* ⊕ *www.cimetierenotredamedesneiges.ca* Ⓜ *Côte-des-Neiges, then Bus 165 southbound.*

NEED A BREAK

✕ **Duc de Lorraine.** Opened in 1952, Duc de Lorraine is a Montréal institution. A light croissant or rich pastry from the city's oldest patisserie makes for a nice break after visiting the Parc Mont-Royal or Oratoire St-Joseph. ⊠ *5002 Côte-des-Neiges, Côte-des-Neiges* ☎ *514/731–4128* ⊕ *www.ducdelorraine.ca* Ⓜ *Côte-des-Neiges.*

Fodor's Choice **Cimetière Mont-Royal.** If you find yourself humming "Getting to Know
★ You" as you explore Mont-Royal Cemetery's 165 acres, blame it
on the graveyard's most famous permanent guest, Anna Leonowens
(1834–1915). She was the real-life model for the heroine of the Rodg-
ers and Hammerstein musical *The King and I.* The cemetery—established in 1852 by the Anglican, Presbyterian, Unitarian, and Baptist
churches—is laid out like a terraced garden, with footpaths that mean-
der between crab-apple trees and past Japanese lilacs. ✉ *1297 chemin
de la Forêt, Côte-des-Neiges* ☎ *514/279–7358* ⊕ *www.mountroyalcem.
com* Ⓜ *Mont-Royal, then Bus 11 westbound.*

St. Joseph's Oratory. Nearly all of Montréal's numerous historic churches
offer free admission, and some, like St. Joseph's Oratory, one of the
world's most visited shrines, offer guided tours. The cost is $5 per per-
son. In summer, tours are offered at 1:30 and 3. Reservations must be
made for winter tours. ✉ *3800 Queen Mary, Côte-des-Neiges* ⊕ *www.
saint-joseph.org/en* ✉ *Free. C$5 for parking. Museum, C$4* ☞ *Tours
are offered at 10:30, 1:30, and 3. Reservations needed for winter tours.*
Ⓜ *Snowdon or Côte des Neiges, then either bus 51, 165 or 166.*

TOWN OF MOUNT ROYAL (TMR)

The Town of Mount Royal, was long a primarily English-speaking,
and for the most part upscale, residential area, filled with classic town
houses and many parks. Just north of Outremont and south of Ville
St-Laurent, it's a notably pretty area, although not a whole lot goes
on here.

GETTING HERE AND AROUND
TMR is a notoriously tricky area to drive to if you don't know Montréal well, and there are no métro stations nearby. The easiest way to
get here from Downtown is by taking the commuter train that leaves
from Central Station and then getting off at the Mont-Royal stop, at
the particularly cute town square. The train ride is notable in itself—it
travels directly under "the mountain" (Parc Mont-Royal), through what
is the second longest tunnel in the country (about 5 km [3 miles]). It
was constructed by the Canadian Northern Railway back in 1910, and
was, at that time, considered quite an engineering feat.

HOCHELAGA-MAISONNEUVE

The neighborhood of Hochelaga-Maisonneuve is one of the best spots to go if you're craving green space, plus it has one of Montréal's best markets. In fact, it's worth the trip on the métro's Green Line just to see the four institutions that make up Montréal's Space for Life, an innovative natural science museum complex—the first in the world to link humans with nature. It includes the Jardin Botanique (Botanical Garden); the Insectarium, which houses the world's largest collection of bugs (but will be closed for most of 2018 for renovations); the Biodôme (also to close for renovations during 2018), a great place to experience different ecosystems under one roof; and the stunning Rio Tinto Alcan Planetarium.

Parc Maisonneuve is a lovely green area, and an ideal place for a stroll or a picnic, and don't miss the Stade Olympique (Olympic Stadium), which played host to the 1976 Summer Olympics; the leaning tower that supports the stadium's roof dominates the skyline here and provides a great viewpoint. The rest of the area is largely working-class residential, but there are some good restaurants and little shops along rue Ontario Est.

Until 1918, when it was annexed by Montréal, the east-end district of Maisonneuve was a city unto itself, a booming, prosperous industrial center full of factories making everything from shoes to cheese. The neighborhood was also packed with houses for the almost entirely French-Canadian workforce who kept the whole machine humming.

Maisonneuve was also the site of one of Canada's earliest experiments in urban planning. The Dufresne brothers, a pair of prosperous shoe manufacturers, built a series of grand civic buildings along rue Morgan—many of which still stand—including a theater, public baths, and a

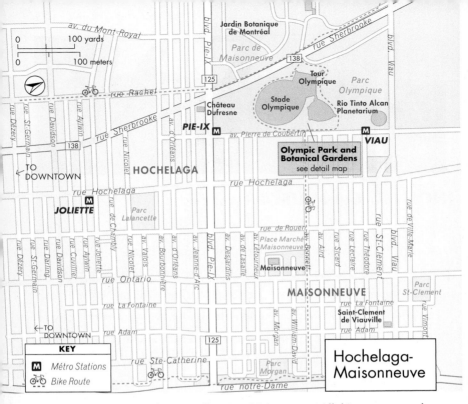

Map labels (Hochelaga-Maisonneuve):

0 / 100 yards
0 / 100 meters

av. du Mont-Royal
Jardin Botanique de Montréal
Parc de Maisonneuve
blvd. Pie-IX
rue Sherbrooke
blvd. Viau
138
Tour Olympique
Parc Olympique
rue Rachel
125
Château Dufresne
Stade Olympique
Rio Tinto Alcan Planetarium
rue Sherbrooke
PIE-IX
M
av. Pierre de Coubertin
M
VIAU
rue St-Germain
rue Davidson
av. Aylwin
rue Nicolet
av. d'Orléans
138
TO DOWNTOWN
HOCHELAGA
Olympic Park and Botanical Gardens
see detail map
rue Hochelaga
rue Hochelaga
JOLIETTE
M
Parc Lalancette
rue de Chambly
av. Yatois
av. d'Orléans
av. Jeanne-d'Arc
blvd. Pie-IX
av. Desjardins
av. de Lasalle
rue de Rouen
Place Marché Maisonneuve
av. Letourneux
rue St-Germain
rue Aird
rue Sicard
rue Leclerce
rue Théodore
blvd. Viau
rue de Ville-Marie
rue Dezery
rue Darling
rue Davidson
rue Cuvillier
de Joliette
av. Aylwin
rue Nicolet
av. Bourbonnière
rue Ontario
Maisonneuve
MAISONNEUVE
Parc St-Clement
rue La fontaine
rue La fontaine
TO DOWNTOWN
rue Adam
Saint-Clement de Viauville
rue Adam
125
av. Morgan
av. William-David
rue Vimont
KEY
M Métro Stations
Bike Route
rue Ste-Catherine
Parc Morgan
rue notre-Dame

Hochelaga-Maisonneuve

---

bustling market, as well as Parc Maisonneuve. All this was supposed to make working-class life more bearable, but World War I put an end to the brothers' plans and Maisonneuve became part of Montréal, twinned with the east-end district of Hochelaga.

GETTING HERE AND AROUND
It's not necessary to drive to the area, as the Pie-IX and Viau métro stops on the Green Line provide easy access to all the sites, including the Insectarium and the Jardin Botanique. For bikers, it's a straight shot across the path on rue Rachel.

TIMING
If traveling with kids, you'll probably want to dedicate more time to exploring the area to see the sites. One of the city's major markets—Marché Maisonneuve—is on the corner of rue Ontario and avenue Bennett, and is well worth a stop.

TOP ATTRACTIONS

FAMILY
Fodor's Choice
★

Jardin Botanique (*Botanical Garden*). Creating one of the world's great botanical gardens in a city with a winter as harsh as Montréal's was no mean feat, and the result is that no matter how brutal it gets in January there's one corner of the city where it's always summer. With 181 acres of plantings in summer and 10 greenhouses open all year, Space for Life

Montréal's Jardin Botanique is the second-largest attraction of its kind in the world (after England's Kew Gardens). It grows more than 26,000 species of plants, and among its 30 thematic gardens are a rose garden, an alpine garden, and—a favorite with the kids—a poisonous-plant garden.

You can attend traditional tea ceremonies in the Japanese Garden, which has one of the best bonsai collections in the West, or wander among the native birches and maples of the Jardin des Premières-Nations (First Nations Garden). The Jardin de Chine (Chinese Garden), with its pagoda and waterfall, will transport you back to the Ming Dynasty. In the fall, all three cultural gardens host magical mixes of light, color, plant life and sculpture during the annual Gardens of Light spectacle. ⊠ *4101 rue Sherbrooke Est, Hochelaga-Maisonneuve* ☎ *514/872–1400* ⊕ *www.espacepourlavie.ca* ⊠ *C$21 (includes Insectarium)* ☉ *Closed Mon. Nov.–mid-May* Ⓜ *Pie-IX or Viau.*

Maisonneuve. World War I and the Depression killed early 20th-century plans to turn this industrial center into a model city with broad boulevards, grand public buildings, and fine homes, but just three blocks south of the Olympic site a few fragments of that dream have survived the passage of time.

A magnificent beaux arts building, site of the old public market, which has a 20-foot-tall bronze statue of a farm woman, stands at the northern end of tree-lined avenue Morgan. Farmers and butchers have moved into the modern building next door that houses the **Marché Maisonneuve**, which has become one of the city's major markets, along with Marché Jean-Talon and Marché Atwater. The old market is now a community center and the site of summer shows and concerts.

Monumental staircases and a heroic rooftop sculpture embellish the public baths across the street. The **Théâtre Denise Pelletier**, at the corner of rues Ste-Catherine Est and Morgan, has a lavish Italianate interior; **Fire Station No.** 1, at 4300 rue Notre-Dame Est, was inspired by Frank Lloyd Wright's Unity Temple in suburban Chicago; and the sumptuously decorated **Église Très-Saint-Nom-de-Jésus**, has one of the most powerful organs in North America. The 198-acre **Parc Maisonneuve,** stretching north of the botanical garden, is a lovely place for a stroll. ✉ *Hochelaga-Maisonneuve* Ⓜ *Pie-IX or Viau.*

WORTH NOTING

Château Dufresne. The adjoining homes of a pair of shoe manufacturers, Oscar and Marius Dufresne, provide a glimpse into the lives of Montréal's Francophone bourgeoisie in the early 20th century. The brothers built their beaux-arts palace in 1916 along the lines of the Petit-Trianon in Paris, and lived in it with their families—Oscar in the eastern half and Marius in the western half.

Worth searching out are the domestic scenes on the walls of the Petit Salon, where Oscar's wife entertained friends. Her brother-in-law relaxed with his friends in a smoking room decked out like a Turkish lounge. During the house's incarnation as a boys' school in the 1950s, the Eudist priests who ran it covered the room's frieze of nymphs and satyrs with a modest curtain that their charges lifted at every opportunity. ✉ *2929 rue Jeanne-d'Arc, Hochelaga-Maisonneuve* ☎ *514/259–9201* ⊕ *www. chateaudufresne.com* 🖥 *C$14* ⊗ *Closed Mon. and Tues.* Ⓜ *Viau.*

FAMILY **Rio Tinto Alcan Planetarium.** In early 2013, Montréal got a new, ultramodern, C$48 million planetarium, one of only a handful of planetariums worldwide to have two circular theaters—one for astronomy exhibits and the other a high-tech multimedia venue. Part of the Space for Life complex, this state-of-the-art facility delivers a futuristic experience unlike any other. The permanent exhibit, EXO: Our Search for Life in the Universe, lets the whole family have fun exploring life on earth and (perhaps) in the universe through interactive and hands-on stations. Hours can vary seasonally so check ahead before you visit. ✉ *4801 av. Pierre-de-Coubertin, Hochelaga-Maisonneuve* ☎ *514/868–3000* ⊕ *www.espacepourlavie.ca/planetarium* 🖥 *C$21* Ⓜ *Viau.*

Tour Olympique. The world's tallest tilting structure—take that, Pisa!—is the 890-foot tower that was supposed to hold the Stade Olympique's retractable roof. It looked great on paper, but never worked in practice, and the current roof is a permanent fixture. If you want a great view of the city, however, ride the glass-encased funicular that slides up the outside of the tower to the observatory at the top. On a clear day you can see up to 80 km (50 miles). ✉ *4141 av. Pierre-de-Coubertin, Hochelaga-Maisonneuve* ☎ *514/252–4141, 877/997–0919* ⊕ *parcolympique.qc.ca* 🖥 *Observation deck C$24* Ⓜ *Pie-IX or Viau.*

THE ISLANDS

The two islands just east of the city in the St. Lawrence River — Île Ste-Hélène, formed by nature, and Île Notre-Dame, created with the stone rubble excavated from the construction of Montréal's métro — are now used for Montréal's indoor-outdoor playground, Parc Jean-Drapeau.

Expo '67, which the World's Fair staged to celebrate the centennial of the Canadian federation, was brought here by the city's mayor, Jean Drapeau. It was the biggest party in Montréal's history, and it marked a defining moment in its evolution as a modern metropolis.

The spirit of coming here for excitement and thrills lives on. La Ronde, a major amusement park that has the world's highest double wooden roller coaster, is on Île Ste-Hélène. On Île Notre-Dame, there's Casino de Montréal, which includes gaming tables and more than 3,200 slot machines.

For a completely different kind of fun, however, there's much to learn about the Islands' history. At the Stewart Museum at the Old Fort, kids will love watching soldiers in colonial uniforms hold flag-raising ceremonies twice a day, rehearse maneuvers, and even practice drills and fire muskets.

GETTING HERE AND AROUND

Both Île Ste-Hélène and Île Notre-Dame are very accessible. You can drive to them via the Pont de la Concorde or the Pont Jacques-Cartier, take the ferry from the Old Port to Île Ste-Hélène (seasonal), or take the métro from the Berri-UQAM station to Jean-Drapeau.

TIMING

If you're traveling with kids, there's enough here to keep them occupied for a full day, especially in nice weather. Because the Islands are so easy to get to with the ferry, visiting can be tacked on to time spent in Old Montréal.

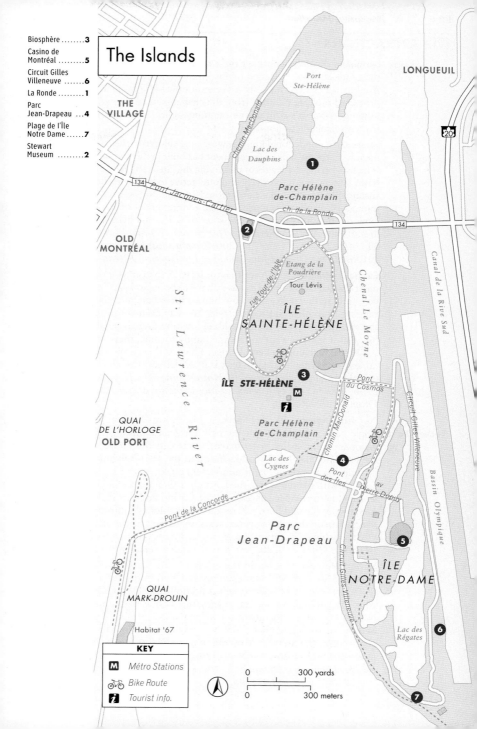

The Islands

LONGUEUIL

THE
VILLAGE

OLD
MONTRÉAL

Port
Ste-Hélène

Lac des
Dauphins

Parc Hélène
de-Champlain

ch. de la Ronde

Pont Jacques-Cartier

chemin MacDonald

rue Tour-de-l'Isle

Étang de la
Poudrière

Tour Lévis

ÎLE
SAINTE-HÉLÈNE

Chenal Le Moyne

Canal de la Rive Sud

St.   Lawrence   River

QUAI
DE L'HORLOGE
OLD PORT

ÎLE STE-HÉLÈNE

Pont
du Cosmos

Parc Hélène
de-Champlain

Lac des
Cygnes

chemin MacDonald

Pont
des Îles

Circuit Gilles-Villeneuve

Bassin Olympique

Pont de la Concorde

Parc
Jean-Drapeau

av.
Pierre-Dupuy

Circuit Gilles-Villeneuve

ÎLE
NOTRE-DAME

QUAI
MARK-DROUIN

Habitat '67

Lac des
Régates

KEY

M Métro Stations

🚲 Bike Route

🛈 Tourist info.

0   300 yards
0   300 meters

TOP ATTRACTIONS

FAMILY **Biosphère.** Nothing captures the exuberance of Expo '67 better than the geodesic dome designed by Buckminster Fuller (1895–1983) as the American Pavilion. It's only a skeleton now—the polymer panels that protected the U.S. exhibits from the elements were burned out in a fire long ago—but it's still an eye-catching sight, like something plucked from a science-fiction movie.

Science of a nonfictional kind, however, is explored in the special environmental center the federal government has built in the middle of the dome. It focuses on the challenges of preserving the Great Lakes and St. Lawrence River system, but it has lively and interactive exhibits on climate change, sustainable energy, and air pollution. Kids and others can use games and interactive displays arranged around a large model of the waterway to explore how shipping, tourism, water supplies, and hydroelectric power are affected. ⊠ Île Ste-Hélène, 160 chemin Tour-de-l'Îsle, The Islands ☎ 514/283–5000, 855/773–8200 ⊕ www.biosphere.ec.gc.ca ⊠ C$15 ⊙ Closed Dec. 21–mid-Jan. (call ahead to confirm) Ⓜ Jean-Drapeau.

Casino de Montréal. You have to be at least 18 to visit Montréal's government-owned casino, but you don't have to be a gambler. The 24-hour-a-day, fully renovated casino now houses three bars and six restaurants, ranging from high-end to deli style. You can even come just to look at the architecture—the main building was the French pavilion at Expo '67. But if you do want to risk the family fortune, there are more than 3,000 slot machines, a keno lounge, a high-stakes gaming area, and 120 tables for playing blackjack, baccarat, roulette, craps, and various types of poker. ⊠ 1 av. du Casino, Île Notre-Dame, The Islands ☎ 514/392–2746, 800/665–2274 ⊕ www.casino-de-montreal.com ⊠ Free Ⓜ Jean-Drapeau, then Bus 167.

FAMILY **Parc Jean-Drapeau.** Île Ste-Hélène and Île Notre-Dame now constitute a
Fodor's Choice single park named, fittingly enough, for Jean Drapeau (1916–99), the
★ visionary (and spendthrift) mayor who built the métro and brought the city both the 1967 World's Fair and the 1976 Olympics. The park includes La Ronde (a major amusement park), acres of flower gardens, a beach with filtered water, the Formula 1 Grand Prix Circuit Gilles Villeneuve, performance spaces, and the Casino de Montréal. There's history, too, at the Old Fort, where soldiers in colonial uniforms display the military methods used in ancient wars. In winter you can skate on the old Olympic rowing basin or slide down iced trails on an inner tube. ⊠ The Islands ☎ 514/872–6120 ⊕ www.parcjeandrapeau.com Ⓜ Jean-Drapeau.

Stewart Museum. Housed in the arsenal of Île Ste-Hélène's 1820s Old Fort, the Stewart Museum encompasses two floors full of interesting historical objects. The permanent collection has close to 27,000 artifacts consisting of military objects, images, rare books, maps, pieces of weaponry; all of which document the history of Montréal, l'Île Ste-Hélène, and the surrounding area, from the early First Nations to today. Open year-round, the Stewart Museum is definitely worth a visit for those interested in the history of New France. ⊠ 20 chemin du Tour-de-l'Îsle, Île Ste-Hélène, The Islands ☎ 514/861–6701 ⊕ www.stewart-museum.org ⊠ C$15 Ⓜ Jean-Drapeau.

DID YOU KNOW?

A relic of Canada's World's Fair Exposition in 1967, the massive Biosphère has withstood fire and ice storms to become a museum devoted to the environment.

WORTH NOTING

Circuit Gilles Villeneuve. In early June you can join the glitterati of Europe and America in the grandstand to watch million-dollar Formula 1 cars shriek around the 4.3-km (2.7-mile) track—if you're lucky enough and rich enough to get a ticket, that is. This is the kind of crowd that uses Perrier to mop up caviar stains from the refreshment tables. During the off season, the track is accessible to everyone. Locals spend sunny summer weekends cycling, rollerblading, and taking walks around this world-famous circuit. ✉ *Île Notre-Dame* ☎ *514/350–0000, 855/790–1245 toll-free* ⊕ *www.circuitgillesvilleneuve.ca* 🖃 *Free outside of special events* Ⓜ *Jean-Drapeau.*

FAMILY **La Ronde.** Every year, it seems, this amusement park, at the eastern end of Île Ste-Hélène, adds some new and monstrous way to scare the living daylights (and maybe even your lunch) out of you. The most recent additions include the Titan, a giant swaying pendulum that will have you—or the kids—soaring and spinning 148 feet above the park, traveling at speeds up to 70 miles per hour, and the Maison Rouge, a haunted house and "labyrinth of terror." Demon, an extreme ride, will—at high speed (of course)—twist you, twirl you, and turn you upside down, then douse you with water jets. The park also aims to terrify you with such stomach-turning champions as the Endor, the Goliath, the Vampire, Monstre, and Vol Ultime. For the less daring, there are Ferris wheels, boat rides, and kiddie rides. The popular **International Fireworks Competition** is held here on Saturday and Wednesday in late June and July. ✉ *22 chemin Macdonald, Île Ste-Hélène* ☎ *514/397–2000* ⊕ *www.sixflags.com/larondeen* 🖃 *C$67, or from C$49 when purchased online* ☺ *Hrs vary seasonally so check ahead* Ⓜ *Jean-Drapeau.*

FAMILY **Plage de l'Île Notre-Dame** (*Île Notre-Dame Beach*). The dress code at the neighboring casino might ban camisoles and strapless tops, but here anything seems to go on warm summer days, when the beach is a sea of oiled bodies. You get the distinct impression that swimming is not uppermost on the minds of many of the scantily clad hordes. If you do want to go in, however, the water is filtered and closely monitored for contamination, and there are lifeguards on duty. A shop rents swimming and boating paraphernalia, and there's a restaurant and picnic areas. ✉ *Île Notre-Dame* ☎ *514/872–6120* ⊕ *www.parcjeandrapeau.com/en/jean-dore-beach-sand-swimming-sun-montreal* 🖃 *C$9* Ⓜ *Jean-Drapeau.*

WHERE TO EAT

EAT LIKE A LOCAL

The combination of multiple cultures and a strong European flair has resulted in all sorts of dishes and flavors that are unique to Québec. Poutine, *tourtière*, steamies, and smoked meat are all part of the province's charm. Sample what's true to this area and you'll end up learning a lot about La Belle Province and its people.

POUTINE

This classic Quebecois dish is basically a plate of french fries topped with gravy and fresh cheese curds. Although it started out as more of a post night-out staple, the new trend is for chic restaurants to reinvent the somewhat greasy dish with improbable toppings (like foie gras or lobster).

TOURTIÈRE

Tourtière is a traditional French Canadian meat pie. It doesn't have a specific filling but can be made with whatever is available; it's frequently made with pork and/or veal, but chefs have been known to use wild game, or in coastal regions,

it can even be made with fish. It's a filling dish, popular around Christmas and New Year as well as sugar shack season in the spring.

TARTE AU SUCRE (SUGAR PIE)

In English Canada, this sweet dessert is also known as a butter tart. Some describe it as a pecan pie, without the pecans. It's a single crust, with the filling on the bottom.

SMOKED MEAT

Montréal-style smoked meat is similar to pastrami, but always made with brisket and cured with a blend of spices that generally contains more pepper and less sugar than New York–style pastrami. Served on rye bread, with a smear of mustard, it's a Montréal specialty.

STEAMIES
In Québec, hot dogs are called "steamies"—both the frankfurter and the bun are steamed until soft and warm. "All-dressed" here means mustard, cabbage (not sauerkraut), onions, and relish—that's all. You can ask for ketchup but you might get a puzzled look.

BAGELS
A Montréal bagel is almost a totally different bagel species from what you'll find elsewhere. Most bagels are boiled before they're baked but in Montréal, they're boiled in honey water, then cooked in a wood-fired oven. The result is a sweeter, denser bagel than its New York counterpart.

QUÉBEC CHEESE
There are more than 300 varieties of cheese made in Québec, where cheese-obsessed locals fuel a creative market of delicious and complex varieties from goat, sheep, and cow's milk. Look for Blue Ermite, made by Benedictine monks—said to be a good "introductory" blue cheese—as well as anything made by Fromagerie du Presbytère, an artisinal cheese company set in an old presbytery in Sainte-Élizabeth-de-Warwick.

MAPLE SYRUP
Did you know that Québec produces three quarters of the world's supply in maple syrup? It's an important part of the Quebecois identity; come springtime, when maple syrup is made, it's not uncommon to see restaurants create entire menus around it. In season, locals will flock to the countryside to have some *tire*—(French for "taffy") warm maple syrup poured directly on snow.

MEAT AND GAME
The vast forests of Québec are filled with wild game; as a result, carnivores are well fed here with bison, duck, wild boar, lamb, and elk. Venison and caribou are favorites among chefs. Québec is also home to Canada's biggest foie gras producers.

ICE WINE
Québec's climate is ideal for making ice wine, a sweet and rich postmeal delicacy. The grapes are harvested by hand once the temperature drops to −8°C (17°F), after which the frozen grapes are pressed until they become a sweet liquor. Ice wine pairs wonderfully well with desserts and Québec-made cheeses.

(top left) A Montréal smoked meat sandwich. (top) Montréal bagels. (bottom) Boiled maple sap being poured on snow to make taffy.

(top left) A Montréal smoked meat sandwich. (top) Montréal bagels. (bottom) Maple syrup being poured on snow to make taffy.

Updated by
Marie-Eve
Vallières

Montréal has one of Canada's most cosmopolitan restaurant scenes with trendy new eateries popping up regularly, their menus heavily influenced by flavors from around the globe, and often with an added touch of French flair.

Montréal's top dining destinations are plentiful, especially as young chefs move to hip destinations in Mile End and the Plateau areas to open new restaurants. Downtown, convenient to many hotels, finds most of its restaurants clustered between rues Guy and Peel and on the side streets that run between boulevard René-Lévesque and rue Sherbrooke. Rue St-Denis and boulevard St-Laurent, between rues Sherbrooke and Jean Talon, have long been, and continue to be, convenient and fashionable areas, with everything from sandwich shops to high-price gourmet shrines. Old Montréal, too, has a collection of well-regarded restaurants, most of them clustered on rue St-Paul, avenue McGill, and place Jacques-Cartier.

You can usually order à la carte, but make sure to look for the table d'hôte, a two- to four-course package deal. It's often more economical, offers interesting specials, and may also take less time to prepare. For a splurge, consider a *menu dégustation,* a five- to seven-course tasting menu that generally includes soup, salad, fish, sherbet (to cleanse the palate), a meat dish, dessert, and coffee or tea. A *menu dégustation* for two, along with a good bottle of wine, will cost around C$250.

Most restaurants will have an English menu or, at the very least, a bilingual menu—but some might only be in French. If you don't understand what a dish is, don't be too shy to ask; a good server will be happy to explain. If you feel brave enough to order in French, remember that in Montréal an *entrée* is an appetizer, and what Americans call an entrée is a *plat principal,* or main dish.

MONTRÉAL DINING PLANNER

RESERVATIONS

Reservations are quickly becoming indispensable in Montréal, especially for weekend dining. Call at least three nights ahead for busy bistros. Because Montrealers eat quite late—an homage to its European roots, perhaps—it's possible to arrive unannounced before 7 pm and get a table—if you're lucky.

HOURS

Montréal restaurants keep unpredictable schedules. Some are closed Sunday, some are closed Monday, some are open every day. Our reviews note closed days but it can't hurt to call and confirm. Kitchens generally stop taking orders at 10 or 11 pm, but many eateries in the Old Port stay open later in the summer, as do hot spots in the Plateau and Mile End. Downtown locations tend to focus on lunch and therefore close earlier. Brunch is over by 3 pm.

DINING WITH KIDS

Kids have become more commonly accepted in bistros, brasseries, and even upscale dining rooms ever since smoking was banned in restaurants. However, minors (less than 18 years of age in Quebec) are not allowed in places that have a bar license.

WHAT TO WEAR

Dress up! Montrealers take pride in their appearance, always preferring to be over- than underdressed. If there was ever a time to pack those fancy designer heels or stylish slacks, this would be it. No running shoes, please. Men should wear a jacket for restaurants in the $$$$ range.

PRICES

Long live the table d'hôte! This cost-cutting special is a regular feature at many Montréal restaurants. Chefs enjoy changing the two-to-three-course special on a daily or weekly basis, often in accordance with market arrivals. ■TIP➔ Upscale restaurants serve elaborate lunch tables d'hôte at cut-rate prices; if your appetite doesn't match that of your wallet, make sure to take advantage of this preset menu. Some restaurants will also offer early-bird or late-night prix-fixe deals. There isn't a one-size-fits-all when it comes to payment policies in Montréal. Most small eateries are cash-only; bistros and upscale restaurants normally accept both debit and credit, but it's never a given. Some may only accept one or the other. Best to call ahead if you are limited to one mode of payment.

WHAT IT COSTS IN CANADIAN DOLLARS				
	$	$$	$$$	$$$$
Restaurants	under C$12	C$12–C$20	C$21–C$30	over C$30

Restaurant prices are based on the average cost of a main course at dinner or, if dinner is not served, at lunch.

MONTRÉAL RESTAURANT REVIEWS

Listed alphabetically within neighborhood.

Use the coordinate (✛ B2) at the end of each listing to locate a site on the corresponding map.

OLD MONTRÉAL (VIEUX-MONTRÉAL)

Old Montréal is home to some of the city's hippest and most charming bistros and fine-dining restaurants—all tucked into heritage buildings. Foodies eat wild game and fresh seafood while drinking imported wine. Many of the better restaurants have a reasonable table d'hôte at lunch. Daily changing menus written on chalkboards are a common sight, since market-fresh food is popular.

$$
BRITISH
FAMILY

✗ **Brit & Chips.** There's no need to cross the pond to find perfectly battered fish and delicious chips as it can be found right here in Old Montréal. The cod is a staple but the salmon dipped in Guinness batter is also a menu favorite, and for a Canadian touch, try the haddock covered in golden maple syrup batter. **Known for:** fish and chips; deep-fried dessert; maple syrup batter; long lines at weekday lunch. $ *Average main: C$12 ⊠ 433 rue McGill, Old Montréal ☎ 514/840–1001 ⊕ www. britandchips.com* Ⓜ *Square Victoria ✛ E6.*

$$$$
FRENCH

✗ **Chez l'Épicier.** Menus at this French fusion restaurant are printed on brown paper, but there's nothing down-market about the crisp white linens and the seasonal creative dishes like seared arctic char, almond arancini, or pan-seared foie gras. Should you choose to splurge, the C$85 (add $60 for wine pairings), seven-course tasting menu is a veritable feast for the senses. **Known for:** tasting menu; wine pairings; market cuisine. $ *Average main: C$37 ⊠ 311 rue St-Paul Est, Old Montréal ☎ 514/878–2232 ⊕ www.chezlepicier.com* ☉ *Closed Sun.– Mon.* Ⓜ *Champs-de-Mars ✛ E6.*

$$$$
CANADIAN

✗ **Club Chasse et Pêche.** Despite the name—French for "Hunting and Fishing Club"—this isn't a hangout for the local gun-and-rod set. Impeccable service and top-notch ingredients have made this one of the best restaurants in the city; the name is simply referencing the wood-and-leather decor. **Known for:** chasse (filet mignon) et pêche (lobster) dish; impeccable service; terroir cuisine. $ *Average main: C$38 ⊠ 423 rue St-Claude, Old Montréal ☎ 514/861–1112 ⊕ www.leclubchasseetpeche.com* ☉ *Closed Sun.–Mon.* Ⓜ *Champ-de-Mars ✛ F6.*

$
CAFÉ
Fodor's Choice
★

✗ **Crew Collective Café.** Undoubtedly the most strikingly beautiful coffee shop in Montreal, perhaps even in North America, Crew Collective & Café is housed inside a former 1920s-era bank that's fitted with 50-foot-high vaulted ceilings, intricate tiling, and bronze chandeliers. The cafe doubles as a co-working space for web start-ups, so it's only fitting that patrons be able order their coffee and nibbles directly online, in real-time, without ever having to queue. **Known for:** architectural, lavish space; curated coffee beans. $ *Average main: C$6 ⊠ 360 Rue Saint-Jacques, Old Montréal ⊕ crewcollectivecafe.com/* Ⓜ *Place d'Armes ✛ E6.*

$$$ ITALIAN 🍴 **Da Emma.** The cellar of what used to be Montréal's first women's prison hardly sounds like the ideal setting for an Italian eatery, but grandma Emma's cooking hushes any bad vibes from the 1800s. Stone walls and heavy beams serve as backdrop for Roman dishes like roasted lamb, fettuccine *con funghi*and pasta *al vongole*, which have all foregone fussy presentation to focus on superior fixings. **Known for:** 300-year-old stone walls; homemade burrata; historic building. [$] *Average main: C$30* ✉ *777 rue de la Commune Ouest, Old Montréal* ☎ *514/392–1568* 🕒 *Closed Sun., and Mon.–Fri. 2–6 pm; no lunch Sat.* [M] *Square-Victoria* ✣ *D6.*

$$$$ CANADIAN 🍴 **Garde Manger.** Popular options at this see-and-be-seen locale, steered by local celebrity chef Chuck Hughes, include bountiful platters of seafood, rich lobster poutine, and hearty braised short ribs—vegetarians should probably head elsewhere, since fish and meat are featured prominently on the menu. The bar, where flirting is in high gear, is a fun option for dining and hanging out. **Known for:** seafood platter; lively atmosphere; lobster poutine. [$] *Average main: C$35* ✉ *408 rue St-François-Xavier, Old Montréal* ☎ *514/678–5044* 🌐 *gardemanger.ca* 🕒 *Closed Mon.* [M] *Place-d'Armes* ✣ *E6.*

$$$ CANADIAN 🍴 **Hambar.** As the name suggests, the focus of this restaurant is ham in all its many incarnations. The menu changes seasonally but charcuteries and marinated vegetables imported from Europe are ever-present. [$] *Average main: C$30* ✉ *Hotel St. Paul, 355 rue McGill, Old Montréal* ☎ *514/879–1234* 🌐 *www.hambar.ca* 🕒 *No lunch Sat.–Sun.* ✣ *E6.*

$$$ MODERN GREEK Fodor's Choice ★ 🍴 **Ikanos.** A far cry from the cliché-clad tavernas found elsewhere in the city, Ikanos serves refined Aegean gastronomy in an elegant and sleek environment. No blue-and-white checkered tablecloths in sight; the muted neutral palette puts the spotlight on the food. **Known for:** grilled octopus; Greek wines; loukoumades. [$] *Average main: C$26* ✉ *112 Rue McGill, Old Montréal* ☎ *514/842–0867* 🌐 *www.restaurantikanos.com* 🕒 *Closed daily 2:30–5:30 pm; No brunch Sat.* [M] *Square Victoria* ✣ *D6.*

$$ FRENCH 🍴 **Le Cartet.** As a gourmet grocery shop, takeout counter, and French restaurant rolled into one, this splendid space was quickly adopted by local foodies. The salmon tartare served with pink berries is a strong contender for a healthy lunch, while the duck confit and gratin *dauphinois* is perfectly suited for larger appetites. **Known for:** gourmet boutique; gratin dauphinois; long brunch lines. [$] *Average main: C$15* ✉ *106 rue McGill, Old Montréal* ☎ *514/871-8887* 🌐 *lecartet.com* [M] *Square-Victoria* ✣ *D6.*

$$$ MODERN ITALIAN Fodor's Choice ★ 🍴 **Le Serpent.** The expertise and irreproachable service at Le Serpent truly make it an essential stop on any Montreal foodie itinerary. The industrial-looking space caters to trendy diners, and almost paradoxically, serves sublime Italianate plates that could be mistaken for comfort food if they weren't so elegantly presented. **Known for:** lobster risotto; industrial cool vibe. [$] *Average main: C$30* ✉ *257 Rue Prince, Old Montréal* ☎ *514/316–4666* 🌐 *www.leserpent.ca* 🕒 *Closed Sun.* [M] *Square Victoria* ✣ *D6.*

3

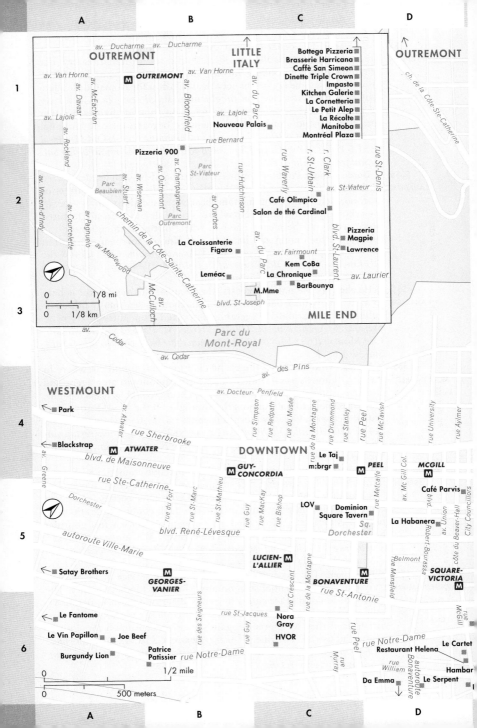

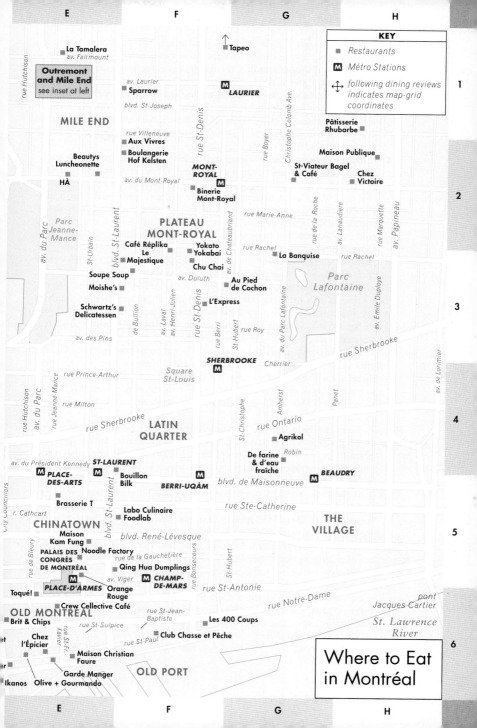

Where to Eat in Montréal

KEY

■ *Restaurants*

Ⓜ *Métro Stations*

⟷ *following dining reviews indicates map-grid coordinates*

La Tamalera
av. Fairmount

Outremont and Mile End
see inset at left

MILE END

Sparrow
av. Laurier
blvd. St-Joseph

rue Villeneuve
Aux Vivres
Boulangerie
Hof Kelsten

Beautys
Luncheonette

HÀ

MONT-ROYAL

Binerie
Mont-Royal

av. du Mont-Royal

Ⓜ **LAURIER**

Pâtisserie
Rhubarbe

Maison Publique

St-Viateur Bagel
& Café

Chez
Victoire

Parc
Jeanne-
Mance

**PLATEAU
MONT-ROYAL**

Café Réplika
Le
Majestique

Yokato
Yokabai

Chu Chai

Soupe Soup

Moishe's

Schwartz's
Delicatessen

av. des Pins

rue Marie-Anne

rue Rachel

La Banquise

rue Rachel

Parc
Lafontaine

av. Duluth
Au Pied
de Cochon

L'Express

rue Roy

Ⓜ **SHERBROOKE**

Cherrier

rue Sherbrooke

Square
St-Louis

rue Prince-Arthur

rue Milton

rue Sherbrooke

**LATIN
QUARTER**

rue Ontario

Agrikol

av. du Président Kennedy

Ⓜ **PLACE-
DES-ARTS**

ST-LAURENT

Ⓜ

Bouillon
Bilk

Ⓜ
BERRI-UQÀM

De farine
& d'eau
fraîche

Robin

blvd. de Maisonneuve

Ⓜ **BEAUDRY**

Brasserie T

rue Ste-Catherine

CHINATOWN

Maison
Kam Fung

**PALAIS DES
CONGRÈS
DE MONTRÉAL**

Labo Culinaire
Foodlab

blvd. René-Lévesque

Noodle Factory

rue de la Gauchetière

Qing Hua Dumplings

av. Viger

Ⓜ **CHAMP-
DE-MARS**

Ⓜ

**THE
VILLAGE**

Ⓜ **PLACE-D'ARMES**

Orange
Rouge

rue St-Antonie

Toqué!

Crew Collective Café

rue St-Jean-
Baptiste

rue Notre-Dame

pont
Jacques-Cartier

OLD MONTREAL

Brit & Chips

Chez
l'Épicier

rue St-Sulpice

rue St-Paul

Les 400 Coups

Club Chasse et Pêche

*St. Lawrence
River*

Ikanos

Maison Christian
Faure

Garde Manger

Olive + Gourmando

OLD PORT

$$$
CANADIAN

✕ **Les 400 Coups.** This low-key destination is the perfect spot for an intimate yet elevated meal, where diners can safely anticipate irreproachable dishes (including the $120, five-course tasting menu with wine pairing) and a finely curated wine list. The decor is grandiose and includes a very large mural taking up one long wall, a vintage tin ceiling, and an open kitchen. **Known for:** tasting menu; curated wine list; intimate setting. $ *Average main: C$23* ✉ *400 Notre-Dame Est, Old Montréal* ☎ *514/985–0400* ⊕ *www.les400coups.ca* ⊘ *Closed Sun.–Mon.* ✛ *F6.*

$
BAKERY
FAMILY
Fodor'sChoice
★

✕ **Maison Christian Faure.** The upscale bakery has made its elegant home inside a beautifully renovated gray stone, three-story building in Old Montréal. The prominent pastry display holds rows of French classics like *mille-feuilles* (a delicate layered dessert of puff pastry and airy vanilla-scented custard) and the best Paris-Brest (a dessert made of choux pastry and a praline flavored cream) this side of the pond, as well as seasonal fruit tarts, baskets of buttery brioches and flaky croissants. **Known for:** French-style pâtisseries; historic building; acclaimed pastry chef. $ *Average main: C$6* ✉ *355 Place Royale, Old Montréal* ☎ *514/508–6453* ⊕ *maisonchristianfaure.ca/en* Ⓜ *Place-d'Armes* ✛ *E6.*

$
CAFÉ
FAMILY
Fodor'sChoice
★

✕ **Olive + Gourmando.** Influential types arrive at lunchtime en masse for a table at this bustling bakery and sandwich shop where vegetables are organically grown in a nearby garden and fresh crab is flown in for salads. Crowd pleasers include Le Cubain panini (pancetta, roasted pork, Gruyère) and the "poached egg on your face" breakfast sandwich (spicy poached eggs with herbs and mayonnaise, Comté cheese, speck and slow-roasted tomatoes). **Known for:** organic produce; affordable sandwiches; "poached egg on your face" breakfast sandwich. $ *Average main: C$11* ✉ *351 rue St-Paul Ouest, Old Montréal* ☎ *514/350–1083* ⊕ *www.oliveetgourmando.com* ⊘ *No dinner* Ⓜ *Square-Victoria* ✛ *E6.*

$$$$
PORTUGUESE

✕ **Restaurant Helena.** An airy, colorful restaurant housed inside a welcoming space with alcove windows and stone walls, the cuisine here is traditional Portuguese with plenty of seafood dishes but also a few choices for carnivores. Share a few tapas plates, like the grilled sardines fillets, salted cod tartlet or Portuguese style clams before you delve into the main show. **Known for:** historic building; Portuguese tapas; lunchtime prix-fixe. $ *Average main: C$35* ✉ *438 McGill, Old Montréal* ☎ *514/878–1555* ⊕ *www.restauranthelena.com* ⊘ *Closed Sun. No lunch Sat.* Ⓜ *Square-Victoria* ✛ *D6.*

$$$$
FRENCH
Fodor'sChoice
★

✕ **Toqué!** Frequently named one of Montréal's best restaurants (a very coveted title in this foodie capital), a meal at Toqué! is not so much about sustenance but rather experience. Toqué is slang for "a little stubborn," as in the chef's insistence on using fresh, local ingredients; consequently, the menu changes daily in accordance with market offerings but foie gras, duck and wild venison are on constant rotation. **Known for:** tasting menu; market cuisine; wine pairings. $ *Average main: C$47* ✉ *900 pl. Jean-Paul-Riopelle, Old Montréal* ☎ *514/499–2084* ⊕ *www.restaurant-toque.com* ⊘ *Closed Sun. and Mon. No lunch Sat.* Ⓜ *Square-Victoria* ✛ *E6.*

DOWNTOWN

From top-quality steak to gourmet burgers, there's lots of meat in Downtown. There's also a nightlife vibe here most evenings. There are rich Indian curries, simple Chinese dumplings, whole-animal cooking, dry-aged beef, designer hamburgers, and updated Italian dishes that stretch the definition. The dress code can be as formal as in Old Montréal or completely toned down and hip—it all depends on where you go.

$$ CARIBBEAN Fodor'sChoice ★ 🍴 **Agrikol.** Montreal-based band Arcade Fire is the mastermind behind this Haitian rum house flanked by the most fabulous patio in the city, bar none. Besides the views, the main draw here is the make-your-own Ti' Punch setup—a bottle of rum, ice cubes, sugar cane juice, lime wedges and other fixings. **Known for:** make-your-own Ti' Punch; tropical decor; groovy Haitian atmosphere. [$] *Average main: C$16* ✉ *1844 Rue Amherst, Downtown* ☎ *514/903–6575* 🌐 *www.agrikol.ca* [M] *Beaudry* ✥ *G4.*

$$$$ MODERN FRENCH 🍴 **Bouillon Bilk.** The decor at this restaurant reflects its philosophy: fresh, thoughtful, and simplified (yet not simple). The market-based menu changes often and includes dishes that are just as beautiful to look at as they are delicious. **Known for:** private-import wines; market cuisine; sleek and intimate decor. [$] *Average main: C$32* ✉ *1595 boul. St-Laurent, Downtown* ☎ *514/845–1595* 🌐 *www.bouillonbilk.com* ⏲ *No lunch on weekends.* [M] *St-Laurent* ✥ *E5.*

$$$ BRASSERIE 🍴 **Brasserie T.** The informal sibling of Montréal's famous Toqué! restaurant, Brasserie T is a see-and-be-seen spot in the heart of downtown. It's an excellent place to eat before or after a show at Place des Arts, as well as a budget-friendly way to experience Toqué's expertise. **Known for:** lively atmosphere; legendary salmon tartare; casual French. [$] *Average main: C$22* ✉ *1425 rue Jeanne-Mance, Downtown* ☎ *514/282–0808* 🌐 *www.brasserie-t.com* [M] *Place-des-Arts* ✥ *E5.*

$$ ECLECTIC Fodor'sChoice ★ 🍴 **Café Parvis.** What used to be a fur showroom in the 1970s now hosts Café Parvis, an impeccably designed eatery with floor-to-ceiling windows, half-stripped paint, and luxuriant plants hanging from the ceiling. If morning visits are for artisan coffee and pâtisserie du jour, dinner is for ordering shareable wood-oven baked pizzas (the prosciutto, blue cheese, pear, and caramelized onions is a definite crowd-pleaser) enhanced by the on-point selection of organic wines. **Known for:** photogenic setting; wood-oven baked pizzas; organic wines. [$] *Average main: C$14* ✉ *403 rue Mayor, Downtown* ☎ *514/764–3589* 🌐 *cafeparvis.com* [M] *Place-des-Arts* ✥ *E5.*

$ CAFÉ FAMILY 🍴 **De farine & d'eau fraîche.** This coffee and pastry shop's display is filled with the cutest cakes and cookies that have a strong "high tea in a modern doll house" vibe, but breakfast, lunch, and brunch is also served. Try the house specialty: a soft chocolate ball with a crispy exterior filled with rich, vanilla-flavored custard. **Known for:** casual brunch; chocolate pastries. [$] *Average main: C$10* ✉ *1701 rue Amherst, The Village* ☎ *514/522–2777* 🌐 *dfef.ca* ⏲ *No dinner* [M] *Beaudry* ✥ *G4.*

$$$ BRITISH Fodor'sChoice ★ 🍴 **Dominion Square Tavern.** Antique chairs and a 40-foot brass bar, along with original floors, lamps, and walls from 1927, set the tone at this atmospheric British tavern. Everything on the menu is made from scratch. **Known for:** bangers and mash; atmospheric British tavern; prix-fixe dish of the day. [$] *Average main: C$25* ✉ *1243 rue Metcalfe,*

Downtown ☎ *514/564–5056* 🌐 *www.tavernedominion.com* ⏲ *No lunch on weekends* [M] *Peel* ✣ *D5.*

$$ CUBAN 🍴 **La Habanera.** This ambience-driven Cuban restaurant is one of the most colorful spaces in downtown Montreal and perhaps even one of the most festive. The neon "All you need is love & mojitos" sign, which hangs on a millennial-pink wall among a flock of plastic flamingos, sets the tone, as does the cocktail list. **Known for:** guava-flavoured piña coladas; rum-soaked shrimp; characterful small space. [$] *Average main: C$9* ✉ *1216 Avenue Union, Downtown* ☎ *514/375–5355* 🌐 *www.lahabanera.ca* ⏲ *Closed Sun. and Mon. Closed Tues.–Sat. 2–5:30 pm* [M] *McGill* ✣ *D5.*

$$ ECLECTIC Fodor's Choice ★ 🍴 **Labo Culinaire Foodlab.** Take cutting-edge experimental art and mix it up with food and what you get is Labo Culinaire Foodlab. Located on the third floor of Montréal's Society of Arts and Technology (SAT), Foodlab is an ongoing culinary experiment with rotating themes that range from destinations (i.e. Jerusalem) to dishes inspired by chefs (i.e. Julia Child's cookbook). **Known for:** beautiful terrace; trendsetting chefs; natural wines. [$] *Average main: C$22* ✉ *Société des Arts Technologiques building, 1201 boul. St-Laurent, Downtown* ☎ *514/844–2033* 🌐 *http://sat.qc.ca/en/evenements/labo-culinaire#section* ⏲ *No lunch. Closed Mon. and Sun.* [M] *St-Laurent* ✣ *F5.*

$$ VEGETARIAN 🍴 **LOV.** With its all-white, plant-heavy décor and sustainable approach to food, fashionable and botanical LOV is the kind of vegan restaurant that even die-hard carnivores will line up for. Stéphanie Audet, one of the rare women chefs in Montreal, works tirelessly with local farmers to limit the restaurant's footprint. **Known for:** vegan poutine; biodynamic wines; upscale vegetarian cuisine. [$] *Average main: C$13* ✉ *1232 Rue de la Montagne, Downtown* ☎ *514/287–1155* 🌐 *www.lov.com* [M] *Peel* ✣ *C5.*

$$ INDIAN FAMILY 🍴 **Le Taj.** Refined Le Taj carries a piece of Montréal's history with its ornate mud wall originally made for India's pavilion at World Expo '67. With northern Indian cuisine in mind, which isn't as spicy as its southern counterpart, *thalis*—platters comprising a variety of curries—are ideal for sampling unfamiliar flavors. **Known for:** vegetarian-friendly; multi-flavored platters; all-you-can-eat lunch buffet. [$] *Average main: C$18* ✉ *2077 rue Stanley, Downtown* ☎ *514/845–9015* 🌐 *www.restaurantletaj.com* ⏲ *No lunch Sat.* [M] *Peel* ✣ *C4.*

$$ AMERICAN FAMILY 🍴 **m:brgr.** The atmosphere is lively at this "burger bar" that is generally packed with students and families drawn by designer mac 'n' cheese, Angus beef hot dogs, and pulled pork sandwiches. However, the build your own specialty burger with toppings like applewood bacon, grilled pineapple, and even decadent truffle shavings or foie gras is why we keep going back. **Known for:** deep-dish cookie; build-your-own burger. [$] *Average main: C$18* ✉ *2025 rue Drummond, Downtown* ☎ *514/906–0408* 🌐 *www.mbrgr.com* ⏲ *Closed Jan.–May on Mon.* [M] *Peel* ✣ *C4.*

CHINATOWN

Montréal's Chinatown may be small but it's packed with big taste, including delicious soup-filled dumplings, delicate and sweet Dragon's Beard candy and a dim sum–filled brunch.

3

$$ 🍴 **Maison Kam Fung.** A family-run restaurant for three generations, there
CHINESE are more than 60 dished on rotation on any given day making this *the*
FAMILY place for dim sum feasts. Waiters clatter up and down the aisles pushing a parade of trolleys bearing such treats as firm dumplings stuffed with pork and stir-fried squid and shrimp. **Known for:** dim sum ; Peking duck; Cantonese and Szechuan dishes. [$] *Average main: C$15* ✉ *1111 rue St-Urbain, Chinatown* ☎ *514/878–2888* [M] *Place-d'Armes* ✥ *E5.*

$ 🍴 **Noodle Factory.** The dining room is small and not much to look at,
CHINESE but no matter—the food here is the main attraction, and locals come
FAMILY in droves for the house-made noodles and dumplings. If you time your visit right, you might see the staff through the huge kitchen window working on the dough. **Known for:** cash only; General Tao chicken; house-made noodles. [$] *Average main: C$10* ✉ *1018 rue St-Urbain, Chinatown* ☎ *514/868–9738* 🌐 *www.restonoodlefactory.com* 💳 *No credit cards* [M] *Places-d'Armes* ✥ *E5.*

$$ 🍴 **Orange Rouge.** Located in the heart of Chinatown, Orange Rouge pays
MODERN ASIAN tribute to its neighborhood with creative interpretations of traditional dishes that might ruffle the feathers of authenticity sticklers but will please Asian food aficionados. The chef takes liberties by combining familiar flavors with a surprising twist like the unusual, slightly herbaceous chrysanthemum salad or the intriguing foie gras steam buns. **Known for:** roasted duck; inventive Asian food; trendy decor. [$] *Average main: C$20* ✉ *106 De La Gauchetière Ouest, Chinatown* ☎ *514/861–1116* 🌐 *orangerouge.ca* 🕑 *Closed Sun. and Mon. No lunch Sat.* ✥ *E6.*

$ 🍴 **Qing Hua Dumplings.** Groups of students and other budget-conscious
CHINESE connoisseurs of hearty chows crowd the tables at this hole-in-the-wall
FAMILY restaurant for soup dumplings just like they make them in northeast China with a price that's right: just C$9 for 15 dumplings. Demand is high for the lamb-and-coriander dumplings; the boiled shrimp, leek, and egg version; and the fried dumplings with chicken and curry. **Known for:** soup dumplings; cash only; affordable eats. [$] *Average main: C$10* ✉ *1019 boul. St-Laurent, Chinatown* ☎ *514/903–9887* 💳 *No credit cards* [M] *Place-d'Armes* ✥ *F5.*

THE PLATEAU AND MILE END

THE PLATEAU MONT-ROYAL

Dotted with bistros and cafés, the Plateau has a bohemian edge that can't be found anywhere else in the city. Chef-owned eateries favor market cuisine served in a decor of brick walls and hardwood floors. Noisy French-style bistros, like L'Express, are local institutions, as are cafés populated by poets and academics with laptops. There's vegetarian cooking, and Thai, along with sushi and stubborn little bakeries that refuse to mechanize.

$$$ 🍴 **Au Pied de Cochon.** Not for the timid, the menu at this famous bistro—
BISTRO one of Anthony Bourdain's favorites—is an ode to nose-to-tail cooking.
Fodor's Choice ★ Martin Picard is a local celebrity chef and wild restaurateur, serving pickled bison tongue, guinea hen liver mousse, a whole pig's head for two, pork hocks braised in maple syrup; but his foie gras obsession is what truly sets him apart, lavishing the stuff on hamburgers and, brace yourselves, poutine. **Known for:** foie gras poutine; Au Pied de

Cochon food truck; celebrity chef. $ *Average main: C$25* ✉ *536 av. Duluth Est, The Plateau* ☎ *514/281–1114* ⊕ *www.aupieddecochon.ca* 🌑 *Closed Mon. and Tues.* Ⓜ *Mont-Royal* ✛ *F3.*

$$
VEGETARIAN
FAMILY

✕ **Aux Vivres.** A favorite among vegans, celiacs, and vegetarians; dishes and beverages served here are creative, inspiring, and delicious—not to mention packed with vitamins. A large chalkboard holds specials of the day; try their gigantic sandwiches, such as the Sirocco (grilled eggplant and hummus), which comes on chapati bread, or for something a little earthier, go with the Dragon bowl, a crowd favorite of steamed bok choy, organic rice, tempeh, marinated veggies, and tamari sauce. **Known for:** Dragon bowl; uncheesecake; vegan- and celiac-friendly. $ *Average main: C$12* ✉ *4631 boul. St-Laurent, The Plateau* ☎ *514/842–3479* ⊕ *www.auxvivres.com* Ⓜ *Mont-Royal* ✛ *F2.*

$$
DINER
FAMILY
Fodor's Choice
★

✕ **Beautys Luncheonette.** The Schkolnick family has been serving brunch at this Montréal landmark since 1942 and very little has changed since, both in decor and classic menu. Standard picks include the Mish Mash omelet, with sliced frankfurters, salami, green peppers, and fried onions; and the Superbeautys 2 with two eggs, pancakes, bacon and sausage, and a toasted bagel; although Beauty's Special—bagel, lox, and cream cheese—is the ultimate classic. **Known for:** historic venue; Beauty's special; long lines on the weekend. $ *Average main: C$12* ✉ *93 av. du Mont-Royal Ouest, The Plateau* ☎ *514/849–8883* ⊕ *www.beautys.ca* Ⓜ *Mont-Royal* ✛ *E2.*

$
CANADIAN
FAMILY

✕ **Binerie Mont-Royal.** Authentic Quebecois food is the specialty at this tiny greasy spoon that's been in business since 1938. Sit at the long counter and make your way through a filling breakfast of eggs, ham, toast, and, as the restaurant's name suggests—beans. **Known for:** Authentic Quebecois food; tourtière (meat pie); beans. $ *Average main: C$10* ✉ *367 av. du Mont-Royal Est, The Plateau* ☎ *514/285–9078* ⊕ *www. labineriemontroyal.com* ▭ *No credit cards* 🌑 *Closed Mon. No dinner Sun., Tues. and Wed. Closed daily 2 pm–5 pm* Ⓜ *Mont-Royal* ✛ *F2.*

$
BAKERY

✕ **Boulangerie Hof Kelsten.** The mastermind behind this photogenic bakery had been making bread for Montréal's best restaurants for years before he decided to open up his own place, now a favorite with locals who line up every weekend for fresh baguettes. In addition to serving a delicious rye and caraway seed loaf as well as chocolate babka, Hof Kelsten is also an excellent lunch option thanks to sandwiches like homemade gravlax with seasoned cream cheese or chopped liver with crispy onions. **Known for:** chocolate babka; Jewish cuisine; trendy bakery. $ *Average main: C$8* ✉ *4524 boul. St-Laurent, The Plateau* ⊕ *hofkelsten.com* 🌑 *Closed Mon. and Tues.* Ⓜ *Mont-Royal* ✛ *F2.*

$
TURKISH
FAMILY

✕ **Café Replika.** College students, freelancers and local hipsters flock to this understated Turkish café for two reasons: the gourmet coffee and the food. Between the Nutella and sea salt cookie, the feta and sausage omelet and the boreks (a traditional flaky pastry sprinkled with sesame seeds), it's hard to pick just one thing off Replika's menu. **Known for:** latte art; Turkish fare; friendly owners. $ *Average main: C$6* ✉ *252 Rue Rachel Est, The Plateau* ☎ *514/903–4384* ⊕ *www.cafereplika.com* Ⓜ *Mont-Royal* ✛ *F3.*

$$
MODERN FRENCH

✕ **Chez Victoire.** A beacon of the French cultural diaspora in Montréal, Chez Victoire is the epitome of Plateau-Mont-Royal's joie de vivre and warmth; fittingly, the creative menu features French-inspired seasonal market cuisine. Take a seat at the long bar and order the house-made charcuterie platter or opt for a booth to share the classic tomato and mozzarella di bufala salad, the roasted bone marrow, or the famous smoked meat burger. **Known for:** organic wines; house-made charcuterie; smoked meat burger. $ *Average main: C$19* ✉ *1453 av. du Mont-Royal Est, The Plateau* ☎ *514/521–6789* ⊕ *chezvictoire.com* Ⓜ *Mont-Royal* ✦ *H2.*

$$
THAI

✕ **ChuChai.** Vegetarians and meat eaters love this casual Thai restaurant where no meat is served but the chefs prepare meatless versions of such classics as calamari with basil, crispy duck with spinach, chicken with green beans, fish with three hot sauces, and beef with yellow curry and coconut milk—substituting the real thing for soy and seitan. Chu-Chai is known for their *miam kram*—an appetizer of coconut, ginger, pepper, nuts, and lime—and their mock duck with soy sauce. **Known for:** vegetarian Thai fare; mock duck; Miam Kram appetizer. $ *Average main: C$20* ✉ *4088 rue St-Denis, The Plateau* ☎ *514/843–4194* ⊕ *www.chuchai.com* ⊙ *Closed Sun. and Mon. No lunch Tues. and Wed.* Ⓜ *Mont-Royal* ✦ *F3.*

$$
MODERN ASIAN

✕ **HÀ.** Located at the foot of Mount Royal, this unassuming but contemporary local hotspot serves some of the best Vietnamese fare in the city on one of the most enjoyable patios in Montreal. Simple yet edgy are the operative words here, with steamed buns attractively blackened with squid ink; the Ginger-Carrot crispy tofu and the Caramel-Soya Sauce Cornish hen are also surprising novelties. **Known for:** squid ink steamed buns; stunning terrace; authentic Vietnamese food. $ *Average main: C$15* ✉ *243 Avenue du Mont-Royal Ouest, The Plateau* ☎ *514/848-0336* ⊕ *www.restarantha.com* ⊙ *Closed Mon. Closed daily from 3–5:30* Ⓜ *Mont-Royal* ✦ *E2.*

$
CANADIAN
FAMILY
Fodor's Choice
★

✕ **La Banquise.** Québec is notorious for poutine—french fries topped with cheese curds and gravy—and La Banquise has been the place for an authentic experience since 1968 with an extensive menu featuring 28 varieties. Neophytes might want to stick with La Classique but mouthwatering novelties like La Taquise (guacamole, sour cream, tomatoes) and Obélix (smoked meat) are quite alluring. **Known for:** open 24 hours; cash only; smoked meat poutine. $ *Average main: C$9* ✉ *994 rue Rachel Est, The Plateau* ☎ *514/525–2415* ⊕ *www.labanquise.com* ▭ *No credit cards* Ⓜ *Mont-Royal* ✦ *G3.*

$$
MODERN
CANADIAN
Fodor's Choice
★

✕ **Le Majestique.** With its bric-à-brac décor, retro knickknacks, and sceney vibes, Majestique is a quirky wine bar that's open until the wee hours with an excellent selection of small plates. The snazzy ambience only adds to the charm of this fine-dining-meets-casual-savoir-faire; the salmon confit, the quinoa croquette and rotating choice of fresh oysters are musts. **Known for:** buzzy oyster house; quirky wine bar; foot-long piglet hotdog. $ *Average main: C$12* ✉ *4105 Boulevard St-Laurent, The Plateau* ☎ *514/439-1850* ⊕ *www.restobarmajestique.com* ⊙ *Brunch on Sun. only.* Ⓜ *Mont-Royal* ✦ *F3.*

3

$$$ ✕ **L'Express.** This iconic Montreal bistro hasn't changed much since its
FRENCH opening in 1980 and it's just as well—regulars would throw a fit if it
FAMILY did. Quintessential French fare is fairly priced and appetizing, out-
Fodor'sChoice standing even, with dishes like steak tartare with fries, salmon with
★ sorrel, and calf's liver with tarragon. **Known for:** steak tartare; lively
atmosphere; late-night dining. Ⓢ *Average main: C$22* ✉ *3927 rue St-
Denis, The Plateau* ☎ *514/845–5333* ⊕ *www.restaurantlexpress.com/
en/* Ⓜ *Sherbrooke* ✛ *F3.*

$$ ✕ **Maison Publique.** Local celebrity chef Derek Dammann teamed up with
MODERN BRITISH famed British chef Jamie Oliver to open this pub-style restaurant that
perfectly blends Canadian and British traditions. The interior is dark and
cozy; the handwritten menu changes frequently based on what's in season,
with a few constants like foie gras toast with gherkins, Welsh rarebit,
and roasted bone marrow served with the "brunch for 2" on weekends.
Known for: Welsh rarebit; breakfast quiche; celebrity chef owners. Ⓢ *Average main: C$20* ✉ *4720 rue Marquette, The Plateau* ☎ *514/507–0555*
⊕ *www.maisonpublique.com* ☾ *Closed Mon. and Tues.* Ⓜ *Laurier* ✛ *H2.*

$$$$ ✕ **Moishe's.** Elegant and old-school, Montréal's premier steak house
STEAKHOUSE has been in the Lighter family since 1938 and they have consistently
Fodor'sChoice remained hands-on when it comes to selecting and aging their own
★ antibiotics-and-hormone-free steaks, sourced from local farmers. Do
not skip Moishe's famous Monte Carlo—potato skins filled with potato
mixed with milk, butter, cream, and chives. **Known for:** Monte Carlo
potato; quality, aged steaks; classic steak house. Ⓢ *Average main:
C$40* ✉ *3961 boul. St-Laurent, The Plateau* ☎ *514/845–3509* ⊕ *www.
moishes.ca* Ⓜ *St-Laurent* ✛ *F3.*

$ ✕ **Patisserie Rhubarbe.** This small and tastefully decorated bakery is,
BAKERY simply put, a Montréal treasure; locals come from all over the city to
FAMILY pick up delicious desserts like lemon tarts and Paris-Brest that taste as
Fodor'sChoice good as they look. Brunch is a relaxed affair with exquisite brioche
★ French toast with apples and caramel or scrambled eggs with truffle oil.
Known for: afternoon tea; Paris-Brest; worthwhile but long wait for a
table. Ⓢ *Average main: C$10* ✉ *1479, avenue Laurier Est, The Plateau*
☎ *514/903–3395* ⊕ *www.patisserierhubarbe.com* ☾ *Closed Mon. and
Tues.* Ⓜ *Laurier* ✛ *H1.*

$$ ✕ **Schwartz's Delicatessen.** This Montréal classic has zero frills decor-wise
DELI and consistently long lines but that's all really beside the point because
FAMILY you simply haven't really eaten in Montréal if you haven't eaten at
Fodor'sChoice Schwartz's, Canada's oldest deli. The cooks do such an excellent job
★ at curing, smoking, and slicing beef brisket that it is no surprise that
even when it's 20 below zero, locals (and celebrity visitors) don't mind
lining up for a thick and legendary smoked meat sandwich on rye with
mustard (and cherry cola if you want the full experience). **Known for:**
smoked meat sandwiches; long wait for a table; local institution. Ⓢ *Av-
erage main: C$14* ✉ *3895 boul. St-Laurent, The Plateau* ☎ *514/842–
4813* ⊕ *www.schwartzsdeli.com* Ⓜ *Sherbrooke* ✛ *F3.*

$ ✕ **Soupe Soup.** With multiple locations in all the right areas of Montreal,
CANADIAN SoupeSoup offers creative soups and sandwiches to those after a no-
FAMILY nonsense healthy lunch. The menu is written on a huge chalkboard and
changes daily. **Known for:** healthy "fast" food; creative soup options;

reliable local chain. $ *Average main: C$9* ✉ *80 av. Duluth Est, The Plateau* ⊕ *www.soupesoup.com* ⊗ *Visit website for each location's operating hrs* Ⓜ *Mont-Royal* ✛ *F3.*

$
CAFÉ
FAMILY
Fodor'sChoice
★

✕ **St-Viateur Bagel & Café.** Even New Yorkers have been known to (collective gasp!) prefer Montréal's light and crispy bagel to its bulkier Manhattan cousin. The secret is dough boiled in honey-sweetened water before baking in a wood-burning oven. **Known for:** delicious bagels; classic and creative options; local favorite. $ *Average main: C$6* ✉ *1127 av. Mont-Royal Est, The Plateau* ☎ *514/528–6361* ⊕ *www. stviateurbagel.com* Ⓜ *Laurier* ✛ *G2.*

$$
JAPANESE

✕ **Yokato Yokabai.** Frequently cited as the best ramen house in Montreal bar none, Yokato Yokabai is indeed a discreet restaurant that deserves to be visited by all noodle lovers—especially when temperatures drop below freezing point. The décor features dark wood paneling and minimal knickknacks and immediately transports diners to a Japanese hole-in-the-wall. **Known for:** Tonkotsu ramen; atmospheric décor; long waits. $ *Average main: C$14* ✉ *4185 Drolet, The Plateau* ☎ *514/282-9991* ⊕ *www.yoka.ca* ⊗ *Closed daily 3–5* Ⓜ *Mont-Royal* ✛ *F3.*

OUTREMONT

Outremont caters to affluent French-speaking professionals with restaurants that look as good as the food being served. There are plenty of charming outdoor terraces in the warm months.

$$
BISTRO
FAMILY
Fodor'sChoice
★

✕ **La Croissanterie Figaro.** The self-proclaimed "un coin perdu de Paris" is famous for its wraparound patio, Parisian vibe, and 100-year-old corner building. It's hard to know which architectural detail to admire first—the art deco chandelier, the art nouveau bar, the stained glass or the woodwork. **Known for:** charming setting; croissant with ham and cheese; opens early and closes late. $ *Average main: C$15* ✉ *5200 rue Hutchison, Outremont* ☎ *514/278–6567* ⊕ *www.lacroissanteriefigaro. com* Ⓜ *Outremont* ✛ *B3.*

$$$
BISTRO
Fodor'sChoice
★

✕ **Leméac.** This sophisticated French bistro pleases Montrealers with its flawless classics and its heated wraparound outdoor terrace; not to mention the late-night two-course table d'hôte menu at just C$27. Regulars gravitate toward dishes such as the calf liver, salmon, or beef tartare, grilled Cornish hen, and hanger steak—all served with ceremonial aplomb on white linen tablecloths. **Known for:** wraparound outdoor terrace; salmon tartare; late night special. $ *Average main: C$30* ✉ *1045 rue Laurier Ouest, Outremont* ☎ *514/270–0999* ⊕ *www. restaurantlemeac.com* Ⓜ *Outremont* ✛ *B3.*

$$$
WINE BAR

✕ **M.Mme.** With a simple but slick decor of exposed brick walls, natural woods, and leather chairs and banquettes, the scene-stealer in this trendy wine bar is the magnificent backlit glassed-in cellar containing over 650 bottles, but the surprise is the excellent, if a little pricey, food. Two menus are available; one comprising a half-dozen sharing plates—including a delightful charcuterie platter and a steak tartare—and a more robust option, offering elegantly presented dishes like suckling pig shoulder, duck magret, and Arctic char, all from a bright, open kitchen. **Known for:** prix-fixe special; suckling pig shoulder; elegant wine bar. $ *Average main: C$21* ✉ *240 Avenue Laurier Ouest, Outremont* ☎ *514/274-6663* ⊕ *www.mmme.ca* ⊗ *Closed Sun.* Ⓜ *Laurier* ✛ *C3.*

3

$$ ✕**Pizzeria 900.** No one does pizza quite like these pizzaiolos; they are,
MODERN ITALIAN   after all, legally certified by the *Associazione of Vera Pizza Napolitana*
in Italy. Using all-natural and nonprocessed ingredients, and adhering
to traditional pizza-making methods (like using a 900-degree oven), Pizzeria 900 is one of the most sought-after pizza spots in town with one
of the most sought-after patios. **Known for:** prix-fixe lunch; Neapolitan-style pizza; stylish space. $ *Average main: C$15* ✉ *1248 rue Bernard
Ouest, Outremont* ☎ *438/386–0900* ⊕ *no900.com* Ⓜ *Outremont* ✛ *B2.*

MILE END

As Montréal's equivalent of Brooklyn and Shoreditch, Mile End caters
mostly to hip creatives. Between hipster-run cafés and locally sourced
revisited British gastropubs, this place sets the trends and constantly
pushes the limits of culinary experimentation.

$$ ✕**BarBounya.** The menu at this beautifully designed eatery features
MEDITERRANEAN   Turkish-inspired cuisine with a focus on meze, small dishes served
hot or cold and meant to be ordered in large quantities for sharing.
The local poached lamb *köfte* with sunchokes has become a classic, as
has the *tune lakerda* and braised quince—which are only enhanced by
BarBounya's extensive wine list, consisting mostly of private imports.
Known for: Turkish tapas; private-import wines; homemade kaymak.
$ *Average main: C$16* ✉ *234, av. Laurier W, Mile End* ☎ *514/439–
8858* ⊕ *www.barbounya.com* ⊘ *Closed Mon. No dinner on Sun.* ✛ *C3.*

$ ✕**Café Olimpico.** Open daily from 7 am to midnight, this Mile End staple
CAFÉ   is a popular spot for great Italian coffee in Montréal's most fashionable
FAMILY   neighborhood. Families and business types alike head to Café Olimpico
in the morning to kickstart their days and the patio is overflowing with
cool types on the odd sunny day. **Known for:** gourmet coffee; sunny
patio; authentic Montréal feel. $ *Average main: C$3* ✉ *124 rue St-
Viateur Ouest, Mile End* ⊕ *www.cafeolimpico.com* ⊟ *No credit cards*
Ⓜ *Rosemont* ✛ *C2.*

$ ✕**Kem CoBa.** Only one word accurately describes the all-natural goodness
CAFÉ   at this ice cream stand: yum. Flavors change frequently based on what
FAMILY   chefs find at the market, but the lightly salted butter ice cream is a staple;
Fodor's Choice   partner it with the apple sorbet and you'll have yourself an apple pie on
★   a cone. **Known for:** cash only; eccentric soft serve flavors; local favorite.
$ *Average main: C$5* ✉ *60 av. Fairmount Ouest, Mile End* ☎ *514/419–
1699* ⊟ *No credit cards* ⊘ *Closed Oct.–Apr.* Ⓜ *Laurier* ✛ *C3.*

$$$$ ✕**La Chronique.** It's an elegant place with white walls and high ceilings
FRENCH   flooded with light, but people don't come here for the ambience; they
come for the excellent food. Without fuss or fanfare, La Chronique has
steadily been one of the best French restaurants in town since it opened
in 1995. **Known for:** tasting menu; seared foie gras; excellent French
cuisine. $ *Average main: C$36* ✉ *104 av. Laurier Ouest, Outremont*
☎ *514/271–3095* ⊕ *www.lachronique.qc.ca* ⊘ *Closed Mon. No lunch
on weekends* Ⓜ *Laurier* ✛ *C3.*

$ ✕**La Tamalera.** The kitschy-cool décor includes a display of religious
MEXICAN   icons as well as vibrantly colorful furniture, while the menu is Mexican
FAMILY   street cuisine at its best. The food here is simple and the menu small,
but everything is fresh and delicious. **Known for:** corn-based homemade
tacos; Mexican-inspired brunch; vibrant decor. $ *Average main: C$10*

✉ *226 av. Fairmount Ouest, Mile End* ☎ *438/381–5034* ⊕ *www.lata-maleramontreal.com* ▭ *No credit cards* ☽ *Closed Mon. No dinner Sat. and Sun.* Ⓜ *Laurier* ✛ *E1.*

$$$
CANADIAN
Fodor's Choice
★

✕ **Lawrence.** There are lines outside this hip and trendy establishment before the restaurant even opens for weekend brunch. The chef's British background means that the homemade scones and clotted cream here are required eating. **Known for:** long lines for brunch; arctic char and sea urchin; British-inspired fare. Ⓢ *Average main: C$21* ✉ *5201 boul. St-Laurent, Mile End* ☎ *514/503–1070* ⊕ *www.lawrencerestaurant. com* ☽ *Closed Mon-Wed. Closed 3-5:30 Thurs.–Sun.* Ⓜ *Laurier* ✛ *C3.*

$$
AMERICAN
FAMILY

✕ **Nouveau Palais.** Hipsters head to this laid-back '70s diner for one thing: delicious, classic greasy spoon dishes with a modern twist (a close second is the decor; think wood paneling and vinyl seats). The Palace Hamburger is gaining a reputation among Montrealers as one of the best in the city, and the sweet-potato pie also has fans. **Known for:** open late; Palace Hamburger; 70s vibe. Ⓢ *Average main: C$15* ✉ *281 rue Bernard Ouest, Mile End* ☎ *514/273–1180* ⊕ *www.nouveaupalais.com* ☽ *Closed Mon. No lunch on Tues.* Ⓜ *Rosemont* ✛ *C1.*

$$
PIZZA
FAMILY
Fodor's Choice
★

✕ **Pizzeria Magpie.** Although a few inspired appetizers are available, it's really all about the pizza and oysters at this unpretentious, casual spot. Tucked away on a small side street in The Village, this classic pizzeria with white-washed walls and pressed tin ceiling turns out some of the best wood-burning oven pizza the city has to offer. **Known for:** Margherita pizza; affordable oysters; homemade desserts. Ⓢ *Average main: C$15* ✉ *1237 rue Amherst, The Village* ☎ *514/544–2900* ⊕ *www.pizzeriamag-pie.com* ☽ *Closed Mon. No lunch on weekends* Ⓜ *Beaudry* ✛ *C2.*

$
BRITISH

✕ **Salon de thé Cardinal.** If it wasn't for the trendy young clientele, you'd think that time had stood still at Salon de thé Cardinal, where you can find a good old-fashioned afternoon tea served with dainty mismatched tableware and in a Victorian-style space filled with antiques, thick runner rugs, and carved wood. Food-wise, the menu varies between sweet (blueberry scones, bourbon cookies, various English cakes) and savory (ploughman's plate, cucumber sandwiches), both complemented by a plethora of fragrant teas. **Known for:** Victorian tea-room; freshly baked scones; delicious teas. Ⓢ *Average main: C$11* ✉ *5326 boul. St-Laurent, Mile End* ☎ *514/903-2877* ⊕ *www.thecardinaltea.com* ☽ *Closed Mon., Tues., and Wed.* Ⓜ *Laurier* ✛ *C2.*

$$
MODERN BRITISH

✕ **Sparrow.** Part cocktail bar, part British restaurant, the aviary decor motifs are welcoming at this oh-so-hip spot—where diners can get a traditional English breakfast in the morning, followed by a Sunday roast and a good old-fashioned basil gimlet. Brunch favorites include red-velvet pancakes and the smoked trout hash. **Known for:** famous Sparrow burgers; Sunday roast; great cocktails. Ⓢ *Average main: C$13* ✉ *5322 boul. St-Laurent, Mile End* ☎ *514/507–1642* ⊕ *www.sparrow-lemoineau.com* Ⓜ *Laurier* ✛ *F1.*

LITTLE ITALY

Little Italy offers a nostalgic look back at what La Bella Italia used to be 30 years ago, as old men congregate in front of their favorite café and chat about politics and last night's soccer game. With its location just steps away from Jean-Talon Market, it's only fitting that historic Piccola

Italia would go on to become the sought-after dining destination that it is today. It's now neighbored by the trendsetting Mile-Ex and Rosemont area, where chefs, moving away from Old Montréal and Downtown's expensive rents, benefit from splendid spaces and eager locals, which include young professionals and diners hungry for new experiences.

$$
PIZZA
FAMILY

✕**Bottega Pizzeria.** Nobody questions the authenticity of the Neapolitan-style pizza here, seeing as there's a 3,500-kilogram wood-burning pizza oven made from Vesuvian rock in the kitchen which cooks pizza in 90 seconds flat, at 500 degrees Celsius (932 °F). There are just a few toppings available but all are fabulously flavoursome, like fresh tomatoes, vegetables, and top quality salumi. **Known for:** gelato to-go; Neapolitan-style pizza; arancini. Ⓢ *Average main: C$19* ⊠ *65 rue St-Zotique Est, Little Italy* ☎ *514/277–8104* ⊕ *www.bottega.ca* ⊘ *Closed Mon. Lunch on Thurs. and Fri. only.* Ⓜ *Beaubien* ✛ *D1.*

$$
MODERN
CANADIAN
FAMILY
Fodor'sChoice
★

✕**Brasserie Harricana.** Instagram-famous for its dusty pink chairs and pleasing, contemporary space, this seriously cool brasserie is home to 41 home-brews—sold by the bottle at the boutique upstairs—and a solid menu that includes monkfish burgers, beer-can chicken, and a hearty ribeye. Waiters are masters at their craft; don't hesitate to ask for beer pairings with your meal. **Known for:** trendy microbrewery; architectural space; fried beer-can chicken. Ⓢ *Average main: C$14* ⊠ *95 Rue Jean-Talon Ouest, Little Italy* ☎ *514/303-3039* ⊕ *www.brasserieharricana. com* Ⓜ *De Castelnau* ✛ *D1.*

$
CAFÉ

✕**Caffè San Simeon.** In the heart of Little Italy, this historic coffee shop filled with regulars chatting away in Italian, is one of the city's best places (that is not run by hipsters) to get an espresso, latte, cappuccino, or the signature smooth Malibu—a lukewarm drink shorter than a cappuccino but longer than a macchiato, made by combining a short shot of espresso with frothed milk. Visit a few times and you won't even have to order: the experienced baristas will prepare your drink when they see you walk in. **Known for:** old-school Italian cafe; Malibu coffee; open late and early. Ⓢ *Average main: C$5* ⊠ *39 rue Dante, Little Italy* ☎ *514/272–7386* ⊕ *www.caffesansimeon.com* ▭ *No credit cards* Ⓜ *Jean-Talon* ✛ *D1.*

$$
SOUTHERN
Fodor'sChoice
★

✕**Dinette Triple Crown.** Dinette Triple Crown is relatively small (a counter with just eight stools) but the real draw here is not indoors; rather, locals know to ask for a picnic basket (fully equipped with cutlery, dishes, and a tablecloth) that will be enjoyed in Little Italy Park across the street. Fried chicken with fluffy mashed potatoes and gravy, braised greens, and biscuits, along with pulled pork sandwiches and brisket, will have you speaking with a southern drawl in no time. **Known for:** large selection of bourbon; fried chicken; picnic baskets. Ⓢ *Average main: C$15* ⊠ *6704 rue Clark, Little Italy* ☎ *514/272–2617* ⊕ *www.dinettetriplecrown.com* ⊘ *Closed Mon.–Wed.* Ⓜ *Beaubien* ✛ *D1.*

$$$
MODERN ITALIAN
Fodor'sChoice
★

✕**Impasto.** This unpretentious, industrial-chic Little Italy restaurant has garnered a great reputation, thanks in part to its celebrity-chef owners, Stefano Faita and Michele Forgione. Start by sharing the artisanal salumi platter, move on to a primi of some of the best fresh pasta dishes in town like the *pansotti* with walnut sauce, the melt-in-your-mouth ricotta gnocchi or the *Porchetta del nonno* (grandpa's pork roast), a must-order if it's on the menu. **Known for:** modern Italian fare; stylish decor; Grandma's pork roast. $ *Average main: C$24* ⊠ *48 rue Dante, Little Italy* 🕾 *514/508–6508* ⊕ *www.impastomtl.ca* ☽ *Closed Sun. and Mon. Lunch on Thurs. and Fri. only* Ⓜ *Jean-Talon* ⊹ *D1.*

$$$
BISTRO

✕ **Kitchen Galerie.** With its small ingredient-based menu, this homey bistro is an example of excellence through simplicity. The chefs do everything—the shopping, the chopping, the cooking, the greeting, and the serving, and the focus is on meats, fish, and vegetarian dishes all inspired by what local farmers bring to the adjacent Jean-Talon market that morning. **Known for:** dishwasher-cooked pot de foie gras; market cuisine; communal seating. $ *Average main: C$30* ⊠ *60 rue Jean-Talon Est, Little Italy* 🕾 *514/315–8994* ⊕ *www.kitchengalerie.com* ☽ *Closed Sun. and Mon.* Ⓜ *Jean-Talon* ⊹ *D1.*

$
BAKERY

✕ **La Cornetteria.** This lovely little bakery, which magically transports its patrons (or at least, their tastebuds) to Italy, specializes in the cornetto, the Italian version of the croissant. Freshly baked every morning, these delightful pastries are available plain or filled with Nutella, ricotta cream, or almond paste. **Known for:** nutella cornetto; traditional cannolis; stracchino sandwiches. $ *Average main: C$4* ⊠ *6528 boul. St-Laurent, Little Italy* 🕾 *514/277–8030* ⊕ *www.lacornetteria.com* ▭ *No credit cards* Ⓜ *Beaubien* ⊹ *D1.*

$$
ECLECTIC

✕ **La Récolte.** One could visit La Récolte (literally, "the harvest") every week and never eat the same meal twice, for the blackboard menu is entirely based on locally sourced market finds; in fact, resourceful La Récolte prides itself into serving Montréal's most eco-friendly brunch (try that leek-and-mushroom Benedictine if it's available). Not that their environmental responsibility overshadows their creativity (case in point, their delectable butternut squash mille-feuille); the balance between refined techniques and market-based cuisine seems to be a hit if the consistently long queues outside are any indication. **Known for:** long lines; market cuisine; leek-and-mushroom Benedictine. $ *Average main: C$19* ⊠ *764 rue Bélanger, Rosemont* 🕾 *514/508-5450* ⊕ *la-recolte.ca* ☽ *No dinner on Sun. Closed Mon. and Tue.* Ⓜ *Jean-Talon* ⊹ *D1.*

$
MIDDLE EASTERN
FAMILY

✕ **Le Petit Alep.** This casual Middle Eastern spot is comfortable and homey but still has style, with music, ivy, exposed-stone walls and a lovely terrasse come summer. The menu is perfect for grazing and excellent sharing options include the *mouhamara* (pomegranate-and-walnut spread), *sabanegh* (spinach-and-onion pies), *fattouche* (a salad with pita chips and mint), and *yalandji* (vine leaves stuffed with rice, chickpeas, walnuts, and tomatoes). **Known for:** Armenian cuisine; atmospheric decor; daily specials. $ *Average main: C$11* ⊠ *191 rue Jean-Talon Est, Rosemont* 🕾 *514/270–6396* ⊕ *www.petitalep.com* ☽ *Closed Sun. and Mon.* Ⓜ *Jean-Talon* ⊹ *D1.*

$$$
MODERN
CANADIAN

✕ **Manitoba.** Bringing a taste of the forest to adoring local foodies, food writers, and adventurous eaters, Manitoba was one of the most percussive restaurant openings of recent years and remains one of the city's top food spots. Serving perhaps the most distinctive fare in the city, with a Boreal hunter-gatherer premise, dishes may include rabbit liver pâté and cedar jelly, deer steak, and fried lichen. **Known for:** Boreal cuisine; deer steak. $ *Average main: C$21* ⊠ *271 rue St-Zotique Ouest, Little Italy* 🕾 *514/270–8000* ⊕ *restaurantmanitoba.com* ☽ *Closed Sun. Dinner only on Sat.* Ⓜ *Parc* ⊹ *D1.*

$$$ MODERN CANADIAN 🍴 **Montréal Plaza.** You won't see anything too familiar on the menu at this fresh, light-filled restaurant with its high ceilings, clean white walls and tablecloths, and modern mix of wood, glass, and sliding industrial windows that open to outdoor seating in summer. You *will* find whimsical yet unpretentious dishes that surprise and delight, like brochettes of duck hearts, baloney cannelloni, and "Chinatown" razor clam—just be sure to order everything with a side of deep-fried Brussels sprouts. **Known for:** affordable wines; creative menu; deep-fried Brussels sprouts stalks. [$] *Average main: C$22* ✉ *6230 rue St-Hubert, Rosemont* ☎ *514/903-6230* 🌐 *www.montrealplaza.com* [M] *Beaubien* ✥ *D1.*

$ SPANISH 🍴 **Tapeo.** Bringing tapas uptown, this Spanish-inspired eatery is a chic yet casual place to drink imported wines and share a few small plates. The Tapeo version of the classic *patatas bravas* served with a spicy tomato sauce and aioli is always a good choice, as are the roasted vine tomatoes and the grilled chorizo. **Known for:** patatas bravas; chef's table; house churros. [$] *Average main: C$11* ✉ *511 rue Villeray, Villeray* ☎ *514/495–1999* 🌐 *www.restotapeo.com* 🕒 *Closed Mon. No lunch on weekends.* [M] *Jarry* ✥ *F1.*

WESTMOUNT

This upscale area, predominantly Anglophone, is a far cry from the French-speaking Montréal foreigners often picture. You'll see polished moms in Prada sunglasses pushing strollers, as well as dressed-down locals walking their dogs along rue Sherbrooke and avenue Greene. Westmount is a relatively new foodie destination, and provides much-needed sustenance after hitting the area's luxury boutiques.

$$$ JAPANESE FUSION 🍴 **Park.** Sustainable, organic, and fresh every day is the philosophy of this high-end sushi place. The menu is eclectic, with excellent sashimi—some specimens flown in directly from Japan—noodles, and Japanese dishes mixed with a variety of influences from the chef's multiple backgrounds—Korean, Argentinian, and Canadian. **Known for:** homemade kimchi BLT on focaccia; creative menu; omakase. [$] *Average main: C$23* ✉ *378 av. Victoria, Downtown* ☎ *514/750–7534* 🌐 *www.parkresto.com* 🕒 *Closed Sun.* [M] *Vendôme* ✥ *A4.*

SUD-OUEST

Low rent and proximity to Downtown make the Sud-Ouest area, consisting of Verdun, Saint-Henri, and Petite-Bourgogne, attractive to small chef-owned restaurants. Choices in this off-the-tourist-trail area run the gamut from fast food to high-end restaurants, with interesting ethnic eats as well.

$$ SOUTHERN FAMILY 🍴 **Blackstrap.** Memphis-style barbecue is the name of the game at this popular, self-serve spot owned and operated by a champion pit master honing his skill behind the smoker and Missouri-imported barbecue pits. Pork, brisket, chicken, and ribs all get a secret-rub treatment and are then cooked slowly for up to 16 hours. **Known for:** "burnt ends" poutine; Memphis-style barbecue; locally sourced meat. [$] *Average main: C$15* ✉ *4436 rue Wellington, Verdun* ☎ *514/507–6772* 🌐 *www.blackstrapbbq.ca* [M] *De l'Église* ✥ *A4.*

Joe Beef, known for its excellent organic rib steak and famous lobster spaghetti, is located in the Sud-Ouest area of Montréal.

$$
BRITISH

✕ **Burgundy Lion.** This multilevel restaurant filled with young professionals lures in patrons with its lively atmosphere and deliciously updated English food. The signature fish-and-chips is deservedly popular, as are other classics like bangers and mash and shepherd's pie. **Known for:** fish and chips; afternoon tea; lively atmosphere. $ *Average main: C$20* ✉ *2496 rue Notre-Dame Ouest, Verdun* ☎ *514/934–0888* ⊕ *www.burgundylion.com* Ⓜ *Lionel-Groulx* ✛ *A6.*

$$$$
MODERN
CANADIAN
Fodor's Choice
★

✕ **HVOR.** The clean and minimalistic Scandinavian décor of Hvor, pronounced "vor" (Danish for "here") is the perfect blank slate for the playful flavor and ingredient combinations on display. Through partnerships with local organic farmers and artisans, as well as an urban garden fitted with 2000 plants and even beehives, HVOR's menu showcases the best of Québec's terroir with inventive plates like hay-smoked beet in bannock crust and lamb shoulder with brined wild mushrooms. **Known for:** Scandinavian decor; 100% organic fine dining; tasting menu with wine pairings. $ *Average main: C$31* ✉ *1414 Notre Dame Ouest, Verdun* ☎ *514/937-2001* ⊕ *www.hvor.ca* ☾ *Closed Sun. and Mon.* Ⓜ *Lucien-L'Allier* ✛ *C6.*

$$$$
MODERN
CANADIAN
Fodor's Choice
★

✕ **Joe Beef.** Eating out here is a little like being invited to a dinner party by a couple of friends who just happen to be top-notch chefs. Everything written on the chalkboard menu is simple, hearty and just delicious, from the fresh oysters to the organic rib steak and the now famous lobster spaghetti. **Known for:** lobster spaghetti; leafy patio; celebrity chef. $ *Average main: C$35* ✉ *2491 rue Notre-Dame Ouest, Verdun* ☎ *514/935–6504* ⊕ *www.joebeef.ca* ☾ *Closed Sun. and Mon. No lunch* Ⓜ *Lionel-Groulx* ✛ *A6.*

$$$$ MODERN CANADIAN Fodor's Choice ★ 🍴 **Le Fantôme.** Equal parts whimsy and polish, Le Fantôme—widely touted as one of Canada's best restaurants—offers an exciting dining experience. Rather than a typical à-la-carte menu, diners will find a prix-fixe 6-to-9 course gastronomic odyssey fueled by the chef's weekly inspiration, be it wild boar and mushroom spaghetti or black bass with fennel compote. **Known for:** chef's inspiration menu; peanut butter foie gras and jelly sandwich;. [$] *Average main: C$70* ✉ *1832 Rue William, Verdun* ☎ *514/846-1832* 🌐 *restofantome.com* 🕒 *Closed Mon.* [M] *Georges-Vanier* ✥ *A6.*

$$ MODERN ITALIAN Fodor's Choice ★ 🍴 **Le Vin Papillon.** First and foremost a wine bar, this tiny 30-seat spot also dishes out delicious vegetable-centric, market-based cuisine. The cuisine features local and seasonal ingredients, and the flavors are simple enough to go well with the stars of the show: the many wines on offer. **Known for:** Italian tapas; Brussels sprouts; extensive wine list. [$] *Average main: C$14* ✉ *2519 rue Notre-Dame Ouest, Verdun* 🌐 *vinpapillon.com* 🕒 *Closed Sun. and Mon.* [M] *Lionel-Groulx* ✥ *A6.*

$$$ MODERN ITALIAN 🍴 **Nora Gray.** The crowd that fills this casual and lively spot nightly is hip, and the simple, modern Southern Italian comfort food and impeccable service keeps them coming back. Start your meal with the roasted cauliflower frittata or the Dungeness crab salad with confit Meyer lemon and deer carpaccio. **Known for:** Southern Italian cuisine; wild boar chop; old-world wine list. [$] *Average main: C$30* ✉ *1391 rue St-Jacques, Verdun* ☎ *514/419–6672* 🌐 *noragray.com* 🕒 *Closed Sun. and Mon.* [M] *Lucien L'Allier* ✥ *C6.*

$ BAKERY FAMILY 🍴 **Patrice Pâtissier.** Pick up a pastry to go at the counter or choose one of the plated desserts to enjoy on-site at Patrice Pâtissier, a beautifully designed pastry shop and lunch spot, overseen by one of Québec's renowned pastry chefs. The green dessert—a savvy combination of pistachios, green apples, cilantro, olive oil and a white chocolate and yogurt mousse—has become a classic. **Known for:** the green dessert; kouign amann; celebrity chef. [$] *Average main: C$4* ✉ *2360 rue Notre-Dame Ouest, Local 104, Verdun* ☎ *514/439–5434* 🌐 *patricepatissier.ca* 🕒 *Closed Mon. and Tues.* [M] *Lionel-Groulx* ✥ *B6.*

$ ASIAN 🍴 **Satay Brothers.** Bringing southeast Asia to southwest Montreal, Satay Brothers is ioperated by two brothers obsessed with the street food found in Singapore, Malaysia, Thailand, and Cambodia. The eclectic and oddly charming space—think red walls, illuminated Chinese lanterns, a mishmash of Asian patterns and decor—features communal seating and a long bar facing the kitchen which fires out steamed pork buns, *laksa* soup, papaya salad and, of course, satays to keep the constant and lively crowd fed. **Known for:** festive ambiance; papaya salad; long lines. [$] *Average main: C$9* ✉ *3721 Notre-Dame Rue Ouest, Verdun* ☎ *514/933-3507* 🌐 *www.sataybrothers.com* 🕒 *Closed Mon. and Tues.* [M] *Lionel-Groulx* ✥ *A5.*

WHERE TO STAY

Updated by
Joanne Latimer

Montréal is a city of neighborhoods with distinct personalities, which creates a broad spectrum of options when it comes to deciding on a place to stay. The Downtown core has many of the big chain hotels you'd find in any city, while Old Montréal, the Plateau, and other surrounding areas have unique *auberges* (inns) and boutique hotels.

Most of the major hotels in Downtown—the ones with big meeting rooms, swimming pools, and several bars and restaurants—are ideal for those who want all the facilities along with easy access to the department stores and malls on rue Ste-Catherine, the museums of the Golden Square Mile, and nightlife on rues Crescent and de la Montagne. If you want something a little more historical, consider renting a room in one of the dozen or so boutique hotels that occupy the centuries-old buildings lining the cobbled streets of Old Montréal. Most of them offer all the conveniences along with the added charm of stone walls, casement windows, and period-style furnishings.

If your plans include shopping expeditions to avenue Mont-Royal and rue Laurier with maybe a few late nights at the jazz bars and dance clubs of Boulevard St. Laurent and rue St-Denis, then the place to bed down is in one of Plateau Mont-Royal's small but comfortable hotels. Room rates in the area tend to be quite reasonable, but be careful: the hotels right in the middle of the action—on rue St-Denis, for example—can be noisy, especially if you get a room fronting the street.

PLANNING

LODGING PLANNER
RESERVATIONS
Montréal is always hosting a festival or an international convention, so the hotels are consistently booked. This takes visitors by surprise. Many of the quaint auberges have a small number of rooms, so they fill up fast. It's necessary to book months ahead for the Grand Prix, the Jazz Festival, the World Film Festival, and all holiday weekends.

	NEIGHBORHOOD VIBE	PROS	CONS
Old Montréal	Cobblestone streets, boutique hotels, designer clothes, and historic architecture; very touristy, although it quiets down at night.	Quaint; easy access to bike paths; nice to walk along the waterfront; hip restaurants and mixology options are in the Old Port.	Can be desolate in the late evening outside hotel lobbies; parking is scarce; depending on the exact location, métro and bus access can be limited.
Downtown	Montréal's center for hustle and bustle, mostly on rue Sherbrooke, rue Ste-Catherine, and boulevard de Maisonneuve.	Extremely convenient; big-name hotel chains; central location; pools; garage parking; perfect for families as well as business travelers; near the outdoor Quartier Spectacle.	Traffic congestion is relentless; not as many dining options as other neighborhoods, and what is there tends to be at either extreme—fast food or very pricey (and not always worth it).
The Latin Quarter	Hopping with university kids and moviegoers, this area boasts a crazy mix of cafés, handmade chocolate shops, and folks carrying library books.	Festival central; easy métro access; right between the Plateau and Downtown; local characters abound.	Uneven gentrification means dodgy pockets; litter; bad roads.
The Plateau and Environs	Scattered auberges, Airbnb rentals and B&Bs host the artsy crowd and academics, with streets filled with local boutiques and hip restaurants; perfect for strolling.	Stumbling distance to the best bistros and pubs; unique shopping that focuses on local designers and craftspeople.	Limited métro and taxi access; limited hotel selections; can be noisy at night; panhandlers galore.
Mont-Royal and Environs	There are only a few hotels in this quiet section of the city, located in the shadow of the immense Parc du Mont-Royal.	Unhurried pace; lots of green space; lower rates.	Limited métro access; few dining options.

■TIP➔ From mid-November to early April rates often drop, and throughout the year many hotels have two-night, three-day, double-occupancy packages at substantial discounts.

FACILITIES

When pricing accommodations, ask what's included. You can assume that all rooms have private baths, phones, and TVs unless otherwise noted. If no meals are included in the room rate, "No meals" is stated toward the end of the review. Breakfast is noted when it's included in the rate.

Most hotels are wired, with a business center in the lobby. Smaller auberges may not have televisions and air-conditioning, but often have Wi-Fi.

Bathtubs, plush bathrobes, and fluffy white duvets are popular here for winter comfort. Bigger hotels have day spas and health clubs, as well as some of the city's finest restaurants.

WITH KIDS

Most of the chain hotels—Le Square Phillips Hotel and Suites, for example—have great pools. Avoid smaller auberges, however, because noise travels and the charming ambience doesn't go far with children. Hotels in the Old Port are popular with families because they're near the Centre des Sciences de Montréal and the Lachine Canal bike path.

Given that they are in a major city, the hotel rooms here are generous. Budget rooms and auberges are the exception, with rooms measuring less than 300 square feet. Otherwise, expect standard sizes of about 400–700 square feet.

PARKING

Parking is a sore point in Old Montréal and downtown. Your car will feel like a tank on the narrow streets, and you can expect to pay heftily for valet service in this part of town. Elsewhere, there's often parking available under the large-scale hotels. This is a blessing in winter, when you don't want to shovel snow and de-ice your car. If possible, avoid taking your car.

PRICES

Aside from during the Grand Prix and the Jazz Festival, it's possible to get a decent hotel room in high season for C$200 to C$300. Take advantage of Web-only deals or phone the hotel directly to ask about promotions.

WHAT IT COSTS IN CANADIAN DOLLARS			
$	**$$**	**$$$**	**$$$$**
Hotels	under C$199	C$200–C$299	C$300–C$399	over C$400

Hotel prices are the lowest cost of a standard double room in high season.

MONTRÉAL HOTEL REVIEWS

Reviews are listed alphabetically within neighborhoods. Use the coordinate (✛ B2) at the end of each listing to locate a site on the corresponding map. Hotel reviews have been shortened; for full information, visit Fodors.com.

OLD MONTRÉAL (VIEUX-MONTRÉAL)

Let's start with the name. Nobody says "Old Town." That's an American phrase. You may call it Old Montréal, but street signs are in French and say "Vieux-Montréal." Either way, it's full of charm—from narrow, cobblestone streets to horse-drawn carriages. You can find boutique hotels, auberges, and cozy bed-and-breakfasts nestled inside heritage buildings. Most properties have exposed beams, stone walls, wooden floors, and thick, casement windows. History buffs find this area pleasing, as do people who want to wander around boutiques and art galleries. But know that this is no place for stilettos. Bring your walking shoes and expect to stumble on film crews and the occasional Hollywood actor taking a smoke break. We're talking to you, Brad Pitt.

$ HOTEL Fodor's Choice ★

🏨 **ALT Montreal Griffintown.** Savvy young hipsters and budget-conscious creative types flock to ALT in Griffintown for its highly affordable set rates, and for sleek rooms with designer furnishings, expansive views, and no set check-out time. **Pros:** contemporary design; Starbucks in lobby; on-site parking. **Cons:** no valet; no king-size beds and no guarantee of a tub; no restaurant on-site. [$] *Rooms from: C$179* ✉ *120 rue Peel, Old Montréal* ☎ *514/375–0220* 🌐 *althotels.ca* 🛏 *154 rooms* 🍴 *No meals* [M] *Bonaventure* ✥ *C6.*

$$$ B&B/INN

🏨 **Auberge Bonaparte.** Stately and distinguished inside a 19th-century building, the freshly updated Auberge Bonaparte is a true gem, with old-world charm—a cozy lobby, exposed stone walls, and original wood details—and old-fashioned good service, as well as modern, comfortable rooms, a great restaurant, and an excellent location. **Pros:** three-course breakfast included; views of the Basilica's private gardens; perfect for theater lovers—the Centaur Theatre is next door. **Cons:** downstairs restaurant can be a bit noisy on weekends; not family-friendly; parking lot is down the street. [$] *Rooms from: C$300* ✉ *447 rue St-François-Xavier, Old Montréal* ☎ *514/844–1448* 🌐 *www.bonaparte.ca* 🛏 *31 rooms* 🍴 *Breakfast* [M] *Place-d'Armes* ✥ *F5.*

$$$ B&B/INN Fodor's Choice ★

🏨 **Auberge du Vieux-Port.** This showcase for 19th-century architecture—think casement windows, exposed beams and brick—is the gold standard for intimate boutique hotels, attracting A-listers and well-heeled romantics with its mix of old-world charm and modern comfort. **Pros:** new loft options offer more space and high ceilings; expansive rooftop deck; some rooms have decks and fireplaces. **Cons:** sometimes noisy in street-facing rooms; some rooms are very small. [$] *Rooms from: C$300* ✉ *97 rue de la Commune Est, Old Montréal* ☎ *514/876–0081, 888/660–7678* 🌐 *www.aubergeduvieuxport.com* 🛏 *51 rooms* 🍴 *Breakfast* [M] *Place-d'Armes or Champ-de-Mars* ✥ *F6.*

$$$ B&B/INN Fodor's Choice ★

🏨 **Épik Montreal.** With its rustic stone walls and exposed beams, this inn was the first of its kind in the Old Port when it opened in the late 1980s, and the new owners continue to honor its tradition of calm excellence while adding modern comfort and contemporary design accents throughout. **Pros:** guests can use refrigerator downstairs; bountiful breakfast served under stained-glass skylight; soundproof shutters. **Cons:** rooms need to be booked far in advance; lobby's chic cocktail bar isn't suitable for kids; king-size beds are pricey. [$] *Rooms from: C$300* ✉ *171 rue St-Paul Ouest, Old Montréal* ☎ *514/842–2634* 🌐 *www.epikmontreal.com* 🛏 *10 rooms* 🍴 *Breakfast* [M] *Place-d'Armes* ✥ *E6.*

$$$$ HOTEL Fodor's Choice ★

🏨 **Hôtel Gault.** Once a cotton factory in the 1800s, this heritage boutique hotel has loftlike rooms with soaring ceilings, cast-iron columns, freestanding tubs, heated floors, and an artsy vibe that doesn't sacrifice comfort for style. **Pros:** some rooms have private terraces; 24/7 room service; quiet location. **Cons:** a bit hard to find; $35 valet; no pool. [$] *Rooms from: C$400* ✉ *449 rue Ste-Hélène, Old Montréal* ☎ *514/904–1616, 866/904–1616* 🌐 *www.hotelgault.com* 🛏 *30 suites* 🍴 *No meals* [M] *Square-Victoria* ✥ *E5.*

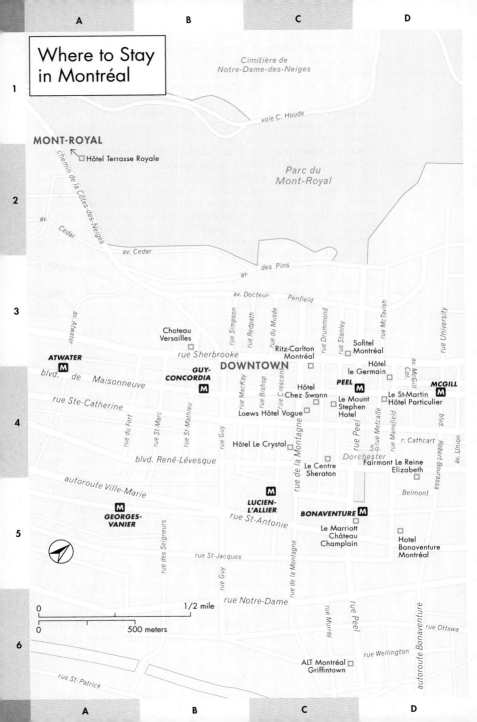

Where to Stay in Montréal

Cimitière de Notre-Dame-des-Neiges

voie C. Houde

MONT-ROYAL

□ Hôtel Terrasse Royale

chemin de la Côte-des-Neiges

Parc du Mont-Royal

av. Cedar

av. Cedar

av. des Pins

av. Docteur- Penfield

rue Simpson

rue Redpath

rue du Musée

rue Drummond

rue Stanley

rue McTavish

rue University

Chateau Versailles □

rue Sherbrooke

Ritz-Carlton Montréal □

Sofitel Montréal □

ATWATER Ⓜ

DOWNTOWN

Hôtel le Germain □

blvd. de Maisonneuve

GUY-CONCORDIA Ⓜ

Hôtel Chez Swann □

PEEL Ⓜ

av. McGill Col.

MCGILL Ⓜ

rue MacKay

rue Bishop

rue Crescent

Le Mount Stephen Hotel

Le St-Martin Hôtel Particulier □

rue Ste-Catherine

Loews Hôtel Vogue □

rue Peel

rue Metcalfe

rue Mansfield

r. Cathcart

blvd. Robert-Bourassa

Union av.

rue du Fort

rue St-Marc

rue St-Mathieu

rue Guy

Hôtel Le Crystal □

rue de la Montagne

Sq. Dorchester

Fairmont Le Reine Elizabeth

blvd. René-Lévesque

Le Centre Sheraton □

Belmont

autoroute Ville-Marie

GEORGES-VANIER Ⓜ

LUCIEN-L'ALLIER Ⓜ

BONAVENTURE Ⓜ

rue des Seigneurs

rue St-Antoine

rue Guy

rue St-Jacques

Le Marriott Château Champlain □

Hotel Bonaventure Montréal □

rue de la Montagne

rue Notre-Dame

rue Murray

rue Peel

rue Ottawa

autoroute Bonaventure

rue St-Patrick

rue Wellington

ALT Montréal Griffintown □

0 _____ 1/2 mile

0 _____ 500 meters

A   B   C   D

1   2   3   4   5   6

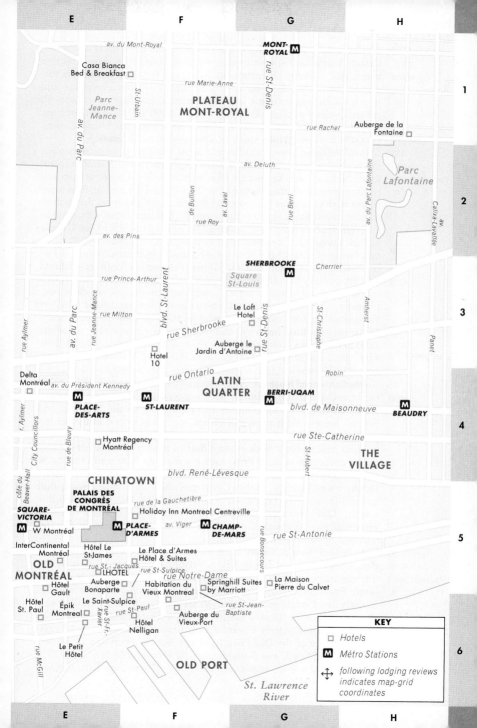

$$$$ HOTEL FAMILY Fodor's Choice ★ 🏨 **Hôtel Le St-James.** Civility reigns at one of the city's most celebrated Grande Dame hotels, with its discrete staff, lavish furnishings, marble baths, and celebrity clientele who appreciate the splendor of this former Mercantile bank. **Pros:** 20-foot ceilings; luxurious experience and stately lobby; most rooms have fireplaces. **Cons:** lacks curb appeal; expensive daily pet fees. [$] *Rooms from: C$500* ✉ *355 rue St-Jacques, Old Montréal* ☎ *514/841–3111, 866/841–3111* 🌐 *www.hotellestjames.com* 🛏 *62 rooms* 🍴 *No meals* [M] *Square-Victoria* ✥ *E5.*

$$$ HOTEL Fodor's Choice ★ 🏨 **Hôtel Nelligan.** There's a cultivated air of refinement echoing through this landmark on rue St. Paul, named for Quebec's most passionate poet, Emile Nelligan, and known for its romance-inspiring lobby atrium and rooftop terrace offering views of the Old City and the harbor. **Pros:** cozy rooms with enormous bathrooms; breakfast with a view on the rooftop terrace; excellent pub grub at the resto-bar, Méchant Bœuf. **Cons:** popular event space; pricey valet parking. [$] *Rooms from: C$359* ✉ *106 rue St-Paul Ouest, Old Montréal* ☎ *514/788–2040, 877/788–2040* 🌐 *www.hotelnelligan.com* 🛏 *105 rooms* 🍴 *No meals* [M] *Place-d'Armes* ✥ *F6.*

$$ HOTEL 🏨 **Hôtel St. Paul.** Forget fussy oil paintings or rococo furniture—behind its 19th-century facade, the St. Paul has a slick new lobby with jewel-toned velvet sofas and dramatic contemporary design, which is contrasted by the serene and neutral room decor. **Pros:** panoramic Old Port views; fashionable lobby design; great location on a north–south artery. **Cons:** underlighted hallways and elevators can be spooky; off-white sofas in the rooms look tired. [$] *Rooms from: C$295* ✉ *355 rue McGill, Old Montréal* ☎ *514/380–2222, 866/380–2202* 🌐 *www.hotelstpaul.com* 🛏 *120 rooms* 🍴 *No meals* [M] *Square-Victoria* ✥ *E6.*

$$ HOTEL 🏨 **InterContinental Montréal.** After extensive room renovations in 2016, the InterContinental definitely got its groove back, catering to a variety of travelers—from families and their pets, to the business and fitness cliques—with personal service, a great gym and saltwater lap pool, a solid in-house restaurant and bar (and the city's only absinthe bar), as well as decor with enough flair to banish all traces of cookie-cutter corporate design. **Pros:** kids get a teddy bear and crayons at check-in; easy underground access to shopping and nightlife; trendy, locally owned café in lobby. **Cons:** gets the convention crowd; dull ground-floor entry. [$] *Rooms from: C$289* ✉ *360 rue St-Antoine Ouest, Old Montréal* ☎ *514/987–9900, 800/361–3600* 🌐 *www.montreal.intercontinental.com* 🛏 *357 rooms* 🍴 *No meals* [M] *Square-Victoria or Place-d'Armes* ✥ *E5.*

$$ HOTEL Fodor's Choice ★ 🏨 **La Maison Pierre du Calvet.** With its Victorian accents, glassed-in garden, Louis XIII and Louis XIV furnishings and storied past as the 18th-century home of a notorious Freemason who entertained Benjamin Franklin, the opulent boutique hotel debuted modern updates in early 2018 while preserving its sense of old-world tranquillity and character. **Pros:** enchanted garden setting for breakfast; quiet, cobblestoned location; stately library. **Cons:** limited room service; at easternmost edge of the Old Port; opulence not for everyone. [$] *Rooms from: C$295* ✉ *405 rue Bonsecours, Old Montréal* ☎ *514/282–1725, 866/282–1725* 🌐 *www.pierreducalvet.ca* 🛏 *9 rooms* 🍴 *Breakfast* [M] *Champ-de-Mars* ✥ *G5.*

$$$
HOTEL
FAMILY
Fodor'sChoice
★

Le Petit Hôtel. The hip little sister of the Auberge du Vieux Port, this boutique hotel marries creative design with old stone walls, exposed beams, a counter coffee bar and a seven-foot orange sculpture in the narrow lobby, and—contrary to its name—not-so-petite rooms. **Pros:** bicycles to borrow; chic lobby café; cribs, playpens, and baby-sitters available. **Cons:** small bathrooms have no tubs; steep fee for valet parking ; no restaurant on site. $ *Rooms from: C$325* ✉ *168 rue St-Paul Ouest, Old Montréal* ☎ *514/940–0360, 877/530–0360* ⊕ *www.petithotelmontreal.com* ⤳ *28 rooms* ⦿ *Breakfast* Ⓜ *Square-Victoria* ✛ *E6.*

$$$
HOTEL
FAMILY
Fodor'sChoice
★

Le Place d'Armes Hôtel & Suites. Three splendidly ornate Victorian commercial buildings were merged to create Old Montréal's largest boutique hotel, pleasing honeymooners and business execs alike with its old-fashioned grandeur, exposed brick walls in rooms, hammam, roof-top terrace, and unobstructed views of the Basilique Notre-Dame-de-Montréal. **Pros:** best (Turkish) spa in town; best Japanese tavern in town (hamachi bibimbap [marinaded yellowtail]). **Cons:** late sleepers may be disturbed by the noontime Angelus bells at the Basilica; steep approach from métro is slippery in winter; no pool. $ *Rooms from: C$300* ✉ *55 rue St-Jacques, Old Montréal* ☎ *514/842–1887, 888/450–1887* ⊕ *www.hotelplacedarmes.com* ⤳ *134 rooms* ⦿ *No meals* Ⓜ *Place-d'Armes* ✛ *F5.*

$$$$
HOTEL

Le Saint-Sulpice. With its sought-after address beside the Basilica's chapel, this boutique hotel is blessed with a magical garden terrace, casement windows that actually open, luxurious suites—both in space and decor—and a lively lobby restaurant with one of the city's best menus. **Pros:** in-room massage service; celebrity-spotting; proximity to the Basilique Notre-Dame de Montréal. **Cons:** church bells may disturb late sleepers; too posh for comfort with kids; pricey summer rates. $ *Rooms from: C$500* ✉ *414 rue St-Sulpice, Old Montréal* ☎ *514/288–1000, 877/785–7423* ⊕ *www.lesaintsulpice.com* ⤳ *108 rooms* ⦿ *No meals* Ⓜ *Place-d'Armes* ✛ *F6.*

$$
HOTEL

LHOTEL. Housed in a stately 19th-century bank in the financial district, the dignified facade accurately suggests its grand and elegant interior with high ceilings, antique furnishings, and large windows, but the iconic Robert Indiana Love sculpture sitting outside also hints at the colorful rooms, bright art deco breakfast room, and extraordinary contemporary art collection within, including works by Jasper Johns, Andy Warhol, and Damien Hirst. **Pros:** decent room rates in Old Montréal; spacious high-ceiling rooms; excellent art collection and close to other galleries. **Cons:** some rooms are dated; buffet continental breakfast is pricey and not included; rue St-Jacques is dull after 6 pm. $ *Rooms from: C$268* ✉ *262 rue St-Jacques Ouest, Old Montréal* ☎ *514/985–0019, 877/553–0019* ⊕ *www.lhotelmontreal.com* ⤳ *55 rooms* ⦿ *No meals* Ⓜ *Square-Victoria* ✛ *E5.*

$$$
HOTEL
FAMILY

Springhill Suites by Marriott. Convenient and quiet, with large rooms and underground parking—rarities in Old Montréal—this all-suites hotel attracts families and business travelers who return for the free breakfast buffet, lobby market, saltwater pool (!), and fitness center. **Pros:** free, bountiful breakfast with healthy options; saltwater pool;

CLOSE UP

Lodging Alternatives

There are many reasons for travelers to consider apartment rentals or other lodging alternatives. Airbnb rentals are hugely popular here and you can find hundreds of options in different budgets and neighborhoods.

Below, you'll find our favorite, reputable providers of short- and long-term rentals. Most will fill advanced grocery orders for a service fee.

LOFT AND APARTMENT RENTALS

Fully furnished lofts—some with closed bedrooms—and apartments are available through these esteemed companies:

D-Luxe Properties. D-Luxe Properties rents stylish apartments and lofts in Montréal's best neighborhoods for long-term stays of at least one month. ☎ *888/393–1972* 🌐 *www.d-luxe.ca* 💳 *No credit cards.*

Habitation du Vieux Montréal. Habitation du Vieux Montréal rents out apartments in one building in the Old Port on St. Laurent Boulevard at the corner of St. Paul. ☎ *514/892–1238* 🌐 *www.habitationvieuxmontreal.ca* 💳 *No credit cards* ✥ *F6.*

Lofts du Vieux-Port. This agency has apartment-style lofts scattered throughout the Old Port. ☎ *888/660–7678* 🌐 *www.loftsduvieuxport.com* 💳 *No credit cards.*

B&BS

Some B&Bs are off the grid. They prefer to remain private and hush-hush. To find them, simply walk the streets of the Village, specifically rues St-Andre, St-Christophe, and St-Timothée, below rue Sherbrooke. Or, ask any of the friendly locals, who'll be more than glad to point you in the direction of their friend's B&B. *For more information on B&Bs, see Travel Smart Montréal and Québec City.*

—Joanne Latimer

well-stocked lobby store. **Cons:** popular with families so pool can be crowded; difficult access on a narrow street; poor views. [$] *Rooms from: C$325* ✉ *445 rue St-Jean-Baptiste, Old Montréal* ☎ *514/875–4333, 888/287–9400* 🌐 *www.springhillsuites.com* 🛏 *124 rooms* 🍴 *Breakfast* [M] *Champ-de-Mars* ✥ *F5.*

$$$$ HOTEL Fodor's Choice ★ 🏨 **W Montréal.** A chic showcase for your Prada luggage, the W Montréal lives up to the brand's reputation for a hip take on luxury and style, providing its A-list clientele with excellent service and sleek, modern decor, notably peekaboo bathrooms, a trendy bar, and a lobby designed for lingering and entertaining. **Pros:** bright, airy rooms; convenient downtown location; well-connected concierge; luxe pet program (daily fee). **Cons:** fee for in-room Wi-Fi (free in the lobby); lobby noisy at night; showers afford no privacy. [$] *Rooms from: C$400* ✉ *901 Square Victoria, Old Montréal* ☎ *514/395–3100* 🌐 *www.whotels.com/montreal* 🛏 *180 rooms* 🍴 *No meals* [M] *Square-Victoria* ✥ *E5.*

DOWNTOWN

The hub for countless festivals, Downtown is a convenient place to unpack your bags. This is where you'll find the major chain hotels, with underground parking, pools, and all the amenities that families enjoy. A few new boutique hotels have appeared in recent years, providing more options for couples without kids. From Downtown, it's just a short trip—via bike path, métro, or taxi—to the city's other neighborhoods of interest, so this is a good central point from which to see the city Since the outdoor festival "quartier" was renovated, even more people are attracted to Downtown's hotel. But be warned, construction slows traffic to a crawl these days. Go by foot or métro whenever possible.

4

$ HOTEL **Château Versailles.** History lovers and lovers of the romantic variety, too, appreciate the luxury within the Versailles' two elegant beaux art mansions, with high ceilings, plaster moldings, antique furnishings, and a twinkling chandelier in the entryway. **Pros:** elaborate decor and breakfast; spacious rooms with fireplaces; easy access to museum district. **Cons:** at busy intersection; too staid for children—and possibly some adults. [$] *Rooms from: C$199* ✉ *1659 rue Sherbrooke Ouest, Downtown* ☎ *514/933–3611, 888/933–8111* 🌐 *www.versailleshotels.com* 🛏 *65 rooms* 🍴 *Breakfast* [M] *Guy-Concordia* ✥ *B3.*

$$ HOTEL FAMILY **Delta Montréal.** Business travelers and jazz festival performers cycle through the Delta's airportlike lobby every year, taking advantage of the hotel's minimalist and quiet rooms, saltwater pool, squash courts, high-tech gym, and family-friendly restaurant. **Pros:** two squash courts and saltwater pool; excellent soundproofing; kid-friendly amenities and deals. **Cons:** drab lobby needs a makeover; no safes in room; restaurant is not great. [$] *Rooms from: C$279* ✉ *475 av. du Président-Kennedy, Downtown* ☎ *514/286–1986, 877/286–1986* 🌐 *www.deltamontreal.com* 🛏 *456 rooms* 🍴 *No meals* [M] *McGill or Place-des-Arts* ✥ *E4.*

$$$ HOTEL Fodor's Choice ★ **Fairmont Le Reine Elizabeth.** Reopened in summer 2017 after a $140 million renovation, Le Reine Elizabeth's retro-chic makeover includes 1960s-inspired interiors; a huge market and food hall; a new spa; creative meeting hubs; and a variety of trendy dining and lounging options—all the while preserving the property's iconic heritage (John and Yoko's 1969 "bed-in" suite [1742] has been carefully restored and enhanced with artifacts from the day). **Pros:** craft cocktails at Nacarat Bar; excellent dining options; luxurious, contemporary rooms. **Cons:** daily fee for Wi-Fi; conventioneers abound. [$] *Rooms from: C$359* ✉ *900 boul. René-Lévesque Ouest, Downtown* ☎ *514/861–3511, 800/441–1414* 🌐 *www.fairmont.com* 🛏 *950 rooms* 🍴 *No meals* [M] *Bonaventure* ✥ *D5.*

$ HOTEL FAMILY **Hotel Bonaventure Montreal.** From the Brutalist concrete facade to its slick, modern new lobby, the Bonaventure delivers style and value, along with a heated outdoor pool, 2½ acres of rooftop gardens, and updated bedrooms with dark wood furniture, mini-refrigerators, and granite countertops. **Pros:** almost every room has a view of the rooftop garden; easy access to the métro and the Underground City; year-round heated pool. **Cons:** lots of business traffic; elevator ride to reception is not so welcoming; Brutalist exterior not for everyone. [$] *Rooms from:*

C$199 ✉ *900 rue de la Gauchetière, Downtown* ☎ *514/878–2332, 800/267–2575* 🌐 *www.hotelbonaventure.com* 🛏 *402 rooms* 🍴 *No meals; Breakfast* [M] *Bonaventure* ✥ *D5.*

$$ HOTEL 🏨 **Hôtel Chez Swann.** Drawn to its Baz Luhrmann–style flamboyance, young culture vultures love that Chez Swann fully commits to the idiosyncratic design, with swirly black ceilings in the hallways, original art, custom furniture, textured rugs, sink-in sofas, a spin room, and free calls within North America. **Pros:** quirky design; in-room spa treatments; downtown location. **Cons:** no bathtubs; no pets; not suitable for kids. [$] *Rooms from: C$200* ✉ *1444 rue Drummond, Downtown* ☎ *514/842–7070* 🌐 *www.hotelchezswann.com* 💳 *No credit cards* 🛏 *23 rooms* 🍴 *Breakfast* [M] *Peel* ✥ *C4.*

$$$$ HOTEL 🏨 **Hôtel Le Crystal.** Le Crystal's luxury suites are all about dramatic style and comfort, designed to showcase the rooms' sleek kitchens, spa-style bathrooms, separate soaking tubs, and floor-to-ceiling windows. **Pros:** best city view from the treadmills; Starbucks on-site; saltwater pool; outdoor year-round whirlpool hot tub; walking distance to Centre Bell. **Cons:** not suitable for kids; only full suites, so no basic rooms; right on the sidewalk of a busy intersection. [$] *Rooms from: C$400* ✉ *1100 rue de la Montagne, Downtown* ☎ *514/861–5550* 🌐 *www.hotellecrystal.com* 🛏 *131 suites* 🍴 *No meals* [M] *Lucien-L'Aller* ✥ *C4.*

$$ HOTEL 🏨 **Hôtel le Germain.** The lobby in this sleek boutique hotel is peppered with creative types and international hipsters who appreciate stylish details like the sliding "wall" of louvered blinds, the bedding designed by Québec fashion icon Marie Saint Pierre, and designer bathrobes, as well as extras like in-room Nespresso machines, luxury car service, deluxe free breakfast, and the Tesla charging station. **Pros:** views of Mont-Royal or the skyscrapers along avenue du Président-Kennedy; chef Daniel Vézina heads the restaurant; connectivity panels project your laptop onto a 42-inch screen. **Cons:** on a charmless urban street; parking is scarce, and the valet isn't cheap; lacks curb appeal. [$] *Rooms from: C$230* ✉ *2050 rue Mansfield, Downtown* ☎ *514/849–2050, 877/333–2050* 🌐 *www.legermainhotels.com/fr/montreal* 🛏 *101 rooms* 🍴 *Breakfast* [M] *Peel or McGill* ✥ *D4.*

$$ HOTEL 🏨 **Hyatt Regency Montréal.** Overlooking the Place des Arts plaza, where the Just for Laughs and International Jazz festivals stage their free events, the Hyatt has loyal clients who return for the minimal-chic rooms and the hotel's fantastic location—right downtown, across from the Musée d'Art Contemporain, beside the Complexe Desjardins shopping mall, and an easy walk to Chinatown. **Pros:** two large outdoor terraces; indoor pool and lounge; dinner served until 11:30 pm. **Cons:** strange approach to lobby via elevator; no lunch served; busy bar and reception areas. [$] *Rooms from: C$299* ✉ *1255 rue Jeanne-Mance, Downtown* ☎ *514/982–1234, 800/361–8234* 🛏 *595 rooms* 🍴 *No meals* [M] *Place-des-Arts or Place-d'Armes* ✥ *E4.*

$ HOTEL FAMILY 🏨 **Le Centre Sheraton.** At this magnet for conventioneers, hockey fans, and businesspeople, the high-tech gym inspires exercise with views of the city, the lobby bar draws boisterous guests for drinks and networking, and the morning crowd shares newspapers at the in-house Starbucks café. **Pros:** expected Sheraton Signature comforts;

rooms have views of the mountain or St. Lawrence River; close to the Centre Bell for hockey and concerts. **Cons:** lobby marred by convention signs; lively scene not for everyone; executive club lounge on the 37th floor costs extra. [$] *Rooms from: C$199* ✉ *1201 boul. René-Lévesque Ouest, Downtown* ☎ *514/878–2000, 800/325–3535* 🌐 *www.sheraton.com/lecentre* 🛏 *825 rooms* 🍴 *No meals* [M] *Bonaventure or Peel* ✥ *C4.*

$ HOTEL 🏨 **Le Marriott Château Champlain.** An icon from the 1967 Olympics, this 36-floor skyscraper overlooking Place du Canada is always full of business guests, families and prom parties, due to its value, expansive views of the city from cozy rooms, and the indoor links to the métro and Underground City. **Pros:** expansive views; park-side location; top three floors have private lounges. **Cons:** can be noisy with parties; off-putting reception desk. [$] *Rooms from: C$199* ✉ *1050 rue de la Gauchetière Ouest, Downtown* ☎ *514/878–9000, 800/200–5909* 🌐 *www.marriott.com* 🛏 *611 rooms* 🍴 *No meals* [M] *Bonaventure* ✥ *C5.*

$$$$ HOTEL Fodor's Choice ★ 🏨 **Le Mount Stephen Hotel.** Set in a restored neoclassical landmark once owned by a Canadian railway pioneer, as well as a new 11-story tower behind the original mansion, this modern boutique hotel features contemporary guest rooms with state-of-the-art comforts (chromatherapy showers, Japanese toilets, heated floors, and Nespresso machines) as well as ornate interiors that include original features like 300-year-old stained-glass windows and intricate woodwork. **Pros:** unique historic property with opulent interior; high-end experience; Insta-worthy Bar George. **Cons:** not family-friendly; rates match the luxury; British-inspired restaurant may be too proper for some. [$] *Rooms from: C$450* ✉ *1440 Drummond St., Downtown* ☎ *514/313–1000* 🌐 *www.lemountstephen.com* 🛏 *90 rooms* 🍴 *No meals* ✥ *C4.*

$$$ HOTEL FAMILY 🏨 **Le St-Martin Hôtel Particulier.** Sober and chic, this tasteful hotel is in a great location for shopping, museums, and restaurants, and made special with features like a year-round heated pool, hardwood accents, fireplaces, soundproofed windows, and a French fusion restaurant. **Pros:** windows are soundproof; soaker tub and TV in bathrooms; very good restaurant. **Cons:** reception is just steps from the sidewalk and gets crowded at checkout; small outdoor pool often in shade; guests must be over the age of 25. [$] *Rooms from: C$319* ✉ *980 boul. de Maisonneuve Ouest, Downtown* ☎ *514/843–3000, 877/843–3003* 🌐 *www.lestmartinmontreal.com* 💳 *No credit cards* 🛏 *113 rooms* 🍴 *No meals* [M] *Peel* ✥ *D4.*

$$ HOTEL FAMILY Fodor's Choice ★ 🏨 **Loews Hôtel Vogue.** Serious shoppers like the location—just a five-minute walk from Holt Renfrew, La Maison Ogilvy, La Maison Simons, and other destinations boutiques—but the hotel's appeal multiplied 10-fold with a multimillion dollar renovation that made the rooms and lobby more fitting (i.e., gorgeous) for regulars like Oscar winners and business elite. **Pros:** chic lobby; huge bathrooms with flat-screen TVs; toys available for kids. **Cons:** fee for high speed Wi-Fi; valet parking fee. [$] *Rooms from: C$249* ✉ *1425 rue de la Montagne, Downtown* ☎ *514/285–5555, 800/465–6654* 🌐 *www.loewshotels.com* 🛏 *142 rooms* 🍴 *No meals* [M] *Peel* ✥ *C4.*

4

$$$$ HOTEL Fodor's Choice ★ 🏨 **Ritz-Carlton Montréal.** The legacy, the elegance, the celebrity chef, the new pool—all good reasons to splurge on a room at the fully renovated "Ritz," the city's grandest hotel and icon in the Golden Square Mile, near museums, McGill University, and all the best boutiques. **Pros:** revived style, but still plenty of history; state-of-the-art bathrooms and soundproof windows; high-end shopping and galleries within a five-minute walk; infinity pool with patio. **Cons:** poor métro access; Sherbrooke Street can be dull on weeknights. [$] *Rooms from: C$425* ✉ *1228 rue Sherbrooke Ouest, Downtown* ☎ *514/842–4212, 800/363–0366* 🌐 *www.ritzmontreal.com* 🛏 *129 rooms* 🍴 *No meals* [M] *Peel or Guy-Concordia* ✥ *C4.*

$$ HOTEL Fodor's Choice ★ 🏨 **Sofitel Montréal.** At the foot of Mont-Royal, in the heart of downtown, this exquisite 17-story hotel uses its understated elegance (if the exquisite lobby carpets, made by the same company that carpeted Versailles for King Louis XIV can be called understated), excellent service and details, and convenient location to attract a well-heeled international crowd. **Pros:** bright and tailored rooms; chef Olivier Perret helms the exceptional restaurant; within walking distance of museums, McGill, the Bell Centre, and destination boutiques. **Cons:** no pool; scarce street parking; obstructed views in the east-facing rooms. [$] *Rooms from: C$259* ✉ *1155 rue Sherbrooke Ouest, Downtown* ☎ *514/285–9000* 🌐 *www.sofitel.com* 🛏 *258 rooms* 🍴 *No meals* [M] *Peel* ✥ *C3.*

CHINATOWN

$$ HOTEL FAMILY 🏨 **Holiday Inn Montreal Centre-Ville.** Fresh from a $9.5 million renovation, this ode to Feng Shui on the edge of Chinatown has a massive goldfish pond in the lobby and a pagoda restaurant-bar, huge guest rooms with dark wood furnishings, and an enviable location across from the Palais des Congrès convention center and a five-minute walk to Old Montréal. **Pros:** kids 18 and under stay and eat for free; great access to convention center; indoor pool open until 11 pm. **Cons:** exterior is a little kitschy; sidewalk approach isn't charming; some views of downtown are unflattering. [$] *Rooms from: C$200* ✉ *99 av. Viger Ouest, Chinatown* ☎ *514/878–9888, 888/878–9888* 🌐 *www.ihg.com/holidayinn/hotels/us/en/montreal/yulca/hoteldetail* 🛏 *235 rooms* 🍴 *No meals* [M] *Place-d'Armes* ✥ *F5.*

THE LATIN QUARTER

Bustling with moviegoers and university kids rushing to cafés and libraries, the Quartier Latin is alive with expectation. No, it isn't as pristine as the Old Port, since gentrification has been slow and uneven, but it's full of local flavor—artisanal chocolate shops, gastropubs, and hippie shops. The panhandlers are funny, not dangerous, and beg in two languages.

$ B&B/INN 🏨 **Auberge le Jardin d'Antoine.** Budget travelers flock to this small, shabby-chic hotel for its free Wi-Fi, metro access, kitchenettes, and deluxe Continental breakfast, but its best-selling point is its location right on rue St-Denis, among the Latin Quarter's trendy restaurants, movie theaters, and poutine joints. **Pros:** lively neighborhood; budget and standard rooms have been upgraded; good coffee machines in rooms. **Cons:** a quarter of the rooms are outdated; the lively location means it can be noisy; panhandlers near the front door. $ *Rooms from: C$113* ✉ *2024 rue St-Denis, Latin Quarter* ☎ *514/843–4506, 800/361–4506* ⊕ *www.aubergelejardindantoine.com* ⇖ *25 rooms* ⦾ *Breakfast* Ⓜ *Berri-UQAM* ✛ *G3.*

$$ Ⅱ **Hotel 10.** Its exterior may be part art nouveau classic from 1914 and part brick-and-concrete contemporary, but the sleek and modern interiors, contemporary furnishings and art throughout, and hip clientele makes this centrally located hotel *all* cool. **Pros:** rooms are bright and modern; car-rental on-site; proximity to nightlife on the main. **Cons:** drivers must choose between iffy street parking or C$30 valet; weekend party atmosphere can be alienating for some; trendy is not everyone's cup of tea. $ *Rooms from: C$249* ✉ *10 rue Sherbrooke Ouest, Latin Quarter* ☎ *514/843–6000, 866/744–6346* ⊕ *www.hotel10montreal. com* ⇖ *136 rooms* ⦾ *No meals* Ⓜ *St-Laurent* ✛ *F3.*
HOTEL
Fodor's Choice
★

$$ Ⅱ **Le Loft Hotel.** Inside an art deco landmark, this chic hotel has loftlike rooms with high ceilings and lots of space, as well as sleek IKEA kitchens, king beds, funky art, leather sectionals, and expansive views of the cityscape. **Pros:** 10-foot ceilings; good for longer stays; superior soundproofing. **Cons:** street parking is scarce; a bit hard to find. $ *Rooms from: C$229* ✉ *334 Terrasse St-Denis, Latin Quarter* ☎ *888/414–5638* ⊕ *www.lofthotel.ca* ⇖ *29 rooms* ⦾ *Breakfast* Ⓜ *Berri-UQAM* ✛ *G3.*
HOTEL

THE PLATEAU MONT-ROYAL

Full of artists and academics, the Plateau is a bustling neighborhood with a high density of bistros, brewpubs, martini bars, cupcake emporiums, designer boutiques, and parks. This is no place for quiet contemplation. In the summer, join the crowds at outdoor markets and street fairs. There aren't many places to stay, but they include some lovely auberges and B&Bs.

$ Ⅱ **Auberge de la Fontaine.** Built out of two adjoining houses with a signature yellow front door, laquered-barn-board facade, and welcoming flower boxes, this turn-of-the-20th-century residence overlooks Parc Lafontaine and one of the city's major bicycle trails. **Pros:** most rooms have whirlpool baths; near bars and restaurants; some rooms have private balconies with park views. **Cons:** lobby is serviceable but lacking glamour; some rooms are unrenovated and quite small; parking can be difficult. $ *Rooms from: C$199* ✉ *1301 rue Rachel Est, The Plateau* ☎ *514/597–0166, 800/597–0597* ⊕ *www.aubergedelafontaine. com* ⇖ *21 rooms* ⦾ *Breakfast* Ⓜ *Mont-Royal* ✛ *H1.*
B&B/INN
FAMILY

$ Ⅱ **Casa Bianca Bed & Breakfast.** Popular with love-struck couples visiting friends on The Plateau, the "casa" is an ode to French Renaissance Revival architecture and promotes an organic vegetarian ethic while offering original details like a terra-cotta fountain, hardwood floors, and elaborate moldings from 1890. **Pros:** facing Mont-Royal; claw-foot tubs; private terrace with flowers; yoga classes. **Cons:** only five rooms, so book early; creaky hardwood floors; no soundproofing in bedrooms; vegetarian not for everyone. $ *Rooms from: C$139* ✉ *4351 av. de l'Esplanade, The Plateau* ☎ *514/312–3837, 866/775–4431* ⊕ *www. casabianca.ca* ⇖ *5 rooms* ⦾ *Breakfast* Ⓜ *Mont-Royal* ✛ *F1.*
B&B/INN

4

CÔTES-DES-NEIGES

With its street-side fruit markets, bookstores, and multicultural vibe, Côtes-des-Neiges has much to offer the more relaxed tourist who isn't looking for a hipster hot spot. The mom-and-pop restaurants serve a United Nations of food choices, too, alongside a thriving Irish pub (McCarold's) and the ubiquitous Starbucks outlets.

$ HOTEL **Hôtel Terrasse Royale.** Basic but a good home base, the Hôtel Terrasse Royale, near the Oratoire St-Joseph, is a serviceable hotel in a busy neighborhood with convenient access to a métro station (across the street) and proximity to multicultural markets and restaurants, where you can dine cheaply and well. **Pros:** practical kitchens; interesting neighborhood; easy access to métro. **Cons:** location can be noisy; dull exterior; lobby needs a renovation. [$] *Rooms from: C$149* ✉ *5225 chemin de la Côte-des-Neiges, Côte-des-Neiges* ☎ *514/739–6391, 800/567–0804* 🌐 *www.terrasse-royale.com* 🛏 *56 rooms* 🍴 *No meals* [M] *Côte-des-Neiges* ✣ *A2.*

NIGHTLIFE

Updated by
Chris Barry

If nightlife in Montréal could be distilled into a cocktail, it would be one part sophisticated New York club scene (with the accompanying pretension), one part Parisian joie-de-vivre (and, again, a dash of snobbery), and one part Barcelonan stamina (which keeps the clubs booming until dawn).

Hot spots are peppered throughout the city. There are compact clusters along rue Crescent, boulevard St-Laurent (known as "The Main"), avenue Mont-Royal, and rue St-Denis. Prominent rue Ste-Catherine plows through town, connecting most of these nighttime niches, and farther east, near Beaudry métro station, it becomes the main drag for the Village, also called Gay Village. For whatever reason, the streets named after saints contain most of the clubs: rue Ste-Catherine, boulevard St-Laurent, rue St-Paul, and rue St-Denis. The Old Port is currently Montréal's hottest neighborhood, with a steady stream of chic venues opening in this cobblestone district.

Montréal's nightlife swings with a robust passion. From the early evening "5-à-7" after-work cocktail circuit, to the slightly later concerts and supper clubs (restaurant–dance club hybrids where people dance on the tables after eating off them), on into the even later dance club scene, all tastes, cultural backgrounds, and legal ages join the melee. Clubbing is, to say the least, huge in Montréal. Some restaurants are even installing discotheques in their basements.

As for what to wear on a Montréal night out: if you have a daring outfit in your closet that you've hesitated to wear—bring it. Montrealers like to get dressed up to go out to bars and clubs, even if the temperature is below freezing. And remember, most club regulars don't even know where they're going until midnight, so don't go out too early.

Montréal Nightlife

OUTREMONT Tame thirty-somethings relax over cocktails

MILE END Hipster spots with decent prices

LE PLATEAU-MONT-ROYAL Rock & Roll and house dancing clubs abound

LATIN QUARTER Students plus resto-lounges for young professionals

DOWNTOWN Densely packed with bars, clubs, and theaters

THE VILLAGE Gay bars and partying 'til dawn

OLD PORT Thriving 5 à 7 scene

CASINO DE MONTRÉAL Gaming and live musical shows 24/7

Map labels

rue Jarry

blvd. De l'Acadie
rue Durocher

Parc Jarry

r. St-Denis
av. Henri-Julien

r. Beaubien

BEAUBIEN Ⓜ

Parc Père-Marquette

av. Van Horne
Ⓜ **OUTREMONT**
av. Stuart
av. Lajoie
r. Bernard

r. de Bellechasse
r. des Carrières

av. Parthenais
r. Fullum

ch. de la Côte-Ste-Catherine
Hartland
av. McEachran
r. St-Viateur
blvd. St-Laurent
av. de Gaspé

av. Fairmount

r. de Bordeaux

ROSEMONT Ⓜ

Ⓜ **ÉDOUARD-MONTPETIT**

Cimetière Mont-Royal

av. du Parc
av. Bloomfield
av. Durocher

Parc Sir-Wilfred Laurier
av. Laurier
Ⓜ **LAURIER**

blvd. St-Joseph
r. Gilford

av. Papineau
av. de Lorimier
r. Parthenais
r. Fullum

MILE END

r. de Lanaudière
r. de Brébeuf
r. Garnier
av. de Lorimier
av. de Bordeaux

Chemin Remembrance
Voie C. Houde

av. du Parc
r. Clark
av. de l'Esplanade

MONT-ROYAL Ⓜ
av. du Mont-Royal
r. Marie-Anne
r. Rachel

Parc du Mont-Royal

r. St-Urbain
av. Duluth

LE PLATEAU-MONT-ROYAL

r. de Mentana
r. du Parc-Lafontaine
r. Roy

Parc Lafontaine

av. Cedar
av. Docteur-Penfield
r. McTavish
r. Peel

r. Prince-Arthur
r. de Bleury
blvd. St-Laurent
av. des Pins

r. Sherbrooke
r. de Champlain
r. de Bordeaux
av. de Lorimier
r. Fullum
r. Ontario

r. Sherbrooke
blvd. de Maisonneuve

r. University
r. Jeanne-Mance
r. Milton
SHERBROOKE Ⓜ
r. Ontario

LATIN QUARTER

r. de la Visitation
r. Plessis
r. Panet

GUY-CONCORDIA Ⓜ

PEEL Ⓜ
PLACE-DES-ARTS Ⓜ
Ⓜ **McGILL**
r. Ste-Famille
ST-LAURENT Ⓜ
BERRI-UQÀM Ⓜ

blvd. de Maisonneuve Ⓜ **PAPINEAU**
BEAUDRY Ⓜ

DOWNTOWN

blvd. René-Lévesque
r. Ste-Catherine
r. de la Gauchetière

THE VILLAGE

r. St-Hubert
r. St-Denis
r. Notre-Dame

autoroute Ville-Marie

Ⓜ **GEORGES-VANIER**

BONAVENTURE Ⓜ

LUCIEN-L'ALLIER Ⓜ
r. Guy
r. Notre-Dame

Ⓜ av. Viger
SQ.-VICTORIA
PL.-D'ARMES Ⓜ

CHAMP-DE-MARS Ⓜ

r. St.-Paul

OLD PORT

Lachine Canal
r. St-Patrick
r. Augustin-Cantin
r. Grand Trunk
r. Charon

Parc Leber

av. Pierre-Dupuy

Pont de la Concorde

Île Ste-Hélène

JEAN-DRAPEAU Ⓜ
Parc Jean-Drapeau

Île Notre-Dame

Parc Floral

St. Lawrence River

autoroute B
Pont Victoria
autoroute Bonaventure

Pont Jacques-Cartier

CASINO DE MONTRÉAL

0 — 1/2 mile
0 — 500 meters

MONTRÉAL NIGHTLIFE BEST BETS

Best for music: Club Soda

Best bubbles: La Champagnerie

Best water view: Terrasse sur l'Auberge

Best martini: Six Resto Lounge

Best comfort food: McKibbins Irish Pub

Best off-the-beaten path: Le Lab

Best for a date: Reservoir

Best patio: Le Sainte-Elisabeth

Best for expense accounts: Suite 701

Best wine bar: Pullman

PLANNING

EVENTS INFORMATION

Check out Cult MTL (⊕ *www.cultmontreal.com*), which is updated frequently with information on the various goings-on about town. The "Friday Preview" section of the *Gazette* (⊕ *www.montrealgazette.com*), the English-language daily paper, has a thorough list of events at the city's concert halls, clubs, and dance spaces.

The following websites provide comprehensive information about Montréal's nightlife scene: ⊕ *www.tourisme-montreal.org*, ⊕ *www.nightlife. ca*, and ⊕ *www.go-montreal.com*.

HOURS

The bars stop serving around 3 am and shut down shortly thereafter (with the exception of sanctioned "after-hour" haunts). On the weekends, expect them to be packed to the gills until closing. The club scene picks up right after the bars close, and then extends until dawn.

LATE-NIGHT TRANSPORTATION

The best way to get around the city after hours is by taxi. Taxis are generally easy to hail on the street, cost roughly C$8 to C$20 to most nightlife spots, and are available if the white or orange light is on.

The Montréal métro's Green and Orange lines have their last nighttime departures at 12:35 am weekdays, 1:05 am Saturday, and 12:30 am Sunday; the Yellow Line runs until 1 am weekdays, 1:30 am Saturday, and 1 am Sunday; and the Blue Line takes its last run at 12:45 am on Sunday and weekdays, and 1:15 am on Saturday. For more information, visit ⊕ *www.stm.info*.

NIGHTLIFE REVIEWS

OLD MONTRÉAL (VIEUX-MONTRÉAL)

Once a tourist trap full of overpriced souvenirs, Old Montréal is now home to a mix of top-notch restaurants and chic lounges. During the summer you can enjoy stunning views of the river from some of the city's best rooftop terraces. Excellent dining can be found along rue St-Paul, while rue McGill is a big part of the 5-à-7 scene.

BARS AND LOUNGES

La Champagnerie. Sharpen your swords! This chic bar for champagne and other sparklers is the perfect place to break open a bottle—literally. The staff like to open the bottles of bubbly with sabers, a practice that adds an element of fun to an accessible venue. Finger foods include oysters, steak (and other kinds of) tartares, and caviar. ⊠ *343 rue St-Paul Est, Old Montréal* ☎ *514/903–9343* ⊕ *www.lachampagnerie.ca* ⊘ *Closed Mon.* Ⓜ *Champs-de-Mars.*

Modavie Wine Bar. With a Mediterranean menu, an attractive sidewalk terrasse, and a sophisticated interior that places dark wood against stone walls, this jazz bar is pleasing to the eyes *and* ears. Despite being spread out over two floors, the space still feels cozy. Live duos play during the first part of the week, while weekends showcase full bands. There's never a cover charge. ⊠ *1 rue St-Paul Ouest, Old Montréal* ☎ *514/287–9582* ⊕ *www.modavie.com* Ⓜ *Champ-de-Mars.*

Philémon Bar. You can grab a glass of one of Philémon's well-priced private import cavas, proseccos, or champagnes to accompany the menu at this sleek bar, which serves more than the usual pub fare (oysters, anyone?). It's packed with locals Thursday through Saturday—in fact, it's become quite the singles hangout. Bouncers keep the ratio of guys to gals at a comfortable level. ⊠ *111 rue St-Paul Ouest, Old Montréal* ☎ *514/289–3777* ⊕ *www.philemonbar.com* Ⓜ *Place-d'Armes.*

Suite 701. This bar inside the chic Place-d'Armes Hotel is *the* place for drinks in Old Montréal—try the Moon Light martini, plump with fresh raspberries. You may want to linger over a plate of the crispy gnocchi. Upstairs, a rooftop patio (Terrasse Place d'Armes) overlooks Notre-Dame Cathedral and serves finger food with a whole other selection of cocktails. ⊠ *701 côte de la Place-d'Armes, Old Montréal* ☎ *514/904–1201* ⊕ *www.suite701.com* Ⓜ *Place-d'Armes.*

Terrasse sur l'Auberge. For an unbeatable view of the Old Port and numerous Montréal landmarks, head to this unpretentious patio on the roof of the Auberge du Vieux-Port Hotel. Open from the end of May through mid-October (2–11 weekdays, 1–11 on weekends), it's a great place to watch the International Fireworks Festival—if you're early enough to snag a table—and enjoy cocktails and a light tapas menu. The cod croquettes are a must-try and pair nicely with the clear sangria (made with sparkling wine). ⊠ *97 rue de la Commune Est, Old Montréal* ☎ *514/876–0081* ⊕ *www.terrassesurlauberge.com* Ⓜ *Place-d'Armes or Champs-de-Mars.*

5

Wunderbar. The local tradition of the cocktail hour has been reinvented thanks to this sexy watering hole inside a sleek W Hotel. From 5 until 10 pm in the summer, five signature cocktails, beers, and appetizers are priced between C$5 and C$10. In the winter, the bar takes on an after-hours vibe, opening only after 10 pm. ✉ *901 sq. Victoria, Old Montréal* ☎ *514/395–3100* 🌐 *www.wunderbarmontreal.com* ⊗ *Closed Sun.* Ⓜ *Square-Victoria.*

LIVE MUSIC

Biddle's Jr. A recent addition to the live-music scene in the heart of Old Montreal, this lively jazz bar and restaurant builds on a name that is synonomous with jazz in Montreal. Owned by the son of the late Philly-born, Montreal-based jazz great, Charles Biddle, Biddle's Jr. is home to superior live music and drinks as well as excellent food offerings; the buttermilk fried chicken with red coleslaw, pickles, and fries will knock your jazzy socks off. ✉ *209 Notre-Dame Ouest, Old Montréal* ☎ *514/504-5299* 🌐 *www.biddlesjr.com* Ⓜ *Place-d'-Armes.*

DOWNTOWN

From expensive restaurants to lowly bars, Downtown offers something for every taste and budget. Rue Crescent, with its lively mix of restaurants, pubs, and clubs, is where you'll find most of the action, with neighboring rue Bishop not far behind.

BARS AND LOUNGES

Fodor's Choice ★ **Brutopia.** House-brewed concoctions like Raspberry Blond Beer or Scotch Ale attract locals and tourists alike, and lately the kitchen has been serving up delicious tapas-style pub food. In addition to the unique brews, check out the sprawling outdoor seating, the art gallery on the third floor, and nightly live music. A typical crowd at Brutopia is under 30, but older folk shouldn't feel out of place. With live music ranging from traditional Irish folk to the occasional punk or psychedelic '60s garage band, this pub serves as a refreshing alternative to the slightly more upscale, trendy bars and nightclubs that mark the Crescent Street strip. ✉ *1219 rue Crescent, Downtown* ☎ *514/393–9277* 🌐 *www.brutopia.net* Ⓜ *Guy-Concordia.*

Burgundy Lion. This British pub serves food that's a notch above the usual. Scotch eggs and the ploughman's lunch are paired with an English take on Québec's beloved poutine—with Stilton cheese and caramelized onions—though it's the fish-and-chips that really shines. Be sure to grab a pint of the Burgundy Lion Ale, or any of the many other beers on draft. Two patios are open in the summer for alfresco drinking. Note that it can get loud in the evenings. ✉ *2496 rue Notre-Dame Ouest, Downtown* ☎ *514/934–0888* 🌐 *www.burgundylion.com* Ⓜ *Lionel-Groulx.*

Fodor's Choice ★ **Dominion Square Tavern.** Busy nearly every night of the week, this bar with a relaxed 1920s atmosphere is one of the hottest spots downtown for a drink after work, a tasty bite before the hockey game, or an old-fashioned cocktail to unwind and plan the rest of the evening. It opens at 11:30 am weekdays and 4:30 pm weekends. Kitchen closes at midnight daily. ⊠ *1243 rue Metcalfe, Downtown* ☎ *514/564–5056* ⊕ *www.tavernedominion.com.*

Fodor's Choice
★

Furco. Making its name through word of mouth alone, Furco has become one of the trendiest downtown bars, and for good reason. It's all about the industrial-chic interior, the warm amber lighting, and the relaxed, inviting vibe. A nice mix of clientele, great food (the menu changes weekly), and good pours also help make this a popular after-work hangout for locals, and the perfect retreat from the Quartier des Spectacles, a stone's throw away. Furco doesn't take reservations, so go early if you want to nab a seat. ⊠ *425 rue Mayor, Downtown* ☎ *514/764–3588* ⊕ *www.barfurco.com* Ⓜ *Place-des-Arts or McGill.*

Hurley's Irish Pub. For years this pub has been serving up a bounty of whiskeys and brews (19 different beers on tap), with a healthy dose of Irish atmosphere on the side. Despite its cavernous size, the arrangement of seating areas, flanked by bars, makes it feel cozy, and there's a stage for live entertainment. It still fills up quickly, so unless you don't mind standing while you sip your Guinness, come early to snag a seat. ⊠ *1225 rue Crescent, Downtown* ☎ *514/861–4111* ⊕ *www.hurleysirishpub. com* Ⓜ *Guy-Concordia.*

Le Sainte-Elisabeth. In the Quartier des Spectacles (the local performing-arts district), this European pub is popular in part because of its friendly service and good selection of domestic and imported beers, as well as whiskey and cognac. With one of the city's most beautiful backyard terraces, this is a great place to enjoy the fall colors. ⊠ *1412 rue Ste-Elisabeth, Downtown* ☎ *514/286–4302* ⊕ *www.ste-elisabeth.com* Ⓜ *Berri.*

Fodor's Choice
★

Pullman. At this sophisticated yet relaxed wine bar, let yourself be guided by the expertise of the sommeliers. The tapas-style cuisine is top notch, and the green beans with truffle oil and roasted almonds are great. During cooler months things get going at 4:30 pm, but in summer don't arrive until the sun starts to set. ⊠ *3424 av. du Parc, Downtown* ☎ *514/288–7779* ⊕ *www.pullman-mtl.com* Ⓜ *Place-des-Arts.*

Six Resto Lounge. With a prime view of the Quartier des Spectacles, this huge terrace overlooking Place des Arts is the perfect place for preshow drinks. In cooler weather you can relax in the purple-and-slate-gray lounge, where the bar takes center stage. Open 5–11:30 pm. ⊠ *Hyatt Regency Hotel, 1255 rue Jeanne-Mance, Downtown* ☎ *514/982–1234* ⊕ *montreal.hyatt.com/en/hotel/dining/SIXResto-Lounge.html* Ⓜ *Place-des-Arts.*

Stogie's Lounge. If the surprisingly trendy interior and views of rue Crescent aren't a big enough draw, then check out the conspicuous glass humidor housing a seemingly infinite supply of imported cigars. Thanks to being grandfathered in, the bar still allows smoking Cubans on-site, despite Québec's tough no-smoking law. ⊠ *2015 rue Crescent, Downtown* ☎ *514/848–0069* ⊕ *www.stogiescigars.com* Ⓜ *Guy-Concordia or Peel.*

COMEDY CLUBS

The Montréal Just For Laughs comedy festival, which takes place every July, has been the largest such festival in the world since its inception back in 1983.

But Montrealers don't have to wait until summer to get their comedy fix, as there are several Downtown clubs covering all things funny.

Comedy Nest. For decades, this comedy club has been showering Montrealers with humor from some of the biggest names out there: Jim Carrey, Tim Allen, and Russell Peters included. For a mere $5, Comedy Lab Wednesdays, when local comics work out new material, are always good for a laugh and will also secure you one free ticket for the weekend's activities. Arrive early to get a decent spot near the stage (or perhaps away from it). ⊠ *Pepsi Forum, 2313 rue Ste-Catherine Ouest, 3rd fl., Downtown* ☎ *514/932–6378* ⊕ *www.comedynest.com* Ⓜ *Atwater.*

Montreal Improv. The heart of the city's improv comedy scene offers shows in both English and French. The Friday night Main Event Smackdowns, where the audience determines the winner, are especially good for a laugh. ■TIP→ Get here early as the $8 tickets usually sell out quickly. ⊠ *3697 boul. St-Laurent, Downtown* ☎ *514/507–3535* ⊕ *www.montrealimprov.com* Ⓜ *Sherbrooke.*

DANCE CLUBS

Club Electric Avenue. Generation X will get along just fine here, as classics from the '80s and '90s boom out over a devoted, nostalgic crowd. In the basement of the Newtown lounge, these digs have great sound, excellent service, and sexy interior design. It's open Thursday to Saturday from 10 pm. ⊠ *1469 rue Crescent, Downtown* ☎ *514/285–8885* Ⓜ *Guy-Concordia.*

Salsathèque. Though neon lights and disco balls abound, this flashy club is all about the Latin lover—dance lover, that is. Merengue, bachata, and salsa (of course) are the specialties, but themed evenings keep things interesting with R&B, reggae, and Top 40 hits. Check the website to learn the week's schedule and sign up for the guest list to avoid a cover. ⊠ *1220 rue Peel, Downtown* ☎ *514/875–0016* ⊕ *www.salsatheque.ca* ⊗ *Closed Mon. and Tues.* Ⓜ *Peel.*

LIVE MUSIC

Club Soda. The grandaddy of the city's rock clubs has evolved into one of the dominant venues for jazz, reggae, techno, and rhythm and blues. Club Soda is a tall, narrow concert hall with high-tech design and 500 seats—all of them with great sight lines. ⊠ *1225 boul. St-Laurent, Downtown* ☎ *514/286–1010* ⊕ *www.clubsoda.ca* Ⓜ *St-Laurent.*

House of Jazz. The food is good but the music is outstanding. For more than 30 years, this institution has been plying the city with the best in jazz, with a little blues and soul thrown in for good measure. A flashy, over-the-top interior that includes mirrored walls adds to the experience. Dress up and be prepared to pay a cover. ⊠ *2060 rue Aylmer, Downtown* ☎ *514/842–8656* ⊕ *www.houseofjazz.ca* Ⓜ *McGill or Place-des-Arts.*

McKibbin's Irish Pub. This beautiful old sandstone mansion includes three floors of food, drink, and good Irish *craic* (a Gaelic term that means having fun with amiable companions). This isn't hard to do with more than 20 different stouts, lagers, and ales on tap. There's live entertainment nearly every night of the week, so head to the basement if you're looking for a bit of quiet (or a good chin-wag). The house fries are excellent for noshing, but beware of the Rim Reaper—chicken wings made with the world's hottest pepper. ⊠ *1426 rue Bishop, Downtown* ☎ *514/288–1580* ⊕ *www.mckibbinsirishpub.com* Ⓜ *Guy-Concordia.*

Fodor's Choice ★ **Upstairs Jazz Bar & Grill.** Five nights a week, the cheerful Joel Giberovitch greets you personally near the entrance to his club, which despite the name is actually downstairs. Giberovitch loves what he does, and the constant stream of local and imported jazz musicians makes this the favored jazz hangout in the city. The eclectic menu makes a nice accompaniment to the live music—try the home-cut fries with smoky mayo. Cover charges start at C$6 and range up to C$45 for name performers during Jazz Fest. The third set is free (usually around 11 pm), and other sets are also free if you sit on one of the cozy terraces. ⊠ *1254 rue Mackay, Downtown* ☎ *514/931–6808* ⊕ *www.upstairsjazz.com* Ⓜ *Guy-Concordia.*

THE VILLAGE

Head east along rue Ste-Catherine to enjoy the colorful Gay Village—you'll know you've arrived when you're amid a sea of pretty pink balls and rainbow flags hung in the streets. It's developing a bit of a reputation for fine dining as of late, though it's still mainly known as a place for late-night partying.

GAY AND LESBIAN NIGHTLIFE

Cabaret Mado. Makeup, glitter, and glamorous costumes abound at this nightclub with drag-queen entertainment. Mado herself is a Québec celebrity (so much so that she's immortalized in wax at the Grévin museum inside the Centre Eaton). During the nightly performances, even the clientele may get involved, thanks to karaoke and improv evenings. ⊠ *1115 rue Ste-Catherine Est, The Village* ☎ *514/525–7566* ⊕ *www.mado.qc.ca* Ⓜ *Beaudry.*

Fodor's Choice ★ **Club Unity.** Unity is actually the club's third incarnation on this spot. Small, semiprivate lounges are scattered throughout the two-story complex, and the beautiful rooftop terrace is one of the finest in the Village. Unity is one of the longest running, most popular gay dance clubs in town—although some have been known to complain you'll often find as many straight girls here as you will gay men. Open weekends from 10 pm to 3 am. ⊠ *1171 rue Ste-Catherine Est, The Village* ☎ *514/523–2777* ⊕ *www.clubunitymontreal.com* Ⓜ *Beaudry.*

Le Stud. Once a men-only establishment, Le Stud has been known to let in some women. A small dance floor and trance music have brought in a whole different crowd. It's packed most nights. ⊠ *1812 rue Ste-Catherine Est, The Village* ☎ *514/598–8243* ⊕ *www.studbar.com* Ⓜ *Papineau.*

Fodor's Choice ★ **Sky.** This massive complex houses a bar, restaurant, and dance club popular with both gay men and women. The best time to come is during the summer, as the pièce de résistance is the beachlike roof deck with city views and a pool (possibly the hottest destination in the Village). ✉ *1478 rue Ste-Catherine Est, The Village* ☏ *514/529–6969* ⊕ *www. complexesky.com* Ⓜ *Beaudry.*

PLATEAU MONT-ROYAL

The restaurants and bars along St-Denis and Mont-Royal are popular with everyone from rambunctious students to serious food-lovers. Boulevard St-Laurent ("The Main"), especially between rue Sherbrooke and avenue des Pins, is home to the see-and-be-seen crowd, with merrymakers spilling out at all hours of the night.

BARS AND LOUNGES

Fodor's Choice ★ **Big in Japan Bar.** Keep your eyes peeled for the red door: there's no sign above this inconspicuous speakeasy. Once you're past the faux suede curtains, the contemporary design and intricate seating plan will win you over—as will the sake and whiskey selection. Lines form on weekends, but weeknights aren't too bad. ✉ *4175 boul. St-Laurent, The Plateau* ☏ *438/380–5658* Ⓜ *St-Laurent.*

Fodor's Choice ★ **Bily Kun.** This Czech-themed bar is a favorite hangout of Plateau locals. There's live jazz during the cocktail hour, or you can groove to a DJ later in the evening. Try an absinthe-laced apple cocktail from the extensive alcohol menu as you nibble on a few tapas. Bily Kun gets packed, though the high ceilings help alleviate the feeling of claustrophobia. ✉ *354 av. du Mont-Royal Est, The Plateau* ☏ *514/845–5392* ⊕ *www. bilykun.com* Ⓜ *Mont-Royal.*

Fodor's Choice ★ **Le Lab.** Fabien Maillard is Montréal's mixologist extraordinaire, and the name of his unpretentious bar is entirely apt. Creating cocktails is his passion and it's shared by the friendly, skilled staff. The potent potions—including a $28 Zombie loaded with liquor—are inspired by everything from old, classic recipes to the fruits of the season. The entire menu changes twice a year, and there are also monthly specials. Call to reserve on weekends; it's packed despite being off the beaten track. ✉ *1351 rue Rachel Est, The Plateau* ☏ *514/544–1333* ⊕ *www. barlelab.com* ☾ *Closed Mon.* Ⓜ *Sherbrooke.*

Fodor's Choice ★ **Reservoir.** It's all about the beer at this friendly restaurant and bar, and it's all brewed right on the premises. With everything from India pale ales to German-inspired wheat beers, they've got you covered. Packed almost every night of the week, the upstairs patio is the ideal spot for watching locals stroll along the quaint cobblestone avenue. ✉ *9 av. Duluth Est, The Plateau* ☏ *514/849–7779* ⊕ *www.brasseriereservoir. ca* Ⓜ *Sherbrooke.*

Suwu. This self-described "hip-hop eatery" and neighborhood bar invites you to relax and pull up a chair or cozy couch. Simple but intense dishes like truffle-oil popcorn and a grilled cheese mac-and-cheese sandwich (yes, you read that right) are paired with powerful cocktails (try the signature Wu-Tang) to help make this one of the hottest destinations

on The Main—without any of the usual pretension. Open nightly from
5 to 3. ⊠ *3581 boul. St-Laurent, The Plateau* ☎ *514/564–5074* ⊕ *www.
suwumontreal.com* Ⓜ *St-Laurent.*

DANCE CLUBS

Cactus. Salsa is the favored style of dancing at Cactus, though merengue
and samba pop up during the week as well. Thursday through Saturday, the double-decker dance floor of this restaurant, bar, and club is
packed with patrons enjoying the rigorously authentic Latin music. You
can fuel up on Mexican food at the restaurant downstairs, then dance
the calories away. ⊠ *4461 rue St-Denis, The Plateau* ☎ *514/849–0349*
⊕ *www.elcactus.ca* Ⓜ *Mont-Royal.*

LIVE MUSIC

Casa del Popolo. One of the city's treasured venues for indie rock, jazz,
reggae, blues, folk, and hip-hop, this neighborhood bar is ideal for discovering up-and-coming local acts or forgotten international giants still
touring. While you enjoy the music, take a look at the original art and
sample some of the tasty vegetarian food. ⊠ *4873 boul. St-Laurent, The
Plateau* ☎ *514/284–3804* ⊕ *www.casadelpopolo.com* Ⓜ *Mont-Royal.*

Divan Orange. Grab a seat on the "orange sofa" and catch emerging
musical talent (both Francophone and Anglophone) at this popular Plateau bar Tuesday through Sunday. Credit cards aren't accepted. ⊠ *4234
boul. St-Laurent, The Plateau* ☎ *514/840–9090* ⊕ *www.divanorange.
org* Ⓜ *Mont-Royal.*

SUPPER CLUBS

Buonanotte. In business on The Main since 1991, this restaurant, lounge,
and weekend supper club continues to pull out all the stops. There's
top-notch Italian cuisine, a comprehensive wine list, well-known DJs,
and even a concierge. Celebrities are known to drop by when in town.
⊠ *3518 boul. St-Laurent, The Plateau* ☎ *514/848–0644* ⊕ *www.buon-
anotte.com* Ⓜ *St-Laurent.*

MILE END

Mile End is becoming well-known for inspired cuisine, affordable
lounges, and relaxed bars, and is slowly becoming a second village to
the hipster gay crowd, who tend to forgo the main Village.

BARS AND LOUNGES

Bar Waverly. Named for the street that epitomizes the Mile End, this
neighborhood bar has a warm staff, friendly ambience, and a great
selection of scotch. Owners Richard Holder and Olivier Farley have
been in the business for years, and it shows. Nightly DJs provide an
edgier vibe, while huge floor-to-ceiling windows make it perfect for
people-watching. ⊠ *5550 boul. St-Laurent, Mile End* ☎ *514/903–1121*
⊕ *www.barwaverly.com* Ⓜ *Laurier.*

La Buvette chez Simone. Arrive early (it opens at 4 pm but the kitchen only
gets going at 5 pm) at this easygoing wine bar—it's always busy and
they don't take reservations. Lots of wines are available by the glass, in
2- and 4-ounce pours, with an emphasis on French varietals. Dress is
casual, though the after-work crowd ups the glam factor. Lively but not

5

obnoxious, La Buvette's a great place to catch up with friends. ⊠ *4869 av. du Parc, Mile End* ☎ *514/750–6577* ⊕ *www.buvettechezsimone. com* Ⓜ *Laurier or Mont-Royal.*

Whisky Café. Known for its happy hour, this bar, café, and cigar lounge is elegant but unpretentious—it's the perfect spot for a romantic rendezvous. The selection of more than 150 varieties of scotch, plus an impressive choice of wines, champagnes, and ports, leaves most everyone's thirst quenched. ⊠ *5800 boul. St-Laurent, Mile End* ☎ *514/278–2646* ⊕ *www.whiskycafe.com* Ⓜ *Rosemont.*

THE ISLANDS

Casino de Montréal, which is on Île Notre-Dame, is several minutes away by car, bicycle, or métro from Downtown. The casino might be the only vestige of nightlife on the islands, but it's worth visiting for the excellent cabaret shows and good selection of bars and restaurants, and, of course, to try your hand at gambling.

CASINOS

Casino de Montréal. Music (including cabaret), food, gambling: there's something for everyone at the Casino de Montréal, which is open around the clock. On Île Notre-Dame, it's easily accessible by car, bicycle, or bus. The casino has more than 3,000 slot machines, a keno lounge, a high-stakes gaming area, and 120 tables for baccarat, craps, blackjack, roulette, and various types of poker, as well as four new restaurants and three new bars. ⊠ *1 av. du Casino, Île Notre-Dame* ☎ *514/392–2746, 800/665–2274* ⊕ *www.casinosduquebec.com/montreal* Ⓜ *Jean-Drapeau.*

6

PERFORMING ARTS

Updated by
Chris Barry

There's something uniquely Quebecois about the kind of entertainment referred to as a *spectacle*. It's more than just a performance, usually involving some kind of multimedia projection, light show, and, if outdoors, fireworks. It's no wonder, then, that the ultimate spectacle, Cirque du Soleil, was founded in Montréal in the '80s. And it's also hardly surprising that North America's largest French-speaking metropolis should be the continent's capital of French theater.

Montréal is the home of nearly a dozen professional companies and several important theater schools, but there's also a lively English-language theater scene and one of the few remaining Yiddish theaters in North America.

In 2012, the city completed the Quartier des Spectacles, a 70-acre theater district in Downtown with stages for outdoor performances and nearly 80 venues for dance, music, theater, and art.

For a city its size, Montréal offers a remarkable number of opportunities for fans of classical music to get their fill, from operas and symphonies to string quartets.

As for dance, there are several modern dance companies of note, including Montréal Danse and Québec's premier ballet company Les Grands Ballets Canadiens.

PLANNING

DRESS CODE

People tend to get somewhat dressed up for the symphony, the opera, and even theater performances in Montréal, perhaps more so than in several large U.S. cities. Men will wear sleek black pants, a button-down, and even a tie. Some women wear dark jeans, but it's not uncommon to see ladies decked out in skirts and dresses with strappy shoes (even in the dead of winter) and carrying clutches.

EVENTS INFORMATION

The bilingual *Nightlife* (🌐 *www.nightlife.ca*) and French-language *Le Voir* (🌐 *www.voir.ca*) list events and reviews, and are free and widely distributed.

Check out the *Gazette*'s "Friday Preview" section (🌐 *www.montrealgazette.com*) for events listings in English.

TICKETS

Tickets for most performances are available at the box offices of the various venues.

La Vitrine Culturelle. Next to the Quartier des Spectacles theater district, la Vitrine Culturelle (literally: Cultural Window) is the perfect place to get information and buy tickets for just about every type of show in town. Great last-minute deals are often available. ✉ *2 rue Ste-Catherine Est, Downtown* ☎ *514/285–4545* 🌐 *www.lavitrine.com* Ⓜ *St-Laurent.*

Ticketmaster. Tickets for theatrical and musical performances, plus a host of other cultural events, can be bought through Ticketmaster. ✉ *Montréal* ☎ *514/790–1111, 855/985–5000* 🌐 *www.ticketmaster.ca.*

BEST FREE PERFORMANCES

Several of the outdoor concerts at the **Montréal International Jazz Festival** in July are free, as are summertime performances at the **Théâtre de Verdure** inside Lafontaine Park.

Two of the greatest places to catch free classical music indoors are at **Montréal Christ Church Cathedral**, where organ recitals are given throughout the year, and at the **Basilique Notre-Dame de Montréal**, where there are year-round concerts by chamber and choral groups (regular church entry fee required).

PERFORMING ARTS REVIEWS

CIRCUS

Montréal's reinvention of the ancient art of the circus began in the 1980s, when two street performers, Guy Laliberté and Daniel Gauthier, founded the now world-famous Cirque du Soleil. But it didn't stop there. The city is also home to a huge complex, out beyond Mont-Royal in the St-Michel district, housing Canada's National Circus School, En Piste (Circus Arts National Network), and Cirque du Soleil's head office. The school attracts budding acrobats and clowns from all over the world, as well as several other smaller schools, and puts on several performances throughout the year at the complex's performance venue, TOHU Cité des Arts du Cirque (🌐 *www.tohu.ca*).

FAMILY Fodor's Choice ★ **Cirque du Soleil.** This amazing circus is one of Montréal's great success stories. The company—founded in 1984 by a pair of street performers—has completely changed people's idea of what a circus can do.

Its shows, now an international phenomenon, use no animals. Instead, colorful acrobatics flirt with the absurd through the use of music, humor, dance, and glorious (and often risqué) costumes.

Cirque du Soleil is Montréal's hometown circus, founded here in 1984. Today there are several troupes across several countries that perform hundreds of shows per year.

The Cirque has companies in Las Vegas and one each in Orlando and Los Angeles—but none in Montréal (though their HQ and a circus school is in the northern part of the city). However, every couple of years one of its international touring companies returns to where it all began, the Old Port, and sets up the familiar blue-and-yellow tent for a summer of sold-out shows. ⊠ *Montréal* ☎ *514/790–1245, 800/361–4595* ⊕ *www.cirquedusoleil.com.*

Cirque Éloize. This award-winning troupe has been touring the globe since 1993, and with well over 4,000 performances under its belt, shows no signs of slowing down. Constantly evolving, Cirque Éloize uses artistic mediums like video and music to bring the circus arts to the masses. ⊠ *Montréal* ☎ *514/596–3838* ⊕ *www.cirque-eloize.com.*

Les 7 doigts de la main. Literally translated as "the seven fingers of the hand," the name is a play on a French expression about working collectively toward a common goal, and these seven fingers—the seven founding partners of the circus—have done just that, building up a world-renowned circus troop over the past decade or so. Combining acrobatics, theater, and dance, they've performed at special events across the globe, including a Royal Variety Performance for Queen Elizabeth II and at the Olympics in Turin and Vancouver. They even made an appearance on *America's Got Talent.* ⊠ *Montréal* ☎ *514/521–4477* ⊕ *www.7doigts.com.*

CLASSICAL MUSIC

Two symphony orchestras, an opera company of some renown, one of the best chamber orchestras in Canada, and several first-rate choirs make Montréal an ideal destination for music lovers. The music faculties of both McGill University and the Université de Montréal have international reputations, and their campuses' concert halls feature performances by the schools' best talents throughout the academic year. The city's main performance halls are at Place des Arts.

I Musici de Montréal Chamber Orchestra. Arguably the best chamber orchestra in Canada, I Musici, under the direction of Jean-Marie Zeitouni, performs at several places around town. These include the Salle Bourgie at the Musée des Beaux-Arts and the Place des Arts' Nouvelle Salle, but its music is best suited to the wood-paneled **Tudor Hall,** atop the Ogilvy department store. There, about a dozen times a year, you can enjoy a coffee or aperitif while you listen to a late-morning or early-evening concert. ✉ *4672 B rue Saint-Denis* ☎ *514/982–6038 tickets* ⊕ *www.imusici.com.*

Opéra de Montréal. This renowned opera company, the largest Francophone opera in North America, has a varied schedule of classics, including *Le Nozze di Figaro*, *Rigoletto*, and *Silent Night*. Seventy-five minutes before each show, the "pre-Opera" program, done in French with a summary in English, gives attendees a look at the history, music, and artists of the Opéra de Montréal. ✉ *Place des Arts, 260 boul. de Maisonneuve, Downtown* ☎ *514/985–2222, 877/385–2222* ⊕ *www. operademontreal.com* Ⓜ *Place-des-Arts.*

Orchestre Métropolitain du Grand Montréal. The Met may lie in the shadow of the Orchestre Symphonique de Montréal, but its talented conductor and artistic director, Yannick Nézet-Séguin, continues to draw the spotlight. He's in high demand across the world; in addition to his role here, he's the musical director at the Philadelphia Orchestra and the Rotterdam Philharmonic, as well as the principal guest conductor of the London Philharmonic Orchestra. His charismatic approach has brought in the crowds since 2000 and produced highly acclaimed performances. Most shows take place at Place des Arts or Maison Symphonique de Montréal. ✉ *486 rue Ste-Catherine Ouest, #401, Downtown* ☎ *514/598–0870* ⊕ *www.orchestremetropolitain.com* Ⓜ *Place-des-Arts.*

Fodor's Choice ★ **Orchestre Symphonique de Montréal.** Under the direction of influential and renowned conductor Kent Nagano, Montréal's beloved OSM plays programs that include masterful renditions of the classics, with contemporary works thrown into the mix. The orchestra's home, the Maison symphonique de Montréal, is part of the Place des Arts complex. ✉ *1600 rue St-Urbain, Downtown* ☎ *514/842–9951, 888/842–9931* ⊕ *www.osm.ca* Ⓜ *Place-des-Arts.*

Place des Arts. Place des Arts is located in the heart of the Quartier des Spectacles and has been hosting performances since 1963. In 2011, the venue underwent a major face-lift and makeover to stunning effect. The glass-walled Maison Symphonique concert hall is the permanent home of the Montréal Symphony Orchestra; with state-of-the-art acoustics and only 75 feet between the end of the stage and the last row, it's an intimate place for concerts. The Salle Wilfrid Pelletier performance

LATE-NIGHT BITES

Da Emma: Hover over a plate of pasta or roasted lamb at this darkly lit, romantic eatery.

Leméac: One of the best deals in town, their *"fin de soirée"* menu (served from 10 pm to midnight) is C$25, with a choice of 16 starters and 15 mains.

m:brgr: Sometimes nothing but a burger after hours will do, and those at this gourmet Downtown destination hit the spot. The fries are a must.

Rotisserie Panama: For satisfyingly filling and reasonably priced fare, head to this Greek restaurant, which serves some of Montréal's best grilled meat.

Schwartz's Delicatessen: Thanks to this legendary deli's takeout window, you can grab a hot (and huge) smoked-meat sandwich to enjoy back at your hotel room.

For full reviews and locations of these restaurants, see Chapter 3, Where to Eat.

space is used by three resident companies: the Opéra de Montréal, Les Grands Ballets Canadiens, and the popular Jean Duceppe theater company. The venue's four other performance spaces host dance, theater, and festival events.

The other outdoor stages and other venues that make up the Quartier des Spectacles allow for lots of shows and festivals to be staged in one common area. Even if you don't have tickets to something, you can walk around the Quartier during festival season (pretty much all summer) to take in a variety of shows and concerts for free. ⊠ *175 rue Ste-Catherine Ouest, Downtown* ☎ *514/842–2112, 866/842–2112* ⊕ *www.laplacedesarts.com* Ⓜ *Place-des-Arts.*

Pollack Concert Hall. McGill University's concert hall showcases the best talents from its formidable music faculty, with concerts by the McGill Symphony, Opera McGill, the McGill Baroque Orchestra, and the Montréal Chamber Orchestra, among others. ⊠ *555 rue Sherbrooke Ouest, Downtown* ☎ *514/398–4547* ⊕ *www.mcgill.ca/music* Ⓜ *McGill.*

Salle Claude-Champagne. This beautiful concert hall hosts more than 150 symphonic and operatic performances every year by the music faculty of the Université de Montréal. The repertoire includes both classic and contemporary works. ⊠ *220 av. Vincent-d'Indy, Outremont* ☎ *514/343–6427* ⊕ *www.musique.umontreal.ca* Ⓜ *Édouard-Monpetit.*

DANCE

Traditional and contemporary dance companies thrive in Montréal, although many take to the road or are on hiatus in summer. Place des Arts, Montréal's main concert hall, is a popular venue for visiting large-scale productions.

Agora de la Danse. More than just a performance space for contemporary dance, this center actively works in the dance community to encourage creativity and experimentation. Hosting acclaimed artists and companies from around the world, the company is also affiliated with the Université du Québec à Montréal dance faculty. ⊠ *1435 rue Bleury, Downtown* ☎ *514/525–1500* ⊕ *www.agoradanse.com* Ⓜ *Place-des-Arts.*

BJM Danse Montréal. Under artistic director Louis Robitaille, BJM Danse Montréal fuses contemporary music and visual arts with extraordinary technique. Performances are held at Place des Arts and Agora de la Danse, and there are free shows at Théâtre de Verdure in Parc Lafontaine during the summer months. ⊠ *Montréal* ☎ *514/982–6771* ⊕ *www.bjmdanse.ca.*

La Fondation de Danse Margie Gillis. Margie Gillis, one of Canada's most exciting and innovative soloists, works with her own company and guest artists to stage performances at Place des Arts, Agora de la Danse, and other area venues. ⊠ *Montréal* ☎ *514/845–3115* ⊕ *www. margiegillis.org.*

Fodor'sChoice ★ **Les Grands Ballets Canadiens de Montréal.** One of Canada's premier ballet companies, Les Grands have been moving audiences since 1957. Under the artistic direction of Louis Robitaille, the company has continued to evolve a rich body of both classic and contemporary work. Their annual presentation of *The Nutcracker*, which often sells out, has become a Christmas tradition. Performances take place at the Place des Arts. ⊠ *Montréal* ☎ *514/849–8681 tickets* ⊕ *www.grandsballets.com.*

Montréal Danse. Lavish sets and dazzlingly sensual choreography have helped make Montréal Danse one of Canada's most popular contemporary repertory companies. They have a busy touring schedule, but also regularly perform at Place des Arts, Agora de la Danse, and the Théâtre de Verdure. ⊠ *Montréal* ☎ *514/871–4005* ⊕ *www.montrealdanse.com.*

Tangente. For more than 35 years, Tangente has hosted weekly performances of contemporary and experimental dance between September and May—there are currently three venues in the city. They also act as an archive for contemporary dance and experimental performance art, with more than 2,000 files focusing on major international dance schools and festivals, companies and choreographers. Tangente encourages national and international exchanges between dance companies and artists. ⊠ *Montréal* ☎ *514/525–5584* ⊕ *www.tangentedanse.ca.*

FILM

Although many of the movie theaters that once lined rue Ste-Catherine have closed down in recent years to make way for new, stadium-seating megaplexes like the Cineplex Odeon Forum Cinema, Montrealers remain uniquely privileged in the variety of alternatives that are available.

Highlighted by the gorgeous art deco confines of the majestic Imperial theater on Bleury Street in Downtown, the city's various venues offer the opportunity to enjoy productions released each year by the province's thriving French-language film industry in addition to the standard Hollywood fare consistently shown at the megaplexes.

6

Cinéma Banque Scotia. This four-level theater complex is in the center of downtown Montréal. The major attraction is movie-watching in either of the IMAX or the UltraAVX-3D theaters. The food hall offers more than just popcorn—sushi, poutine, and doughnuts are also up for grabs. The lines can be long, so go early or buy tickets online. ✉ *977 rue Ste-Catherine Ouest, Downtown* ☎ *514/842–0549* ⊕ *www. cineplex.com* Ⓜ *Peel.*

Cinéma du Parc. A favorite of Montréal moviegoers for years, this theater focuses on first-run movies from around the world. Retrospectives based on interesting themes and prominent directors are also screened. Located inside the Galeries du Parc mall, near McGill University, it primarily caters to an Anglophone audience. ✉ *inside the Galeries du Parc mall, 3575 av. du Parc, Downtown* ☎ *514/281–1900* ⊕ *www. cinemaduparc.com* Ⓜ *Place-des-Arts.*

Cinéma Impérial. Recognized by the Québec government as a historical monument in 2001, this beautiful, old-fashioned movie theater screens independent films, though on a somewhat irregular basis. It plays host to many cultural events, including the Montréal World Film Festival. ✉ *1432 rue Bleury, Downtown* ☎ *514/884–7187* ⊕ *www.cinemaimperial.com* Ⓜ *Place-des-Arts.*

Cinémathèque Quebecoise. With more than 35,000 films in its collection, and a ticket price of just C$10, Montréal's Museum of the Moving Image is the best place in the city to catch a foreign flick in its original language (with subtitles), in addition to Quebecois and other Canadian productions. The museum also stocks scripts, television shows, and various new media, with a permanent display of old-fashioned cinema equipment. ✉ *335 boul. de Maisonneuve Est, Latin Quarter* ☎ *514/842–9763* ⊕ *www.cinematheque.qc.ca* Ⓜ *Berri-UQAM.*

Cineplex Odeon Forum Cinemas. With 22 screens showing everything from Hollywood blockbusters to indie flicks, choice is the main draw at this massive theater. That, plus the bowling alley, poolroom, and arcade complex. It used to be the home of Montréal's beloved Canadiens ice hockey team (look for the old seating and hockey memorabilia in the lobby). ✉ *2313 rue Ste-Catherine Ouest, Downtown* ☎ *514/904–1274* ⊕ *www.cinemamontreal.com* Ⓜ *Atwater.*

THEATER

There are at least 10 major French-language theater companies in town, some of which have an international reputation. The choices for Anglophones are more limited.

Black Theatre Workshop. The only black English-language company in Québec (and the longest-running in Canada) continues to support and nourish the careers of many prominent artists on the national scene. Expect innovative new productions performed alongside classic plays, such as *A Raisin in the Sun.* Shows take place at the Centaur Theatre and other venues around the city. ✉ *Downtown* ☎ *514/932–1104* ⊕ *www.blacktheatreworkshop.ca.*

Centaur Theatre. Montréal's best-known English-language theater company stages everything from frothy musical revues to serious works, and prominently features works by local playwrights. Its home is in the former stock-exchange building in Old Montréal. ⊠ *453 rue St-François-Xavier, Old Montréal* ☎ *514/288–3161, 514/288–1229* ⊕ *www.centaurtheatre.com* Ⓜ *Place-d'Armes.*

Centre Phi. Packed with intimate screening rooms, recording facilities, exhibition spaces, and a performance space, this center promotes artist-driven film, design, and music from locals as well as international artists. Films are in English and French. ⊠ *407 rue St-Pierre, Old Montréal* ☎ *514/225–0525, 855/526–8888* ⊕ *www.phi-centre.com* Ⓜ *Place-d'Armes or Square-Victoria.*

Geordie Productions. Promoting itself as a theater for all audiences, this accomplished English company has been delighting kids and adults since 1982. The 2017–18 lineup featured productions that included adaptations of *Boys With Cars, A Christmas Carol* and *Around the World in 80 Days.* Most productions are performed at the Centaur Theatre. ⊠ *Downtown* ☎ *514/845–9810* ⊕ *www.geordie.ca.*

Mainline Theatre. Operated by the same people who present the Montréal Fringe Festival every summer, the Mainline opened in 2006 to serve the city's burgeoning Anglo theater community and has been going strong ever since. ⊠ *3997 boul. St-Laurent, The Plateau* ☎ *514/849–3378* ⊕ *www.mainlinetheatre.ca* Ⓜ *St-Laurent or Mont-Royal.*

Monument-National. The highly regarded École Nationale de Théâtre du Canada—aka National Theatre School of Canada—supplies world stages with a steady stream of well-trained actors and directors. It works and performs in the historic and glorious old theater that has played host to such luminaries as Edith Piaf and Emma Albani. (Québec's first feminist rallies in the early 1900s also took place here.) Graduating classes perform professional-level plays in both French and English. The theater also plays host to an assortment of touring plays, musicals, and concerts. ⊠ *1182 boul. St-Laurent, Downtown* ☎ *514/871–2224* ⊕ *www.monument-national.qc.ca* Ⓜ *St-Laurent.*

Segal Centre for the Performing Arts. English-language favorites like *Harvey* and *Inherit the Wind* get frequent billing at this Côte-des-Neiges venue, along with locally written works. The center is best known, however, as the home to the **Dora Wasserman Yiddish Theatre,** which presents such musical works as *The Jazz Singer* and *The Pirates of Penzance* in Yiddish. ⊠ *5170 chemin de la Côte-Ste-Catherine, Côte-des-Neiges* ☎ *514/739–2301, 514/739–7944* ⊕ *www.segalcentre.org* Ⓜ *Côte-Ste-Catherine.*

Théâtre Denise Pelletier. With an objective to introduce younger audiences to theater, the Pelletier, which celebrated its 50th year in 2014, puts on French-language productions in a beautifully restored Italianate hall. It's a 15-minute walk from the métro station. ⊠ *4353 rue Ste-Catherine Est, Hochelaga-Maisonneuve* ☎ *514/253–8974* ⊕ *www.denise-pelletier.qc.ca* Ⓜ *Joliette or Pie-IX.*

6

Théâtre Jean Duceppe. Named for one of Québec's most beloved actors, this theater makes its home in the smallest and most intimate of the four auditoriums in Place des Arts. It primarily stages major French-language productions. ✉ *175 rue Ste-Catherine Ouest, Downtown* ☎ *514/842–2112* ⊕ *www.duceppe.com* Ⓜ *Place-des-Arts.*

Théâtre du Nouveau Monde. A season's offerings at this theater might include works by locals Michel Tremblay and Patrice Robitaille, as well as works by Shakespeare, Molière, Camus, Ibsen, Chekhov, and Arthur Miller. ✉ *84 rue Ste-Catherine Ouest, Downtown* ☎ *514/866–8668* ⊕ *www.tnm.qc.ca* Ⓜ *St-Laurent.*

Théâtre Outremont. Inaugurated in 1929, the theater rapidly became a local favorite and had its heyday in the '70s before it fell into disarray. After reopening its doors in the early '90s, the theater has regained much of its steam with mostly theater and live music acts. ✉ *1248 av. Bernard, Outremont* ☎ *514/495–9944* ⊕ *www.theatreoutremont. ca* Ⓜ *Outremont.*

Théâtre du Rideau Vert. The oldest professional French theater company in North America, Théâtre du Rideau Vert has been winning over audiences with its contemporary productions since 1948. Many popular Francophone actors got their big break here. ✉ *4664 rue St-Denis, The Plateau* ☎ *514/844–1793* ⊕ *www.rideauvert.qc.ca* Ⓜ *Mont-Royal.*

Théâtre Ste-Catherine. With approximately 100 comfortable seats, this independent alternative theater features comedy and improv shows most nights. On Sunday there's a free improv workshop that's open to all, with participants later showing off what they learned as that evening's entertainment. The theater also houses Le Nouveau International, a nonprofit organization run by a thriving community of artists working year-round to produce theater, comedy, improv, films, a bimonthly magazine, and sketch shows. ✉ *264 rue Ste-Catherine Est, Latin Quarter* ☎ *514/284–3939* ⊕ *www.theatresaintecatherine. com* Ⓜ *Berri-UQAM.*

Théâtre St-Denis. This is one of several theaters hosting events that are part of the Just For Laughs Festival, and touring Broadway productions, concerts, musicals, and dance performances can often be seen here. ✉ *1594 rue St-Denis, Latin Quarter* ☎ *514/849–4211* ⊕ *www. theatrestdenis.com* Ⓜ *Berri-UQAM.*

7

SHOPPING

Updated by
Elizabeth
Warkentin

Montrealers *magasinent* (shop) with a vengeance, whether they're scurrying down busy Ste-Catherine downtown checking out department store bargains, hunting for Danish antiques in the Gay Village, browsing designer wares on St. Laurent, or sampling gourmet eats at one of the city's markets. For many locals, doing the *magasinage* is practically an art form.

Yet one of North America's top shopping cities is in a state of flux. Where, until recently, boulevard St-Laurent and rue St-Denis, were the "it" streets to shop, increasingly this honor is now being shared with Old Montréal, an area that has been enjoying a renaissance. In the last decade or so, Montréal's patron saint of shopping streets, Ste-Catherine, has been undergoing a metamorphosis as a significant cohort of young, educated professionals moves into condos Downtown and retailers scramble to meets their needs and tastes. The changing face of retail and the prevalence of online shopping has also contributed to the transformation of Ste-Catherine and other Downtown streets, with the corresponding downward slide of many traditional brick-and-mortar stores. That being said, Montréal's most important shopping street has also welcomed new arrivals such as the trendy Vancouver-based Aritzia; Lolë, Montréal's more stylish version of Lululemon; an elegant Club Monaco spread out over two floors of the Beaux Arts–style Dominion Square Building; and a branch of hip Montréal-brand, Frank and Oak, initially an online-only retailer. Moreover, the city's two luxury department stores, Ogilvy and Holt Renfrew, are set to merge into one mammoth luxury department store and Four Seasons Hotel complex slated to open by 2019.

Meanwhile, City Hall is planning (and has been for a while now) an epic—and highly controversial—face-lift for Ste-Catherine. If implemented, the commercial epicenter will be reimagined into a new outdoor pedestrian shopping mall with heated sidewalks and longer shopping hours. For now, the downtown core, including Old Montréal, Chinatown, and the Quartier des Spectacles, is a tourist zone, and as such, stores are permitted to stay open 24/7.

PLANNING

HOURS

Most shops open by 10 am Monday through Saturday and close at 6 pm Monday through Wednesday. Stores stay open until 9 pm on Thursday and Friday, but on Saturday they usually close at 5 pm. On Sunday, most downtown shops open noon to 5 pm. There are, however, exceptions. Large chain stores in the *centre ville* often stay open weeknights until 9, and boutiques in areas that draw a drinks-and-dinner crowd, such as in the Plateau and in Old Montréal, can stay open even later in summer.

SALES TAX

Visitors must pay 5% in federal tax, called the GST (or TPS in Québec), and an additional 9.975% in Québec tax on most goods and services. Now that the U.S. greenback is worth roughly 20% more than the Canadian dollar, deals can be easier to find than they were a few years ago.

MONTRÉAL SHOP REVIEWS

OLD MONTRÉAL (VIEUX-MONTRÉAL)

7

The old part of the city has more than its share of garish souvenir shops, but fashion boutiques and shoe stores with low to moderate prices line rues Notre-Dame and St-Jacques, from rue McGill to Place Jacques-Cartier. With gentrification in the west end of the area, high-end fashion boutiques and spas abound, especially along rue St-Paul Ouest. The area is also rich in art galleries and crafts shops along rue St-Paul and tucked inside the narrow rue des Artistes. Use the Place-d'Armes, Champ-de-Mars, or Square-Victoria métro stations.

ART

DHC/ART. DHC/ART aims to showcase compelling contemporary art from around the world. A free iPhone app takes you through the exhibits, and podcasts provide a fascinating look at the artists themselves. Check the website or call before you visit as DHC closes regularly for installations. ⊠ *451 and 465 rue St-Jean, Old Montréal* ☎ *514/849–3742, 888/934–2278* ⊕ *www.dhc-art.org* ☽ *Closed Mon. and Tues.* Ⓜ *Square-Victoria or Place-d'Armes.*

Galerie d'Art Émeraude. In a new building facing the historic Marché Bonsecours, Galerie d'Émeraude is part of the Bourget group of galleries in Old Montréal. Galerie d'Émeraude specializes in Quebecois and Canadian art, including the works of British-born painter Michael Foer. Foer was inspired by the paintings of the Group of Seven, also known as the Algonquin Group, whose paintings of the Canadian landscape initiated the first major Canadian national art movement. ⊠ *301 rue St. Paul Est, Old Montréal* ☎ *514/845–2121* ⊕ *www.galerieemeraude.com* Ⓜ *Champ-de-Mars.*

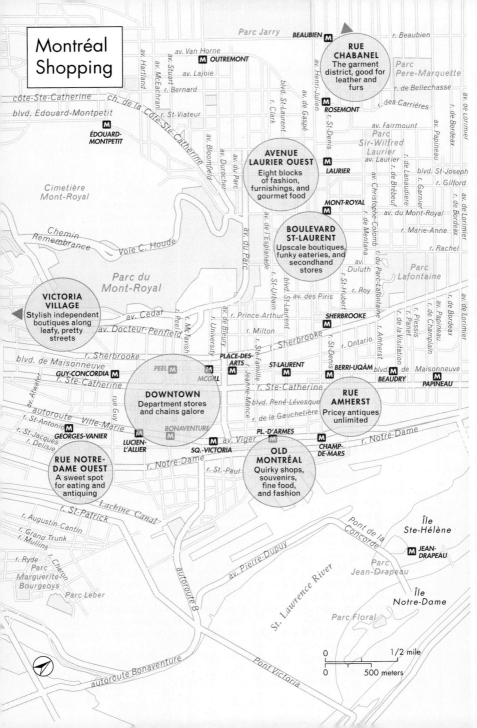

Montréal Shopping

RUE CHABANEL
The garment district, good for leather and furs

AVENUE LAURIER OUEST
Eight blocks of fashion, furnishings, and gourmet food

BOULEVARD ST-LAURENT
Upscale boutiques, funky eateries, and secondhand stores

VICTORIA VILLAGE
Stylish independent boutiques along leafy, pretty streets

DOWNTOWN
Department stores and chains galore

RUE AMHERST
Pricey antiques unlimited

RUE NOTRE-DAME OUEST
A sweet spot for eating and antiquing

OLD MONTRÉAL
Quirky shops, souvenirs, fine food, and fashion

Parc Jarry

Cimetière Mont-Royal

Parc du Mont-Royal

Parc Père-Marquette

Parc Sir-Wilfrid Laurier

Parc Lafontaine

Lachine Canal

Parc Marguerite Bourgeoys

Parc Leber

St. Lawrence River

Île Ste-Hélène

Parc Jean-Drapeau

Île Notre-Dame

Parc Floral

0   1/2 mile
0   500 meters

CLOSE UP

Montréal's Best Shopping Streets

Most visitors to Montréal will have Downtown and Old Montréal on the itinerary, but for an authentic experience à la Montréalaise you should also venture into some of the other neighborhoods.

Avenue Laurier Ouest. Shops and boutiques along the eight blocks between boulevard St-Laurent and chemin de la Côte-Ste-Catherine sell medium- to high-end fashions, home furnishings, decorative items, artwork, books, kitchenware, toys and children's items, and gourmet food. There are plenty of restaurants, bars, and cafés in which to rest your feet and check out your purchases. The street is about a 10-minute walk from the Laurier métro station.

Boulevard St-Laurent. Affectionately known as The Main, St-Laurent has restaurants, boutiques, and nightclubs that cater mostly to an upscale clientele. Still, the area has managed to retain its working-class immigrant roots and vitality to some degree: high-fashion shops are interspersed with ethnic-food stores, secondhand clothing and decor boutiques, and hardware stores. Indeed, a trip up this street takes you from Chinatown to Little Italy.

Rue Amherst. Antiques shops began springing up in the Gay Village in the early 1990s, most of them on rue Amherst between rues Ste-Catherine and Ontario. Copious cafés and brunch spots nearby will fuel your quest. The area used to be less expensive than rue Notre-Dame, but it's not always the case these days. Use the Beaudry métro station.

Rue Bernard. Only a few blocks away from the Outremont métro station, this chic villagey street is well worth a detour. The street boasts many sidewalk cafés—called *terrasses* in local parlance—for fine or casual dining, as well as specialty food stores, decor shops, and some of the best ice cream in Montréal at Le Glacier Bilboquet.

Rue Chabanel. The eight-block stretch of Chabanel just west of boulevard St-Laurent is the heart of the city's garment district. The goods seem to get more stylish and more expensive the farther west you go. If you're lucky, you might come across signs for designer sample sales. Many of the city's furriers have also moved into the area. A few places on Chabanel accept credit cards, but bring cash anyway. If you pay in cash, the price will often include the tax. From the Crémazie métro station, take Bus 53 north.

Rue Notre-Dame Ouest. The fashionable place for antiquing is a formerly run-down five-block strip of Notre-Dame between rue Guy and avenue Atwater. Most of the action is at the western end of the strip, as are many of the restaurants and cafés that have sprung up to cater to shoppers. Walk east from Lionel-Groulx métro station.

Victoria Village. The carriage-trade area for wealthy Westmount citizens, who live on the leafy slopes of Mont-Royal, has morphed into a shopping destination for all Montrealers with an eye for style. Independent boutiques offer distinctive home decor, shoes, gifts, stationery, and fashion along rues Victoria and Sherbrooke, with the epicenter between Victoria and Claremont. Cafés and fine specialty food shops also abound. Vendôme is the closest métro station.

7

Images Boréales. If the friendly and knowledgeable staff doesn't win you over, the vast collection of Inuit and Iroquois art will. With more than 2,000 pieces of sculpture in soapstone and serpentine, authentic drawings, and beautiful jewelry, the hardest part will be choosing what to buy. ⊠ *446 pl. Jacques-Cartier, Old Montréal* ☎ *514/875–6134* ⊕ *www. imagesboreales.com* Ⓜ *Champ-de-Mars.*

CLOTHING

Boutique Denis Gagnon. This creative designer, whose creations have been exhibited at the Montréal Museum of Fine Arts, is much beloved on the Montréal fashion scene. In this sleek, subterranean boutique, Gagnon's couture designs stand alongside his ready-to-wear collection. He's also well-known for his shoes. ⊠ *170B rue St-Paul Ouest, Old Montréal* ☎ *514/935–6360* ⊕ *www.denisgagnon.ca* Ⓜ *Place-d'Armes.*

Boutique Philippe Dubuc. One of the city's favorite menswear designers, Philippe Dubuc's collections are characterized by richly textured fabrics, exquisite tailoring, and lots of grays, blues and blacks. ⊠ *417 rue St. Pierre, Old Montréal* ☎ *514/282–1465* ⊕ *www.dubucstyle.com* Ⓜ *Square Victoria.*

Fodor's Choice
★ **Espace Pepin.** Talented owner and painter Lysanne Pepin has an eye for design, and as you pass through the gauzy curtains, her boutique-cum-atelier is an intriguing—and beautiful—space to explore. Filled with romantic clothes, funky shoes, and a carefully edited mix of local and international labels, you'll also find eclectic housewares and furniture for home and office. ⊠ *350 rue St-Paul Ouest, Old Montréal* ☎ *514/844–0114* ⊕ *www.pepinart.com* Ⓜ *Square-Victoria.*

U&I. Stylish locals flock to this sleek boutique in Old Montréal, which is stocked with unisex avant-garde finds from North America and Europe, with an emphasis on Montréal and Canadian brands. Cydwoq and Canada Goose hang alongside coats from the sleek Montréal label Mackage and pieces from U&I's own label. ⊠ *215 St. Paul Ouest, Old Montréal* ☎ *514/508–7704* ⊕ *www.boutiqueuandi.com* Ⓜ *Place-d'Armes.*

HOUSEWARES

Fodor's Choice
★ **À Table Tout Le Monde.** Should you require the most refined disposable plates for a picnic on the mountain (or in your hotel room), you can stop in at this shop and pick up a few Wasara pieces designed in Japan. The sophisticated shop features fine designs from around the world, including Goyer Bonneau (for functional ceramics) and Bousquet (for playful porcelain designs). Of course, it's not all disposable. Quite the contrary. ⊠ *361 rue St-Paul Ouest, Old Montréal* ☎ *514/750–0311* ⊕ *www.atabletoutlemonde.com* ☉ *Closed Mon.* Ⓜ *Square-Victoria.*

MALLS AND SHOPPING CENTERS

Marché Bonsecours. The silver-domed Marché Bonsecours, the city's main public market in the 1800s, has been restored and renovated with a modern edge. The 15 boutiques inside sell First Nations artwork, Quebecois designer fashions, jewelry, kitchenware, and more. The paintings of Michel Sylvain on display at Art et Antiquités Médius capture eloquent Montréal street scenes. Soak it all up over a cup of coffee from Le Café des Arts or a full meal and an artisinal beer at Pub BreWskey. ⊠ *350 rue St-Paul Est, Old Montréal* ☎ *514/872–7730* ⊕ *www.marche-bonsecours.qc.ca* Ⓜ *Champ-de-Mars.*

TOP MONTRÉAL SHOPPING EXPERIENCES

Some of the best deals can be found at **La Maison Simons** department store, where there's something cheap and chic for everyone, from teenyboppers to mesdames and monsieurs on a budget. Along rue Ste-Catherine and in the underground malls, check out trendy Quebecois fashion emporiums like **Le Château**. Montréal's luxury lane runs from **Ogilvy** up to **Holt Renfrew** on rue Sherbrooke, though the two are meant to merge into a megaluxury shopping and hotel (Four Seasons) complex at the corner of Ste-Catherine and De la Montagne by the end of 2018, with designer fashion from **Marie Saint Pierre** and custom pearl jewelry from **Boutique Laura Aline** lining the route.

The path of luxury continues west along rue Sherbrooke, where you'll find the Montréal Museum of Fine Arts, as well as high-end galleries and antiquarians such as **Galerie Alan Klinkhoff** and le **Petit Musée**.

Funky fashionistas will want to hit Mile End and the Plateau. In Mile End, hipster territory includes **General 54** and **Unicorn**, with **Citizen Vintage** for recycled fashions. Moving down Montréal's beloved Main—boulevard St-Laurent—check out vintage, decor, fashion, and design shops.

Closer to Downtown, **Boutique 1861** and **M0851** are worth the walk. One-of-a-kind independent shops line avenue Mont-Royal and rue St-Denis.

SPA

Le Scandinave Les Bains Vieux-Montréal. A bastion of urban chic in historic Old Montréal, this spa is especially popular on cold winter days. Inspired by the age-old tradition of public baths, the Scandinave prides itself on offering guests an authentic yet contemporary experience with an accent of privacy and total relaxation. The posh interior of slate, marble, and wood contrasts nicely with the bubbling pool and misty steam rooms. The ultimate meltdown is the zero-stress chamber of absolute quiet and darkness to intensify the peacefulness. All you need to bring along is your bathing suit; the spa provides sandals, bathrobes, and towels. For extra relaxation, sign up for a massage with one of their professional masseuse. ⊠ *71 rue de la Commune Ouest, Old Montréal* ☎ *844/220–2009* ⊕ *www.scandinave.com* Ⓜ *Place-d'Armes.*

DOWNTOWN

Montréal's largest retail district takes in rues Sherbrooke and Ste-Catherine, boulevard de Maisonneuve, and the side streets between them. Because of the density and variety of the stores, it's the best shopping bet if you're in town overnight or for a weekend. The area bounded by rues Sherbrooke, Ste-Catherine, de la Montagne, and Crescent has antiques and art galleries in addition to designer salons. Fashion boutiques and art and antiques galleries line rue Sherbrooke. Rue Crescent holds a tempting blend of antiques, fashions, and jewelry displayed beneath colorful awnings. Rue de la Montagne is the corridor of chic, between the high-end Holt Renfrew and Ogilvy department stores, with designer boutiques—including top Québec labels—en route. Rue Ste-Catherine is the main shopping thoroughfare, with most of the chain stores and department stores. To get here, take the métro to the Peel, McGill, or Guy-Concordia stations.

ANTIQUES

Antiquités Pour La Table. Armoires and sideboards brimming with fine crystal and china line the walls at this beautiful store, while chandeliers, linens, and other vintage pieces make up the rest of the treasures. *Phone before you visit as hours can vary.* ✉ *762 av. Atwater, Downtown* ☎ *514/989–8945* ⊕ *www.antiquesforthetable.com* Ⓜ *St-Henri.*

Grand Central. "Grand" is the right word to describe this antiques emporium—it's filled to the brim with elegant chandeliers and candelabras, armchairs and secretaries, and other decorative elements from the 18th and 19th centuries. These items would add a touch of refinement to almost any home. ✉ *2448 rue Notre-Dame Ouest, St-Henri, Downtown* ☎ *514/935–1467* ⊕ *www.grandcentralinc.ca* Ⓜ *Lionel-Groulx.*

Viva Gallery. Unique along the Notre-Dame antiques stretch, this shop sells exquisite Asian furniture—armoires, chests, chairs, and wooden screens with fine carvings—complemented by paintings from Xiaoyang Yu that depict life in Beijing. ✉ *1970 rue Notre-Dame Ouest, Downtown* ☎ *514/932–3200* ⊕ *www.vivagalerie.com* ☉ *Closed Sun., Mon., Wed., and Fri.* Ⓜ *Lucien-L'Allier.*

ART

Edifice Belgo. Built more than a century ago, Edifice Belgo houses more than two dozen art galleries exhibiting the works of both established and emerging artists. Galerie Roger Bellemare is one of the best galleries for contemporary art. Galerie Trois Points showcases the work of Montréal and Québec artists. For wearable art, visit designer Véronique Miljkovitch's atelier on the second floor. ✉ *372 rue Ste-Catherine Ouest, Downtown* ☎ *514/861–2953* ☉ *Closed Sun.–Tues.* Ⓜ *Place-des-Arts.*

Galerie Alan Klinkhoff. The Klinkhoffs know art. Open since 1950, the gallery boasts several floors of Canadian works from both contemporary and historical artists. ✉ *1448 rue Sherbrooke Ouest, Downtown* ☎ *514/284–9339, 416/233–0339 Toronto office* ⊕ *www.klinkhoff.ca* ☉ *Closed Sun.* Ⓜ *Guy.*

BOOKS AND STATIONERY

Indigo. At this branch of the largest bookstore chain in Canada, a vast selection of classic literature, novels, music, and magazines (in English and French) are sold alongside housewares, fashion accessories, and baby gifts. Famous authors sometimes drop by for book signings. ✉ *1500 av. McGill College, corner of rue Ste-Catherine, Downtown* ☎ *514/281–5549* ⊕ *www.chapters.indigo.ca* Ⓜ *McGill.*

Paragraphe. This cornerstone of Montréal's English-language literary scene carries the usual selection of mysteries and thrillers, but also stocks a wide range of Canadian works. It's a favorite with visiting authors, who stop by to read from their latest releases. Sip on a coffee from the adjacent Second Cup coffee shop while you peruse the stacks. ✉ *2220 av. McGill College, Downtown* ☎ *514/845–5811* ⊕ *www.paragraphbooks.com* Ⓜ *McGill.*

Renaud-Bray. Tucked away in the basement level of the Complexe Desjardins shopping mall, this outlet of the vast French-language book chain is chockablock with French and English books, magazines, and music. ⊠ *150 Ste-Catherine Ouest, Downtown* ☎ *514/288–4844* ⊕ *www.renaud-bray.com* Ⓜ *Place-des-Arts.*

Fodor'sChoice ★ **The Word.** Deep in the heart of the McGill University neighborhood, or ghetto as it's known by locals, this small shop is bursting with used books (including first editions) and specializes in philosophy, poetry, and literature. The award-winning Montréal landmark, open since 1975, shuns modern technology (including a cash register) in favor of timeless appeal. There's not even a sign, so keep your eyes peeled as you walk along Milton, though the bargain books lining the window are a good clue. ⊠ *469 rue Milton, Downtown* ☎ *514/845–5640* ⊕ *www. wordbookstore.ca* ☾ *Closed Sun.* Ⓜ *McGill.*

CLOTHING

Abe & Mary's. This upmarket clothing destination on rue de La Montagne holds racks of IRO Paris, 3x1, Vilebrequin, and Mr & Mrs Italy, as well as apothecary brands such as Molton Brown, Voyage & Cie, and Bond No. 9. The sleek white café also beckons with fresh salads, wraps, soups, and other health-conscious choices. ⊠ *2170 rue De La Montagne, Downtown* ☎ *514/908–4088* ⊕ *www.abeandmarys.com* Ⓜ *Guy-Concordia or Peel.*

Aritzia. At more than 10,000 square feet, Aritzia's gleaming glass-fronted, two-story location on Ste-Catherine Street is the Vancouver brand's largest in Canada, opening its doors in 2015 to great fanfare among the twentysomething fashionista set. Offering pretty, minimalist classics like embroidered bib-front sleeveless white dresses, lightweight shirt dresses and slip dresses for summer, this is the place to shop if you're looking for on-trend women's clothing at reasonable prices. Along with its own collections, Aritzia also carries popular labels like Mackage, Citizens of Humanity, and Rag and Bone. ⊠ *1125 rue Ste-Catherine Ouest, Downtown* ☎ *514/285–0791* ⊕ *www.aritzia. com* Ⓜ *Peel.*

Fodor'sChoice ★ **Arthur.** Everything about this shop, from the immaculate hardwood floors to the classic bespoke men's shirts featuring damask silk linings and hand-sewn button holes speaks of quality, tradition, and style. Armenian-Canadian tailor Arthur der Shahinian has been creating bespoke suits for men (and some women) since 1978, first from his modest digs at Marché Jean-Talon, now from his elegant atelier-cum-boutique on Crescent Street. Still, Mr. der Shahinian and his son Tavit haven't compromised their principles of quality and friendly, professional service. At 66, der Shahinian is the youngest shirtmaker in Montréal, a fact that speaks volumes about what has been happening to the fashion industry in the last quarter decade or so. The der Shahinians also custom-make men's shoes. ⊠ *2165 rue Crescent, Downtown* ☎ *514/843–0522* ⊕ *www.arthurmontreal.com* Ⓜ *Guy-Concordia.*

BEDO. Nailing the trends season after season, BEDO is an affordable way to replenish your wardrobe without breaking the bank. Well regarded by the fashion-obsessed of both sexes, the company collaborated with star designer Denis Gagnon to put out an affordable collection of his avant-garde creations. ✉ *Centre Eaton, 705 rue Ste-Catherine Ouest, Downtown* ☎ *514/849–3385* ⊕ *www.bedo.ca* Ⓜ *McGill.*

Café Boutique Eva B. On the secondhand fashion map for decades, Eva B has all kinds of clothes, shoes, jewelry, and even eyeglasses on offer. Budget at least 30 minutes to scour the labyrinth of racks and the "pool," a large platform in the back where everything is a dollar. Just watch your step; the floor is uneven. Nosh on a samosa or something else from the in-store café if you get hungry in the process. ✉ *2015 boul. St-Laurent, Downtown* ☎ *514/849–8246* ⊕ *www.eva-b.ca/en* Ⓜ *St-Laurent.*

COS. Housed in an historic greystone on Ste-Catherine Street, the upmarket-feeling but mostly midmarket-priced boutique brand of Swedish fashion group H&M, COS (Collection of Style) has a bit of a cult following among fashion-lovers for its simple, stylish basics with modern lines and understated tones. ✉ *1310 rue Ste-Catherine Ouest, Downtown* ☎ *514/878–3838* ⊕ *www.cosstores.com/ca/en* Ⓜ *Guy-Concordia or Peel.*

Editorial Boutique. Designer duds happily share space with inexpensive but chic items at this low-key downtown boutique with a devoted cult following. Brands include Citizens of Humanity, Erin Wasson, Luv U Always, For Love of Lemons, Unif, and Jeffrey Campbell. ✉ *1455 rue Stanley, Downtown* ☎ *514/849–3888* ⊕ *www.editorialboutique. com* Ⓜ *Peel.*

Fodor's Choice ★ **E.R.A. Vintage Wear.** With a reputation as the best vintage shop in the city, this upscale boutique specializes in vintage clothing, shoes, and accessories from the 1920s through the mid-1980s. Each handpicked item is carefully cleaned, repaired, and altered as necessary to give it a more contemporary flavor. High-profile clients like Julianne Moore and Cate Blanchett have been known to drop by. This location is bright, spacious, and loaded with irresistible treasures. ✉ *999 rue du College, loft 44, Downtown* ☎ *514/543–8750* ⊕ *www.eravintagewear.com* ☉ *Closed Sun.* Ⓜ *Place St-Henri.*

Fodor's Choice ★ **Frank and Oak.** More than a store outfitting young, creative professionals in quality denim and plaid essentials as well as rich velvets and airy chiffons in contemporary styles, the 5,000-square-foot Montréal flagship of this formerly online-only Canadian brand is an experience—a welcoming space where people can drink specialty coffee, meet friends, get a shave and haircut, attend regular events like whiskey tastings, and enjoy high-tech shopping. ✉ *1420 rue Stanley, Downtown* ☎ *514/228–3761* ⊕ *www.frankandoak.com* Ⓜ *Peel.*

Harricana. Yesterday's old fur coats and stoles are transformed into everything from car coats and ski jackets to baby wraps and throw pillows at this designer shop. For summer, vintage scarves become flirty little tops. The recycled furs, leather, silks and woolen items are sold at dozens of shops, but the best place to see what's available is this combination atelier and boutique. ✉ *416 rue McGill, Downtown* ☎ *514/787–3790* ⊕ *www.harricana.qc.ca* Ⓜ *Square Victoria.*

Harry Rosen. This is Canada's premier high-end menswear destination. Stocked with both casual and formal attire, wallets, watches, and hats, this 22,000-square-foot flagship store caters to the classically tailored male. Brands include 7 For All Mankind, Michael Kors, Cole Haan, Tom Ford, and Armani. ⊠ *Cours Mont-Royal, 1455 rue Peel, Downtown* ☎ *514/284–3315* ⊕ *www.harryrosen.com* Ⓜ *Peel.*

Le Château. This Québec chain features its own line of reasonably priced fashions for men and women. You'll find chic suits, dresses, and evening wear, plus shoes, handbags, and jewelry galore. The flagship store is on rue Ste-Catherine, but there's also a factory outlet at the Marché Central. ⊠ *Centre Eaton, 705 rue Ste-Catherine Ouest, Downtown* ☎ *514/284–9166* ⊕ *www.lechateau.com* Ⓜ *McGill.*

Lululemon. This Canadian sports-and-yoga wear chain offers plenty of styles, colors, and cuts to please both guys and gals. You'll also find headbands, scarves, jewelry, and more. ⊠ *970 rue Ste-Catherine Ouest, Downtown* ☎ *514/394–0770* ⊕ *www.lululemon.com* Ⓜ *Peel.*

Fodor's Choice **Marie Saint Pierre.** The leading female designer in Québec (and one who's
★ celebrated throughout Canada), Marie Saint Pierre is known for her signature pleats and ruffles—think sleek and sophisticated rather than frilly. Now she's lending her avant-garde touch to bridal, with a wedding collection that's available only at this flagship boutique. ⊠ *2081 rue de la Montagne, Downtown* ☎ *514/281–5547* ⊕ *www.mariesaint-pierre.com* Ⓜ *Peel or Guy-Concordia.*

Olam. The fashions here don't come cheap, but French-influenced owner Charles Abitbol believes in quality fashion for women of all ages. Abitbol sources funky and whimsical fashions for the younger set, as well as more classic pieces with clean lines from European, American, and local Québec designers such as Yumi, Sanctuary Clothing, Desigual, and Mélissa Nepton. The Fat Boy beanbag chairs may entice you to hang a while in the vast loftlike upstairs space, but like the Taschen design books and the colonial-inspired Québec and French-made wooden furniture, these are also for sale. ⊠ *1374 rue Ste-Catherine Ouest, Downtown* ☎ *514/875–9696* Ⓜ *Peel.*

Roots. Bring the great outdoors in, courtesy of this beloved Canadian chain with a beaver emblem. There are lots of casual neutrals for men, women, and kids, with pops of colorful sportswear thrown in for good measure. Quality leather goods are also available. ⊠ *1025 rue Ste-Catherine Ouest, Downtown* ☎ *514/845–7995* ⊕ *www.roots.com* Ⓜ *Peel.*

Fodor's Choice **Shan.** Designed in Montréal and sold around the world, this is couture
★ swimwear at its finest. In a rainbow of colors, these sexy cuts are meant to be displayed—though one of the ethereal cover-ups just might make one reconsider. Men can also shop the collection of swim trunks, briefs, and ready-to-wear. ⊠ *2150 rue Crescent, Downtown* ☎ *514/287–7426* ⊕ *www.shan.ca* Ⓜ *Peel or Guy-Concordia.*

Tristan & America. Appealing to the just-out-of-university set, this chain sells contemporary yet classic fashions that are perfect for young professionals. There has been a push toward casual weekend wear in recent years, with flirty lace tops, leggings, and ponchos and capes hitting the shelves. ⊠ *1001 rue Ste-Catherine Ouest, Downtown* ☎ *514/289–9609* ⊕ *www.tristan-america.com* Ⓜ *Peel.*

Winners. Tucked away on the lowest level of Place Montréal Trust lies this huge discount store stocked with clothing, shoes, housewares—you name it. Allow adequate time if you really want to rummage but if you're not at leisure, head straight to the runway collections and the sale racks for the best bargains. The Alexis Nihon (Atwater métro) location, on the edge of Westmount, can also be a good bet for snagging a deal on designer labels and Italian shoes. ⊠ *Place Montréal Trust, 1500 av. McGill College, Downtown* ☎ *514/788–4949* ⊕ *www.winners.ca* Ⓜ *McGill.*

CLOTHING: MEN'S ONLY

Fodor's Choice
★

Henri Henri. The best men's hat store in Canada carries a huge stock of homburgs, fedoras, and derbies, as well as cloth caps and other accessories. Prices range from about C$155 to C$1,000, the top price fetching you a top-of-the-line Panama hat. ⊠ *189 rue Ste-Catherine Est, Downtown* ☎ *514/288–0109, 888/388–0109* ⊕ *www.henrihenri. ca* Ⓜ *St-Laurent or Berri-UQAM.*

L'Uomo Montréal. You'll come to this store for the selection of European menswear and accessories, but you'll stay for the impeccable service and attention to detail. Expect suits from Kiton and Borrelli, bags from Prada, shoes from UK brand Edward Green, and ties from Massimo Bizzocchi. ⊠ *1452 rue Peel, Downtown* ☎ *514/844–1008, 877/844–1008* ⊕ *www.luomo-montreal.com* ☉ *Closed Sun.* Ⓜ *Peel.*

Tozzi. Known around Montréal as one of the top menswear destinations, Tozzi is a one-stop shop for the dapper gentleman. Suits, polos, jeans, watches, sunglasses, and cologne—this boutique offers just about everything in a minimalist, serene environment. ⊠ *2115 rue Crescent, Downtown* ☎ *514/285–2444* ⊕ *www.boutiquetozzi.com* Ⓜ *Guy-Concordia or Peel.*

DEPARTMENT STORES

Fodor's Choice
★

Holt Renfrew. This upscale department store is Canada's answer to Bergdorf Goodman. Gucci, Chanel, and all the usuals are complemented by up-and-coming designers and Holt's own in-house line. Just try and walk past the wall of handbags on the ground floor without being tempted to buy one or two. Even if your budget doesn't allow for much more than window-shopping, a trip to Café Holt downstairs is a must. Tartines—open-face sandwiches—are made here from bread flown in from Paris's Poilâne bakery and come in several enticing combinations. Holt Renfrew purchased Ogilvy, Montréal's other chic department store, a few blocks south, and the two are currently in the process of merging into a megaluxury complex and hotel. ⊠ *1300 rue Sherbrooke Ouest, Downtown* ☎ *514/842–5111* ⊕ *www.holtrenfrew.com* Ⓜ *Peel or Guy-Concordia.*

Hudson's Bay (formerly La Baie). Hudson's Bay department store is a descendant of the Hudson's Bay Company, the great 17th-century fur-trading company that played a pivotal role in Canada's development. The Bay, as it's known by Canadians, has been a department store since 1891 and is known for its duffel coats and signature red, green, and white-striped blankets. Besides fashions, housewares, and toys, there's also a portrait studio, beauty salon, and spa. ⊠ *585 rue Ste-Catherine Ouest, Downtown* ☎ *514/281–4422* ⊕ *www.thebay.com* Ⓜ *McGill.*

La Maison Simons. Find the *trends du jour* at a great price from the youth-oriented labels on the ground floor of this bustling department store. Upstairs, the fare is more mature, ranging from respectable and affordable twin sets to luxe offerings from the likes of Chloé and Missoni. The store's fashion-forward men's suits and casual wear are also worth checking out. ✉ *977 rue Ste-Catherine Ouest, Downtown* ☎ *514/289–1840, 877/666–1840* ⊕ *www.simons.ca* Ⓜ *Peel.*

Fodor's Choice ★ **Ogilvy.** Founded in 1865, this department store boasts a vast selection of clothing and accessories for men and women. The Louis Vuitton boutique is more than 3,000 square feet and has a "bag bar." It's also a good place to rest weary feet. ■ **TIP→ Ogilvy was purchased by Holt Renfrew, Montréal's other posh department store, and the two are in the process of merging into a megaluxury store and hotel on rue Ste-Catherine so expect some potential disruption during your visit.** ✉ *1307 rue Ste-Catherine Ouest, Downtown* ☎ *514/842–7711, 855/842–7711* ⊕ *www.ogilvycanada.com* Ⓜ *Peel.*

FOOD

Divine Chocolatier. Tucked away in a small basement space on Crescent Street, this adorable little chocolaterie owned by Belgian *maître chocolatier* Richard Zwierzynski has lived here for 25 years, and been in existence since 1976. With its stuffed teddy bears, shoe- and bottle-shape chocolate decorations, and antique porcelain plates adorning the walls, a visit to Divine feels like stepping into a 19th-century ice-cream parlor. Chocolate massage oil and chocolate tablets made from the mold of an illustration from the Kama Sutra will tickle the fancy, but it's the chocolate truffles, assorted chocolates, and the dark chocolate ganache cheesecake that people come for again and again. ✉ *2158 rue Crescent, Downtown* ☎ *514/282–0829* ⊕ *www. divinechocolatier.com* Ⓜ *Guy-Concordia.*

Marché Atwater. Heading down Atwater Avenue toward Lachine Canal, you can't miss the art deco tower of Atwater Market. This is the best spot to pick up local produce, fresh flowers, and gourmet meats and cheeses. In summer, bring a blanket and enjoy a perfect picnic by the canal or have a drink at the Canal Lounge Cafe, a cafe and bar on a barge. ✉ *138 av. Atwater, Downtown* ☎ *514/937–7754* ⊕ *www.marchespublics-mtl.com* Ⓜ *Lionel-Groulx.*

LINGERIE

La Senza. The two-story flagship of this Québec-based chain is packed with bright, cheerful push-up bras, panties, and negligees. Sleepwear is also available. ✉ *1133 rue Ste-Catherine Ouest, Downtown* ☎ *514/281–0101* ⊕ *www.lasenza.com* Ⓜ *Peel.*

MALLS AND SHOPPING CENTERS

Centre Eaton de Montréal. In addition to the 175 stores in downtown's largest mall, there's free Wi-Fi in the spacious lower-level food court. Early 2013 brought the opening of a branch of the Musée Grévin, a wax museum that replicates more than a hundred local and international celebrities. ✉ *705 rue Ste-Catherine Ouest, Downtown* ☎ *514/288–3708* ⊕ *www.centreeatondemontreal.com* Ⓜ *McGill.*

Les Cours Mont-Royal. A variety of chic independent boutiques are mixed in with quality chains like DKNY and Desigual in this graceful mall, once a grand hotel. Drop by Spa Diva or the top-notch salon Pure if you're in need of a beauty break. The elegant atrium sometimes hosts runway shows. ⊠ *1455 rue Peel, Downtown* ☎ *514/842–7777* ⊕ *www. lcmr.ca* Ⓜ *Peel.*

Place Ville Marie. Stylish shoppers head to the 80-plus retail outlets in Place Ville Marie, part of the city's vast underground network. After a shopping spree, be sure to check out the recently opened rooftop observation deck (see www.ausommetpvm.com), where you'll get a 360-degree view of the city and you'll also find the restaurant/brasserie and terrace Les Enfants Terribles. ⊠ *Boul. René-Lévesque and rue University, Downtown* ☎ *514/861–9393* ⊕ *www.placevillemarie.com* Ⓜ *McGill or Bonaventure.*

SHOES

Browns. This local institution stocks fashionable footwear and accessories for men and women. Besides its own label, Browns carries shoes by Emporio Armani, Michael Kors, Cole Haan, Steve Madden, and Stuart Weitzman. Comfortable couches make shopping a pleasant experience inside this gleaming white-and-silver flagship. ⊠ *1191 rue Ste-Catherine Ouest, Downtown* ☎ *514/987–1206, 866/720–7463* ⊕ *www.browns-shoes.com* Ⓜ *Peel.*

THE VILLAGE

The Gay Village is known for its excellent furniture stores as much as for its vibrant nightlife. Rue Amherst is nearly overflowing with antiques shops; plenty of unique treasures are just waiting to be discovered, most being midcentury modern. The Beaudry métro station is your best bet.

ANTIQUES

Fodor's Choice
★

Antiquités Curiosités. A sea of chairs, lamps, and other 1930s to 1980s furnishings and accessories awaits you at Antiquités Curiosités, but it's the beautifully restored Mad Men–era teak pieces that are the biggest draw. Retro curiosities like rotary phones also tickle the fancy. ⊠ *1769 rue Amherst, The Village* ☎ *514/525–8772* Ⓜ *Beaudry.*

Fodor's Choice
★

Boutique Spoutnik. Mod, space-aged, kitsch, this boutique has it all. From Russell Spanner dressers to vintage needlepoint dog-portraits-turned-cushions to ceramic lamps in atomic designs circa 1950, Spoutnik is a veritable Aladdin's Cave of retro treasures. Owner Sylvie Rochon takes her work seriously, carefully curating her collection and adding her own artistic touches to vintage objects, and has been featured in several Québec publications. ⊠ *2120 rue Amherst, The Village* ☎ *514/525–8478* ⊕ *www.boutiquespoutnik.com* ☾ *Closed Sun. and Mon.* Ⓜ *Sherbrooke.*

MONTRÉAL'S MARKETS

If food is your first love, head to Montréal's markets, especially in the bountiful days of the autumn harvest.

Marché Jean-Talon in the north end of the city has an Italian flavor; the surrounding streets are home to some of the finest pizza and café lattes anywhere. **Marché Atwater** has an indoor hall, packed with eateries, butchers, bakeries, and fine food emporiums.

The markets are a great place to pick up nonperishables such as jam from Île d'Orléans or cranberries harvested late September to mid-October; or maple syrup and butter, year-round.

THE PLATEAU, MILE END, LITTLE ITALY, AND OUTREMONT

THE PLATEAU MONT-ROYAL

The Plateau has long been recognized as one of North America's hippest neighborhoods, and though trends typically come and go, its cachet endures. Rue St-Denis is home to both independent boutiques and chain stores selling local and international fashion, as well as numerous jewelry stores, all at prices for every budget. Boulevard St-Laurent and avenue Mont-Royal both offer opportunities for vintage shopping, with St-Laurent also known for contemporary furniture and decor stores.

CLOTHING

Fodor'sChoice
★
Boutique 1861. This boutique stocks romantic, lacy, and affordable finds from local and international designers, including Arti Gogna and Champagne & Strawberry. With everything white—hardwood floors, couches, and armoires—the boudoir vibe is irresistible. Just look for the pink-and-black cameo signage. The name comes from the smaller branch at 1861 rue Ste-Catherine. ⊠ *3670 boul. St-Laurent, The Plateau* ☎ *514/670–6110* ⊕ *www.1861.ca.*

Kanuk. This company's snowy owl trademark has become something of a status symbol among the shivering urban masses. These Québec-made coats and parkas are built to keep an Arctic explorer warm and dry. Try on coats in a variety of styles and lengths, with optional fur hoodies. Rain gear is also on offer. ⊠ *485 rue Rachel Est, The Plateau* ☎ *514/284–4494, 877/284–4494* ⊕ *www.kanuk.com* ☉ *Closed late Mar.–early Sept. Closed Sun.* Ⓜ *Mont-Royal.*

Fodor'sChoice
★
M0851. Sleek, supple leather clothing and bags from the Québec designer Frédéric Mamarbachi have a cult following from Antwerp to Tokyo. The rough-hewn wood floors and concrete walls of this branch give it an industrial-chic vibe. ⊠ *3526 boul. St-Laurent, The Plateau* ☎ *514/849–9759* ⊕ *www.m0851.com* Ⓜ *St-Laurent or Sherbrooke.*

7

FOOD

Fodor's Choice ★ **La Vieille Europe.** For a taste of the old Main, where generations of immigrants came to shop, look no farther than this deli packed with sausages, cheeses, European chocolates, jams, and atmosphere. Pick up a rich shot of espresso on your way out. *Call ahead as hours vary seasonally.* ✉ *3855 boul. St-Laurent, The Plateau* ☎ *514/842–5773* Ⓜ *St-Laurent or Sherbrooke.*

HOUSEWARES

Fodor's Choice ★ **Arthur Quentin.** Check out this elegant shop for fine French tableware from Gien and Maintenon. There's also gourmet kitchen gear, as well as designer messenger bags, maps, pens, and clothing. ✉ *3960 rue St-Denis, The Plateau* ☎ *514/843–7513* ⊕ *www.arthurquentin.com* Ⓜ *Sherbrooke.*

Zone. This multilevel labyrinth of affordable housewares is especially busy on weekends. It's filled with fine and funky designs for the kitchen, bath, and living room. There is a large location in Westmount and on Monkland, in NDG, as well. ✉ *4246 rue St-Denis, The Plateau* ☎ *514/845–3530* ⊕ *www.zonemaison.com* Ⓜ *Sherbrooke or Mont-Royal.*

LINGERIE

Fodor's Choice ★ **Deuxième Peau.** Tucked away in a basement, the tiny "Second Skin" sells a fine assortment of French lingerie. It's hard to miss the curvy mannequins in their ground-floor window, adorned in the likes of Aubade, Chantelle, and Prima Donna. While you're feeling brave and beautiful, kill two birds with one stone and try on a bathing suit from their tasteful collection of fine French, Spanish, and Australian designers. ✉ *4457 rue St-Denis, The Plateau* ☎ *514/842–0811* ⊕ *www.deuxiemepeau.com* Ⓜ *Mont-Royal.*

SHOES

John Fluevog. Unusually curved lines, from the heels of his shoes to the interior design of his funky boutique, have cultivated a devout following for the Canadian shoe designer. Belts and bags are also available, letting you create a quirky yet coordinated outfit. Look to the soles for curious and inspiring messages. ✉ *3857 rue St-Denis, The Plateau* ☎ *514/509–1627* ⊕ *www.fluevog.com* Ⓜ *Sherbrooke.*

OUTREMONT

Avenue Laurier in Outremont is a good destination for those in pursuit of a little luxury.

CLOTHING

Billie. One of Montréal's favorite boutiques, Billie has rows of bookcases, drawers, and shelves that give the feeling of raiding your best friend's closet. Look for chic dresses and blouses from Alice + Olivia, cozy sweaters from Repeat Cashmere, and eclectic shoes by Cynthia Vincent. If you are shopping for kid sizes, be sure to visit Bille Le Kid at 1001 avenue Laurier Ouest. ✉ *1012 av. Laurier Ouest, Outremont* ☎ *514/270–5415* ⊕ *www.billieboutique.com* Ⓜ *Laurier.*

Fodor's Choice ★ **Lyla.** Some of the finest lingerie in the city—including brands like Eres and La Perla—is stocked at this lovely little shop. The staff is extremely helpful in finding what fits and flatters. Two other reasons to stop and shop: exquisite fashion from Europe and a great selection of swimsuits and darling cover-ups. ✉ *400 av. Laurier Ouest, Outremont* ☎ *514/271–0763* ⊕ *www.lyla.ca* Ⓜ *Laurier.*

Mimi & Coco. You'll want to snap up several of the locally designed T-shirts at Mimi & Coco, perhaps pairing them with luxe knitwear from Italy. Beautiful floor-to-ceiling windows create a bright, inviting interior, even on cloudy days. The shop also sells dog collars and leashes, with profits going to a nonprofit foundation that works to promote animal rescue and adoption. Come at lunchtime and sample one of Mandy's gourmet salads from the in-store counter. ✉ *201 av. Laurier Ouest, Outremont* ☎ *514/906–0349* ⊕ *www.mimicoco.com* Ⓜ *Laurier.*

Fodor's Choice
★

Très Chic Styling. Stylish Hervé Léger dresses at two for C$500? Style-savvy co-founders Maryam Rafa and Angelica Koinis believe that women should look good and dress well without having to spend a small fortune. Designer denim and fabulous cocktail dresses for half off (or more) have built their reputation. ✉ *1069 av. Laurier Ouest, Outremont* ☎ *514/274–3078* ⊕ *www.tcstyling.com* Ⓜ *Laurier.*

CLOTHING: MEN'S ONLY

Michel Brisson. This is the go-to place for art directors, architects, and other men with an eye for European design from Etro, Jil Sander, or Dries Van Noten. The Laurier store is sleek, with clean lines and lots of gray, while the Old Montréal location injects a bit of warmth with rich wood paneling. ✉ *1074 av. Laurier Ouest, Outremont* ☎ *514/270–1012* ⊕ *www.michelbrisson.com* Ⓜ *Laurier.*

FOOD

Yannick Fromagerie. This cheese shop is the go-to destination for the city's top chefs and cheese aficionados. Yannick Achim carries 400 varieties, buying from local dairies and stocking an astonishing international selection. You'll find Pikauba cheese from Québec beside pecorino made with raw sheep's milk and laced with black truffles. Cheese lovers here eagerly trade advice on building the perfect after-dinner cheese plate. ✉ *1218 rue Bernard O., Outremont* ☎ *514/279–9376* ⊕ *www.yannick-fromagerie.ca* Ⓜ *Outremont.*

MILE END

Just north of the Plateau, the Mile End offers an eclectic mix of artsy boutiques and shops stocked with up-and-coming Montréal designers.

CLOTHING

Bodybag by Jude. When Nicole Kidman wore one of this designer's zip denim dresses, Judith Desjardins's star was set. The designer has a penchant for all things British, so look for cheeky checks and plaids. ✉ *17 rue Bernard Ouest, Mile End* ☎ *514/274–5242* ⊕ *www.bodybagbyjude.com* Ⓜ *Rosemont.*

Citizen Vintage. If you're a slave to all things vintage, then this Mile End boutique has your name on it. Bright, spacious, and carefully curated by the owners (who scour North America for their finds), this store makes shopping easy, as everything is arranged by color. The stock changes almost daily, so don't feel you can only visit once. ✉ *5330 boul. St-Laurent, Mile End* ☎ *514/439–2774* ⊕ *www.citizenvintage.com* Ⓜ *Laurier.*

7

It's well worth the métro ride up to Little Italy's busy Marché Jean-Talon to see French Canadian farmers sell their local produce and prepared food.

Fodor's Choice
★

Éditions de Robes. Owner Julie Pesant has stocked her boutique with top quality Montréal-made-and-designed dresses in a multitude of styles that can easily be dressed up or down with a simple change of accessories. From peplums to lace, satin to jersey, long and short, they're all here. There's also an outpost at 2122 rue Crescent near the Montréal Museum of Fine Arts. ⊠ *178 rue St-Viateur Ouest, Mile End* ☎ *514/271–7676* ⊕ *www.editionsderobes.com* ☉ *Closed Mon.* Ⓜ *Laurier.*

General 54. The Mile End neighborhood earned its reputation for all things cool with funky shops like this one. The natural-hue clothes—most by local designers—are feminine and elegant, and owner Jennifer Glasgow sells her eponymous clothing line here. The location on The Main is warm and welcoming, with exposed brick and intricately patterned floors. ⊠ *5145 boul. St-Laurent, Mile End* ☎ *514/271–2129* ⊕ *www.general54.com* Ⓜ *Laurier.*

Mousseline. With sizes running from 2 to 22, this place makes finding the perfect fit a snap. Choosing from among the casual wear by fashion labels like James Perse, Pas de Calais, and Danish designer Noa Noa might be a bit more difficult. Be sure to pick up a comforting sweater from Autumn Cashmere. ⊠ *220 av. Laurier Ouest, Mile End* ☎ *514/878–0661* ⊕ *www.boutiquemousseline.com* Ⓜ *Laurier.*

Unicorn. Young Quebecois designers like Barilà, Valérie Dumaine, and Mélissa Nepton are the stars of this beautiful Mile End boutique, which also stocks unique national and international labels. All the black and white in the window display hints at the minimalist aesthetic within. ⊠ *5135 boul. St-Laurent, Mile End* ☎ *514/544–2828, 855/544–2828* ⊕ *www.boutiqueunicorn.com* Ⓜ *Laurier.*

Fodor's Choice ★ **Vestibule.** This cheerful boutique is a dream come true for owner Audrey Morissette, who adores all things whimsical and feminine. Uniting her love of fashion and decor, the shop is filled with pretty items ranging from jewelry to clothing to candles, as well as ceramics and other household items. ✉ *5157 boul. St-Laurent, Mile End* ☎ *514/419–3868* ⊕ *www.boutiquevestibule.com* Ⓜ *Laurier.*

LITTLE ITALY
Little Italy is a gourmet shopper's paradise.

FOOD
Fodor's Choice ★ **Marché Jean-Talon.** This is the biggest and liveliest of the city's public markets. On weekends in summer and fall, crowds swarm the half-acre or so of outdoor produce stalls, looking for the fattest tomatoes, sweetest melons, and juiciest strawberries. Its shops also sell sausage, fish, cheese, bread, pastries, and other delicacies. Early in the morning you might rub elbows with the city's top chefs. The market is in the northern end of the city, but is easy to get to by métro. ✉ *7070 av. Henri-Julien, Little Italy* ☎ *514/937–7754* ⊕ *www.marchespublicsmtl.com* Ⓜ *Jean-Talon.*

Fodor's Choice ★ **Marché Milano.** A huge expansion in 2013 made this popular Italian grocer, in business since 1954, even more popular, as customers line up for prepared foods at the takeout counter. There's a vast selection of cheeses, oils, vinegars, and baked goods. For some elbow room, go during the week. ✉ *6862 boul. St-Laurent, Little Italy* ☎ *514/273–8558* ⊕ *www.milanofruiterie.com* Ⓜ *De Castelnau or Jean-Talon.*

FURS
Labelle Fourrure. This family business has remained a fixture on Montréal's fur map for a century by adapting to the fashions of the day and offering good service and value for your dollar. ✉ *6570 rue St-Hubert, Little Italy* ☎ *514/276–3701* ⊙ *Closed Sun.* Ⓜ *Beaubien.*

WESTMOUNT

Stylish locals, quaint architecture, and upscale boutiques make Westmount a chic shopping destination. Rue Sherbrooke Ouest is a pleasant mix of hip shops, florists, and home decor stores. Avenue Victoria is a smaller version of the same, with a few grocery stores and vintage shops thrown in. The closest métro is Vendôme, or you can take Bus 24 west from Downtown.

ART
Galerie de Bellefeuille. This gallery has a knack for discovering important new talents. It represents many of Canada's top contemporary artists as well as some international ones. Its 5,000 square feet hold a good selection of sculptures, paintings, and limited-edition prints. ✉ *1366 and 1367 av. Greene, Westmount* ☎ *514/933–4406* ⊕ *www.debellefeuille.com* Ⓜ *Atwater.*

7

CHILDREN'S CLOTHING

FAMILY **Oink Oink.** This pigtail-covered boutique offers three levels of fun for babies, kids, and young adults. Innovative and kooky gifts, books, clothing, and even scooters are available. ✉ *1343 av. Greene, Westmount* ☎ *855/939–2634, 514/939–2634* ⊕ *www.oinkoink.com* Ⓜ *Atwater.*

CLOTHING

James. The home of hippie-chic in Montréal, this boutique is packed with flowing tunics, embroidered blouses, and white cotton dresses. Add a good mix of designer jeans and funky moccasins by Minnetonka and you'll understand why James is a Victoria Village mainstay. ✉ *4910 rue Sherbrooke Ouest, Westmount* ☎ *514/369–0700* Ⓜ *Vendôme.*

JoshuaDAVID. One of Victoria Village's best boutiques may be small, but it's packed with a great selection of contemporary labels, including Diane von Furstenberg, Alexander McQueen, and plenty of Rich & Skinny denim. Rings by Kara Ross add bling to any outfit. ✉ *4926 rue Sherbrooke Ouest, Westmount* ☎ *514/788–4436* ⊕ *www.shopjoshuadavid.com* Ⓜ *Vendôme.*

Fodor'sChoice **Pretty Ballerinas.** This little boutique showcases beautiful ballerina flats ★ handmade in Spain. Available in a wide variety of colors and styles, you'll find it difficult to limit yourself to just one pair. You'll also find Barbour handbags—a canvas tote might be the perfect accessory to complement your new flats. ✉ *392 av. Victoria, Westmount* ☎ *514/489–3030* ⊕ *www.prettyballerinas.ca* Ⓜ *Vendôme.*

Fodor'sChoice **TNT.** The 6,000 square feet of women's clothing, shoes, and accesso-★ ries include an eclectic mix of labels: Stella Forest, Lauren Moshi, and Michael Stars hang near shoes from House of Harlow and Dolce Vita. ✉ *4100 rue Ste-Catherine Ouest, Westmount* ☎ *514/935–1588* ⊕ *www. tntfashion.ca* Ⓜ *Atwater.*

Fodor'sChoice **WANT Apothecary.** Set in pleasant surroundings inspired by a 19th-cen-★ tury pharmacy, this boutique keeps its customers coming back with interesting and quality goods and doting service. As well as items from the local leather-goods label WANT, the shop stocks beauty and skin care products and clothing by Acne, Fillppa K, and Nudie Jeans. ✉ *4960 rue Sherbrooke Ouest, Westmount* ☎ *514/484–3555* ⊕ *www.wantapothecary.com* Ⓜ *Vendôme.*

SHOES

Tony's. A fixture in Westmount since 1937, Tony's is one of the area's top shoe stores. It might seem small from the outside, but it's filled with fine specimens for men, women, and kids—and at good prices, too. ✉ *1346 av. Greene, Westmount* ☎ *514/935–2993, 888/488–6697* ⊕ *www.tonyshoes.com* Ⓜ *Atwater.*

SPORTS AND
THE OUTDOORS

Updated by
Chris Barry

Most Montrealers would probably claim they hate winter, but the city is full of cold-weather sports venues—skating rinks, cross-country ski trails, and toboggan runs—that see plenty of action. During warm-weather months, residents head for the tennis courts, bicycle trails, golf courses, and two lakes for boating and swimming.

You don't have to travel far from Montréal to find good downhill skiing or snowboarding. The many ski centers in the Laurentians and Eastern Townships are within an hour's drive from the city *(see the Side Trips from Montréal chapter for directions)*. As for cross-country, excellent trails can be found right in Parc du Mont-Royal, or on the Islands (Île Ste-Hélène and Île Notre-Dame).

Despite the bitter winters (or perhaps because of them), Montréal has fallen in love with the bicycle, with enthusiasts cycling year-round. More than 600 km (372 miles) of bike paths crisscross the metropolitan area, and bikes are welcome on the first car of métro trains during off-peak hours.

The city is truly passionate about Canada's national sport, hockey. If you're here during hockey season, try to catch a Montréal Canadiens game at Centre Bell, or at the very least find yourself a good sports bar.

BIKING

Weather permitting, one of the best ways to discover Montréal is on a bicycle. This is an incredibly bike-friendly metropolis, and there are thousands of designated bike paths connecting diverse neighborhoods across the island, running along the river, and through parks and forests. If you like to bike but would rather not do it on city streets, ferries at the Old Port can take you to Île Ste-Hélène and the south shore of the St. Lawrence River, where riders can connect to hundreds of miles of trails in the Montérégie region.

Bixi. Available 24 hours a day, seven days per week, April through November, these bikes are a convenient way to explore the city. Public bicycle rental stations are located as far west as Notre-Dame-de-Grace, a western Montréal neighborhood, east to the Olympic Park, and as far south as Parc Jean-Drapeau and even Longueuil (a south shore neighborhood). There's a fee of C$5 for a 24-hour period and C$14 for 72 hours, which include 30 minutes' bike rental for each separate trip; extra charges are incurred for longer rides. The transaction is easily done with the swipe of a credit card (a security deposit is also required).

> **TOP FIVE SPORTS EXPERIENCES**
>
> ■ Catch a Montréal Canadiens game.
>
> ■ Bike around the Old Port, then take the ferry across to Parc Jean-Drapeau to finish your ride.
>
> ■ Go white-water rafting on the Lachine Rapids.
>
> ■ Ice-skate for free on Île Ste-Hélène's huge rink.
>
> ■ Hike up to the top of Mont-Royal for a fantastic view of the city.

Monthly and yearly subscriptions are also available for longer stays. The bikes are designed for quick (but unlimited) trips; to minimize extra charges, always keep your next Bixi station in mind. ⊠ *Montréal* ☎ *514/789–2494, 877/820–2453* ⊕ *montreal.bixi.com.*

Fodor's Choice ★ **Féria de Vélo de Montréal** (*Montréal Bike Festival*). The biggest bike celebration in North America includes the **Tour la Nuit**, a 22-kilometer (14-mile) nighttime ride through the city. The weeklong festival culminates in as many as 50,000 cyclists taking over the streets for the **Tour de l'Île**, a 50-km (31-mile) ride along a route encircling Montréal. ⊠ *Montréal* ☎ *514/521–8356, 800/567–8356* ⊕ *www.velo.qc.ca.*

Fitz & Follwell Co. This company's bike tour of Montréal highlights is popular, but go deeper and try "Hoods & Hidden Gems" to really learn what makes the city tick. They also offer bike rentals, walking tours, and snow tours in winter. ⊠ *115 av. du Mont-Royal Ouest, The Plateau* ☎ *514/840–0739* ⊕ *www.fitzandfollwell.ca.*

Lachine Canal. The most popular cycling trail on the island begins at the Old Port and winds its way to the shores of Lac St-Louis in Lachine. Pack a picnic lunch; there are plenty of green spaces where you can stop and refuel along the way. ⊠ *Montréal.*

Le Pôle des Rapides. This 100-km (62-mile) network of bicycle trails follows lakefronts, canals, and aqueducts. The trails are open April 15 to October 15. ⊠ *Montréal* ☎ *514/732–7303* ⊕ *www.pistescyclables.ca* Ⓜ *Verdun, Angrignon, LaSalle, Charlevoix, Lionel-Groulx.*

Vélo Montréal. For longer cycling excursions, renting a bike from this company is your best bet. Each rental includes a bicycle helmet, bottle cage, lock, and rear carrier rack. Packages start at C$10 for one hour or C$15 for two hours and go all the way to C$120 for a full week or C$165 for two weeks. They also lease tandem bikes, a fun alternative for couples. ⊠ *3880 rue Rachel Est, Hochelaga-Maisonneuve* ☎ *514/259–7272* ⊕ *www.velomontreal.com* Ⓜ *Pie-IX.*

8

The Route Verte

Stretches of what's called the most extensive route of biking trails in North America pass right through the very heart of Downtown Montréal.

The Route Verte (Green Route) is a free 5,000-km (3,100-mile) network of paths, shared roadways, and paved shoulders that traverse the province of Québec.

The cycling group Vélo Québec began first talking about the possibility of a province-wide bike network back in the 1980s, but it wasn't until 1995 that the government announced it would fund the C$88.5-million project to be built over the next 12 years.

More than 320 km (200 miles) of the Route Verte cover the streets of the city. It passes through Downtown, stretches up Mont-Royal, hugs the coast near the Lachine Canal, and extends out to Parc Jean-Drapeau, to name just a few of the major areas covered.

For more information, including maps, suggested routes, and other trip-planning tools, check out ⊕ *www.routeverte.com.*

BOATING

In Montréal you can climb aboard a boat at a Downtown wharf and be crashing through Class V white water minutes later.

Lachine Rapids Tours. Discover the rapids on a large jet boat—and bring a change of clothes. There are daily departures (every two hours) May through October from Clock Tower Pier in the Old Port. The price includes all gear, and the trip lasts an hour. Another option is a 20-minute ride in a 12-passenger boat that reaches speeds up to 80 kph (50 mph). Boats leave the Old Ports' Jacques Cartier Pier every half hour between 10 am and 6 pm from May to October. Trips are narrated in French and English. ⊠ *47 de la Commune Ouest, Old Montréal* ☎ *514/284–9607* ⊕ *www.jetboatingmontreal.com* ⊠ *Jet boat C$69, 20-minute speed boat ride C$27* Ⓜ *Champ-de-Mars.*

GOLF

Montréal golf enthusiasts have several excellent golf courses available to them, many less than a half-hour drive from Downtown. If you're willing to trek a bit farther (about 45 minutes), you'll find some of the best golfing in the province. For a complete listing of the many golf courses in the area, Tourisme Québec (⊕ *www.bonjourquebec.com*) is the best place to start.

Club de Golf Métropolitain Anjou (*Anjou Metropolitan Golf Club*). One of the longest courses in the province, the Championship course features an undulating landscape with five lakes and some tricky bunkers, all calling for accurate shots. Beginners and improvers can hone their skills on the short Executive course, where more accomplished players will also enjoy a quick round. A clubhouse featuring a steak house and bistro, several banquet halls, a pro shop with an indoor practice range (winter only), and an outdoor driving range all serve to make this a top-notch facility. A dress code is in effect. The club is in Anjou, a 20-minute drive from downtown Montréal. ✉ *9555 boul. du Golf* ☎ *514/353–5353* ⊕ *www. golfmetropolitainanjou.com* ✉ *Championship Course, C$28–C$53; Executive Course, C$15* ⏱ *Championship Course: 18 holes, 7005 yards, par 3, 4, and 5; Executive Course: 6 holes, 1022 yards, par 3* ☞ *Facilities: Driving range, golf carts, restaurant* Ⓜ *Honoré-Beaugrand.*

The Falcon. Soon after this club opened in 2002, it rapidly became recognized as one of the best courses in Québec. Designed by Graham Cooke, it winds through a verdant, well-wooded landscape dotted with water hazards and sand traps, and offers an exciting challenge. Five sets of tees accommodate different skill levels. It's 25 minutes west of downtown in the picturesque and largely Anglophone village of Hudson (which is worth a visit in itself). Recent improvements include a C$2 million clubhouse. Early-bird specials profit those who don't mind a teeing off at 7 am. ✉ *59 rue Cambridge, Hudson* ☎ *450/458–1997* ⊕ *www.falcongolf. ca* ✉ *C$40–C$58 weekdays, C$40–C$72 weekends and holidays* ⏱ *18 holes, 7096 yards, par 72* ☞ *Facilities: Driving range, putting green, golf carts, rental clubs, lessons, restaurant, clubhouse, practice facilities.*

Golf Dorval. The two original courses here, designed by Graham Cooke, were combined into a single challenging par-72 golf course with a rolling parkland setting. There are four levels of difficulty, finishing with a long, narrow par-4 18th hole with a slope up to the green. A lighted driving range with 50 stations and two putting greens are also available. There's a dress code. The course is a 20-minute drive from downtown Montréal. Reserve a weekday morning three days in advance and get two tickets and one cart for C$92–C$96. ✉ *2000 av. Reverchon, Dorval* ☎ *514/631–4653* ⊕ *www.golfdorval.com* ✉ *C$31–C$50* ⏱ *18 holes, 6643 yards, par 72* ☞ *Facilities: Driving range, putting green, golf carts, rental clubs, lessons, snack bar.*

Golf Ste-Rose. With lovely views of the Rivière des Mille-Îles, hardwood forests, and myriad ponds, this course may be the most beautiful in Québec. It's a short hop over the bridge to the island of Laval. The course features four sets of tees to accommodate different skill levels. Recently renovated to improve the pace of play, the 18-hole course was designed by John Watson, one of the great names of Canadian golf course architecture. ✉ *1400 boul. Mattawa, Ste-Rose* ☎ *450/628–6072, 450/628–3573* ⊕ *www.golfsterose.groupebeaudet.com* ✉ *C$27–C$52* ⏱ *18 holes, 6134 yards, par 70* ☞ *Facilities: Driving range, golf carts, rental clubs, restaurant, bar.*

HOCKEY

Ice hockey is nothing short of an institution in Montréal, the city that arguably gave birth to the sport back in the late 19th century. Although variations of the game are said to have been played in other U.S. and Canadian cities as early as 1800, the first organized game of modern hockey was played in Montréal in 1875, and the first official team, the McGill University Hockey Club, was founded in Montréal in 1880. The

city's beloved Montréal Canadiens is the oldest club in the National Hockey League and, as Montrealers are keen to tell you, one of the most successful teams in North American sports history.

McGill University Redmen Hockey. Formed in 1877, this was the first organized hockey club in Canada. It is now one of the top university men's ice hockey programs in Canada, and the Redmen were a Canadian University cup finalist in 2011. Games against cross-town rivals the Concordia Stingers or the UQTR Patriotes are always emotional duels. Home games take place at Percival Molson Stadium. ⊠ *475 av. des Pins Ouest, Downtown* ☎ *514/398–7006* ⊕ *www.redmenhockey.com* Ⓜ *McGill.*

Fodor's Choice **Montréal Canadiens.** The team meets National Hockey League rivals at
★ the Centre Bell from October through April (and even later if they make the playoffs). The "Habs" (the nickname's taken from Habitants, or early settlers) have won 24 Stanley Cups, although they've been struggling in the standings for several years now and haven't won a cup since the 1992–93 season. Nevertheless, Les Canadiens are a great source of pride to the city's sports fans, and tickets for their local games continue to be a hot commodity. Buy tickets in advance to guarantee a seat. ⊠ *1909 av. des Canadiens-de-Montréal, Downtown* ☎ *877/668–8269, 514/790–2525* ⊕ *canadiens.nhl.com* Ⓜ *Lucien-L'Allier or Peel.*

ICE-SKATING

Come the winter months, you don't have to look very far to find an ice-skating rink in Montréal. There are municipally run outdoor—and some indoor—rinks in virtually every corner of the city.

Accès Montréal. For information on the numerous ice-skating rinks (at least 195 outdoor and 21 indoor) in the city, it's best to call or check the city's website. Outdoor rinks are open from December until mid-March, and admission is free. The rinks on Île Ste-Hélène and at the Old-Port are especially large, but there is a C$6.95 admission charge (free admission for children under 6) to skate at the latter. ⊠ *Montréal* ☎ *514/872–1111* ⊕ *www.ville.montreal.qc.ca.*

Atrium le 1000 de la Gauchetière. Inside the tallest building in Montréal, this skating rink lies under a glass atrium, allowing sunlight to shine down on the rink year-round. After working up an appetite, hit any one of the 14 restaurants in the surrounding food court. ⊠ *1000 rue de la Gauchetière, Downtown* ☎ *514/395–0555* ⊕ *www.le1000.com* ⊡ *C$8; skate rental C$7* Ⓜ *Bonaventure.*

JOGGING

Most city parks have jogging paths, and you can also run the trail along the Lachine Canal.

Parc du Mont-Royal. The gravel Olmsted Road in Parc du Mont-Royal is a superb place for a tranquil jog surrounded by nature. For a panoramic view of downtown, head to the Kondiaronk lookout. ⊠ *Montréal* ☎ *514/843–8240* ⊕ *www.lemontroyal.qc.ca* Ⓜ *Mont-Royal.*

RACING

Grand Prix. Every year in early June, the Gilles Villeneuve Circuit plays host to this Formula One race, which attracts more than 100,000 fans. Tickets start at C$99 for general admission (one day) and from C$200 for grandstand tickets (three days). Be sure to book your room early for that entire week, as hotels operate at maximum capacity (and maximum cost). ⊠ *Parc Jean Drapeau, 222 Circuit Gilles Villeneuve, The Islands* ☎ *514/350–0000* ⊕ *www.circuitgillesvilleneuve.ca.*

SKIING AND SNOWBOARDING

There are pros and cons to skiing in the Eastern Townships and the Laurentians. The slopes in the Townships are generally steeper and slightly more challenging, but it requires more time to get out to them. Also, the Townships' centers tend to be quieter and more family-oriented, so if it's après-ski action you're looking for, you might prefer heading out to a Laurentian hill like Mont St-Sauveur where, for many, partying is as much the experience as is conquering the slopes.

As for cross-country skiing, you needn't even leave the city to find choice locations to pursue the sport. There's a network of winding trails stretching throughout Parc du Mont-Royal, and the Lachine Canal offers a 12-km (7-mile) stretch of relatively flat terrain, making for both a scenic and relatively simple cross-country excursion.

For more information on skiing in the Eastern Townships and the Laurentians, see Chapter 9, Side Trips from Montréal.

Tourisme Québec. The "Ski-Québec" brochure available from the tourism office has a wealth of information about skiing in and around the city, and the website has a complete lists of all the hills and trails in the province. ⊠ *Montréal* ☎ *514/873–2015, 877/266–5687* ⊕ *www.bonjourquebec.com.*

CROSS-COUNTRY

Cap-St-Jacques Regional Park. The best cross-country skiing on the island is on the 32 km (20 miles) of trails in the 900-acre Cap-St-Jacques park in the city's west end, about a half-hour drive from downtown. ⊠ *20099 boul. Gouin Ouest, Pierrefonds* ☎ *514/280–6871* ⊕ *www.ville.montreal.qc.ca* Ⓜ *Henri-Bourassa, then Bus 68 west.*

Mont-Royal. Within the city itself, "the mountain" (as it's known) is essentially a toboggan run, but its modest slope makes it ideal for beginners and little ones learning to ski. It's also a good place to get in a quick cross-country workout. ⊠ *Parc du Mont-Royal* ☎ *514/843–8240* ⊕ *www.lemontroyal.qc.ca.*

DOWNHILL

Mont St-Sauveur. If you're looking for the complete ski package, including shopping and nightlife, this mountain village is a good choice. At the gateway to the Laurentians, the 40 trails here are only an hour north of the city, helping make them a local hangout for Montréal residents. ☎ *450/227–4671* ⊕ *www.montsaintsauveur.com.*

Mont Sutton. A quaint village, a beautiful mountain—lots of glades—and plentiful snow make this the best skiing in the Eastern Townships (and possibly the province). It gets busy, but multiple chairlifts can handle nearly 12,000 people per hour. ✉ *Sutton* ☎ *450/538–2545, 866/538–2545* ⊕ *www.montsutton.com.*

Mont Tremblant. This huge resort is the best in the Laurentians for skiing, though it can be pricey. Sleep, ski, and eat in total comfort; there are plenty of high-end hotels on-site, some with luxury spas. The pedestrian village is like something out of Disney, with charming storefronts and colorful rooftops. Four slopes, 96 runs, and 14 lifts await two hours north of Montréal. ✉ *1000 chemin des Voyageurs, Mont-Tremblant* ☎ *866/356–2233* ⊕ *www.tremblant.ca.*

SWIMMING

Most of the city's municipal outdoor pools are open from mid-June through August. Admission is free on weekdays. On weekends and holidays there's a small fee of no more than C$4 at some pools, depending on the borough.

Parc-Plage l'Île Notre-Dame. The west side of Île Notre-Dame is home to the city's man-made beach with probably the cleanest water (tested and monitored) in Montréal, which makes the entrance fee worth it. ✉ *The Islands* ☎ *514/872–6120* ⊕ *www.parcjeandrapeau.com* ✉ *C$9* Ⓜ *Jean-Drapeau, then Bus 167.*

9

SIDE TRIPS FROM MONTRÉAL

WELCOME TO
SIDE TRIPS FROM MONTRÉAL

TOP REASONS TO GO

★ **Ski at Mont-Tremblant:** Heading 150 km (90 miles) north of Montréal takes you to some of the best skiing east of the Rockies, as well as fine hotels and restaurants, a lively ski village, and great golf courses.

★ **Take a driving tour of Eastern Township wineries:** The vineyards here resemble those in the Niagara Region and Okanagan Valley.

★ **Visit Abbaye St-Benoit-du-Lac:** The Benedictine monks built this splendid church—with its fairy-tale castle bell tower—on the shores of Lake Memphrémagog.

★ **Spend a night among wolves in Parc Omega:** Go with an experienced guide to explore the lives of these great predators in their natural habitat—the magnificent Outaouais region.

★ **Go leaf peeping ... anywhere:** From mid-September through mid-October the entire Laurentians, Eastern Townships, and Outaouais are ablaze with spectacular fall foliage.

The Laurentians resort area begins 60 km (37 miles) north of Montréal. The Eastern Townships start approximately 80 km (50 miles) east of the city in a southern corner of the province. The Outaouais lies about 110 km (68 miles) to the west, bordering Ontario. All three are an easy drive from Montréal.

1 The Laurentians.
With its ski hills and lakes, this is sheer paradise for those looking for a quick break from the hustle and bustle of urban life. Quaint villages, many steeped in colorful history, line the delightful countryside—all hardly a stone's throw away from the center of Montréal.

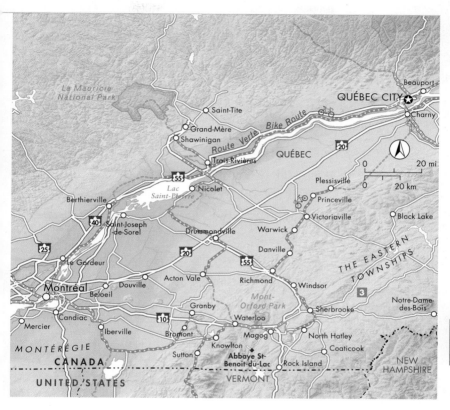

2 The Outaouais.
The ruggedly beautiful Outaouais is an excellent place to go camping and spot wildlife—and that's especially true of Gatineau and Parc Omega.

3 The Eastern Townships. A favorite ski and sun destination for those looking to get away from it all, this is also an increasingly popular culinary tourism destination for its artisan food producers and wineries. Settled by British Loyalists fleeing the American

Revolution, the region's redbrick villages, charming bed-and-breakfasts, and excellent regional dining are a blend of New England and Nouvelle France.

Updated by
Elizabeth
Warkentin

In the minds of many who live here, one of Montréal's great-est attributes is its proximity to the sheer physical beauty of the surrounding countryside. From downtown Montréal you can head in pretty well any direction and within an hour or so, you'll be, if not in the wilderness, then at least in the thick of cottage country. The three most popular side-trip destinations from Montréal are the Laurentians, the Eastern Townships, and the Outaouais—each possessing its own distinct characteristics and flavor.

Most people traveling to this region do so by car, making it easy to spend as much or as little time in any given area as desired. However, Québec has created the Route Verte (Green Route), a 5,000-km (3,100-mile) network of bike trails in the southern part of the province. Many of the trails are currently open for access.

THE LAURENTIANS

The Laurentians (les Laurentides) range is a delightful year-round desti-nation for getting outdoors, whether it's for golf and white-water rafting in the summer or skiing and dog sledding in the winter. Along with its stunning natural beauty, it's also known for its authentic Québec food—all of this to be found less than an hour's drive from downtown Montréal, traffic allowing.

The main tourist region, which actually encompasses only a small part of the Laurentian mountain range, is divided into two major regions: the Lower Laurentians (les Basses Laurentides) and the Upper Laurentians (les Hautes Laurentides). But don't be fooled by the designations; they don't signify great driving distances. The rocky hills here are relatively low, but many are eminently skiable, with a few peaks above 2,500 feet. Mont-Tremblant, at 3,150 feet, is the region's highest.

The P'tit Train du Nord—the former railroad line that's now a 200-km (124-mile) "linear park" used by cyclists, hikers, skiers, and snowmobilers—made it possible to transport settlers and cargo easily to the Upper Laurentians. It also opened up the area to skiing by the early 1900s. Before long, trainloads of skiers replaced settlers and cargo as the railroad's major trade. At first a winter weekend getaway for Montrealers who stayed at boardinghouses and fledgling resorts, the Upper Laurentians soon began attracting international visitors.

Ski lodges and private family cottages for wealthy city dwellers were accessible only by train until the 1930s, when Route 117 was built. Today there's an uneasy peace between the longtime cottagers, who want to restrict development, and resort entrepreneurs, who want to expand. At the moment, commercial interests seem to be prevailing. A number of large hotels have added indoor pools and spa facilities, and efficient highways have brought the country even closer to the city—45 minutes to St-Sauveur, 1½–2 hours to Mont-Tremblant.

Sadly, apart from the well-trod tourist resorts of St-Sauveur and Mont-Tremblant, the Laurentians has been on a bit of an economic downswing in the last decade or so. Many of the grand old lodges and lakefront hotels have closed, leaving a gap in availability of finer accommodations for tourists; interesting dining options are also harder to come by than in the Eastern Townships.

The resort area begins at St-Sauveur-des-Monts (Exit 60 on Autoroute 15) and extends north to Mont-Tremblant. Beyond, the region turns into a wilderness of lakes and forests best visited with an outfitter. Fishing guides are concentrated around Parc du Mont-Tremblant. To the first-time visitor, the hilly areas around St-Sauveur, Ste-Adèle, Morin Heights, Val-Morin, and Val-David up to Ste-Agathe-des-Monts form a pleasant hodgepodge of villages, hotels, and inns that seem to blend one into another. Tourisme Laurentides in Mirabel provides information and offers a daily lodging-booking service. Its main information center is at the Porte du Nord complex at Exit 51 on Autoroute 15.

9

WHEN TO GO

The Laurentians are a big skiing destination in winter, but the other seasons all have their own charms: you can drive up from Montréal to enjoy the fall foliage; to hike, bike, play golf, camp, or fish; or to engage in spring skiing—and still get back to the city before dark. The only slow periods are early November (aka "mud season"), when there isn't much to do, and June, when the area has plenty to offer but is plagued by black flies. Control programs have improved the situation somewhat.

GETTING HERE AND AROUND

Autoroute 15 is the fastest and most direct route from Montréal to the most in-demand spots in the Laurentians. This limited access highway peters out at Ste-Agathe and morphs into Autoroute 117, which runs all the way to Rouyn-Noranda. Exit numbers on Autoroute 15 reflect the distance from Montréal. Autoroute 15 starts at the New York–Québec border where it connects to Interstate 87, so it's also the most direct route for most visitors from the United States. The highway crosses into

Montréal on the Champlain Bridge and follows the Décarie and Metropolitan expressways across the island. Visitors arriving from Boston and points east on Interstate 91 can follow Autoroute 55 from the border north to Autoroute 10 (the Autoroute des Cantons de l'Est) and then drive west until it merges with Autoroute 15 at the Champlain Bridge.

VISITOR INFORMATION

Contact Tourisme Laurentides (Porte du Nord). ⌧ *1000 Hwy. 15 N, St-Jérôme* ✛ *Exit 51, Autoroute 15N* ☎ *450/224–7007 from Montréal area, 800/561–6673 from rest of North America* ⊕ *www.laurentides.com.*

OKA

40 km (25 miles) west of Montréal.

If you like apples and delicious cheese, Oka is sure to be a highlight of your trip. It was once the home of Cistercian monks, but the urban sprawl has driven them from their abbey, on the shores of Lac des Deux-Montagnes, to seek solace farther north in St-Jean-de-Matha in the Lanaudière region, but the cheese they made famous is still produced by a private firm here and is available in local shops. The rolling hills around the little town of Oka are where you'll find many of the apple orchards. If you love cider, follow the *Route des Vergers,* stopping at various properties along this "Orchard Route" to sample the local wares. There's also a winery on the route: La Roche des Brises, whose whites and reds include the portlike *L'été Indien* (Indian Summer).

GETTING HERE AND AROUND

To get from Montréal to Oka, take Autoroute 15 North to Autoroute 640 West.

EXPLORING

Parc d'Oka (*Oka National Park*). Beautifully surrounded by low hills, this park has a lake fringed by a sandy beach and plenty of opportunities for outdoor sports, including hiking and biking trails, kayaking, canoeing, fishing, and, in winter, snowshoeing and cross-country skiing. Locals also consider it to be one of the top camping destinations. Administered by the province along environmentally conscious lines—they implemented the Ecological Integrity Monitoring Program (EIMO) in 2004—it has nearly 900 campsites, and you can rent bicycles, cross-country skis, snowshoes, canoes, and kayaks from the office. Note that the strip at the far eastern end of the beach is "clothing optional," or, in effect, "clothing nonexistent." ⌧ *2020 chemin Oka* ☎ *450/479–8365, 800/665–6527 activities* ⊕ *www.sepaq.com* 🖱 *C$9.*

EN ROUTE

Hudson. A quick detour on the ferry (C$11 one-way; *traverseoka.ca*) across Lac des Deux-Montagnes brings you to this small town with old houses now used for art galleries, boutiques, and Christmas shops. In winter there's an "ice bridge": basically a plowed path across a well-frozen lake. Taking a walk across the bridge is a singular experience. If you happen to visit on a Saturday from May to October, make a stop at the popular **Finnegan's Market** (*www.finnegansmarket.com*). Open from 9 to 4, the flea market sells antiques, jewelry, crafts, and preserves, among other goods. ⌧ *Hudson.*

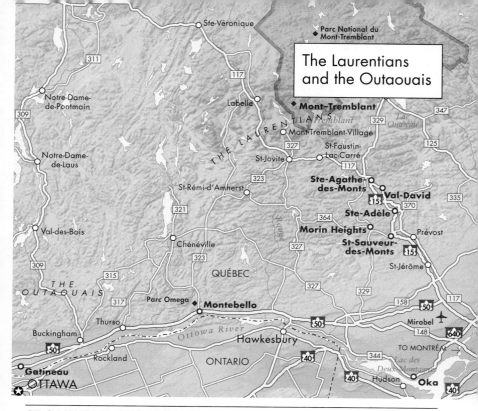

ST-SAUVEUR-DES-MONTS

85 km (53 miles) north of Oka, 63 km (39 miles) north of Montréal.

Just a 45-minute drive from Montréal (or 90 minutes when the traffic's heavy, as it frequently is), St-Sauveur is probably the busiest little town in Québec, especially on weekends. Its rue Principale bristles with bars and restaurants that serve everything from lamb brochettes and spicy Thai stir-fries to steaks and burgers. On summer weekends, the street is so jammed with cars and the sidewalks so packed with visitors that it's sometimes called Crescent Street North after the action-filled street in Montréal. Despite the glitz and the sea of condos that surround it, however, the town has managed to retain a bit of rural charm in its fine old church and veranda-fronted clapboard homes.

St-Sauveur in winter is no less busy. The "mountains" surrounding the town hardly qualify as Alpine—none has a vertical drop of more than 700 feet—but they're close to Montréal, well serviced by lifts, and lit at night, so the winter sports scene here is very lively. Whether you ski or not, the après-ski scene in St-Sauveur is worth sampling.

GETTING HERE AND AROUND

Take Highway 15 north from Montréal and get off at Exit 60. The best way to explore the main street is to find a parking lot and walk around. Driving through town is difficult in winter, impossible in summer.

VISITOR INFORMATION

Contact Tourist Welcome Bureau of Pays-d'en-Haut. ✉ *1014 rue Valiquette, Ste-Adèle* ☎ *450/229-6637* 🌐 *www.lespaysdenhaut.com.*

EXPLORING

FAMILY **Mont-St-Sauveur Water Park.** Slides, a giant wave pool, a wading pool, and snack bars will all keep the kids occupied here. The river rafting attracts an older, braver crowd; the nine-minute ride follows the natural contours of steep hills. On the tandem slides, plumes of water flow through figure-eight tubes and makes for a great time. But if you'd rather stay dry, take an adventure through the trees on their zip line or enjoy a fast ride with the Viking Alpine Coaster. ✉ *350 rue St-Denis* ☎ *450/227–4671* 🌐 *www.sommets.com/en/* 🎟 *C$36.*

Musée du ski des Laurentides. The Laurentians are one of the oldest ski regions in North America, and ski buffs will enjoy this little museum tracing the long history of this area with great photos, artifacts, and some interesting models of early ski lifts. It also houses the Temple de la Renomée du ski (the Ski Hall of Fame). ✉ *30 rue Filion* ☎ *450/227–2564* 🌐 *www.museeduskideslaurentides.com* 🎟 *Free, though donation of $3 suggested.*

WHERE TO STAY

$ B&B/INN 🏨 **Relais St-Denis.** Once a wartime refuge for well-heeled English children and their governesses, this inn and spa now offers everyone a refuge from everyday stress, with a fireplace and a whirlpool bath in every room and a year-round outdoor heated pool and steam room. **Pros:** variety of spa services and in-room massage packages; kitchenette in all rooms and suites; walking distance to restaurants, outlet shopping, and activities; most rooms have gas fireplaces. **Cons:** not much to occupy the kids; decor is basic and "businesslike," could use updating. [$] *Rooms from: C$159* ✉ *61 rue St-Denis* ☎ *450/227–4766, 888/997–4766* 🌐 *www.relaisstdenis.com* 🛏 *42 rooms* 🍴 *No meals.*

SHOPPING

SHOPPING CENTERS

Factoreries St-Sauveur. If you feel like shopping and can't resist a bargain, this could be your dream destination. With 35 stores, including Jones New York, Guess, Parasuco, and Rockport selling designer clothing at reduced prices, there's really no reason not to go. Be warned, however, that it can get very crowded and difficult to find parking in the surrounding lots. ✉ *100 rue Guindon* ☎ *450/240–0880* 🌐 *www.tanger-outlet.com/saintsauveur.*

Rue Principale. Small fashion boutiques, restaurant terraces, and cute gift shops in old French-Canadian and Victorian homes adorned with bright awnings and flowers line this popular tree-lined shopping street. ✉ *St-Sauveur-des-Monts.*

One of the most popular times to visit the region is in fall, when the mountains are splashed with a spectrum of warm yellows, oranges, and reds.

SPORTS AND THE OUTDOORS
SKIING

Sommet St-Sauveur. The hills surrounding St-Sauveur might be relatively low, but this vibrant ski resort is long-established and perennially popular for good reason. It has an extensive skiable area, good snow-making and lift capacity, and many trails that are lit at night, making it possible for energetic Montrealers to drive up after work for a couple hours of skiing. There are several other hills in the area, but Mont-St-Sauveur is the largest, with a 700-foot vertical drop and 142 acres of skiable terrain. Seventeen of its 38 trails are for beginners and intermediates, 16 are for experts, and 5 are rated extreme. Mont-Avila has 13 trails (2 beginner, 3 intermediate, 5 difficult, 3 extremely difficult), a snow park, a fun tubing park, and the Viking, a toboggan-style ride in a cart that twists and turns on a track through the forest. ✉ *350 av. St-Denis, St-Sauveur* ☎ *450/227–4671* ⊕ *www.sommets.com.*

Station de Ski Mont-Habitant. More than 55 years in operation, Mont-Habitant is one of the last of the independent ski operations in St-Sauveur. This mountain has always been a favorite with families and with beginner and intermediate skiers because the vertical drop is just 600 feet and the 10 trails are relatively gentle. Mont-Habitant also has St-Sauveur's only beach, which makes it very popular in the summer. ✉ *12 chemin des Skieurs* ☎ *450/227–2637, 866/887–2637* ⊕ *www. monthabitant.com* ✍ *C$41 day pass.*

MORIN HEIGHTS

10 km (6 miles) west of St-Sauveur-des-Monts, 73 km (45 miles) north-west of Montréal.

If St-Sauveur is too busy and overdeveloped for your liking, Morin Heights is a great alternative, with plenty of restaurants, bookstores, boutiques, and craft shops to explore free from the crowds. The town's British architecture and population reflect its settlers' heritage; most residents here speak English.

In summer, windsurfing, swimming, and canoeing on the area's two lakes—Claude and Lafontaine—are popular. In fall and winter, come for the foliage and the alpine and Nordic skiing.

GETTING HERE AND AROUND

From Montréal to Morin Heights, take Autoroute 15 North, then take Exit 60.

WHERE TO STAY

Morin Heights is true cottage country, and thus options for accommodation are slim. Your best bet might be to rent a cottage, or as they're known by French-speaking locals, a *chalet* ⊕ *www.chaletsauquebec. com.* The Montréal pages for ⊕ *craigslist.com* and ⊕ *kijiji.ca* are full of posts advertising private chalet rentals in the Laurentians. If you'd prefer to go through a third party, most area real estate agents broker short- and long-term cottage and chalet rentals as well; try Remax Laurentides *(450/227–8411).*

$

B&B/INN

⚀ **Hotel Alila.** This auberge by the main road is one of the best-equipped spa destinations in the area, and its outdoor terrace is a pleasant place to relax. **Pros:** some rooms have beautiful views of the Rivière du Nord; whirlpool baths and fireplaces in some units. **Cons:** isolated from village; close to highway; no breakfast; in need of refurbishment. $ *Rooms from: C$108* ⊠ *500 Rte. 364, Morin-Heights* 🕾 *450/644–0168* ⊕ *www. alila.ca* ⮐ *29 rooms* ⦿❙ *No meals.*

SHOPPING

SPAS

Amerispa Spa Nordique. Only 45 minutes outside of Montréal, this is a great place to escape and unwind. Hidden in a Laurentian forest of maples, firs, and birches is a beautifully rustic pavilion housing a spa with hot tubs and cold pools, eucalyptus-scented steam baths, and thermal and Nordic waterfalls. The Elixir Ice Cider Massage with companion body wrap gets good reviews. ⊠ *160 rue Watchorn, Morin-Heights* 🕾 *450/226–7722, 866/263–7477* ⊕ *www.amerispa.ca.*

STE-ADÈLE

12 km (7 miles) north of Morin Heights, 85 km (53 miles) north of Montréal.

While Ste-Adèle is not as pretty as St-Sauveur, this town has a lot to offer, with attractions and activities to please families, outdoors enthusiasts, and visitors who want to experience something of the local culture. With a permanent population of more than 10,000, it's the largest community in the lower part of the Laurentians, and has good boutiques, restaurants, summer theater (performed in French), and art galleries. Active types can find horseback riding, golf, and lengthy bike trails in summer and skiing in winter.

GETTING HERE AND AROUND

From Montréal to Ste-Adèle, take Autoroute 15 North and then take Exit 67.

VISITOR INFORMATION

Contact Tourist Welcome Bureau of Pays-d'en-Haut. ⊠ *1014, rue Valiquette* ☏ *450/229–6637* ⊕ *www.lespaysdenhaut.com.*

EXPLORING

FAMILY **Au Pays des Merveilles.** Fairy-tale characters such as Snow White, Little Red Riding Hood, and Alice in Wonderland wander the grounds, playing games with children. Small fry may also enjoy the petting zoo, amusement rides, wading pool, and puppet show. A ride called Le Petit Train des Merveilles (the Little Train of Wonders) is a nod to the historic train that launched the tourism industry in the Laurentians. There are 45 activities, enough to occupy those aged two to eight for about half a day. Check the website for discount coupons. The theme park is completely accessible to strollers and wheelchairs. ⊠ *3795 Chemin de la Savane* ☏ *450/229–3141* ⊕ *www.paysmerveilles. com* ⊠ *C$20.*

WHERE TO STAY

$ 📺 **Le Chantecler.** A longtime favorite with Montrealers, this hotel has
HOTEL   seen better days, but it remains a good choice for active types wanting
FAMILY to expend some energy. **Pros:** friendly, helpful staff; lakeside rooms; year-round activities. **Cons:** can be hard to get a reservation; rooms in need of renovation; restaurant sometimes closed. $ *Rooms from: C$155* ⊠ *1474 chemin Chantecler* ☏ *450/229–3555, 888/910–1111* ⊕ *www.lechantecler.com* ⇱ *179 rooms* ⫱*No meals.*

SPORTS AND THE OUTDOORS

GOLF

Club de Golf Chantecler. Club de Golf Chantecler. Every hole here will provide panoramic views of the surrounding Laurentian scenery. Opened in 1950, this semiprivate club offers a mountainside course with long and narrow fairways and three sets of tees for different skill levels. Just one hour from Montreal, it's easy and convenient for a day trip. ⊠ *2520 chemin du Club* ☏ *450/476–1339, 450/229–3742* ⊕ *www. groupebeaudet.com* ⊠ *C$28.04–C$34.75* ⚑ *18 holes, 6120 yards, par 72* ⚐ *Facilities: Putting green, golf carts, pull carts, rental clubs, pro-shop, restaurant, bar.*

SKIING

Ski Mont-Gabriel. Part of Les Sommets chain of ski resorts, Mont Gabriel has five lifts, 18 superb downhill trails, which are primarily for intermediate and advanced skiers, and a vertical drop of 656 feet. It's about 19 km (12 miles) northeast of Ste-Adèle. ⊠ *1501 chemin du Mont-Gabriel* ⊕ *www.sommets.com/en/ski-mountains/sommet-gabriel/* ⊠ *C$39 day ski pass.*

VAL-DAVID

33 km (20 miles) west of Ste-Adèle, 82 km (51 miles) north of Montréal.

Val-David is a major destination for mountain climbers, hikers, and campers. It's also a place that many Québec artists and artisans call home, a fact suggested by the several galleries and marvelous art shops in town.

GETTING HERE AND AROUND

The village is just a couple of kilometers east of Exit N6 on Autoroute 15, making it easy to get to by car, but it's also accessible by bicycle: Le P'tit Train du Nord cycling trail runs right through town.

VISITOR INFORMATION

Contact Tourist Bureau of Val-David. ✉ *2525 rue de l'Église, Val-David* ☎ *888/322–7030, 819/324–5678* 🌐 *www.valdavid.com.*

EXPLORING

FAMILY **Village du Père Noël** (*Santa Claus Village*). Santa is not just for Christmas here. In his summer residence kids can sit on his knee and speak to him in French or English, then have fun in the grounds, which contain bumper boats, a petting zoo with goats, sheep, horses, and colorful birds; games; and a large outdoor pool in the summer. There is a snack bar, but visitors are encouraged to bring their own food (there are numerous picnic tables). During the cold winter months, the park transforms into a winter wonderland with skating rinks and tubing fun for the kids. ✉ *987 rue Morin, Val-David* ☎ *819/322–2146, 800/287–6635* 🌐 *www.noel.qc.ca* 🎟 *C$20.*

WHERE TO EAT

$$ CANADIAN FAMILY Fodor's Choice ★ 🍴 **Au Petit Poucet.** For a true Quebecois treat, stop by this rustic cabin for breakfast or lunch. Founded in 1945, it's a big draw with tourists and locals alike. **Known for:** copious breakfast options; the restaurant's famous homemade country bread. [$] *Average main: C$20* ✉ *1030 Rte. 117, Val-David* ☎ *819/322–2246, 888/334–2246* 🌐 *www.aupetit-poucet.com* 🕒 *No dinner.*

WHERE TO STAY

$ B&B/INN Fodor's Choice ★ 🏨 **La Maison de Bavière.** Walking into this charming B&B is like being transported to a cozy Bavarian mountain inn. **Pros:** directly across from the P'tit Train du Nord cycling and cross-country ski trail; two-minute walk to the village of Val-David; lovely backyard facing the rushing Rivière du Nord; within the grounds of the Parc des Amoureux; vegans, allergy sufferers, and others on special diets are catered to with options like soy yogurt or hot cereal served with caramelized nuts and banana puree. **Cons:** only four rooms; common room is small and right off the rooms, so guests need to keep voices down. [$] *Rooms from: C$140* ✉ *1470 chemin de la Rivière, Val-David* ☎ *819/322–3528, 866/322–3528* 🌐 *www.maisondebaviere.com* 🛏 *4 rooms, 2 self-catering studios* 🍽 *Some meals.*

SHOPPING

CERAMICS

1001 Pots. One of the most interesting events in Val-David is this ceramic exhibition, held from July through mid-August, which started in 1988. On view is the Japanese-style pottery of 1001 Pots' founder Kinya Ishikawa—as well as pieces by up to 100 other ceramists. Ishikawa's studio also displays work by his wife, Marie-Andrée Benoît, who makes fish-shaped bowls with a texture derived from pressing canvas on the clay. There are workshops for adults and children throughout the exhibition, and there is always at least one artisan on site. While you're there, take the time to enjoy tea in one of the three beautiful gardens and learn the art of the Japanese tea ceremony. ⊠ *2435 rue de l'Église, Val-David* ☏ *819/322–6868* ⊕ *www.1001pots.com* ✉ *C$2 for exhibition* ✆ *C$2 admission.*

HOUSEHOLD

Atelier Bernard Chaudron, Inc. If you're looking for an interesting conversation piece to bring back home with you, check out master craftsman Bernard Chaudron's hand-forged, lead-free pewter household objects that include oil lamps, hammered-silver beer mugs, pitchers, candleholders, and animal-themed knife rests. ⊠ *2347 rue de l'Église, Val-David* ☏ *819/322–3944, 888/322–3944* ⊕ *www.chaudron.ca.*

SPORTS AND THE OUTDOORS

SKIING

Centre de Ski Vallée-Bleue. Family-run and family-focused, this ski hill suits everyone, from beginners to advanced level skiers and snowboarders, with 19 trails, 3 lifts, and a vertical drop of 365 feet. ⊠ *1418 chemin Vallée-Bleue, Val-David* ☏ *819/322–3427, 866/322–3427* ⊕ *www.vallee-bleue.com* ✉ *C$38 ski pass.*

STE-AGATHE-DES-MONTS

9

5 km (3 miles) north of Val-David, 96 km (60 miles) northwest of Montréal.

The wide, sandy beaches of Lac des Sables are the most surprising feature of Ste-Agathe-des-Monts, a tourist town best known for its ski hills. Water activities include canoeing, kayaking, swimming, and fishing. Ste-Agathe is also a stopover point on the Linear Park, the bike trail between St-Jérôme and Mont-Laurier.

GETTING HERE AND AROUND

From Montréal to Ste-Agathe-des-Monts, take Autoroute 15 North. Take Exit 89 to reach QC–329 South, and then take QC–117.

VISITOR INFORMATION

Contact Tourist Bureau of Ste-Agathe-des-Monts. ⊠ *24 rue St-Paul est* ☏ *819/326–3731, 888/326–0457* ⊕ *www.sainte-agathe.org/en/.*

WHERE TO STAY

$ ⌕ **Hôtel Spa Watel.** If you're looking for a room with a double-size
HOTEL   Jacuzzi, a fireplace, and a balcony with a superb view of Lac des Sables, try this white-painted, lodge-style hotel, which is also convenient for the boutiques and cultural activities in Ste-Agathe. **Pros:** adjacent to three beaches; indoor and outdoor pools; year-round

outdoor spas. **Cons:** not all rooms have a Jacuzzi, fireplace, and lake view; some lake-view rooms are off an enclosed glass balcony, motel style, so they don't receive direct air from outside. [$] *Rooms from: C$140* ✉ *250 rue St-Venant* ☎ *819/326–7016, 800/363–6478* 🌐 *www.hotelspawatel.com* 🛏 *31 rooms* 🍴 *Some meals.*

CAMPING

In the woods near a lively resort area, Au Parc des Campeurs has activities for all age groups, from sport competitions to outings for the kids. There's a sandy beach where you can rent canoes and kayaks and launch your boat from the town's marina. Reservations for this campground (open mid-May through September) are recommended. ✉ *2 chemin du Lac-des-Sables, Ste-Agathe-des-Monts* ☎ *819/324–0482 or 800/561–7360* 🌐 *www.camping-steagathe.com.*

SPORTS AND THE OUTDOORS

BOAT TOURS

***Alouette V* and VI.** These sightseeing boats offer guided 50-minute tours of Lac des Sables. They run at least seven times a day from mid-June to mid-August and five times a day from mid-August to mid-October. The first boat leaves the dock at 11:30 am. ✉ *Municipal Dock, rue Principale* ☎ *819/326–3656, 866/326–3656* 🌐 *www.croisierealouette.com* 🎟 *C$22 for 50-minute cruise.*

MONT-TREMBLANT

25 km (16 miles) north of Ste-Agathe-des-Monts, 100 km (62 miles) north of Montréal.

At more than 3,000 feet, Mont-Tremblant is one of the highest peaks in the Laurentians and a major draw for skiers. The resort area at the foot of the mountain (called simply Tremblant) is spread around 14-km (9-mile) -long Lac Tremblant and is consistently—and justifiably—ranked among the top ski resorts in eastern North America.

The hub of the resort is a pedestrians-only village that gives an architectural nod to the style of New France, with dormer windows and colorful steep roofs on buildings that house pubs, restaurants, boutiques, sports shops, a movie theater, self-catering condominiums, and hotels. A historical town this is not: built for the resort, it may strike you as a bit of Disney in the mountains.

GETTING HERE AND AROUND

The easiest way to get here is by car. Drive north on Autoroute 15 until it ends just beyond Ste-Agathe-des-Monts and then continue on Route 117 (a four-lane highway) for another 30 km (18 miles) to the Mont-Tremblant exit (Exit 119). The resort's parking lots are vast, but they fill up quickly. A shuttle bus links them to the main resort and ski area. Mont-Tremblant has two tourist offices, one in the village and one in the downtown area.

VISITOR INFORMATION

Contact Tourisme Mont-Tremblant. ✉ *5080 Montée Ryan* ☎ *877/425–2434, 819/425–2434* 🌐 *www.mont-tremblant.ca.*

EXPLORING

FAMILY Fodor's Choice ★ **Parc National du Mont-Tremblant.** This vast wildlife sanctuary has more than 400 lakes and rivers and is home to nearly 200 species of birds and animals, so it's great for wildlife watching. Cross-country skiers, snowshoers, and snowmobilers enjoy the park's trails in winter and camping, fishing, canoeing, and hiking are the popular summer activities. The park was once the home of the Algonquins, who called this area Manitonga Soutana, meaning "mountain of the spirits." ✉ *Mont-Tremblant* ☎ *800/665–6527* 🌐 *www.sepaq.com* 🎫 *C$9 per day.*

La Diable Vistors' Centre. The park entrance closest to Mont-Tremblant is at La Diable Vistors' Centre, just beyond the village of Lac-Supérieur and about a half-hour drive from the resort. ✉ *3824 chemin du Lac Supérieur, Lac Supérieur* ☎ *819/688–2281 visitor center, 800/665–6527 Sépaq (government national park agency)* 🌐 *www.sepaq.com/pq/mot.*

WHERE TO EAT

$$ ITALIAN 🍴 **Auberge du Coq de Montagne.** Five minutes from the ski slopes and right on Lac Moore, this rustic restaurant, which opens onto a terrace during the summer months, looks a bit shabby from the outside but has garnered much praise for its Italian dishes. These include tried-and-true favorites such as veal marsala and veal *fiorentina* (cooked with spinach and cheese). **Known for:** Italian dishes like veal marsala; homemade pasta. [$] *Average main: C$20* ✉ *2151 chemin du Village* ☎ *819/425–3380* 🌐 *www.aubergeducoqdemontagne.com* 🕒 *Closed Easter Mon.–late May; early Oct.–mid-Dec.*

$ CANADIAN FAMILY 🍴 **Creperie Catherine.** This is a great place to refuel in the Mont-Tremblant area if you want to take a break from the hustle and bustle of the Village. Ten minutes by car, this restaurant was recently part of the popular Food Network TV show *You Gotta Eat Here*, and rightly so, as they offer some of the best and most creative crepe dishes. **Known for:** escargot crepe with signature béchamel sauce; Catherine's Special (eggs, ham, and cheese); banana split. [$] *Average main: C$12* ✉ *977 rue Labelle* ☎ *819/681–4888* 🌐 *www.creperiecatherine.ca.*

$$$$ FRENCH 🍴 **Restaurant Le Cheval de Jade.** "The Jade Horse" is quite haute—an elegant dining room with lace curtains, white linens, and ivory china—and the food is the real thing. Local, seasonal ingredients and organic produce are used to create classic French fare such as bouillabaisse, grilled veal chop, and duck with fresh truffles. **Known for:** classic French cuisine; elegant dining. [$] *Average main: C$35* ✉ *688 rue de St-Jovite* ☎ *819/425–5233* 🌐 *www.chevaldejade.com* 🕒 *Closed Sun. and Mon. No lunch.*

WHERE TO STAY

$$$$ HOTEL FAMILY Fodor's Choice ★ 🏨 **Fairmont Tremblant.** The centerpiece of the Tremblant resort area takes its cues from the grand 19th-century railroad "castle hotels" scattered throughout Canada. **Pros:** poolside barbecue during the summer; dogs (under 50 lbs.) allowed; easy access to ski hills and the village; all-new restaurants and bar. **Cons:** it's in the fairly busy village rather than more scenic grounds; valet parking $25 plus tax, and public parking (fees may apply) a 10-minute walk away. [$] *Rooms from: C$320* ✉ *3045 chemin de la Chapelle* ☎ *819/681–7000, 800/257–7544* 🌐 *www.fairmont.com/tremblant* 🛏 *314 rooms* 🍽 *Breakfast.*

9

RENTING A SKI CHALET IN MONT-TREMBLANT

If you think you'd like to spend more than a few days in the Laurentians you might want to consider renting a chalet from a private owner. There are generally plenty to choose from, and not only is a private rental often less expensive than staying at a hotel, it's a lot homier as well, especially if you are traveling with children. And even with the many restaurants in Mont-Tremblant, every once in a while it's nice to buy groceries and come home to cook your own dinner.

Options range from cozy little cottages for four to multibedroom properties where you could have a real house party with family and friends. If you fill a place to capacity the cost can be very competitive, particularly if you don't mind being outside the main hub of the resort or out of the peak season. Some places offer weekend rates as well as renting by the week. Very good sources for chalet rentals in this part of the province are the websites 🌐 *www.chalets-mont-tremblant.com* and 🌐 *www.chaletsauquebec.com*, and the Montréal pages for 🌐 *craigslist.com* and 🌐 *kijiji.ca* are full of posts advertising private chalet rentals in the Laurentians. If you'd prefer to go through a third party, most area real estate agents broker short- and long-term cottage and chalet rentals as well. Try Remax Laurentides at 286 Principal in St-Sauveur (*450/227–8411*) for starters.

$$$ HOTEL FAMILY 🏨 **Le Grand Lodge.** At this Scandinavian-style log-cabin hotel, on 13½ acres on the shore of Lac Ouimet, you'll find great year-round amenities and activities for families and sports lovers and a resorty feel that survives its busy conference trade schedule. **Pros:** peaceful environment with woods and walking trails behind hotel; ice rink and ice path in winter; private beach on the lake. **Cons:** rooms and suites lacking in style; pool very narrow; gas fireplaces as opposed to wood-burning. [$] *Rooms from: C$206* ✉ *2396 rue Labelle* ☎ *819/425–2734, 800/567–6763* 🌐 *www.legrandlodge.com* 🛏 *112 rooms* 🍴 *Breakfast.*

SPORTS AND THE OUTDOORS

GOLF

Mont-Tremblant. The same company that operates the ski resort also runs two of the most challenging and popular championship golf courses in Québec. **Le Géant** (the Giant) was designed by Thomas McBroom to take full advantage of the fantastic scenery. **Le Diable** (the Devil), with long narrow fairways and strategically placed red sand bunkers, was designed by Michael Hurdzan and Dana Fry. Also at Le Diable, you can find the reputable Tremblant Golf Academy. ✉ *Mont-Tremblant* ☎ *866/356–2233, 866/783–5634* 🌐 *www.tremblant.ca* 🎫 *C$119 weekdays, C$139 weekends* ⛳ *Le Diable, 18 holes, 7056 yards, par 71; Le Géant, 18 holes, 6836 yards, par 72* ☞ *Facilities: Le Diable: Driving range, putting green, golf carts, caddies (digital/GPS), rental clubs, pro shop, golf academy/lessons, restaurant, bar; Le Géant: Driving range, putting green, golf carts, rental clubs, pro shop, gold academy/lessons, restaurant, bar.*

SKIING

Mont-Tremblant. With a 2,116-foot vertical drop, 654 acres of skiable terrain, 95 trails, 18 acres of ramps and jumps for snowboarders, and enough state-of-the-art snowmaking equipment to blanket a small city, Mont-Tremblant is truly one of the great ski resorts of North America, arguably the best east of the Rockies. Its 14 lifts—including two heated gondolas and five high-speed, four-passenger chairlifts—can handle 27,230 skiers an hour. It has some of the toughest expert runs on the continent, but it also has long, gentle runs like the 6-km (3.7-mile) Nansen and dozens of exciting trails for intermediate skiers. Its altitude and location, as well as all that snowmaking equipment, gives it some of eastern Canada's most reliable ski conditions, especially now that winters are getting warmer. All this doesn't come cheap, mind you. A day lift ticket costs about C$85, but for serious skiers there is no better mountain in Québec. ⊠ *1000 chemin des Voyageurs* ☎ *866/356–2233, 819/681–3000* ⊕ *www.tremblant.ca* ✉ *One-day lift ticket C$85 (C$99 during Christmas holidays).*

NIGHTLIFE AND PERFORMING ARTS

Festi Jazz. Tons of fun and completely free, the very popular five-day jazz festival in early August draws in at least 15,000 tourists and locals to Mont-Tremblant. The concerts take place under the stars on two outdoor stages and in at least 10 restaurants, bars, and hotels in the Village or St-Jovite (downtown area). ⊠ *Mont-Tremblant* ⊕ *www. jazzmttremblant.com.*

Festival International du Blues de Tremblant (*Tremblant International Blues Festival*). People don't just flock to Mont-Tremblant for outdoor fun. This place is becoming a music lovers' paradise, especially for 10 days in July when the Blues Festival takes place with more than 130 shows. Artists such as Otis Taylor, JJ Grey & Mofro, and Thornetta Davis entertain fans on outdoor stages and in intimate clubs right in the Village. ⊠ *Mont-Tremblant* ☎ *819/681–3000* ⊕ *blues.tremblant.ca/en/.*

THE OUTAOUAIS

First settled in the mid-19th century and long known for its logging, the Outaouais (pronounced: ewt–away) region is now a nature lover's paradise as well, with 20,000 lakes, countless rivers, 400 km (249 miles) of hiking trails, and 2,730 km (1,696 miles) of snowmobile trails.

To fully experience the majesty of the Outaouais wilderness you could spend close to a week here, but simply driving to any of the region's major provincial parks is a good one-day journey. Montebello, a little country village on the banks of the Ottawa River, is only a 1½-hour drive from Montréal, and is where you'll find Le Château Montebello, the largest log structure ever built. From there you can find excursions to take you to the surrounding countryside, or if you'd prefer, you can simply take in nearby Omega Park, a safari adventure where you'll bear witness to many of the region's creatures interacting within their natural environment. It encompasses an enormous body of land located in the southwest corner of the province.

WHEN TO GO

The Outaouais is beautiful at any time of year, but unless you're looking to spend several days there it's best to go in summer and stay in the lower region, around Montebello. Making your way up to the provincial parks in the north is a lengthy journey at best, but in winter, potentially hazardous road conditions could well add several more hours to your trip.

GETTING HERE AND AROUND

To get to the Outaouais take Autoroute 15 North roughly 40 km (25 miles) until you get to Autoroute 50 West heading toward Lachute. Drive another 70 km (43 miles) past Lachute and you'll soon be in Montebello. Continue on another 15 km (9 miles) to reach Gatineau.

VISITOR INFORMATION

Contact Tourisme Outaouais. ✉ *103 rue Laurier, Gatineau* ☏ *819/778–2222* ⊕ *www.tourismeoutaouais.com.*

MONTEBELLO

130 km (80 miles) west of Montréal.

Located on the banks of the Ottawa River, this little village is best known for the Fairmont Le Château Montebello, a spectacular hotel touted as the largest log cabin in the world. Given the town's relative proximity to Ottawa, the nation's capital, more than a few world leaders and dignitaries have visited Montebello for one of the many international summits hosted by the Château since it was built in 1930. The Outaouais in general is well-known for the rugged beauty of its wilderness, and even in this more populated southern section of the region there's still excellent fishing, hunting, canoeing, hiking, and wildlife-spotting, with a series of hiking paths starting right beside the Château Montebello. Even if an expedition into the bush isn't quite your thing, you can still get up close to the local wildlife in a more controlled environment at Parc Omega, home to a wide variety of indigenous species and domestic animals.

GETTING HERE AND AROUND

From Montréal, take Autoroute 50 West for 130 km (80 miles); it's about a 90-minute trip.

VISITOR INFORMATION

Contact Montebello Tourist Information Office. ✉ *Gare de Montebello, 502-A rue Notre-Dame* ☏ *819/423–5602* ⊕ *www.tourismeoutaouais.com.*

EXPLORING

FAMILY **Parc Omega.** In the 1,800 acres of hills, valleys, rivers, and streams that make up the park, visitors drive along designated trails to view wild animals roaming free in their beautiful natural environment. These include bear, Alpine ibexes, buffalo, wolves, elk, and more. There are also walking trails among nonaggressive species like white-tailed deer, with caged golf-cart rental available in summer to save the legwork. Also in summer, you can visit farm animals in the restored 19th-century Léopold's Farm and see a birds of prey show. ✉ *399 Rte. 323 N*

☎ *819/423–5487* ⊕ *www.parc-omega.com* ⊟ *C$23–C$28, depending on season* ⊙ *Last admission 2 hrs before closing.*

WHERE TO EAT AND STAY

$
CANADIAN

✕ **La Belle Bédaine Casse-Croûte.** If you're looking for elegant dining keep on going, but if you're after a bit of local color, a cold beer, a good burger, a steamie (hot dog), or maybe a sample of Québec's famed poutine, then La Belle Bédaine (which translates as "the happy belly") is just the place. Its good and basic menu comes with a terrace overlooking the river. **Known for:** breakfast menu; steamies; poutine. $ *Average main: C$7* ✉ *664 rue Notre-Dame* ☎ *819/423–5053* ⊟ *No credit cards.*

$$$
ITALIAN

✕ **Le Napoleon.** In what is basically a one-street town, this restaurant's reputation for serving outstanding food at affordable prices stands out, and the knowledgeable, personable waitstaff does, too. Though the cuisine is primarily Italian, some Mediterranean, French, and Quebecois influences are also in evidence, backed up by a fairly extensive and reasonably priced wine list. **Known for:** great wine list; good food at good prices. $ *Average main: C$23* ✉ *489 rue Notre-Dame* ☎ *819/423–5555* ⊕ *www.le-napoleon.com* ⊟ *No credit cards* ⊙ *No lunch.*

$$$$
HOTEL
FAMILY
Fodor's Choice
★

🏨 **Fairmont Le Château Montebello.** On a bank of the Ottawa River, with its own marina, this grand log-built hotel provides rustic luxury, local flavor, beautiful grounds, great views, and heaps of activities—no wonder it's an annual family destination for many well-heeled Canadians. **Pros:** great place to bring children; indoor tennis; magnificent fireplace in lobby; state-of-the-art conference facility; beautiful pool and spa. **Cons:** small bathrooms; 90-minute drive from Montréal; no nearby restaurants of note; pricey, and a C$25 per room per night resort fee is added to your bill at checkout; carpeting in some rooms look a bit worn as does some of the furniture in the lounge. $ *Rooms from: C$350* ✉ *392 rue Notre-Dame* ☎ *819/423–6341, 866/540–4462* ⊕ *www.fairmont.com/montebello* ⇄ *211 rooms* ⍩ *No meals.*

GATINEAU

205 km (127 miles) west of Montréal.

This town on the northern edge of the Ottawa River is best known for the nearby Gatineau Park and the many outdoor activities that can be done here. For more history, visit the Canadian Museum of History, which emphasizes the changes the country has undergone, from the prehistoric past to the present day. From Gatineau, it's a short walk over the Alexandra Bridge to visit Ottawa, the nation's capital. The view from either side of the river is stunning.

GETTING HERE AND AROUND

From Montréal, take Autoroute 50 west for 205 km (127 miles); it's about a two-hour trip.

VISITOR INFORMATION

Contact Gatineau Tourist Information Office. ✉ *103 rue Laurier* ☎ *819/778–2222, 800/265–7822* ⊕ *www.tourismeoutaouais.com.*

9

EXPLORING

FAMILY **Canadian Museum of History.** Formerly known as the Canadian Museum of Civilization, this superb institution officially changed its name in 2013 when it received C$25 million in funding from the Canadian government in order to renovate and expand. More than 50,000 square feet of the existing museum has been renovated, and a new Canadian History Hall showcasing the people and events that have shaped Canada over the last 15,000 years was added in 2017. Other highlights include the First Peoples Hall, which has some 2,000 objects on display, and the Children's Museum. ⊠ *100 rue Laurier* ☎ *819/776–7000, 800/555–5621* ⊕ *www.historymuseum.ca* ✉ *C$20.*

FAMILY **Gatineau Park.** This massive park—nearly 364 square km (140 square miles)—brings nature lovers from all over throughout the year. You can hike up King Mountain on a challenging trail that takes you 300 meters (980 feet) above the Ottawa Valley, explore Lusk Cave, go camping, view the Luskville Falls, or swim at one of the six beaches here (there are also 50 lakes). In winter the cross-country skiing trails cover approximately 200 km (125 miles) of the park. From June to mid-October, you can use the park's south entrance on Taché Boulevard; stop at the reception center for visitor information. ⊠ *Gatineau* ☎ *819/827–2020* ⊕ *www.canadascapital.gc.ca/places-to-visit/gatineau-park* ✉ *C$10 per vehicle.*

WHERE TO EAT AND STAY

$$
CANADIAN
Fodor'sChoice
★

✕ **Edgar.** Wonderful homemade pastries such as pear-and-almond tarts, lemon-curd doughnuts, and chai scones have brought renown to this little place (only 11 seats), but there's more to it than that. Breakfast and lunch are always busy, and weekend brunch, served until 2 pm, brings a line out the door. **Known for:** weekend brunch; homemade pastries; cute terrace. $ *Average main: C$17* ⊠ *60 rue Bégin* ☎ *819/205–1110* ⊕ *www.chezedgar.ca* ▭ *No credit cards* ☉ *No dinner. Closed Mon.*

$$$$
HOTEL

⌂ **Moulin Wakefield Mill Hotel and Spa.** Part heritage mill with original features, part modern environmentally friendly building, this waterside hotel and spa on the edge of Gatineau Park has lots of character, wonderful views of the MacLaren Falls, and plenty of pampering on offer. **Pros:** walking distance to Gatineau Park; great views; pets allowed. **Cons:** hotel caters mostly to adults; expensive; hardwood floors in rooms in the main building are in need of refinishing. $ *Rooms from: C$299* ⊠ *60 chemin Mill* ☎ *888/567–1838, 819/459–1838* ⊕ *www.wakefieldmill.com* ⇆ *42 rooms* ⦿ *Breakfast.*

THE EASTERN TOWNSHIPS

The Eastern Townships (also known as les Cantons de l'Est, and formerly as l'Estrie) refers to the southeast corner of the province of Québec, which borders Vermont, New Hampshire, and Maine, and is known for its mountains, spas, charming small towns, lush forests, and many vineyards. In winter, the Townships are the place to be for serious ski and snowboard enthusiasts, boasting many of the province's highest peaks and most challenging trails. In summer, boating, swimming, sailing, golfing, in-line skating, hiking, and bicycling take over. And every fall the inns are booked solid with visitors eager to take in the brilliant foliage. Fall is also a good time to visit the wineries (although most are open all year). Because of its mild microclimate, the Townships area has become one of the more prominent wine regions in Canada, with a dozen of Québec's 33 commercial wineries.

There remains a sizable, albeit dwindling, English population here, mostly the descendants of Empire Loyalists who fled first the Revolutionary War and later the newly created United States of America. The Loyalists were followed, around 1820, by the first wave of Irish immigrants. Some 20 years later the potato famine sent more Irish pioneers to the Townships. The area became more Francophone after 1850, as French Canadians moved in to work on the railroad and in the lumber industry, but the region still looks more like New England than New France, with redbrick villages, tidy Protestant churches, and white clapboard farmhouses with big verandas. During the late 19th century, English families from Montréal and Americans from the border states began summering at cottages along the lakes.

WHEN TO GO

The Eastern Townships are best in fall, when the foliage is at its peak; the region borders Vermont and has the same dramatic colors. It's possible to visit wineries at this time, but you should call ahead, since harvest is a busy time.

GETTING HERE AND AROUND

For the Eastern Townships, take Autoroute 10 Est (the Autoroute des Cantons de l'Est) from Montréal, or U.S. 91 from New England, which becomes Autoroute 55 as it crosses the border into the Eastern Townships.

VISITOR INFORMATION

Contact **Tourisme Cantons-de-l'Est.** ✉ *20 rue Don-Bosco Sud, Sherbrooke* ☏ *819/820–2020, 800/355–5755* ⊕ *www.easterntownships.org.*

9

BROMONT

78 km (48 miles) east of Montréal.

The boating, camping, golf, horseback riding, swimming, tennis, biking, canoeing, fishing, hiking, cross-country and downhill skiing, and snowshoeing available here make this a place for all seasons. Bromont has the only night skiing in the Eastern Townships—and there's even a slope-side disco, Le Bromontais. The town also has more than 100 km (62 miles) of maintained trails for mountain bikers.

GETTING HERE AND AROUND

Bromont is about one hour from Montréal on Autoroute 10. Get off at Exit 78.

VISITOR INFORMATION

Contact **Bromont Tourism Office.** ✉ *15 boul. de Bromont* ☏ *877/276–6668, 450/534–2006* ⊕ *www.tourismebromont.com.*

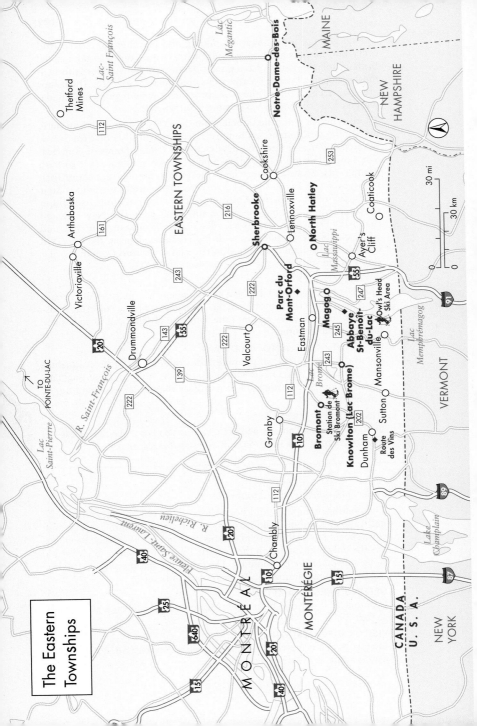

The Eastern Townships

MAINE

Lac Mégantic

Lac Saint-François

NEW HAMPSHIRE

Notre-Dame-des-Bois

Thetford Mines

112

161

EASTERN TOWNSHIPS

Arthabaska

Victoriaville

Cookshire

253

216

Sherbrooke

Lennoxville

North Hatley

Coaticook

243

Ayer's Cliff

Lac Massawippi

55

Victoriaville

55

Drummondville

143

222

Parc du Mont-Orford

Magog

247

Owl's Head Ski Area

20

20

R. Saint-François

222

139

Valcourt

222

Eastman

245

Abbaye St-Benoît-du-Lac

Mansonville

VERMONT

Lac Memphrémagog

TO POINTE-DU-LAC

Lac Saint-Pierre

243

Lac Brome

Sutton

112

Granby

Bromont

Station de Ski Bromont

Knowlton (Lac Brome)

202

Dunham

Route des Vins

10

R. Richelieu

Fleuve Saint-Laurent

112

89

Lac Champlain

20

Chambly

MONTÉRÉGIE

10

15

40

401

CANADA
U. S. A.

87

25

540

MONTRÉAL

NEW YORK

15

40

20

30 mi

30 km

EXPLORING

Fodor's Choice ★ **Route des Vins** (*Wine Route*). Make sure you bring along a designated driver for this Wine Route, which includes 22 wineries. Map out your chosen stops then travel from one to the next to learn about their history, local products and, best of all, sample the wine. Most wineries have an area outdoors where you can enjoy a picnic. ■ **TIP→ Call for hours as they may change from one season to the next.** ⊠ *Bromont* ☎ *888/811–4928* ⊕ *www.laroutedesvins.ca/en.*

Vignoble de l'Orpailleur. Established in 1982, this vineyard produces 11 wines, including its Double Gold medal-winning ice wine at the Finger Lakes International competition. Tours are given three times a day during the summer and you can stop by the museum, where you'll learn about the history and production of wine, from the cultivation of the vines to the bottling process. The patio restaurant is a nice place to take a break. ⊠ *1086 rue Bruce (Rte. 202), Dunham* ☎ *450/295–2763* ⊕ *www.orpailleur.ca.*

Vignoble Domaine Côtes d'Ardoise. This winery, opened in 1980, was one of the first to set up shop in the area, and is considered to be the oldest vineyard still in operation in Québec. On nearly 30 acres of land, 50,000 vines go to produce some award-winning reds, whites, rosés, and ice wines. Visit for a tasting and enjoy a picnic on the grounds. From July through October, a sculpture garden showcases the works of more than 80 artists, primarily from the area. ⊠ *879 rue Bruce (Rte. 202), Dunham* ☎ *450/295–2020* ⊕ *www.cotesdardoise.com.*

Vignoble Les Trois Clochers. This lovely winery is another great stop along the wine route. It produces a dry, fruity white from Seyval grapes as well as several other white, red, and ice wines. In addition to the tastings, you can take a tour of the grounds (reservations required), stroll along the trails, and stop for a picnic before you move on to the next stop. ⊠ *341 chemin Bruce (Rte. 202), Dunham* ☎ *450/295–2034* ⊕ *www.3clochers.com.*

WHERE TO STAY

$ HOTEL **Auberge Château Bromont.** Among the rolling hills of the Townships and with great views of the local countryside from every room, this modern hotel is part of the Domaine Château-Bromont complex, and well priced, considering all the amenities available. **Pros:** outstanding views from each room; friendly staff; close to ski hill and golf course. **Cons:** lack of an elevator makes it difficult for guests on the upper floors, especially those with ski equipment. $ *Rooms from: C$120* ⊠ *95 rue de Montmorency* ☎ *888/276–6668* ⊕ *www.chateaubromont.com* ⇩ *40 rooms* ◎ *Breakfast.*

$$ HOTEL **Hôtel Château Bromont.** Massages, algae wraps, and aromatherapy are just a few of the services at this European-style resort, which also includes a large, Turkish-style *hammam* (steam room) and the Château Bromont Golf Course. **Pros:** outdoor hot tubs; friendly staff. **Cons:** some rooms are small, so check what you're getting when you book; windows facing the interior courtyard/indoor swimming pool do not open and those rooms can feel claustrophobic. $ *Rooms from: C$165* ⊠ *90 rue Stanstead* ☎ *450/534–3433, 888/276–6668* ⊕ *www.chateaubromont.com* ⇩ *156 rooms, 8 suites* ◎ *Breakfast; No meals; Some meals.*

SHOPPING

MARKETS

Fodor's Choice ★   **Bromont Five-Star Flea Market.** The gigantic sign on Autoroute 10 is hard to miss. More than 1,000 vendors at this indoor flea market sell T-shirts, household gadgets, and much more, on weekends (9–5) from April to the end of October. Shoppers come from as far away as Vermont. ⊠ *16 rue Lafontaine* ☎ *888/689–1255, 450/534–0440* ⊕ *www.mapbromont.com.*

SPAS

Fodor's Choice ★   **Balnea Réserve Thermale.** Tucked away in a forest and overlooking a lake, this strikingly contemporary spa takes advantage of its location with airbeds that float among lily pads, and tiers of sundecks with gorgeous views. In addition to steam rooms, saunas, and baths, Balnea also has 30 body treatments: you can bliss out with the gotu kola and green tea wrap, a chocolate and grape-seed massage, or yoga by the lake. Full- and half-day spa packages are available. During the summer, Balnea plays host to Summer of Chefs, a gourmet cooking competition that takes places over 10 Sundays and features 10 of Québec's best chefs who take over the kitchen and create their own menu inspired by ingredients available at the nature reserve. ⊠ *319 chemin du Lac Gale* ☎ *866/734–2110, 450/534–0604* ⊕ *www.balnea.ca.*

SPORTS AND THE OUTDOORS

GOLF

Royal Bromont. Designed by Graham Cooke, one of the most reputable golf course architects, the Royal Bromont was built in 1992 and is located in the center of Bromont. All 18 holes provide wonderful views of the surrounding mountains and, from novice to expert, this golf course is considered to be one of the top places to play. In 1994 the Royal Bromont hosted the Canadian PGA Championships. ⊠ *400 chemin Compton* ☎ *450/534–4653, 888/281–0017* ⊕ *www.royalbromont. com* 🖼 *C$35–C$50* ⚑ *18 holes, 7036 yards, par 72* ☞ *Facilities: driving range, putting green, golf carts, pull carts, rental clubs, pro shop, golf lessons, restaurant, bar.*

SKIING

FAMILY   **Station de Ski Bromont.** Not many metropolises in eastern North America can boast a 1,300-foot ski mountain within an hour's drive of downtown. That height and proximity has made Bromont very popular with Montréal day-trippers and weekenders. But Bromont's 156 trails (102 of them lighted at night) and nine lifts can handle the crowds quite comfortably. Like many other ski hills, Bromont operates as a year-round resort. In summer and early fall, you can take a mountain bike to the summit aboard a chairlift and test your nerves on one of 19 downhill trails, two of which are labeled "easy"—the rest are "hard" to "extreme." Part of the ski hill is converted into the **Bromont Aquatic Park** in summer, with a 24,000-square-foot wave pool and 25 rides and slides. ⊠ *150 rue Champlain* ☎ *450/534–2200, 866/276–6668* ⊕ *www. skibromont.com* 🖼 *Skiing C$42–C$62; aquatic park C$43; mountain biking C$45 per day.*

VENUE

Parc Équestre Olympique Bromont. If you love horses and competitions, the Bromont Equestrian Center is the place to visit. Once an Olympic site, it hosts show jumping, dressage, and pony club events, and, in late July, the annual International Bromont Equestrian competition. ✉ *450 chemin de Gaspé* ☎ *450/534–0787* 🌐 *www.parcequestrebromont.org.*

KNOWLTON (LAC BROME)

49 km (29 miles) northeast of Bromont, 101 km (63 miles) southeast of Montréal.

Knowlton is the quintessential Eastern Townships resort town, with Loyalist-era buildings, old inns, great antiques shops, and enticing pastry shops. Fortunately, it's managed to retain its particular identity, with a main street full of stores selling antiques, art, clothes, and gifts. Interesting little restaurants have taken residence in renovated clapboard houses painted every color of the rainbow. A frequent feature on most menus here is Brome Lake duck, served in many different ways. These internationally renowned birds are raised at a farm on the shores of Brome Lake just a few miles outside town. The main regional tourist office is in Foster, one of the other old villages that constitute Lac Brome, but walking maps of Knowlton are available from many local businesses.

GETTING HERE AND AROUND

To get from Montréal to Knowlton, take Autoroute 10 Est, head toward Autoroute 15 Sud, and take Exit 90 for QC–243.

VISITOR INFORMATION

Contact Lac Brome Tourism Office. ✉ *696 rue Lakeside, Lac Brome* ☎ *450/243–1221* 🌐 *www.tourismelacbrome.com/en/.*

EXPLORING

Fodor's Choice ★ **Musée Historique du Comté de Brome.** Here's a wonderful opportunity to learn about the Loyalists who settled the area after fleeing the American Revolution. Several buildings, including the former County Courthouse dating back to 1859, the old firehall (fire station), and a former school, house an eclectic collection that include 19th-century farm tools, Native Canadian arrowheads, and a military collection that includes uniforms and a World War 1 Fokker aircraft. The museum also maintains the Tibbits Hill Pioneer School, a stone schoolhouse built in 1834 to serve rural families—kids can find out what education was like in the mid-19th century. ✉ *130 chemin Lakeside, Knowlton* ☎ *450/243–6782* 🌐 *www.bromemuseum.com* 🎟 *C$8.*

WHERE TO STAY

$ B&B/INN Fodor's Choice ★ 🏨 **Auberge Knowlton.** A local landmark since 1849, when it was first a stagecoach stop, and later a railway stop, this rustic inn is a special-occasion venue for locals and a delightful option for visitors who relish period style and good regional cuisine. **Pros:** within walking distance of Knowlton's main attractions; dog-friendly; storage, repair kits, and so on, for bicycles; atmospheric restaurant serving good food. **Cons:** on the main road through town, so not the most scenic location; no elevator. [$] *Rooms from: C$130* ✉ *286 chemin Knowlton, Lac Brome, Knowlton* ☎ *450/242–6886* 🌐 *www.aubergeknowlton.ca* 🛏 *12 rooms* 🍴 *No meals.*

NIGHTLIFE AND PERFORMING ARTS

Théâtre Lac Brome. This local theater company stages plays, musicals, and productions of classic Broadway and West End hits from mid-June to Labor Day. It hosts professional and amateur English-language productions, but has also dabbled in bilingual productions as well as contemporary works by Canadian playwrights. The 175-seat, air-conditioned theater is behind the Knowlton Pub. ⊠ *9 Mount Echo Rd., Knowlton* 🖀 *450/242–2270 tickets* ⊕ *www.theatrelacbrome.ca.*

SHOPPING

ANTIQUES

Camlen. Cameron and Helen Brown (get it? Cam + len) import gorgeous antiques from China and Eastern Europe, create reproductions using old wood and sell antique Canadian pieces. Their passion for, and dedication to, the art of furniture making are reflected in the high standard of workmanship. ⊠ *110 Lakeside Rd., Knowlton* 🖀 *450/243–5785* ⊕ *www.camlenfurniture.com.*

CLOTHING

Rococo. Owners Carla Hadlock and Anita Laurent—the latter a former model—know fashion and style, and have many contacts in the business, so their collection of clothing and accessories includes many items obtained straight from manufacturers. You'll love the prices, too, which are a fraction of what you'd pay in a large retail store. ⊠ *293 Knowlton Rd., Knowlton* 🖀 *450/243–6948.*

ABBAYE ST-BENOÎT-DU-LAC

132 km (82 miles) southeast of Montréal.

At this impressive abbey, a bell juts above the trees like a fairy-tale castle. Combine its calm and peaceful surroundings with the chance to pick up some of the products sold here, including sparkling apple wine and some of the best cheese in Québec, and you have an expedition that makes for a very memorable experience.

GETTING HERE AND AROUND

To get to the abbey from Magog, take Route 112 and follow the signs for the side road (Rural Route 2, or rue des Pères) to the abbey.

EXPLORING

Fodor'sChoice ★ **Abbaye St-Benoît-du-Lac.** Built by the Benedictines in 1912 on a wooded peninsula on Lac Memphrémagog, the abbey is home to upward of 50 monks. They sell apples and sparkling apple wine from their orchards, as well as cheeses: Ermite (which means "hermit"), St-Benoît, and ricotta. Gregorian prayers are sung daily, and some masses are open to the public; call for the schedule. Dress modestly if you plan to attend vespers or other rituals, and avoid shorts. If you wish to experience a few days of retreat, there are guesthouses for both men and women. Reserve well in advance (a contribution of C$60 per night, which includes meals, is suggested). ⊠ *1 rue Main, St-Benoît-du-Lac* 🖀 *819/843–4080, 819/843–2861 store* ⊕ *www.st-benoit-du-lac.com* ⊘ *Closed major holidays.*

PARC DU MONT-ORFORD

19 km (12 miles) north of Abbaye St-Benoît-du-Lac, 115 km (72 miles) east of Montréal.

In addition to a multitude of year-round outdoor activities, such as hiking, camping, fishing, and snowmobiling, the provincial park here also serves as a nature reserve.

The annual music performances that make up the Festival Orford always draw crowds to the foot of Mont-Orford.

GETTING HERE AND AROUND

From Montréal, go east on Highway 10 (Autoroute des Cantons de l'Est), take Exit 115 onto QC–112 and go north onto QC–141 (chemin du Mont-Orford). Coming from the east, leave Highway 10 at Exit 118 and go north on QC–141.

EXPLORING

Festival Orford. Every summer, from the end of June to mid-August, a celebration of music and art brings classical music, jazz, and chamber orchestra concerts to Parc du Mont-Orford. It's organized by the Orford Arts Centre, which has been teaching students the art of classical music and performance since 1951. ⊠ *3165 chemin du Parc, Orford* ☎ *819/843–3981 tickets, 800/567–6155 in Canada* ⊕ *www.orford.mu/en.*

FAMILY **Parc du Mont-Orford.** The amount of activities seem almost endless at this 58-square-km (22-square-mile) park. Summertime sees hikers, campers, beach lovers, and canoers enjoying the grounds and in winter, showshoers and cross-country skiers take over. White-tailed deer and blue herons share the park with tourists. The scenery in the fall is spectacular, with vibrant orange, yellow, and red hues spreading across the landscape. ⊠ *3321 chemin du Parc, Orford* ☎ *819/843–9855, 800/665–6527* ⊕ *www.sepaq.com/pq/mor* 🎫 *C$9 a day.*

WHERE TO STAY

$ 🛏 **Estrimont Suites & Spa.** With a Nordic waterfall, Scandinavian baths,
HOTEL and relaxation yurt, plus nearby golf courses, riding stables, and ski hills, this attractive complex fits the bill for an active or relaxing break. **Pros:** very reasonably priced spa packages; excellent place for conferences or business retreats; two outdoor hot tubs in scenic surroundings. **Cons:** only one suite is wheelchair accessible. $ *Rooms from: C$145* ⊠ *44 av. de l'Auberge (Rte. 141 Nord), Orford* ☎ *800/567–7320, 819/843–1616* ⊕ *www.estrimont.ca* 🛏 *95 suites* 🍽 *Breakfast.*

MAGOG

11 km (6 miles) south of Parc du Mont-Orford, 118 km (74 miles) east of Montréal.

This bustling town is at the northern tip of Lac Memphrémagog, a large body of water that reaches into northern Vermont. Its sandy beaches are a draw, and it's also a good place for boating, bird-watching, sailboarding, horseback riding, dog sledding, in-line skating, golfing, bass fishing, and snowmobiling. You might even see Memphré, the lake's sea dragon, on one of the many lake cruises—there have been more than 100 sightings since 1816.

In recent years this formerly depressed textile town has enjoyed something of an economic and cultural rebirth, partially due to the substantial number of artists who have chosen to relocate to this welcoming, and relatively inexpensive, region of the province. The streets downtown are lined with century-old houses that have been converted into boutiques, stores, and eateries.

GETTING HERE AND AROUND

From Montréal to Magog, take Autoroute 10 Est, keep left toward Autoroute 15 Sud, and then take Exit 118 for QC–141.

VISITOR INFORMATION

Contact Memphrémagog Tourism Office. ✉ *2911 chemin Miletta* ☎ *819/843–2744, 800/267–2744* 🌐 *www.tourisme-memphremagog.com.*

EXPLORING

Le Cep d'Argent. The wines from this vineyard have won many awards, including four at a recent Finger Lakes International Wine Competition. The whites are very good, and the dessert wine—similar to a port and flavored with a little maple syrup—goes well with the local cheese. You can take a guided tour of the vineyard and winery, with a tasting of six different wines that's been paired with local foods, for C$20, or participate in a discovery visit for families, in which adult family members can taste five different products for C$13. In the new Interpretation Centre you can learn about the traditional ways of making champagne. ✉ *1257 chemin de la Rivière* ☎ *819/864–4441, 877/864–4441* 🌐 *www.cepdargent.com.*

WHERE TO STAY

$$ B&B/INN 🏨 **Auberge l'Étoile Sur-le-Lac.** The majority of rooms at this popular inn on Magog's waterfront have lake views, including some with fireplaces. **Pros:** right on Lac Memphrémagog; various packages available; direct access to the popular cycling route Verte; Magog attractions all within comfortable walking distance. **Cons:** not recommended for guests who are looking for isolated, peaceful surroundings. [$] *Rooms from: C$180* ✉ *1200 rue Principale Ouest* ☎ *819/843–6521, 800/567–2727* 🌐 *www.etoile-sur-le-lac.com* 🛏 *52 rooms, 8 condos* 🍴 *Some meals.*

$$$$ HOTEL 🏨 **Spa Eastman.** The oldest spa in Québec, once a simple health center, has evolved into a bucolic haven for anyone seeking rest and therapeutic treatments, including lifestyle and weight-management counseling. **Pros:** dinner included in room rate; a totally relaxing and peaceful respite; wheelchair-accessible rooms. **Cons:** no phone or TV might prove too isolating for some. [$] *Rooms from: C$420* ✉ *895 chemin des Diligences, Eastman* ☎ *450/297–3009, 800/665–5272* 🌐 *www.spa-eastman.com* 🛏 *44 rooms* 🍴 *All meals.*

NIGHTLIFE AND PERFORMING ARTS

Auberge Orford. Come by boat and you can moor right alongside this patio bar that overlooks the Magog River. Sometimes there's live entertainment, but when musicians aren't around, the flocks of ducks lining up alongside the café to beg crumbs from patrons' plates keep patrons entertained. ✉ *20 rue Merry Sud* ☎ *819/843–9361, 877/843–9361* 🌐 *www.auberge-orford.com.*

Café St-Michel. In a century-old building, this pub, outfitted in shades of charcoal and ebony, serves Tex-Mex food, pasta, fish-and-chips and local beers. Its patio bar, at Magog's main intersection, may not be peaceful, but it's a great spot to watch the world go by. *Chansonniers* (singers) belt out popular hits for a full house on Friday and Saturday evening starting at 6 pm. ✉ *503 rue Principale Ouest* ☎ *819/868–1062* ⊕ *www.cafestmichel.com.*

Microbrasserie La Memphré. Named after the monster said to lurk in Lake Memphrémagog, La Memphré dates back to the 1800s, when it belonged to Magog's first mayor. Now a microbrewery, it serves Swiss-cheese fondue, sausages with beer mustard, onion soup, and panini—all good accompaniments for a cold one. Hope for a train to go by when you're in the restaurant: if you hear the horns, a pitcher of house beer is only C$12! ✉ *12 rue Merry Sud* ☎ *819/843–3405* ⊕ *www.lamic.ca.*

SPORTS AND THE OUTDOORS
GOLF

Golf Owl's Head. This course, close to the Vermont border, has some spectacular views. Laid out with undulating fairways, bent-grass greens, and 64 sand bunkers, the course, designed by Graham Cooke, is surrounded by mountain scenery. The clubhouse, a stunning timber-and-fieldstone structure with five fireplaces and 45-foot-high ceilings, is a popular watering hole. ✉ *181 chemin Owl's Head, Mansonville* ☎ *450/292–3342, 800/363–3342, 450/292–3666 direct line to golf club* ⊕ *www.owlshead.com* ⛳ *C$44 weekdays, C$52 weekends* ⛳ *18 holes, 6710 yards, par 72* ⛳ *Facilities: driving range, putting green, pitching area, golf carts, pull carts, rental clubs, pro shop, golf lessons, restaurant, bar.*

Manoir des Sables golf course. Between Mount Orford and Lake Memphrémagog, this resort course comes with some of the best scenery in the Eastern Townships and has been voted a favorite course in Québec. The best views are from the second, third, and fourth holes. Several water hazards are dotted around the course, with streams cutting across more than half the fairways and ponds calling for accurate shots onto some greens. ✉ *90 av. des Jardins, Orford* ☎ *819/847–4299, 866/656–4747* ⊕ *www.hotelsvillegia.com* ⛳ *Weekdays C$36, weekends C$40* ⛳ *18 holes, 6352 yards, par 71.*

Mont-Orford Golf Club. This venerable course in the heart of the national park winds through forested land, with the peak of Mont-Orford visible from many of its greens. There are some tricky holes—look out for the pond to the right of the fairway and an uphill putt on the 5th, the two streams cutting across the 8th, and the sharp dog-leg on the 13th. All in all, it's a satisfying challenge and an exceptionally scenic course to play. ✉ *3074 chemin du Parc* ☎ *819/843–5688, 866/673–6731* ⊕ *www.orford.com* ⛳ *C$39 weekdays, C$42 weekends* ⛳ *18 holes, 6095 yards, par 72* ⛳ *Facilities: golf carts, rental clubs, pro shop, lessons, restaurant.*

SKIING

Owl's Head Ski Area. On the Knowlton Landing side of Lake Memphrémagog, Owl's Head is great for skiers seeking sparser crowds—and the views from its peak are truly exceptional. It has eight lifts, a 1,772-foot vertical drop, and 50 trails, including a 4-km (2½-mile) intermediate run, the longest such run in the Eastern Townships. It's also one of the least expensive hills in the Townships. ✉ *40 chemin du Mont-Owl's Head* ☎ *450/292–3342, 800/363–3342* 🌐 *www.owlshead.com* 🎫 *C$55 day ski pass.*

NORTH HATLEY

10 km (6 miles) east of Magog, 133 km (83 miles) east of Montréal.

Along with Frelighsburg and Knowlton, North Hatley is undoubtedly one of Québec's prettiest villages. The small resort town on the tip of Lac Massawippi has a theater as well as some excellent inns and restaurants. Set among hills and farms, it was discovered by rich vacationers in the early 1900s, and has been drawing visitors ever since. It was particularly popular with magnates from the American South who were looking for a cool summer refuge that wasn't controlled by the Yankees. The result is that some of the village's most majestic buildings are more reminiscent of Georgia than Vermont.

GETTING HERE AND AROUND

From Montréal to North Hatley, take Autoroute 10 Est to Autoroute 15 Sud, and then take Exit 121 to get onto Autoroute 55 Sud. Take Exit 29 for QC–108.

WHERE TO EAT AND STAY

$$ AMERICAN

🍴 **Pilsen Pub.** Massawippi pale and brown ales and a vast selection of microbrews and imports are all on tap here. Pub food is served both in the upstairs dining room and in the tavern. **Known for:** a vast selection of microbrews and imports on tap; burgers and homemade soups; lively, welcoming atmosphere. [$] *Average main: C$18* ✉ *55 rue Principale* ☎ *819/842–2971* 🌐 *www.pilsen.ca.*

$$$$ HOTEL Fodor's Choice ★

🏨 **Manoir Hovey.** Overlooking Lac Massawippi, with a private beach, this elegant retreat feels rather like a private estate, with many activities, such as tennis, boating, and bicycling, included in the room rate. **Pros:** lakeside setting; secluded; historic buildings; wheelchair accessible. **Cons:** main restaurant overpriced; grounds often taken over by weddings on weekends; 10% tax added to Saturday night room rate. [$] *Rooms from: C$290* ✉ *575 chemin Hovey* ☎ *819/842–2421, 800/661–2421* 🌐 *www.manoirhovey.com* 🛏 *43 rooms* 🍽 *Some meals.*

NIGHTLIFE AND PERFORMING ARTS

Fodor's Choice ★

Piggery. Enriching the Townships' cultural landscape since 1965, this theater, in a former pig barn in the mountains, is known for showcasing English-language plays, with a focus on Canadian playwrights. Concerts, magic shows, and comedy acts also feature in a season that runs mid-May through October. ✉ *215 chemin Simard* ☎ *819/842–2431* 🌐 *www.piggery.com.*

SHERBROOKE

21 km (12 miles) northeast of North Hatley, 130 km (81 miles) east of Montréal.

Sherbrooke bills itself as the *Reine des Cantons de l'Est* (Queen of the Eastern Townships), and with a population of more than 150,000, it's far and away the region's largest and most important city. The Loyalists who founded the city in the 1790s and who named it for Sir John Coape Sherbrooke, one of Canada's pre-Confederation governors-general, used the power of the Rivière St-François to build a strong industrial base. Though the city's economic importance has waned, it still has significant manufacturing and textile plants, and Wellington Street, in the downtown area, is experiencing a significant face-lift, with trendy restaurants, bars, and clubs now occupying once-vacant lots.

A highlight of the town is the many beautifully painted murals on the sides of downtown buildings, and you can follow a self-guiding 6-km (4-mile) tour of them, starting from the tourist office on rue King.

GETTING HERE AND AROUND

Sherbrooke is easy to get to by car via Autoroute 10. From the United States, it's an easy stop on the way to Montréal if you cross the border via Interstate 91 and take Autoroute 55. There are also frequent bus connections between Montréal and Sherbrooke. The city is large and quite hilly, so getting around on foot can be difficult. However, there's a well-developed bus system.

VISITOR INFORMATION

Contact Sherbrooke Tourism Office. ⊠ *785 rue King Ouest* ☎ *819/821–1919, 800/561–8331* ⊕ *www.destinationsherbrooke.com.*

EXPLORING

FAMILY **Musée de la Nature et des Sciences.** Fun and educational for the whole family, this natural history museum utilizes imaginative multisensory displays with state-of-the-art light and sound effects—the buzzing of mosquitoes may be *too* lifelike—and hands-on displays to enhance the experience. Long-running temporary exhibits include Terra Mutantes, a geological experience portraying the birth of the Appalachian Mountains, and AlterAnima, exploring animal life in a mythical forest. Both will be available until May or June 2020. ⊠ *225 rue Frontenac* ☎ *819/564–3200, 877/434–3200* ⊕ *www.naturesciences.qc.ca* ☒ *C$13* ☾ *Closed Mon and Tues in Sept–May.*

Musée des Beaux-Arts de Sherbrooke. This fine-arts museum has a permanent exhibit on the history of art in the region from 1800 to the present. More than 10 exhibits per year are staged in its three galleries, with an emphasis on artists from the Eastern Townships. ⊠ *241 rue Dufferin* ☎ *819/821–2115* ⊕ *www.mbas.qc.ca* ☒ *C$10* ☾ *Closed Mon.*

WHERE TO EAT

$$$$
BISTRO
FAMILY
✗**Auguste.** Auguste placed Sherbrooke on the foodie map when it opened in 2008, and it continues to impress. Local ingredients take pride of place in this minimalist bistro-style restaurant, which features dishes like mushroom risotto or sweet potato ravioli. **Known for:** pouding chômeur (poor man's pudding) drenched in maple syrup; free

children's dinner menu Sun.–Wed. [$] *Average main: C$33* ✉ *82 rue Wellington N* ☎ *819/565–9559* 🌐 *www.auguste-restaurant.com* 🕒 *No brunch weekdays.*

NIGHTLIFE AND PERFORMING ARTS

Centennial Theatre. On the campus of Bishops University, this 600-seat theater presents a roster of jazz, classical, and rock concerts, as well as opera, dance, mime, and children's theater. ✉ *2600 rue College* ☎ *819/822–9692* 🌐 *www.centennialtheatre.ca.*

Le Vieux Clocher de l'Université de Sherbrooke. Le Vieux Clocher de l'Université de Sherbrooke presents music, from classical to jazz, and a variety of theater and comedy shows. ✉ *2500, boul. de l'Université* ☎ *819/820–1000* 🌐 *www.centrecultureludes.ca/.*

SHOPPING

CRAFTS

Boutique des Métiers d'Art. Stop in this charming little shop filled with crafts made by artists from the Eastern Townships. Jewelry, kitchenware, and clothing are just a few of the items you'll want to take home. ✉ *121 rue Frontenac* ☎ *819/823–0221* 🌐 *www.metiersdartestrie.com* 🕒 *Closed Mon. and Tues.*

NOTRE-DAME-DES-BOIS

72 km (43 miles) east of Sherbrooke, 204 km (127 miles) east of Montréal.

Notre-Dame-des-Bois is a sleepy little one-street village just north of the Maine border. It sits in the shadow of one of the region's tallest and steepest mountains—Mont-Mégantic, which soars 576 meters (1,890 feet) above the surrounding plain, with a height of 3,601 feet above sea level. In 2007, the Mont-Mégantic Observatory area was declared the first International Dark-Sky Reserve, in recognition of the lack of light pollution that provides some of the clearest night skies in Québec, a quality that attracts stargazers, both professional and amateur.

GETTING HERE AND AROUND

Count on a three-hour journey from Montréal, some of it over paved but bumpy secondary roads. To get here, follow Autoroute 10 east past Sherbrooke to its end near Ascot Corner, then follow Route 112 to East Angus, then Route 253 to Cookshire, and finally Route 212 through L'Avenir to Notre-Dame-des-Bois. If you want to make the journey comfortably, plan to stay overnight somewhere rather than just coming for the day.

EXPLORING

Astrolab du Mont-Mégantic (*Mont-Mégantic's Observatory*). Both amateur stargazers and serious astronomers head to this observatory, located in a beautifully wild and mountainous area that in 2007 became the first ever International Dark-Sky Reserve. The observatory is at the summit of the Townships' second-highest mountain (3,601 feet above sea level and 1,890 feet above the surrounding landscape), whose northern face records annual snowfalls rivaling any in North America. A joint venture of the University of Montréal and Laval University, the observatory has a powerful telescope, the largest on the East Coast. In the Astrolab at the welcome center at the mountain's base, you can view an exhibition and a multimedia show to learn about the night sky. ■ **TIP→ Hours vary depending on the season, so check website for updated information.** ✉ *Parc Mégantic, 189 Rte. du Parc* ☎ *819/888–2941, 888/665–6527* 🌐 *www.astrolab-parc-national-mont-megantic.org* 🎫 *Observatory and Astrolab: C$19 daytime, C$21–C$25 at night. Additional fee of C$9 charged to enter Parc Mégantic* ✍ *Reservations essential.*

Parc du Mont-Mégantic. If you're short on time or don't feel like a hike you can take a shuttle bus to the top of Mont-Mégantic for spectacular views of Québec, Maine, New Hampshire, and on really clear days, Vermont. But if you want the full experience, walk up. The park has 50 km (31 miles) of hiking trails that are also open in winter to snowshoers and cross-country skiers. For a real adventure, you can stay overnight in one of the park's rustic shelters. ✉ *189 Rte. du Parc* ☎ *819/888–2941, 800/665–6527* 🌐 *www.sepaq.com/pq/mme/* 🎫 *C$9.*

WHERE TO STAY

$ B&B/INN Fodor's Choice ★

🏨 **Aux Berges de l'Aurore.** From its lofty perch, this delightful century-old inn has spectacular views day and night—it's within the International Dark-Sky Reserve—and is less than a minute's drive from Mont Mégantic National Park and the Astrolab. **Pros:** great scenery; close to area activities; delicious breakfasts; hiking trails on the property. **Cons:** minimum two-night stay holiday weekends and some other times; threadbare towels; no shampoo or conditioner provided; some bathrooms have musty odor. [$] *Rooms from: C$120* ✉ *139 Rte. du Parc* ☎ *819/888–2715* 🌐 *www.auberge-aurore.qc.ca* 🛏 *3 rooms, 2 suites* 🍴 *Breakfast; Some meals.*

QUÉBEC CITY

WELCOME TO QUÉBEC CITY

TOP REASONS TO GO

★ **See the Château Frontenac:** Even if you're not staying at Québec City's most famous landmark, make sure to pop into one of the world's legendary hotels.

★ **Dine at world-class restaurants:** High-end bistros; hip, hole-in-the-wall cafés; amazing breweries and wine bars: Québec City has it all.

★ **Explore La Citadelle:** Québec City's highest perch is the largest fortified base in North America and site of the daily Changing of the Guard in summer.

★ **Play on the Plains of Abraham:** With cross-country skiing and sledding in winter and picnicking, concerts, and in-line skating in summer, this huge park is a popular place for outdoor fun.

★ **From Carnival to Festival:** For three weekends in January and February, the city hosts one of the biggest winter festivals in the world. In July, up to 80,000 people cheer some of the biggest rock and pop stars at the open-air Summer Festival.

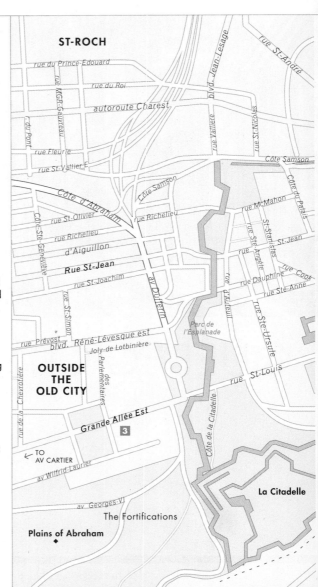

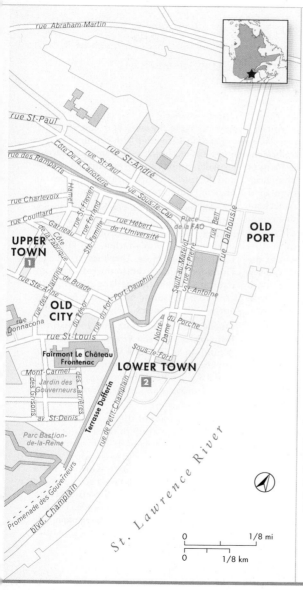

The central portions of Lower Town (Basse-Ville) and Upper Town (Haute-Ville) make up the Old City (Vieux-Québec). You can walk from one to the other, or ride the funicular that runs between them. Beyond the walls, the main street is the Grande-Allée, which approaches the Old City from the west.

1 Upper Town. Crowning Cap Diamant and partially surrounded by the Fortifications, Upper Town hosts the city's main attractions, including the majestic Château Frontenac and La Citadelle, a star-shape fortress. The sweeping views of the St. Lawrence River, the Laurentian Mountains to the north, and the Appalachians to the south are all enchanting.

2 Lower Town. A maze of cobblestone streets with tucked-away cafés, boutique hotels, artisan shops, and art galleries characterizes Lower Town.

3 Outside the Old City. Rue St-Jean, avenue Cartier, the Grande-Allée, and the St-Roch district all have restaurants, shops, and nightlife worth checking out.

10

A WALK THROUGH QUÉBEC CITY'S HISTORY

Exploring Québec City's history can be an all-consuming pastime—and a rewarding one. The walk outlined here takes you through much of it, but feel free to pursue the Old City's inviting little detours.

Outside the Old City

The best place to begin a journey through the history of New France is at the end. Start your tour at the **Wolfe Monument,** on the far west side of the **Plains of Abraham.** It was here in 1759 that British General James Wolfe extinguished France's dreams of a North American empire and set off the English-French divergence that has both enriched and plagued Canada's history.

The Plains of Abraham was where the famous battle took place. Today it's a pleasant and expansive city park with trees, lawns, and meandering paths with sweeping views of the St. Lawrence River.

Make your way over to the Fortifications and the Old City via the northern side of the Plains of Abraham, along the **Grande Allée,** through the residential neighborhood of **Montcalm,** home to gorgeous 19th-century neo-Gothic and Queen Anne–style mansions and **Hôtel du Parlement.**

The Fortifications

The end of the Grand Allée is Porte St-Louis. Turn right down the Côte de la Citadelle, which leads to **La Citadelle.** Something of a microcosm of Canada's sometimes contrarian cultural character, the fortress is home to the Royal 22e Régiment, a crack military unit that speaks French but dresses in the bearskin hats and red tunics of a British guards unit for ceremonial parades. Don't miss the daily Changing of the Guard ceremony.

Upper Town

Beyond **Porte St-Louis,** you can imagine yourself in 17th- and 18th-century France. Steep-roofed houses with small windows crowd a tangle of narrow, curving streets and the rattle of horse-drawn carriages on ancient cobblestones adds to the illusion.

The **Maison Jacquet** on rue St-Louis looks exactly as it did when it was built in 1677 and the **Maison Kent** was once the home of Queen Victoria's father, the Duke of Kent. **Le Couvent des Ursulines** at 12 rue Donnacona has a museum featuring an exhibit of magnificent lace embroidery created by Ursuline nuns in the 19th and early 20th centuries.

Québec City's most famous building, the **Fairmont Le Château Frontenac,** is at the beginning of **Terrasse Dufferin,** which is worth a stroll for sweeping views of the St. Lawrence River before you get on the funicular to reach Lower Town.

Lower Town

Once at the base of this cable-connected elevator, you end up in the 17th-century **Maison Louis-Jolliet,** built before he paddled off to explore the Mississippi River. From here, it's a short walk to **Place Royale,** a square graced by a statue of the Sun King Louis XIV, and considered to be the birthplace of New France. The last jaunt is along **rue du Petit-Champlain,** the oldest street in the city, lined with shops and cafés.

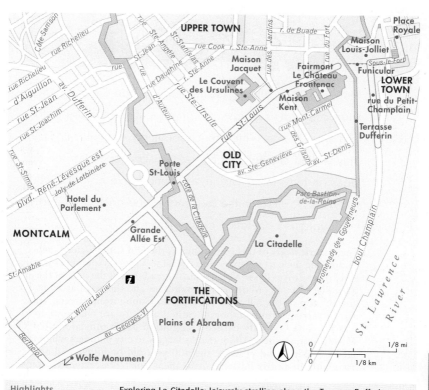

Highlights	Exploring La Citadelle; leisurely strolling along the Terrasse Dufferin; walking along rue du Petit-Champlain in the Old City.
Where to Start	The Wolfe Monument, on the far western side of the Plains of Abraham outside the walls of the city.
Length	About 3 km (2 miles).
Where to End	On rue du Petit-Champlain, in the Lower Town section of the Old City.
Best Time to Go	If you want to avoid crowds in summer, go on a weekday morning.
Worst Time to Go	A cold winter day.
Editor's Choice	Strolling along the tree-lined streets off Grande Allée in Montcalm; riding the funicular from Upper Town to Lower Town; standing in historic Place Royale.

Updated by
Rémy Charest

Québec City's alluring setting atop Cape Diamond (Cap Diamant) evokes a past of high adventure, military history, and exploration. This French-speaking capital city is the only walled city north of Mexico. Visitors come for the delicious and inventive cuisine, the remarkable historical continuity, and to share in the seasonal exuberance of the largest Francophone population outside France.

The historic heart of this community is the Old City (Vieux-Québec), comprising the part of Upper Town (Haute-Ville) surrounded by walls and Lower Town (Basse-Ville), which spreads out at the base of the hill from Place Royale. Many sets of staircases and the popular funicular link the top of the hill with the bottom. Cobblestone streets, horse-drawn carriages, and elaborate cathedrals here are charming in all seasons. The Old City earned recognition as an official UNESCO World Heritage site in 1985, thanks largely to city planners who managed to update and preserve the 400-year-old buildings and attractions without destroying what made them worth preserving. The most familiar icon of the city, Fairmont Château Frontenac, is set on the highest point in Upper Town, where it holds court over the entire city.

Sitting proudly above the confluence of the St. Lawrence and St. Charles rivers, the city's famous military fortification, La Citadelle, built in the early 19th century, remains the largest of its kind in North America. In summer, visitors should try to catch the Changing of the Guard, held every morning at 10 am; you can get much closer to the guards here than at Buckingham Palace in London.

Enchanting as it is, the Old City is just a small part of the true Québec City experience. Think outside the walls and explore St-Roch, a downtown hot spot, which has artsy galleries, foodie haunts, and a bustling square. Cruise the Grande-Allée and avenue Cartier to find a livelier part of town dotted with nightclubs and fun eateries. Or while away the hours in St-Jean-Baptiste, a neighborhood with trendy shops and hipster hangouts.

QUÉBEC CITY PLANNER

WHEN TO GO

Winter can be formidable, but the city stays alive—especially during the popular Winter Carnival. Spring is short and sweet with the *cabanes à sucre* (sugar shacks) bringing fresh maple goodies. In summer, the city's terraces and courtyards open and everyone comes out to enjoy the sunshine. In late September and early October, the region's foliage blazes with color.

GETTING HERE AND AROUND

The Funiculaire du Vieux-Québec, a small elevator up the side of the steep embankment, travels between Upper and Lower towns. Another option, and a good workout, is to take one of the sets of stairs that start in Upper Town and end at the Quartier du Petit Champlain in Lower Town. Renting a car isn't recommended unless you're taking day trips outside the city.

AIR TRAVEL

If you're flying in, Jean-Lesage International Airport is about 19 km (12 miles) northwest of downtown. Driving into town, take Route 540 (Autoroute Duplessis) to Route 175 (boulevard Laurier). The ride takes about 30 minutes. Taxis are available immediately outside the airport exit near the baggage-claim area. A ride into the city costs about C$34.

BUS TRAVEL

Bus service in Québec City is an effective way to go from the Vieux-Québec to other parts of the city, particularly using the Metrobus lines (those with an 800 number). C$8.50 for a one-day ticket, C$3.50 for a one-way trip.

CAR TRAVEL

Montréal and Québec City are linked by Autoroute 20 on the south shore of the St. Lawrence River and by Autoroute 40 on the north shore. On both highways, the ride between the two cities is about 240 km (150 miles) and takes about three hours. U.S. I–87 in New York, U.S. I–89 in Vermont, and U.S. I–91 in New Hampshire connect with Autoroute 20, as does Highway 401 from Toronto. Driving northeast out of Montréal on Autoroute 20, follow signs for Pont Pierre-Laporte (Pierre Laporte Bridge) as you approach Québec City. After you've crossed the bridge, take the exit to boulevard Laurier (Route 175), which becomes the Grande-Allée.

10

CRUISE SHIP TRAVEL

Charming shops and cobblestone streets greet visitors arriving to Québec City by boat. The cruise port, located on rue Dalhousie in Petite Champlain, is on the same street as the Musée de la Civilisation and just a few streets away from Place Royale. Take the (C$2) funicular on Petit-Champlain to get close to the Chateau Frontenac and stroll along Terrasse Dufferin.

TRAIN TRAVEL

VIA Rail, Canada's passenger rail service, has service between Montréal and Québec City. The trip takes less than three hours. One-way tickets cost C$89, but early reservation rates can be as low as C$29. A taxi from the Gare du Palais train station to the Fairmont Le Château Frontenac is about C$8.

VISITOR INFORMATION

Québec City Tourist Information. ✉ *12 rue Sainte-Anne, Upper Town* ☎ *418/641–6290, 877/266–5687* ⊕ *www.quebecregion.com.*

UPPER TOWN

No other place in Canada has so much history squeezed into such a small spot. Upper Town was a barren, windswept cape when Samuel de Champlain decided to build a fort here nearly 400 years ago. Now it's a major tourist destination surrounded by cannon-studded stone ramparts.

Home to the city's most famous sites, Upper Town's Old City offers a dramatic view of the St. Lawrence River and the countryside, especially from a ride on the funicular (C$2) or while walking along the Terrasse Dufferin, in front of the Château Frontenac. Historic buildings that house bars, cafés, and shops and hotels line the neighborhood's winding streets. A 3-mile-long wall neatly splices off this section of the city with entrances on rues St-Jean and St-Louis, Vieux-Québec's two main thoroughfares. The wall itself is a national historic monument. It began as a series of earthworks and wooden palisades built by French military engineers to protect the Upper Town from an inland attack following the siege of the city by Admiral Phipps in 1690. Over the next century, the French expended much time, energy, and money to strengthen the city's fortifications. After the fall of New France, the British were equally concerned about strengthening the city's defenses and built an earth-and-wood citadel atop Cap Diamant. Slowly, the British replaced the palisades that surrounded the city with the massive cut-stone wall that has become the city's trademark attraction. The crowning touch came after the War of 1812, with the construction of the cut-stone, star-shape citadel, perched high on Cap Diamant.

Like La Citadelle, most of the homes that line the narrow streets in Upper Town are made of granite cut from nearby quarries in the 1800s. The stone walls, copper roofs, and heavy wooden doors on the government buildings and high-steepled churches in the area also reflect the Upper Town's place as the political, educational, and religious nerve center of both the province and the country during much of the past four centuries.

GETTING HERE AND AROUND

Many people begin their tours in Upper Town, taking in the Château Frontenac, which is probably Québec City's top site, as well as the spectacular views. The Fortifications border this section of the city. Walk along rue d'Auteuil, between rues St-Louis and St-Jean, to get a good sense of where the wall divides the Old City.

10

Québec City's Terrasse Dufferin offers unobstructed views of the St. Lawrence River, with the peaks of the Laurentians and the Appalachians visible in the distance.

If coming from Lower Town, take the funicular. Otherwise, consider braving one of the many staircases that connect the top of the hill to the bottom and bypass the line, which gets long in the summer. Shops and restaurants provide the opportunity for a quick rest along the way.

TIMING

Plan to spend a whole day visiting the many sights and shops clustered around the Château Frontenac. Rue St-Jean offers many lunch options, or do as the locals do and grab a sandwich and head to a bench in one of the area's parks.

Leave at least a half-day for walking the walls of La Citadelle. Set out early in the morning to catch the Changing of the Guard (10 am in summer). Afterward, picnic on the Plains, or one of the terraces on the Grande Allée and avenue Cartier.

TOP ATTRACTIONS

Basilique Cathédrale Notre-Dame de Québec (*Our Lady of Québec Basilica Cathedral*). François de Laval, the first bishop of New France, once ruled a diocese that stretched to the Gulf of Mexico. Laval's original cathedral burned down and has been rebuilt several times, but the current basilica still has a chancel lamp that was a gift from Louis XIV, the Sun King.

The church's interior includes a canopy dais over the Episcopal throne, a ceiling of painted clouds decorated with gold leaf, and richly colored stained-glass windows. The large crypt was Québec City's first cemetery; more than 900 bodies are interred here, including 20 bishops and four governors of New France. Samuel de Champlain may be buried near the basilica; archaeologists have been searching for his tomb since 1950. There are panels that allow you to read about the history of this church. If you prefer, guided tours of the cathedral and crypt (by appointment only) are also available. The Centre d'animation François-de-Laval uses videos and pictures to illustrate the life of Québec's first bishop and founder of Canada's Catholic Church. A "holy door" was added to the church in 2014. ☒ *16 rue de Buade, Upper Town* ☎ *418/692–2533 church* ⊕ *notredamedequebec.org* ☒ *Basilica free, guided tour C$3.*

Centre Marie-de-l'Incarnation. In the lobby of the museum is the Centre Marie-de-l'Incarnation, a center with an exhibit and books for sale on the life of the Ursulines' first superior, who came from France and cofounded the convent. ☒ *10 rue Donnacona, Upper Town* ☎ *418/692–2523.*

Chapelle des Ursulines (*Ursuline Chapel*). Founded in 1639, the Couvent des Ursulines is the oldest institution of learning for women in North America. Its chapel is where French general Louis-Joseph Montcalm was buried after he died in the 1759 battle that decided the fate of New France. It also houses the finest examples of wood-carving anywhere in Québec, gilded by the nuns themselves. In 2001, Montcalm's remains were transferred to rest with those of his soldiers at the Hôpital Général de Québec's cemetery, at 260 boulevard Langelier. The exterior of the Ursuline Chapel was rebuilt in 1902, but the interior contains the original chapel, which took sculptor Pierre-Noël Levasseur from 1726 to 1736 to complete. The Ursulines is still an active elementary school today. ☒ *2 rue du Parloir, Upper Town* ☎ *418/694–0694* ⊕ *www.ursulines-uc.com* ☒ *Free* ⊙ *Closed Mon. year-round, and closed Tues.–Fri., Nov.–Apr.*

Fodor's Choice ★ **Fairmont Le Château Frontenac.** The most photographed landmark in Québec City, this imposing turreted castle with a copper roof owes its name to the Comte de Frontenac, governor of the French colony between 1672 and 1698. Samuel de Champlain was responsible for Château St-Louis, the first structure to appear on the site of the Frontenac; it was built between 1620 and 1624 as a residence for colonial governors. In 1784 Château Haldimand was constructed here, but it was demolished in 1892. The original portions of the hotel opened the following year, one in a series of château-style hotels built across Canada to attract wealthy railroad travelers. It was remarkably luxurious for the time: guest rooms contained fireplaces, bathrooms, and marble fixtures, and a special commissioner purchased antiques for the establishment. The hotel was designed by New York architect Bruce Price, who also worked on Québec City's train station, Gare du Palais. The addition of a 20-story central tower in 1924 completed the hotel. Since then the Château, as it's called by locals, has accumulated a star-studded guest roster, including Prince William and Kate Middleton, Queen Elizabeth II, Princess Grace of Monaco, Alfred Hitchcock and Ronald Reagan, as well as Franklin Roosevelt and Winston Churchill, who met here in 1943 and 1944 for two wartime conferences. ☒ *1 rue des Carrières, Upper Town* ☎ *418/692–3861* ⊕ *www.fairmont.com/frontenac.*

10

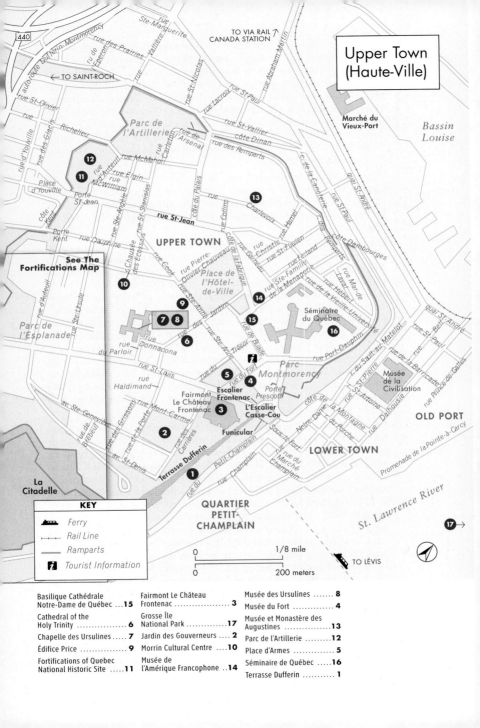

Upper Town (Haute-Ville)

TO VIA RAIL ↗
CANADA STATION

rue Ste-Marguerite

rue des Prairies

autoroute Dufferin-Montmorency

rue de Caperton

rue des Prairies

Vallière

← TO SAINT-ROCH

rue St-Olivier

rue St-Nicolas

rue Lacroix

rue St-Paul

rue St-Vallier

Marché du Vieux-Port

Bassin Louise

rue St-André

rue

Richelieu

rue des Glacis

rue d'Youville

Place d'Youville

côte Kent

Porte St-Jean

Porte Kent

Parc de l'Artillerie

rue d'Auteuil

rue Elgin

rue McMahon

rue McWilliam

rue St-Angèle

rue Ste-Angèle

côte du Palais

rue des Remparts

côte Dinan

côte de la Canoterie

quai St-André

N12

N11

rue St-Jean

UPPER TOWN

rue St-Stanislas

rue Ste-Ursule

rue d'Auteuil

See The Fortifications Map

rue des Écossais

la Chausée des Écossais

rue Cook

rue Ste-Anne

Place de l'Hôtel-de-Ville

côte de la Fabrique

rue Pierre-Olivier-Chauveau

rue Garneau

rue Ste-Famille

rue Christie

rue St-Flavien

rue Ferland

rue Ste-Famille

de la Ménagerie

rue Hamel

côte Dambourges

des Remparts

rue Mar de

rue Hébert

Laval

côte de la Vieille-Université

quai St-André

Parc de l'Esplanade

N10

N9

N7 N8

N6

rue des Jardins

rue Donnacona

rue du Parloir

rue St-Louis

rue Haldimand

N13 Charlevoix

N14

N15

Séminaire du Québec

N16

rue de Brézé

rue St-Flavien

rue Port-Dauphin

rue du Fort

Trésor

ℹ️

Parc Montmorency

rue Port-Dauphin

rue St-Paul

quai St-André

Bell

rue St-Paul

rue de la Barricade

Fairmont Le Château Frontenac

N3

Escalier Frontenac

L'Escalier Casse-Cou

N2

N5

N4

Porte Prescott

côte de la Montagne

rue du Sault-au-Matelot

rue St-Pierre

rue St-Antoine

rue Dalhousie

rue Prince-des-Gaîtes

Musée de la Civilisation

OLD PORT

rue du Marché Champlain

Funicular

Petit-Champlain

Notre-Dame

au Porche

LOWER TOWN

Terrasse Dufferin

N1

rue du

rue Petit-Champlain

sous-le-Fort

Promenade de la Pointe-à-Carcy

av. Ste-Geneviève

rue Mont-Carmel

av. St-Denis

rue des Carrières

rue de la Porte

rue St-Brébeuf

rue des Grisons

La Citadelle

QUARTIER PETIT-CHAMPLAIN

St. Lawrence River

N17 →

KEY

🚢	Ferry
┼┼┼	Rail Line
	Ramparts
ℹ️	Tourist Information

0 ———— 1/8 mile
0 ———— 200 meters

TO LÉVIS

THE HISTORY OF QUÉBEC CITY

Québec City was founded by French explorer Samuel de Champlain in 1608 and is the oldest municipality in the province. In the 17th century, the first French explorers, fur trappers, and missionaries arrived to establish a colony.

French explorer Jacques Cartier arrived in 1535, and although he did attempt to set up a (short-lived) colony, it was Champlain who founded "New France" some 70 years later and built a fort (called Place Royale today) on the banks of the St. Lawrence.

The British were persistent in their efforts to dislodge the French from North America, but the colonists of New France built forts and other military structures, such as a wooden palisade (defensive fence) that reinforced their position on top of the cliff. It was Britain's naval supremacy that ultimately led to New France's demise. After capturing all French forts east of Québec, General James Wolfe led his army to Québec City in the summer of 1759.

After a months-long siege, thousands of British soldiers scaled the heights along a narrow cow path on a moonless night. Surprised to see British soldiers massed on a farmer's field so near the city, French general Louis-Joseph Montcalm rushed out to meet them in what became known as the Battle of the Plains of Abraham. The French were routed in the 20-minute skirmish, which claimed the lives of both Wolfe and Montcalm. The battle symbolically marks the death of New France and the birth of British Canada.

British rule was a boon for Québec City. Thanks to more robust trade and large capital investments, the fishing, fur-trading, shipbuilding, and timber industries expanded rapidly.

Wary of new invasions from its former American colonies, the British also expanded the city's fortifications. They replaced the wooden palisades with a massive stone wall and built a star-shape fortress. Both structures still stand.

The constitution of 1791 established Québec City as the capital of Lower Canada, a position it held until 1840, when the Act of Union united Upper and Lower Canada and made Montréal the capital. When Canada was created in 1867 by the Act of Confederation, which united four colonial provinces (Québec, Ontario, New Brunswick, and Nova Scotia), Québec City was named the province's capital city, a role it continues to play. In Québec, however, the city is known officially as *la capitale nationale,* a reflection of the nationalist sentiments that have marked Québec society and politics since the 1960s.

Fortifications of Québec National Historic Site. In the early 19th century this was just a clear space surrounded by a picket fence and poplar trees. The French began building ramparts along the city's cliffs as early as 1690 to protect themselves from British invaders. However, the colonists had trouble convincing the French government to take the threat of invasion seriously, and when the British invaded in 1759 the walls were still incomplete. The British, despite attacks by the Americans during the American Revolution and the War of

Kids will love watching the Royal 22nd Regiment's Changing of the Guard every summer day at 10 am, from June 24 until the first Monday in September.

1812, took a century to finish them—and they never saw armed conflict. From June to early October, the park is the starting point for walking the city's 5 km (3 miles) of walls. There are two guided tours (adults C$9.80); one starts at the interpretation center and the other begins at Terrasse Dufferin. ⊠ *2, rue d'Auteuil, Upper Town* ⊕ *www.pc.gc.ca/fortifications.*

Fodor's Choice ★ **Jardin des Gouverneurs** (*Governors' Park*). In this small park just south of the Château Frontenac stands the **Wolfe-Montcalm Monument,** a 50-foot-tall obelisk that pays tribute to both a winning (English) and a losing (French) general. The monument recalls the 1759 battle on the Plains of Abraham, which essentially ended French rule here. British general James Wolfe lived only long enough to hear of his victory; French general Louis-Joseph Montcalm died shortly after Wolfe, with the knowledge that the city was lost. On the south side of the park is **avenue Ste-Geneviève,** lined with well-preserved Victorian houses dating from 1850 to 1900. Many have been converted to inns, B&Bs, and hotels. ⊠ *Upper Town.*

Fodor's Choice ★ **La Citadelle.** Built at the city's highest point, on Cap Diamant, the Citadelle is the largest fortified base in North America still occupied by troops. The 25-building fortress was intended to protect the port, prevent the enemy from taking up a position on the Plains of Abraham, and provide a refuge in case of an attack. Having inherited incomplete fortifications, the British completed the Citadelle as protection against French and, eventually, American attacks. However, by the time it was finished in 1832, the attacks against Québec City had ended.

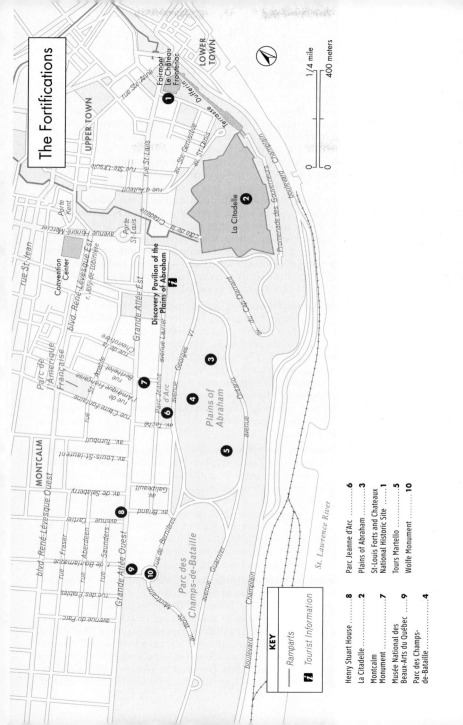

The Fortifications

UPPER TOWN

LOWER TOWN

Fairmont Le Château Frontenac **1**

La Citadelle **2**

Plains of Abraham

Parc des Champs-de-Bataille

Discovery Pavilion of the Plains of Abraham

Convention Center

MONTCALM

Parc de l'Amérique Française

St. Lawrence River

0   1/4 mile

0   400 meters

KEY

Ramparts

i Tourist Information

Henry Stuart House **8**

La Citadelle **2**

Montcalm Monument **7**

Musée National des Beaux-Arts du Québec **9**

Parc des Champs-de-Bataille **4**

Parc Jeanne d'Arc **6**

Plains of Abraham **3**

St-Louis Forts and Chateaux National Historic Site **1**

Tours Martello **5**

Wolfe Monument **10**

Since 1920 the Citadelle has served as a base for Canada's most storied French-speaking military formation, the Royal 22e Régiment (Royal 22nd Regiment), known across Canada as the Van Doos, from the French "vingt-deux" (22). Firearms, uniforms, and decorations from as far back as the 17th century are displayed in the **Musée du Royal 22e Régiment** (Royal 22nd Regiment Museum) in the former powder magazine, built in 1750. If weather permits, you can watch the Changing of the Guard, a ceremony in which troops parade before the Citadelle in red coats and black fur hats while a band plays. The regiment's mascot, a well-behaved goat, watches along. The queen's representative in Canada, the governor-general, has a residence in the Citadelle, and it's open for tours in summer. Québec City's oldest military building, the Cape Diamond Redoubt, was constructed in 1693 under the supervision of the engineer Josué Boisberthelot de Beaucours and is now included in the guided tours. You must take a tour to access the Citadelle, since it's a military base. ■TIP→ The location—set high above the St. Lawrence river with stunning views of the city and surrounding countryside—is worth a visit even if you don't want to pay (or wait) to take a tour. ⊠ *Côte de la Citadelle, Upper Town* 🕾 *418/694–2815* ⊕ *www.lacitadelle.qc.ca* 🖾 *C$16.*

Montcalm Monument. France and Canada jointly erected this monument honoring Louis-Joseph Montcalm, the French general who gained his fame by winning four major battles in North America. His most famous battle, however, was the one he lost, when the British conquered Québec City on September 13, 1759. Montcalm was in the north, at Beauport, when he learned that the British attack was imminent. He quickly assembled his troops to meet the enemy and was wounded in battle in the leg and stomach. Montcalm was carried into the walled city, where he died the next morning. The monument depicts the standing figure of Montcalm with an angel over his shoulder. ⊠ *Cours du Général-De Montcalm, Montcalm.*

Musée des Ursulines. The former residence of Madame de la Peltrie, the laywoman who helped found the convent, is now a museum providing an informative perspective on the Ursuline nuns. It includes an exhibition on the nuns' work in education during the 19th and 20th centuries, and magnificent examples of ornate lace work, such as altar frontals with gold and silver threads intertwined with semiprecious jewels. The Ursulines are famous for their lace, and it took a nun nine years of training to attain the level of a professional lace embroiderer. ⊠ *12 rue Donnacona, Upper Town* 🕾 *418/694–0694* ⊕ *www.museedesursulines.com* 🖾 *C$8.*

Fodor'sChoice   **Musée National des Beaux-Arts du Québec** (*National Museum of Fine Arts*
★   *of Québec*). The 2016 opening of the spectacular new wing of the Musée National des Beaux-Arts du Québec (MNBAQ) increased the museum's space by 90%, provided a remarkable steel-and-glass setting for the collection of 22,000 traditional and contemporary pieces of Québec art, and most of all completely transformed it from a neoclassical museum in the park to a museum with a slick and modern wing right on the city's liveliest avenue, the Grand Allée. Designed by architects Rem Koolhaas and Shohei Shigematsu, the Lassonde Pavilion features three stacked,

cascading galleries; a grand stairwell that spirals dramatically from the top floor to the basement, where a rising almost-mile-long tunnel connects to the museum's three other wings in the park; and views of the neighboring neo-Gothic church from both the rooftop terrace and courtyard. MNBAQ houses works by Jean-Paul Riopelle (1923–2002), Jean-Paul Lemieux (1904–90), Alfred Pellan (1906–88), Fernand Leduc (1916-2014), and Horatio Walker (1858–1938) that are particularly notable, as well as legions of other artifacts. The original museum building in Parc des Champs-de-Bataille was designed by Wilfrid Lacroix and erected in 1933 to commemorate the 300th anniversary of the founding of Québec. Incorporated within is part of an abandoned prison dating from 1867. A hallway of cells, with the iron bars and courtyard, has been preserved as part of a permanent exhibition on the prison's history. ✉ *Parc des Champs-de-Bataille, Upper Town* ☎ *418/643–2150* ⊕ *www. mnbaq.org* 🎫 *C$20* ⊘ *Closed Mon.*

Parc de l'Artillerie (*Artillery Park*). If the ornate china and regimental silver glittering in the beautifully restored officers' mess in this national historic site are any indication, 19th-century British officers knew how to party in style. Visit the gardens and rooms of the restored **Officers' Quarters,** all decorated in the style of the 1830s, and you'll see they lived much the same way.

In July and August, get a taste (literally) of life in the lower ranks with a piece of chewy "soldier's bread" baked in an outdoor oven, share in a tea ceremony, or watch a costumed actor in a French uniform of the 18th century demonstrate shooting with a flintlock musket. Artillery Park's four buildings all have long histories. The Officers' Quarters, for example, were built in 1817 and are housed in the Dauphin Redoubt, which, as the name suggests, were virtually impenetrable to enemy attacks. The British took it over in 1759, and from 1785 until 1871 it served as the mess for the officers of the Royal Artillery Regiment. The old iron foundry houses a magnificent scale model of Québec City built in 1808, allowing visitors to get a sense of the city as it looked then, as well as its geography and history. ✉ *2 rue d'Auteuil, Upper Town* ☎ *888/773–8888, 418/648–7016* ⊕ *www.pc.gc.ca/fra/lhn-nhs/ qc/fortifications/index.aspx* 🎫 *C$4, C$10 for guided tour.*

Parc des Champs-de-Bataille (*Battlefields Park*). These 250 acres of gently rolling slopes have unparalleled views of the St. Lawrence River, and within the park and west of the Citadelle are the Plains of Abraham. The park hosts the popular Summer Festival, Winter Carnival, and many other shows and activities throughout the year. ✉ *835 av. Laurier, Upper Town* ⊕ *www.ccbn-nbc.gc.ca/en.*

Fodor's Choice
★
Parc Jeanne d'Arc. An equestrian statue of Joan of Arc is the focus of this park, which is bright with colorful flowers in summer, and often adorned with seasonal decorations. A symbol of military courage and of France itself, the statue stands in tribute to the heroes of 1759 near the place where New France was lost to the British. The park also commemorates the Canadian national anthem, "O Canada"; it was played here for the first time on June 24, 1880. ✉ *Avs. Laurier and Taché, Upper Town.*

10

QUICK
BITES

Chez Ashton. As far as fast food goes, nothing is more Quebecois than poutine, that rough-and-ready dish made of fries, cheese curds, and gravy. In Québec City, this regional chain, founded in 1969, is the local favorite for hurried lunchers and late-night snackers. ⊠ *54 Côte du Palais, Upper Town* ☎ *418/692–3055* ⊕ *www.chezashton.ca.*

Place d'Armes. For centuries, this wide square was used for parades and military events; today, it's mostly strollers, buskers, and visitors enjoying restaurant terraces. On its west side stands the majestic **Ancien Palais de Justice** (Old Courthouse), a Renaissance-style building from 1887. The plaza is on land that was occupied by a church and convent of the Récollet missionaries (Franciscan monks), who in 1615 were the first order of priests to arrive in New France. The Gothic-style **fountain** in the center pays tribute to their arrival. ⊠ *Rues St-Louis and du Fort, Upper Town.*

FAMILY
Fodor's Choice
★

Plains of Abraham. This park, named after Abraham Martin, who used the plains as a pasture for his cows, is the site of the famous 1759 battle that decided New France's fate. People cross-country ski here in winter and in-line skate in summer. At the **Museum of the Plains of Abraham,** check out the multimedia display, which depicts Canada's history. ⊠ *Museum of the Plains of Abraham, 835 av. Wilfrid-Laurier, Level 0 (next to Drill Hall), Upper Town* ☎ *418/649–6157 Discovery Pavilion and bus-tour information* ⊕ *www.ccbn-nbc.gc.ca* ⊠ *Discovery Pavilion C$14 for 1-day pass (summer only), bus tour and Odyssey exhibition included.*

St-Louis Forts and Châteaux National Historic Site. Venture under the Terrasse Dufferin to see archaeological treasures from the official residence and power base of the French and British governors. Two-year excavations unearthed objects from the first château, built under the direction of Governor Montmagny, to the time the Château St-Louis burned in 1834. Wine bottles, kitchenware—even remains of walls and door frames—give clues to the luxurious life of the governors, who were among the most powerful men in the nation. Don't miss the guided tours and activities. History buffs might consider attending one of the in-depth archaeology conferences held here. ⊠ *Terrasse Dufferin, Upper Town* ☎ *418/648–7016* ⊕ *www.pc.gc.ca* ⊠ *C$4 for guided tours* ⊘ *Closed late-Oct.–late May.*

Terrasse Dufferin. This wide boardwalk with an intricate wrought-iron guardrail has a panoramic view of the St. Lawrence River, the town of Lévis on the opposite shore, Île d'Orléans, the Laurentian Mountains to the north, and the edge of the Appalachians to the south. It was named for Lord Dufferin, governor of Canada between 1872 and 1878, who had this walkway constructed in 1878. Château St-Louis, whose remains can be seen under the walkway, was home to every governor from 1626 to 1834, when it was destroyed by fire. There are 90-minute tours of the fortifications that leave from here. The **Promenade des Gouverneurs** begins at the boardwalk's western end; the path skirts the cliff and leads up to Québec's highest point, Cap Diamant, and also to the Citadelle. ⊠ *Upper Town.*

Wolfe Monument. This tall monument marks the place where the British general James Wolfe died in 1759. Wolfe landed his troops about 3 km (2 miles) from the city's walls; 4,500 English soldiers scaled the cliff and began fighting on the Plains of Abraham. Wolfe was mortally wounded in battle and was carried behind the lines to this spot. ⊠ *Rue de Bernières and av. Wolfe-Montcalm, Montcalm.*

WORTH NOTING

Cathedral of the Holy Trinity. The first Anglican cathedral outside the British Isles was erected in the heart of Québec City's Upper Town between 1800 and 1804. Its simple, dignified facade is reminiscent of London's St. Martin-in-the-Fields, and the pediment, archway, and Ionic pilasters introduced Palladian architecture to Canada. The land on which the cathedral was built was originally given to the Récollets (Franciscan monks from France) in 1681 by the king of France for a church and monastery. When Québec came under British rule, the Récollets made the church available to the Anglicans for services. Later, King George III ordered construction of the present cathedral, with an area set aside for members of the royal family. A portion of the north balcony is still reserved for the use of the reigning sovereign or his or her representative. The church houses precious objects donated by George III, and numerous plaques honor distinguished members of the local English community. The cathedral's impressive rear organ has 3,058 pipes. Even more impressive is the smaller English Chamber Organ, built in 1790, which was donated to the cathedral for the Bicentenial Celebrations in 2004. ⊠ *31 rue des Jardins, Upper Town* ☎ *418/692–2193* ⊕ *www. cathedral.ca* ▧ *Free.*

Édifice Price. Styled after the Empire State Building, this 17-story, art deco structure was the city's first skyscraper when it was built in 1929. It served as headquarters of the Price Brothers Company, a lumber firm founded by Sir William Price, and today is an official residence of the premier of Québec, who uses the top two floors. ⊠ *65 rue Ste-Anne, Upper Town.*

Grosse Île National Park. For thousands of immigrants from Europe in the 1800s, the first glimpse of North America was the hastily erected quarantine station at Grosse Île—Canada's equivalent of Ellis Island. During the time Grosse Île operated (1832–1937), 4.3 million immigrants passed through the port of Québec. For far too many passengers on disease-racked ships, particularly the Irish fleeing the potato famine, Grosse Île became a final resting place. Several buildings have been restored to tell the story of the tragic period of Irish immigration. It's necessary to take a boat tour or ferry to visit the park (some day-long cruises depart from Québec City), and you should reserve in advance.

Croisières AML offers guided cruises that depart for Grosse Île from Berthier-sur-Mer, on the south shore of the St Lawrence. The six-hour tours, offered from May to October, cost C$54, which includes admission to the island (⊕ www.croisieresaml.com). ⊠ *Québec City* ☎ *418/234–8841 Parks Canada, 888/773–8888* ⊕ *www.grosseile.ca* ▧ *C$50, including boat tour or ferry.*

10

Henry Stuart House. If you want to get a firsthand look at how the well-to-do English residents of Québec City lived in a bygone era, this is the place. Built in 1849 by the wife of wealthy businessman William Henry, the Regency-style cottage was bought in 1918 by the sisters Adèle and Mary Stuart. Active in such philanthropic organizations as the Red Cross and the Historical and Literary Society, the sisters were pillars of Québec City's English-speaking community. They also maintained an English-style garden behind the house. Soon after Adèle's death in 1987 at the age of 98, the home was classified a historic site for its immaculate physical condition and the museum-like quality of its furnishings, almost all of them Victorian. Guided tours of the house and garden start on the hour and include a cup of tea and piece of lemon cake. ⊠ *82 Grande Allée Ouest, Upper Town* ☎ *418/647–4347* ⊕ *www. maisonhenrystuart.qc.ca* ✉ *C$8.*

Morrin Cultural Centre. This stately gray-stone building has served many purposes, from imprisoning and executing criminals to storing the national archives. Built between 1808 and 1813, it was the first modern prison in Canada and was converted into Morrin College, one of the city's first private schools, in 1868. That was also when the **Literary and Historical Society of Québec**, forerunner of Canada's National Archives, moved in. The college is no longer in operation, but historical and cultural talks are held in English, and tours of the building, including two blocks of prison cells, the Victorian-era library, and College Hall, are available. ⊠ *44 rue Chaussée des Ecossais, Upper Town* ☎ *418/694–9147* ⊕ *www.morrin.org* ✉ *Library free; guided tours C$11.*

Musée de l'Amérique Francophone. A former student residence of the Séminaire de Québec houses this museum, which focuses on the history of the French in North America. Among other things, you can view about 20 of the museum's 400 landscape and still-life paintings, some from as early as the 15th century, along with French colonial money and scientific instruments drawn from collections created by the priests for the education of their students, starting in 1806. The attached former chapel is used for exhibits, conferences, and cultural activities. An exhibit called The Rediscovered Colony shows artifacts from the first French attempt at colonization of the area in 1540. ⊠ *2 côte de la Fabrique, Upper Town* ☎ *418/692–2843* ⊕ *www.mcq.org* ✉ *C$16.*

Musée du Fort. A 30-minute sound-and-light show reenacts the area's important battles, including the Battle of the Plains of Abraham and the 1775 attack by American generals Arnold and Montgomery. The museum's permanent expositions feature a history on soldiers' weaponry, uniforms, and military insignia; a glossary of lesser-known New France facts; and a diorama on the background of the show and building. A 400-square-foot replica of the city—complete with ships, cannons, and soldiers lined up for battle—is the highlight of the museum and helps guests visualize the area's strategic importance. ⊠ *10 rue Ste-Anne, Upper Town* ☎ *418/692–2175* ⊕ *www.museedufort.com* ✉ *C$9* ⊙ *Closed Jan. 8–24.*

10

Fodor's Choice **Musée et Monastère des Augustines de la Miséricorde de Jésus de l'Hôtel-Dieu**
 ★ **de Québec** (*Augustinian Monastery and Museum*). Augustinian nuns
arrived from Dieppe, France, in 1639 with a mission to care for the sick
in the new colony. They established the first hospital north of Mexico,
the **Hôtel-Dieu**, the large building west of the monastery. The monastery
underwent a complete renovation and expansion, in 2015, and now
includes a quiet, health-conscious restaurant (with silent breakfast!), as
well as accommodations—both contemporary rooms and more basic
but comfortable "cell" rooms with antique furniture—for those looking for a quiet retreat (electronics must be shut off on premises). The
museum houses an extensive collection of liturgical and medical artifacts of all kinds, and it's also worth visiting the richly decorated chapel
designed by artist Thomas Baillairgé (1829–1932), as well as the vaults,
which date to 1659 and were used by the nuns as shelter from British
bombardments. There is still a small order of nuns living in a section
of the monastery. ⊠ *32 rue Charlevoix, Upper Town* ☎ *418/692–2492
tours* ⊕ *www.monastere.ca* ⊠ *C$10 admission, C$15 for guided tours*
⊘ *Closed Mon. and statutory holidays.*

Séminaire de Québec. Behind iron gates, next to the Notre-Dame-de-
Québec cathedral, lies a tranquil courtyard surrounded by austere stone
buildings with rising steeples, structures that have housed classrooms
and student residences since 1663. François de Montmorency Laval,
the first bishop of New France, founded the Québec Seminary to train
priests in the new colony. In 1852 the seminary gave birth to Université
Laval, the first Francophone university in North America. In the 1950s
the university moved to a larger campus in suburban Ste-Foy.

Today priests still live on the premises, and Laval's architecture school
occupies part of the building. The on-site **Musée de l'Amérique francophone** gives tours of the seminary grounds and the interior in summer.
Tours start from the museum, at 2 côte de la Fabrique. The small Second
Empire–style **Chapelle Extérieure,** at the west entrance of the seminary,
was built in 1888 after fire destroyed the 1750 original. Joseph-Ferdi-
nand Peachy designed the chapel; its interior is patterned after that of
the Église de la Trinité in Paris. ⊠ *1 côte de la Fabrique, Upper Town*
☎ *418/692–2843, 866/710–8031* ⊠ *C$16.*

Tours Martello (*Martello Towers*). Of the 16 Martello towers in Canada,
four were built in Québec City because the British government feared
an invasion after the American Revolution. In summer, visitors can tour
Martello Tower No. 1, and watch a presentation on the history of the
four structures. A haunted maze is held for youngsters on Halloween
at Martello Tower No. 2, at avenues Taché and Laurier, and a mystery
dinner show is available by reservation. Martello Tower No. 3, which
guarded the westward entry to the city, was demolished in 1904. Martello Tower No. 4, on rue Lavigueur overlooking the St. Charles River,
only opens to the public for Halloween activities. ⊠ *Battlefields Park,
Upper Town* ☎ *418/648–4071 for information on towers* ⊕ *www.ccbn-
nbc.gc.ca* ⊠ *C$14 for day pass to tower, Discovery Pavilion on Plains
of Abraham, and a bus tour of park.*

LOWER TOWN

Seeing all the bustle and upscale commerce here, it's hard to imagine that 40 years ago, this area was run-down and looking for a new lease on life. Today, after exploring Place Royale and its cobblestone streets, you can walk along the edge of the St. Lawrence River and watch the sailboats and ships go by, shop at the market, or kick back on a *terrasse* (patio) with a local craft beer. Rue Petit-Champlain also has charming places to stop and listen to street musicians, and the scene near the Old Port starts buzzing as soon as the sun goes down.

If there's a cradle of French civilization in North America, you're standing in it when you visit Lower Town. In 1608, Champlain chose this narrow, U-shaped spit of land sandwiched between the frigid waters of the St. Lawrence River and the craggy heights of Cap Diamant as the site for his settlement. Champlain later abandoned the fortified *abitation* (residence) at the foot of Cap Diamant and relocated to the more easily defendable Upper Town.

However, the area continued to flourish as a bustling port and trading center for French merchants, fur traders, and *coureurs des bois* (woodsmen), and France's Native American allies. It was also the base from which dozens of military campaigns and fact-finding missions were launched into the heart of the continent. A bust of France's Sun King, Louis XIV, was erected in the main square, Place du Marché, which was renamed Place Royale in 1686. Destroyed by British cannons that were set up on the opposite shore during the siege of 1759, the port and buildings were rebuilt by the British, and the area quickly regained its role as Canada's leading commercial and business center.

Lower Town went into an economic tailspin in the late 1800s, becoming a slum whose narrow streets were lined with pawnshops, rough-and-tumble taverns, and smoky brothels that catered to sailors and lumberjacks. This lasted until the 1960s, when it received a multimillion-dollar face-lift that remade it into a sanitized version of its 1700s self. Today, once-dilapidated houses and warehouses contain busy boutique hotels, stylish boutiques, chic art galleries, and popular restaurants and bars. Lower Town, home to approximately 850 people, is bounded by the Dufferin-Montmorency Highway to the west, the St. Charles River to the north, the St. Lawrence River to the east, and Petit Champlain shopping area to the south.

10

GETTING HERE AND AROUND

Because Lower Town is the oldest part of the city, many prefer to see it first to get a sense of how the city developed chronologically. If coming from Upper Town, head down L'Escalier Casse-Cou, a stairway steep enough to earn that name, which means "Breakneck Stairs." Have your camera ready; you'll get that quintessential Petit-Champlain photo at the top of the staircase.

TIMING

You'll need one full day to see the area surrounding two of the city's most famous squares, Place Royale and Place de Paris. Pause for lunch before touring the Musée de la Civilisation and the antiques district.

TOP ATTRACTIONS

Église Notre-Dame-des-Victoires (*Our Lady of Victory Church*). The fortress shape of the altar is no accident; this small but beautiful stone church on Place Royale is linked to a bellicose past. Grateful French colonists named it in honor of the Virgin Mary, whom they credited with helping French forces defeat two British invasions: one in 1690 by Admiral William Phipps and the other by Sir Hovenden Walker in 1711. The church itself was built in 1688, making it the city's oldest—it has been restored twice since then. Several interesting paintings decorate the walls, and a model of *Le Brezé*, the boat that transported French soldiers to New France in 1664, hangs from the ceiling. The side chapel is dedicated to Ste. Geneviève, the patron saint of Paris. ⊠ *32 rue Sous-le-Fort, Lower Town* ☎ *418/692–1650* ⊕ *www.notredamedequebec.org* ☞ *Free, C$2 for guided tours.*

L'Escalier Casse-Cou. The steepness of the city's first iron stairway, an ambitious 1893 design by city architect and engineer Charles Baillairgé, is ample evidence of how it got its name: Breakneck Steps. Still, those 59 steps were quite an improvement on the original stairway, built in the 17th century, that linked the Upper Town and Lower Town. There are shops and restaurants at various levels. ⊠ *Lower Town.*

Maison Chevalier. This old stone house (which is actually three houses brought together) was built in 1752 for the shipowner Jean-Baptiste Chevalier. Its classic French style is one rich aspect of the urban architecture of New France. ⊠ *50 rue du Marché-Champlain, Lower Town* ☎ *418/646–3167.*

Maison Louis-Jolliet. Louis Jolliet, the first European to see the Mississippi River, and his fellow explorers used this 1683 house as a base for westward journeys. Today it's the lower station of the funicular. A monument commemorating Jolliet's 1672 trip to the Mississippi stands in the small park next to the house, which is at the foot of the Escalier Casse-Cou (Breakneck Staircase). ⊠ *16 rue du Petit-Champlain, Lower Town* ⊕ *www.funiculaire-quebec.com.*

FAMILY

Fodor'sChoice

★

Musée de la Civilisation (*Museum of Civilization*). Wedged between narrow streets at the foot of the cliff, this spacious museum with a striking limestone-and-glass facade was designed by architect Moshe Safdie to blend into the landscape. Its campanile (bell tower) echoes the shape of the city's church steeples. Two excellent permanent exhibits

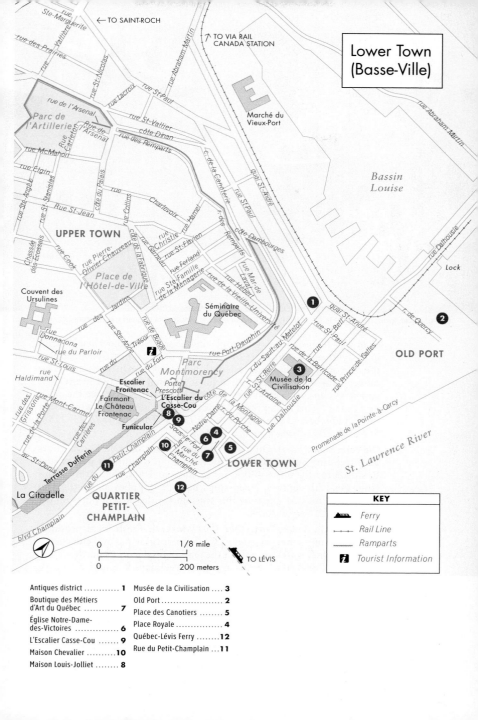

Lower Town (Basse-Ville)

TO SAINT-ROCH →

↑ TO VIA RAIL CANADA STATION

Marché du Vieux-Port

Parc de l'Artillerie

Bassin Louise

Lock

UPPER TOWN

Couvent des Ursulines

Place de l'Hôtel-de-Ville

Séminaire du Québec

OLD PORT

La Citadelle

Parc Montmorency

Escalier Frontenac

Fairmont Le Château Frontenac

L'Escalier du Casse-Cou

Funicular

Musée de la Civilisation

Terrasse Dufferin

LOWER TOWN

QUARTIER PETIT-CHAMPLAIN

Promenade de la Pointe-à-Carcy

St. Lawrence River

TO LÉVIS

0   1/8 mile
0   200 meters

KEY

🚢 Ferry
Rail Line
Ramparts
ℹ Tourist Information

One of Lower Town's top sights is the Place Royale, also one of the oldest public squares in the country.

examine Québec's history. "People of Québec, Now and Then" engagingly synthesizes 400 years of social and political history—including the role of the Catholic church and the rise of the Québec nationalist movement—with artifacts, time lines, original films and interviews, and news clips. It's a great introduction to the issues that face the province today. "This Is Our Story" looks at the 11 aboriginal nations that inhabit Québec. ✉ *85 rue Dalhousie, Lower Town* ☎ *418/643–2158, 866/710–8031* ⊕ *www.mcq.org* 🎫 *C$15.*

Old Port (*Vieux Port*). On warm summer nights, the Old Port harbors an interesting and varied nightlife scene, but daytime is just as fun. Restored for the city's 400th anniversary in 2008, the harbor dates from the 17th century, when ships brought supplies and settlers to the new colony. At one time this was among the busiest ports on the continent. ✉ *Lower Town.*

Fodor's Choice
★

Marché du Vieux-Port (*Old Port Market*). Fresh local produce, including apples, berries, and charcuterie; local wines and ciders; and artisan-crafted wares are sold at the market on the port's northwestern tip (at quai St-André). Stalls are open weekdays 9–6 and weekends 9–5 spring to fall; some stay open daily in winter, when the market is decked out for the holidays. ✉ *160 quai St-André, Lower Town* ⊕ *www.marchevieuxport.com.*

Fodor's Choice
★

Place Royale. The houses that encircle this cobblestone square, with steep Normandy-style roofs, dormer windows, and chimneys, were once the homes of wealthy merchants. Until 1686 the area was called Place du Marché, but its name changed when a bust of Louis XIV was placed at its center. During the late 1600s and early 1700s, when

Place Royale was continually under threat of British attack, the colonists moved progressively higher to safer quarters atop the cliff in Upper Town. After the French colony fell to British rule in 1759, Place Royale flourished again with shipbuilding, logging, fishing, and fur trading. The *Fresque des Québécois*, a 4,665-square-foot trompe-l'oeil mural depicting 400 years of Québec's history, is to the east of the square, at the corner of rue Notre-Dame and côte de la Montagne. ⊠ *Lower Town.*

Musée de la Place Royale. This modern information center, set cleverly within the historic Place-Royale, includes exhibits and a replica of a 19th-century house, where children can try on period costumes. A clever multimedia presentation, also good for kids, offers a brief history of Québec. ⊠ *27 rue Notre-Dame, Lower Town* ☎ *418/646–3167* ⊕ *www.mcq.org* 🎫 *C$16* 🕐 *Closed Mon. Sept.–June.*

OFF THE BEATEN PATH

Fodor's Choice ★

Québec–Lévis Ferry. Crossing the St. Lawrence River on this ferry will reward you with a striking view of the Québec City skyline, with the Château Frontenac and the Québec Seminary high atop the cliff. The view is even more impressive at night. Ferries generally run every 20 or 30 minutes from 6 am until 7 pm, and then every hour until 2:20 am; there are additional ferries from April through November. From late June to August you can combine a Québec–Lévis ferry ride with a bus tour of Lévis, getting off at such sights as the star-shaped Fort No. 1, one of three built by the British between 1865 and 1872 to defend Québec. ⊠ *10 rue des Traversiers, 1 block south of pl. de Paris, Lower Town* ☎ *418/643–8420, 877/787–7483* ⊕ *www.traversiers. gouv.qc.ca* 🎫 *C$4 each way (pedestrians, cyclists, car passengers); C$9 (car, including driver).*

Fodor's Choice ★

Rue du Petit-Champlain. The oldest street in the city was once the main street of a harbor village, with trading posts and the homes of rich merchants. Today it has pleasant boutiques, art galleries, and cafés, and on summer days the street is packed with tourists. Natural-fiber weaving, Inuit carvings, hand-painted silks, local fashion design, and enameled copper crafts are among local specialties for sale here. If you're coming from upper town, take the *Escalier Casse-Cou* (breakneck steps) down, and the funicular back up (or round-trip): both deliver you to the start of this busy, unique street. ⊠ *Lower Town* ⊕ *www.quartierpetitchamplain.com.*

10

QUICK BITES

Bistrot Le Pape-Georges. For a respite from the shoppers on rue du Petit-Champlain, grab an outdoor table at Le Pape-Georges and cool off with a drink and creamy, tangy local cheeses and fruit. This stone-and-wood wine bar, the first of its kind in Québec City when it opened almost 35 years ago, is also nice indoors; there's music on Thursday, Friday, and Saturday nights. Known for: great by-the-glass wine selection; cozy atmosphere. ⊠ *8 rue du Cul-de-Sac, Lower Town* ☎ *418/692–1320* ⊕ *www.quartierpetitchamplain. com/en/commercants/bistrot-pape-georges.*

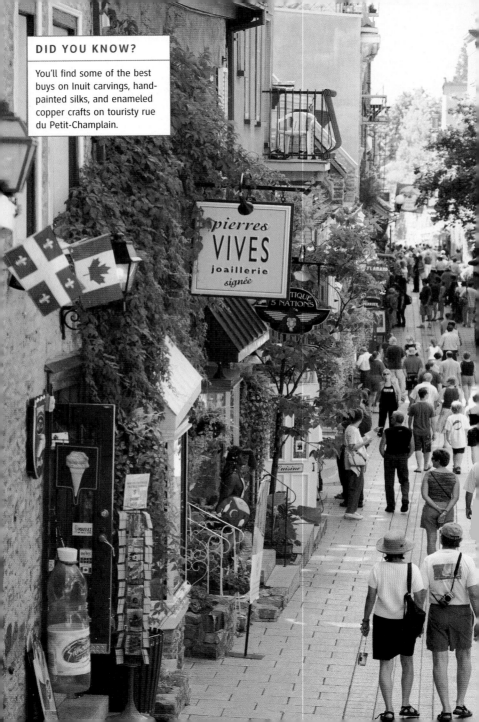

pierres
VIVES
joaillerie
signée

5 NATIONS

WORTH NOTING

Antiques district. Antiques shops cluster around rues St-Pierre and St-Paul, the latter once part of a business district packed with warehouses, stores, and businesses. After World War I, shipping and commercial activities plummeted, and the low rents attracted antiques dealers. Today their shops, together with numerous cafés, restaurants, boutique hotels, and art galleries, have made this one of the town's more popular areas. ⊠ *Lower Town.*

Boutique des Métiers d'Art du Québec. This boutique, run by the Conseil des métiers d'art, a coordinating body that oversees all kinds of arts and crafts disciplines and organizes annual fairs, features the best from Québec in glass art, porcelain, jewelry, woodworking, and much more, most with a stylish, contemporary feel. ⊠ *29 rue Notre-Dame, Lower Town* ☎ *418/694–0267* ⊕ *www.metiersdart.ca.*

FAMILY **Les Grands Feux Loto-Québec.** Throughout the month of August, an international competition of fireworks performances set to music lights up the skies between Old Québec and Lévis, launched from barges on the St. Lawrence River, near the ferry docks. Special shows are presented on the sites before the first rockets launch. ⊠ *Lower Town* ☎ *418/692–3736* ⊕ *www.lesgrandsfeux.com.*

Place des Canotiers. What used to be a vast parking lot across from the Museum of Civilization has been replaced by an elegant and modern park that provides great views of upper town and improves access to the river for locals who now linger and stroll here and also for the cruise ships that often moor here. Even the new multistory parking garage has been dressed up in an elegant wooden facade that gives the area extra character. ⊠ *40, rue Dalhousie, Lower Town* ⊕ *www.capitale.gouv.qc.ca/parcs-et-places-publiques/places-publiques/place-des-canotiers.*

10

OUTSIDE THE OLD CITY

Venture outside the walls for a glimpse of the real Québec City. Head to the St-Jean-Baptiste quarter for hipster hideouts and trendy shops. Grande-Allée and avenue Cartier buzz with clubs and bars inside Queen Anne–style mansions. Cafés, galleries, and good restaurants are popping up regularly in St-Roch, the city's urban core. If you do have a car, it's a beautiful drive on boulevard Champlain, which runs from Lower Town all around the southern edge of Québec City, following the St. Lawrence River: you might want to take a stroll along the Promenade Samuel-de-Champlain, a stunning, modern linear park created for the city's 400th anniversary, in 2008. Above are the cliffs that lead to the Plains of Abraham, and farther on you'll see the Sillery Coves. Any one of the steep hills will take you back toward the main roads that run east–west or the highways that cross north–south: Duplessis, the farthest west; Henri IV; Robert-Bourassa; and Dufferin-Montmorency.

GETTING HERE AND AROUND

It's a 15-minute walk from the Old City to avenue Cartier, but the bus system is excellent here and easy to use. There are many bus stops throughout Upper Town, and a number of lines run up and down boulevard René-Lévesque and Grande Allée. There are many options available from place d'Youville or on rue Honoré-Mercier. If you do choose to walk, take a detour to avenue Laurier or avenue Georges VI for a tour through leafy green streets with gorgeous homes.

St-Roch, on the other hand, is a little less convenient by bus from the Old City. Plan to catch cabs, which aren't hard to find, to take you there and back.

TIMING

There's no need to dedicate more than half a day to see the area around Grande-Allée or the St-Roch neighborhood. Both are great destinations for lunch, an afternoon browsing in the shops, or an evening out at a restaurant or bar.

TOP ATTRACTIONS

Avenue Cartier. The mix of reasonably priced restaurants and bars, groceries and specialty food shops, hair salons, and stores makes Cartier a favorite lunchtime and after-work stop for many downtown

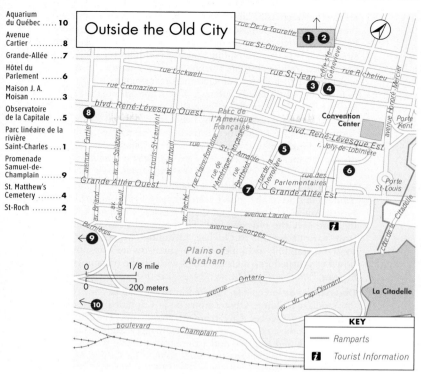

office workers. After business hours the street hums with locals running errands or soaking up the sun on patios. When darkness falls, the avenue's patrons get noticeably younger. The attraction? A half dozen nightclubs and pubs that offer everything from wine and quiet conversation to Latin music and earsplitting dance tunes. ⊠ *Montcalm, Outside the Old City.*

Grande-Allée. One of the city's oldest streets, the Grande Allée was the route people took from outlying areas to come sell their furs in town. In the 19th century the wealthy built neo-Gothic and Queen Anne–style mansions here, which now house trendy cafés, clubs, and restaurants. The street actually has four names: inside the city walls it's rue St-Louis; outside the walls, Grande Allée Est; farther west, Grande Allée Ouest; then finally, boulevard Laurier. ⊠ *Outside the Old City.*

QUICK BITES

La Piazzeta. This colorful, theatrical spot is all about thin-crust square pizza and is a solid stand-by for a good, affordable meal, particularly if you're traveling with children. ⊠ *707 rue St-Jean, Outside the Old City* ☎ *418/529–7489.*

Hôtel du Parlement. The only French-speaking legislature in continental North America, the 125-member Assemblée Nationale du Québec meets behind the stately walls of this Second Empire-style building

10

erected between 1877 and 1886. If the Assemblée is sitting (and your French is up to scratch), see if you can get into the visitors gallery to hear heated exchanges between the federalist-leaning Liberals and the secessionist Parti Québécois. Failing that, the buildings themselves, designed by Québec architect Eugène-Étienne Taché, are worth a visit. The facade is decorated with statues of such important figures of Québec history as Cartier, Champlain, Frontenac, Wolfe, and Montcalm. A 30-minute tour (in English, French, or Spanish) takes in the President's Gallery, the Parlementaire restaurant, the Legislative Council Chamber, and the National Assembly Chamber. Tours may be restricted during legislative sessions. Outdoor tours of the gardens and statues are also available during summer. ✉ *1045 rue des Parlementaires, Outside the Old City* ☎ *418/643–7239, 866/337–8837* ⊕ *www.assnat.qc.ca* ✆ *Free.*

Fodor'sChoice
★
Maison J. A. Moisan. Founded in 1871 by Jean-Alfred Moisan, this place claims the title of the oldest continuously operating grocery store in North America. The original display cases, woodwork, and tin ceilings preserve the old-time feel. The store sells hard-to-find products from various regions of Québec, including cheeses, charcuterie, and some outstanding local ales. The original owner's upstairs home has now been turned into a classic B&B with all the trimmings. ✉ *699 rue St-Jean, Outside the Old City* ☎ *418/522–0685* ⊕ *www.jamoisan.com.*

Observatoire de la Capitale. Located atop the Édifice Marie-Guyart, the city's tallest building, Observatoire de la Capitale offers a spectacular panorama of Québec City from 31 stories up. The site features an overview of the city's history with 3-D imagery, audiovisual displays in both French and English, and a time-travel theme with a 1960s twist. ✉ *1037 rue de la Chevrotière, Outside the Old City* ☎ *418/644–9841* ⊕ *www.observatoirecapitale.org* ✆ *C$14.*

QUICK BITES
Halles du Petit Quartier. This small but busy food and shopping mall on avenue Cartier has restaurants and shops that sell jewelry, fish, flowers, cheeses, pastries, breads, vegetables, fresh coffee, and candies. You'll find some excellent local cheeses, as well as a few Italian and other European specialties—there's no fast food here. If you're looking for picnic snacks for a day trip to the Plains of Abraham, plan to fill your basket here and then head up to the park. ✉ *1191 av. Cartier, Montcalm, Outside the Old City* ☎ *418/688–1635* ⊕ *www.hallesdupetitquartier.com.*

Parc linéaire de la rivière Saint-Charles (*St Charles River Linear Park*). This 32-kilometer (20-mile) stretch of trails and walkways follows the St Charles River from its source at Lake St Charles, to the northwest (which supplies a large part of Québec City's drinking water), all the way to the Bassin Louise Marina, in the Vieux-Port. Many sections are in quiet stretches of forests, or run along wetlands and meadows. The trails immediately west of the harbor offer a green oasis at the heart of the city. It's also possible to rent kayaks and paddle over 11 km (6.5 miles) of the northernmost part of the river. ✉ *Outside the Old City* ☎ *418/691–4710* ⊕ *www.societerivierestcharles.qc.ca.*

Fodor's Choice
★

Promenade Samuel-de-Champlain. This 4-kilometer (2.5-mile) park along the St. Lawrence River is a local favorite, with an amazing view of the river and the two bridges that cross it to the west, as well as some smart, whimsical, and modern landscape design. On a sunny summer day, the place is busy with strollers, bikers, and in-line skaters, as well as kids playing in the fountains and on the lawns. You will find a café and observation tower toward the western end of the park. In summer, special buses will take you from Lower Town to the promenade. ✉ *Boul. Champlain, Outside the Old City* ☎ *418/528–0773, 418/528–0773* ⊕ *www.capitale.gouv.qc.ca/ realisations/promenade-samuel-champlain.*

St. Matthew's Cemetery. The burial place of many of the earliest English settlers in Canada was established in 1771 and is the oldest cemetery remaining in Québec City. Also buried here is Robert Wood, the disavowed half-brother of Queen Victoria. Closed in 1860, the cemetery has been turned into a park. Next door is **St. Matthew's Anglican Church,** now a recently renovated public library. It has a book listing most of the original tombstone inscriptions, including those on tombstones removed to make way for the city's modern convention center. ✉ *755 rue St-Jean, Outside the Old City.*

St-Roch. Hip bars and trendy shops pepper St-Roch, once an industrial area and now a technology hub. There's a fair selection of hotels, most of them catering to business clientele, and new spots are popping up constantly. The "main drags" of the neighborhood are boulevard Charest and rue Saint-Joseph, which offer a mix of office buildings, lunch spots, and after-work hangouts. Jardins Saint-Roch, a large square, provides good people-watching and, occasionally, street performances and art events.

Look for Église St-Roch, a massive stone church, and you'll quickly find rue St-Joseph, the district's other major street, known for trendy shops and entertaining buskers. Shop for new duds here and walk west to go dine in one of the neighborhood's sleek new bistros. The popularity of the area has spawned many new restaurants. When it comes time for an after-dinner drink, there's a plethora of pubs and terraces. Korrigane Brasserie Artisanale is a great choice, and so is Le Cercle, a restaurant, art gallery, and music venue.

Art abounds in the neighborhood, from the famed street-art-covered viaduct and modern sculptures to outdoor theater and circus acts. Complexe Méduse, on rue de St-Vallier, is an avant-garde arts cooperative that houses multimedia artists, a community radio station, galleries, artists-in-residence, and performance spaces.

St-Roch is a long, but downhill jaunt from the Old City and walkable if you have the time. If you're not in the mood for exercise, the best way to reach this neighborhood is by cab. Plan to spend about C$9 each way. There are usually plenty of cabs available for the reverse trip. Taking the bus (800 or 801) is also an option. ✉ *St-Roch, Outside the Old City.*

10

WORTH NOTING

FAMILY **Aquarium du Québec.** Breakfast with the walruses, lunch (carefully) with the polar bears, and spend the afternoon watching the seals do their tricks at this clifftop aquarium overlooking the St. Lawrence and Québec City's two main bridges. When you tire of the mammals, check out the thousands of species of fresh- and saltwater fish in the aquarium's massive, three-level aquatic gallery, or have some hands-on experiences with mollusks, starfish, and stingrays. Don't miss the jellyfish ballet or seahorse tanks. This is the only aquarium in North America with examples of all five species of cold-water seals. ⊠ *1675 av. des Hôtels, Ste-Foy, Outside the Old City* ☎ *866/659–5264, 418/659–5264* ⊕ *www.aquariumduquebec.com* ⊠ *C$19.*

WHERE TO EAT

Bistros, sidewalk cafés, and chic, cutting-edge restaurants make up the dining scene in Québec City. "Grab and go" is more the exception than the rule; be prepared to eat at a leisurely pace. Québec's culinary scene offers variety, including modern international cuisine and inventive farm-to-table bistros, traditional French dishes like foie gras and escargot; distinctly French-Canadian specialties such as *tourtière* (meat pie); and local fare such as ice cider, poutine, and maple sugar pie.

With so many options, choosing where to go can be difficult. Many establishments post their *menu du jour* outside, so you can stroll along and let your cravings guide the way. However, bear in mind that reservations are a must at most restaurants during holidays, Winter Carnival, and in the summer months, when the coveted outdoor terraces open. When ordering, remember that in this French-speaking province, an *entrée* is an appetizer and the *plat principal* is the main course. Plan to tip at least 15% of the bill.

Use the coordinate (✛ B2) at the end of each listing to locate a site on the corresponding map.

WHAT IT COSTS IN CANADIAN DOLLARS			
$	**$$**	**$$$**	**$$$$**
Restaurants under C$12	C$12–C$20	C$21–C$30	over C$30

Restaurant prices are the average cost of a main course at dinner or, if dinner is not served, at lunch.

UPPER TOWN

In addition to quick to-go *boulangeries* (bakeries), cafés, and diners, Upper Town also has its share of legendary restaurants known for market-fresh ingredients and legions of creative chefs and sommeliers.

$$$$ ✕ **Aux Anciens Canadiens.** This establishment is named for a 19th-century
CANADIAN book by Philippe-Aubert de Gaspé, who once resided here. The house, dating from 1675, has servers in period costume and five dining rooms

with different themes. **Known for:** authentic French-Canadian cooking; Lac St-Jean tourtière; historical setting. $ *Average main: C$39* ⊠ *34 rue St-Louis, Upper Town* ☎ *418/692–1627* ⊕ *www.auxancienscanadiens. qc.ca* ☾ *No lunch Mon.–Wed.* ✛ *F3.*

$ ✕**Café-Boulangerie Paillard.** Owned by Yves Simard and his wife, Rebecca, this bakery, pastry counter, sandwich bar, pizza shop (summer only), and ice-cream parlor is known for its selection of nouvelle French pastries, whole grain breads, gourmet sandwiches, and artisanal gelato. Long wooden tables, designed to get customers talking to each other, create a convivial atmosphere. **Known for:** great French pastries; efficient service; delicious sandwiches. $ *Average main: C$10* ⊠ *1097 rue St-Jean, Upper Town* ☎ *418/692–1221* ⊕ *www.paillard.ca* ✛ *E2.*

CAFÉ
Fodor'sChoice
★

$ ✕**Casse-Crêpe Breton.** Crepes in generous proportions are served in this simple, busy café-style restaurant. From a menu of more than 20 fillings, pick your own chocolate or fruit combinations; design a larger meal with cheese, ham, and vegetables; or sip a bowl of Viennese coffee topped with whipped cream. **Known for:** quick service; inexpensive menu; good crepes with lots of options. $ *Average main: C$7* ⊠ *1136 rue St-Jean, Upper Town* ☎ *418/692–0438* ⊕ *www.cassecrepebreton.com* ✛ *E2.*

CAFÉ

$$$$ ✕**Chez Boulay Bistro Boréal.** Chefs Jean-Luc Boulay and Arnaud Marchand, who are both revered in this town, delight patrons with elegant interpretations of cuisine inspired by northern Québec and made entirely from local ingredients. A mix of locals celebrating special occasions and tourists fresh from shopping rue St-Jean dine in this elegant dining room on bison tartare, braised beef ravioli with candied red cabbage, and salmon in a flavorful cranberry glaze. **Known for:** distinctive cuisine; excellent wine list; upscale bistro fare. $ *Average main: C$35* ⊠ *1110 rue St-Jean, Upper Town* ☎ *418/380–8166* ⊕ *www.chezboulay. com* ▭ *No credit cards* ✛ *E2.*

CANADIAN

$ ✕**Chez Temporel.** At this bustling, veteran café, city dwellers of all sorts—struggling writers, musicians, street-smart bohemians, bureaucrats, businessmen, and busy moms and dads—enjoy Wi-Fi and some of the city's best coffee, croque-monsieurs (open-face French-bread sandwiches with ham, tomato, and broiled cheese), sandwiches, and soups. Good, modestly priced beer and wine are also served. **Known for:** great coffee; hearty eats; leisurely atmosphere. $ *Average main: C$9* ⊠ *25 rue Couillard, Upper Town* ☎ *418/694–1813* ✛ *F1.*

CAFÉ

$$$$ ✕**Le Champlain - Fairmont Château Frontenac.** Chef Stéphane Modat has made this elegant dining room one of the city's top gastronomical tables, showcasing unexpected combinations, delicious flavors, locally sourced ingredients, and whimsical presentations (like digging through chocolate "earth" in a flower pot for tasty sweet bites). While service can be a bit stiff, the food is anything-but, and the rewards on the plate are definitely worth any formality. **Known for:** high, creative gastronomy; elegant, romantic dining room; excellent Sunday Brunch. $ *Average main: C$45* ⊠ *Fairmont Le Château Frontenac, 1, rue des Carrières, Upper Town* ☎ *418/692–3861* ⊕ *www.restaurantchamplain.com* ✛ *G3.*

MODERN
CANADIAN
Fodor'sChoice
★

$ ✕**Le Chic Shack.** At this refreshing alternative to the Old City's ubiquitous white-linen bistros, you can get fast food that's also high quality. Burgers made from grass-fed cattle served on soft artisanal brioche

FAST FOOD
FAMILY

10

buns make this a prime locale for lunch goers. **Known for:** great burgers; quality fast food; delicious milk shakes. $ *Average main: C$11* ✉ *15 rue du Fort, Upper Town* ☎ *418/692–1485* ⊕ *lechicshack.ca* ▭ *No credit cards* ✛ *G2.*

$$$$
EUROPEAN

✕ **Le Continental.** If Québec City had a dining hall of fame, Le Continental would be there among the best. Since 1956 this historic spot, steps from the Château Frontenac, has been serving solid, traditionally gourmet dishes. **Known for:** classic gastronomy; tableside "guéridon" service; old-school excellence. $ *Average main: C$60* ✉ *26 rue St-Louis, Upper Town* ☎ *418/694–9995* ⊕ *www.restaurantlecontinental. com* ☽ *No lunch weekends* ✛ *F2.*

$$$
FRENCH

✕ **L'Entrecôte Saint-Jean.** Steak frites (steak with fries) is on menus everywhere in Québec City and in lots of other places throughout the world, but this lively establishment has a 30-year reputation as the master of the dish—*L'entrecôte* is a particular sirloin cut, usually long and relatively thin. At this restaurant, it's all about the sauce. **Known for:** steak frites; unpretentious, well-made food; great patio. $ *Average main: C$27* ✉ *1080 rue St-Jean, Upper Town* ☎ *418/694–0234* ⊕ *www.entrecotesaintjean.com* ▭ *No credit cards* ☽ *No lunch weekends, Sept.–May* ✛ *E2.*

$$$$
FRENCH

✕ **Le Saint-Amour.** At one of the city's most romantic and treasured restaurants, chef Jean-Luc Boulay entices diners with such creations as red-deer steak grilled with a wild-berry and peppercorn sauce, and filet mignon with port wine and local blue cheese. Paul McCartney and Sting have both eaten here. **Known for:** foie gras; seven different kinds of Valrhona chocolate; romantic atmosphere. $ *Average main: C$65* ✉ *48 rue Ste-Ursule, Upper Town* ☎ *418/694–0667* ⊕ *www.saint-amour.com* ☽ *No lunch weekends* ✛ *E3.*

$$
ITALIAN

✕ **Sapristi.** The owners of Les Trois Garçons, a neat burger shop across the street, opened this Italian-leaning restaurant in what was a longtime favorite bar, Le Chantauteuil. The menu is satisfying, with a number of imaginative pizzas and pastas, salads and such. **Known for:** creative pizzas; hip and popular; fried mozzarella. $ *Average main: C$17* ✉ *1001 rue St-Jean, Upper Town* ☎ *418/692–2030* ⊕ *sapristi.ca* ▭ *No credit cards* ✛ *E2.*

LOWER TOWN

Lower Town has its fair share of renowned eateries, and you'll find some of the best terraces in town. Dine after the sun goes down under twinkling lights at L'Echaudé, or satisfy late-night cravings at SSS, which has a special after-hours snack menu. For impeccable upscale fare, go to L'Initiale.

$$
CANADIAN

✕ **Buffet de L'Antiquaire.** Hearty home cooking, generous portions, and rock-bottom prices have made this no-frills, diner-style eatery in the heart of the antiques district, a Lower Town institution. It's a good place to sample traditional Quebecois dishes such as pea soup and *cipaille* (a deep-dish layered pie using poultry, meat, or seafood), and the homemade and delicious sugar pie, crepes, and other desserts. **Known for:** traditional dishes; old-school diner; Québec City institution. $ *Average main: C$12* ✉ *95 rue St-Paul, Lower Town* ☎ *418/692–2661* ✛ *G1.*

$$$$
CANADIAN
Fodor's Choice
★
✕ Chez Muffy. This restaurant, inside the museumlike Auberge Saint-Antoine, has stone walls and attractive wooden floors and exposed beams from the building's warehouse days. Chef Julien Ouellet creates menus that change with the seasons, but fresh, locally sourced ingredients are at the core of the classic, elegant menu. **Known for:** historic warehouse setting; seasonal tasting menu; considered wine list. $ *Average main: C$35* ✉ *10 rue St-Antoine, Lower Town* ☎ *418/692–1022* ⊕ *www.saint-antoine.com* ✛ *G2.*

$$$$
FRENCH
Fodor's Choice
★
✕ Laurie Raphaël Restaurant-Atelier-Boutique. Local and regional products are emphasized here—among local celebrity chef Daniel Vézina's creations are crystallized foie gras with truffle snow, and venison tartare. There are two tasting menus, with three or five "themes" and remarkable wine pairings as an option, starting at C$105. **Known for:** smart, high-end gastronomy; elegant setting; tasting menus. $ *Average main: C$105* ✉ *117 rue Dalhousie, Lower Town* ☎ *418/692–4555* ⊕ *www.laurieraphael.com* ⊗ *Closed Sun.–Tues., and Jan. 1–15* ✛ *G1.*

$$$
CAFÉ
✕ Le Café du Monde. Next to the cruise terminal in the Old Port, this massive restaurant has a spectacular view to equal its food. The outdoor terrace in front overlooks the St. Lawrence River, while the side *verrière* (glass atrium) looks onto l'Agora amphitheater and the old stone Customs House. **Known for:** lively scene; great views; simple, delicious French food. $ *Average main: C$30* ✉ *84 rue Dalhousie, Suite 140, Lower Town* ☎ *418/692–4455* ⊕ *www.lecafedumonde.com* ✛ *H1.*

$$$
FRENCH
✕ L'Echaudé. A mix of businesspeople and tourists frequent L'Echaudé because of its location between the nearby business and antiques districts. For lunch, the flank steak with shallots is a classic, and every day there's excellent fish, tartares, and pasta on the menu. **Known for:** French-inspired dishes; elegant decor; three-course brunch. $ *Average main: C$25* ✉ *73 rue Sault-au-Matelot, Lower Town* ☎ *418/692–1299* ⊕ *www.echaude.com* ✛ *G1.*

$$
CAFÉ
✕ Le Cochon Dingue. The café dishes at this cheerful chain, whose name translates into the Crazy Pig, include delicious tartares, steak with fries, hearty soups, a selection of international dishes like satays and "général Dingue" chicken, as well as substantial desserts like sugar pie with vanilla cream. At the boulevard Champlain location, sidewalk tables and indoor dining rooms artfully blend the chic and the antique; black-and-white checkerboard floors contrast with ancient stone walls. **Known for:** often long waits for a table; affordable bistro chain; good people-watching. $ *Average main: C$14* ✉ *46 boul. Champlain, Lower Town* ☎ *418/692–2013* ⊕ *www.cochondingue.com* ⊗ *No dinner* ✛ *G3.*

10

$$$
CANADIAN
✕ Légende. Set on the ground floor of the Hôtel des Coutellier, in the Old Port area, Légende is set in a large wood and stone room with plush banquettes and an elegant bar. There are a lot of sharing plates—the smartly prepared fish and seafood board (including things like salmon rillettes and welk salad) is particularly delightful. **Known for:** local ingredients, served creatively; open space; vast patio in summer. $ *Average main: C$28* ✉ *255 rue St-Paul, Lower Town* ☎ *418/614–2555* ⊕ *restaurantlataniere.com* ▬ *No credit cards* ✛ *E1.*

$$$$ FRENCH Fodor's Choice ★ 🍴 **L'Initiale.** A contemporary setting and gracious service place L'Initiale in the upper echelon of restaurants in this city, in cost as well as quality. Widely spaced tables favor intimate dining, and the warm brown-and-cream interior is cozy. **Known for:** one of Québec's top chefs; solid tasting menu; chic, intimate atmosphere. [$] *Average main: C$65* ✉ *54 rue St-Pierre, Lower Town* ☎ *418/694–1818* 🌐 *www.restaurantinitiale.com* 🕓 *Closed Sun., Mon., and early Jan.* ⊕ *G2.*

$$$$ ECLECTIC 🍴 **Restaurant Toast!** At this very chic, very intimate restaurant in Le Priori hotel, mod light fixtures are set against stone-and-brick walls, and a secret garden terrace removes all street noise out back, making it perfect for a relaxing night with friends. Enjoy chef Christian Lemelin's local duck carpaccio, a surf and turf of octopus and beef, or his roasted venison with juniper-blueberry sauce. **Known for:** beautiful courtyard; slightly ornate, flavorful dishes; intimate setting. [$] *Average main: C$35* ✉ *17 rue Sault-au-Matelot, Lower Town* ☎ *418/692–1334* 🌐 *www.restauranttoast.com* ⊕ *G2.*

$$ ECLECTIC 🍴 **Simple Snack Sympathique** (*SSS*). Throngs of professionals and young urbanites pack restaurant Simple Snack Sympathique (SSS)—a name that sounds more "quick bite" than elegant restaurant—to dine on artfully prepared dishes, from angel hair pasta with succulent duck confit to tender ribs served alongside crispy fries. It's a chic place to be on Saturday night. **Known for:** creative classics; stylish interior; good cocktails. [$] *Average main: C$20* ✉ *71 rue St-Paul, Lower Town* ☎ *418/692–1991* 🌐 *www.restaurantsss.com* 💳 *No credit cards* 🕓 *No lunch weekends* ⊕ *G1.*

OUTSIDE THE OLD CITY

There are many cute cafés and fine eateries within the walls of the Old City, but don't miss the thriving culinary scene beyond them. Le Café du Clocher Penché is arguably the bistro with the best brunch, and it gives you an excuse to visit trendy St-Roch. Or if you're looking for a little more luxury, head to Louis Hébert to nibble on trendy dishes while playing "spot the politico."

Work up a good appetite by wandering through the streets. No visit to Québec is complete without a picnic in the park; pop into one of the city's little out-of-the-way patisseries for buttery croissants and heavenly brioches.

$$ MODERN ITALIAN 🍴 **Battuto.** Chef Guillaume Saint-Pierre's love for authentic Italian cuisine led him to open this 25-seat restaurant, located off the main Saint-Roch thoroughfares, where he can fully concentrate on that passion with gusto and skill. Italian tradition (there's arancini and vitello tonatto) blend with local flair (fresh fettucini with local corn, bacon and local mushroom). **Known for:** perfect fresh pasta; dolci that blend local flair and Italian know-how; hard-to-get table. [$] *Average main: C$18* ✉ *527, boul. Langelier, St-Roch* ☎ *418/614–4414* 🌐 *www.battuto.ca* 🕓 *Closed Sun. and Mon.* ⊕ *A3.*

$$$$ 🍴 **Bistro B.** Chef François Blais, who first made Panache into one of the city's hot spots, decided on a more casual approach when he opened his own restaurant on avenue Cartier. In true "market cuisine" spirit, the whole menu fits on a blackboard, with a handful of appetizers,

main courses, and desserts that change daily. $ *Average main: C$35* ✉ *1144 av. Cartier, Montcalm* ☎ *418/614–5444* ⊕ *www.bistrob.ca* ▤ *No credit cards* ✛ *A6.*

$$
TAPAS

✕ **Buvette Scott.** A great selection of well-priced wines (many organic or "natural") are matched with simple and sometimes inventive dishes at this popular wine bar. On a side street just off rue St-Jean, in the hip St-Jean-Baptiste neighborhood, it serves the likes of duck breast tataki, mushroom French Toast and beet lasagna with a groovy soundtrack. **Known for:** popular with locals; good wine selection; great little bites. $ *Average main: C$16* ✉ *821, rue Scott, Outside the Old City* ☎ *581/741–4464* ⊙ *Closed Sun.* ✛ *C3.*

$
ECLECTIC
FAMILY

✕ **Chez Cora.** Substantial breakfasts with mounds of fresh fruit are the specialty at this sunny chain restaurant, which is open from 6 am until 3 pm. Whimsy is everywhere, from the plastic chicken decorations to the inventive dishes, often named after the customers or family members who inspired them. **Known for:** hearty and healthy breakfasts; a fun menu with whimsical touches; unfussy atmosphere. $ *Average main: C$12* ✉ *545 rue du Parvis, St-Roch, Outside the Old City* ☎ *418/524–3232* ⊕ *www.chezcora.com* ⊙ *No dinner* ✛ *B2.*

$$
MODERN
AMERICAN

✕ **Chez Victor.** This cozy burger joint with brick-and-stone walls attracts an artsy crowd to rue St-Jean. A wide range of topping combinations and daily special burgers are available, and french fries are served with a dollop of homemade mayonnaise (there are five varieties available) and poppy seeds. **Known for:** hearty burgers; cozy atmosphere; good selection of local beers; poutine. $ *Average main: C$17* ✉ *145 rue St-Jean, St-Jean-Baptiste* ☎ *418/529–7702* ⊕ *www.chezvictorburger.com* ✛ *A4.*

$$$
CANADIAN

✕ **Ciel!** Spectacular views of the whole city are not the only reason to climb up here, thanks to chef David Forbes' solid farm-to-table approach. The food is unfussy, creative, and delicious (try the pan-seared scallops with mushroom gnocchi and celery emulsion), and service is friendly and well-managed. **Known for:** spectacular views; rotating restaurant; tasty farm-to-table dishes. $ *Average main: C$30* ✉ *1225 cours du General Montcalm, Outside the Old City* ☎ *418/640–5802* ⊕ *www.cielbistrobar.com* ✛ *C5.*

$$
CANADIAN

✕ **Le Billig.** This casual crepe shop occupies a large space with lovely exposed-brick walls. Buckwheat flour crepes are filled with simple ham and cheese, or fancier combos like duck confit with onion marmalade. **Known for:** great crepes, often original; good cider selection; buckwheat and wheat options. $ *Average main: C$16* ✉ *481 rue St-Jean, St-Jean-Baptiste, Outside the Old City* ☎ *418/524–8341* ▤ *No credit cards* ✛ *B3.*

$$$$
BISTRO

✕ **Le Bouchon du Pied Bleu.** It's worth heading to the outskirts of the St-Roch downtown district for this unique dining experience, inspired by the French *bouchons* (as bistros are called in the city of Lyon). Big salad bowls appear at your table, for starters, and you can help yourself. $ *Average main: C$35* ✉ *179 St-Vallier Ouest, St-Roch* ☎ *418/914–3554* ⊕ *piedbleu.com* ▤ *No credit cards* ⊙ *Closed Mon. and Tues.* ✛ *A2.*

$$$
FRENCH
Fodor's Choice
★

✕ **Le Café du Clocher Penché.** An amiable staff and inventive bistro cuisine (without pretentious fluff) make this establishment a local favorite. The high ceilings and imposing vault door give away the fact that this was once a bank. **Known for:** terroir-driven cuisine; best brunch in the city;

lively lunch scene. [$] *Average main: C$24* ✉ *203 rue St-Joseph Est, St-Roch, Outside the Old City* ☎ *418/640–0597* 🌐 *www.clocherpenche.ca* 💳 *No credit cards* 🕒 *Closed Mon. No dinner Sun.* ⊕ *A2.*

$$ BISTRO 🍴 **Le Café Krieghoff.** Modeled after a typical Paris bistro and named for a Canadian painter who lived up the street (and whose prints hang on the walls), this busy, noisy restaurant with patios in front and back has been a popular place with the locals for over 40 years. Open every day from early morning to late evening, Krieghoff serves specialties that include salmon, quiche, "la Toulouse" (a big French sausage with sauerkraut), steak with french fries, boudin (pig-blood sausage), and "la Bavette" (hanger steak). **Known for:** big bowls of hot chocolate; simple, flavorful dishes; good place to work or study. [$] *Average main: C$15* ✉ *1089 rue Cartier, Outside the Old City* ☎ *418/522–3711* 🌐 *www.cafekrieghoff.qc.ca* ⊕ *A6.*

$$$ MODERN EUROPEAN Fodor's Choice ★ 🍴 **Le Cercle.** As a combination bar, restaurant, art gallery, and concert venue, Le Cercle is the hub of St-Roch's culinary and cultural life. Movie clips are projected onto the walls, and a garage door lets in city sounds, creating a lively setting, especially during summer. **Known for:** vibrant atmosphere; late-night snacks and drinks. [$] *Average main: C$22* ✉ *226–28 St-Joseph Est, St-Roch, Outside the Old City* ☎ *418/948–8648* 🌐 *www.le-cercle.ca* 💳 *No credit cards* ⊕ *A2.*

$$$ BISTRO 🍴 **Le Hobbit Bistro.** Tucked into a converted house that was built in 1846 and open since the 1970s, the nameis obviously inspired by Tolkien and harks to a slightly hippy past, but this restaurant is far from the shire, serving fresh, colorful salads, juicy burgers, and delectable tartares in a rustic-chic setting. Highlights include duck confit with a cranberry and orange compote, bison-cheek risotto, and apple-and-beet salad in a light vinaigrette. **Known for:** local bistro vibe; breakfast with a twist; smart, unpretentious dishes. [$] *Average main: C$25* ✉ *700 rue St-Jean, St-Jean-Baptiste* ☎ *418/647–2677* 🌐 *www.hobbitbistro.com* 💳 *No credit cards* ⊕ *C3.*

$$$ CANADIAN 🍴 **Le Parlementaire.** Despite its magnificent beaux-arts interior and its reasonable prices, the National Assembly's restaurant remains one of the best-kept secrets in town. Chef Yves Légaré prepares contemporary cuisine with products from Québec's various regions. **Known for:** elegant, historic decor; tasty regional dishes. [$] *Average main: C$24* ✉ *1045 rue des Parlementaires, Montcalm, Outside the Walls* ☎ *418/643–6640* 🌐 *www.assnat.qc.ca* 🕒 *Closed weekends July–Labor Day; closed Sat.–Mon., Labor Day–June. No dinner* ⊕ *D4.*

$$ ECLECTIC 🍴 **Noctem Artisans Brasseurs.** A great selection of beers, brewed on premises or coming from some of the best microbreweries in Québec, attract diners here, along with the smart menu of reinvented pub food (fish and waffle, blood sausage pie, braised pork belly with chimichurri sauce and parsley root chips, for example). The decor, with raw plywood and exposed structures, is modern and trendy. **Known for:** great beer selection; creative pub food; trendy decor. [$] *Average main: C$18* ✉ *438, rue du Parvis, St-Roch* ☎ *581/742–7979* 🌐 *www.noctem.ca* ⊕ *B2.*

$$$ ECLECTIC 🍴 **Patente et Machin.** This fun and friendly place has a menu with terrific meats, grilled cheese, and whimsical ideas, like the use of guinea fowl wings in lieu of chicken wings. The food here has personality, humor, and...lots of butter. **Known for:** playful dishes; pleasantly chaotic service; great wine selection. [$] *Average main: C$25* ✉ *82 rue St-Joseph Ouest, St-Roch, Outside the Old City* ☎ *581/981–3999* 💳 *No credit cards* ⊕ *A2.*

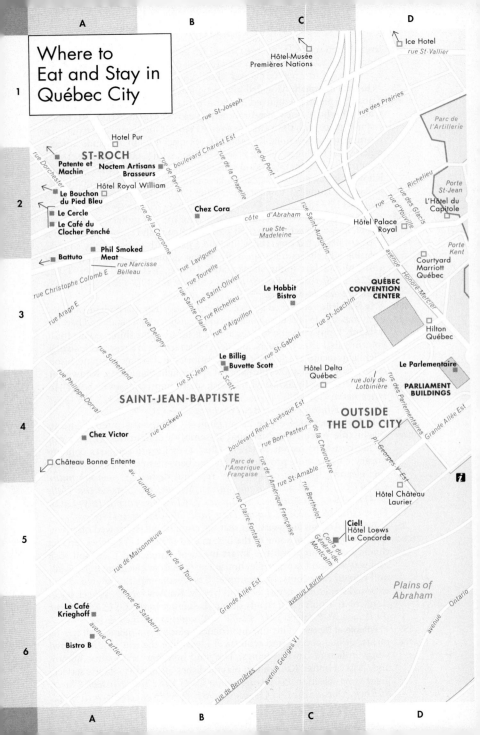

Where to Eat and Stay in Québec City

A   **B**   **C**   **D**

Ice Hotel
rue St-Vallier

Hôtel-Musée
Premières Nations

rue St-Joseph

Parc de
l'Artillerie

rue des Prairies

Hotel Pur

ST-ROCH

Patente et
Machin

Noctem Artisans
Brasseurs

Richelieu

boulevard Charest Est

rue de la Chapelle

rue du Pont

Porte
St-Jean

L'Hôtel du
Capitole

rue Dorchester

rue de Parvis

Hôtel Royal William

Le Bouchon
du Pied Bleu

rue de la Couronne

Chez Cora

Le Cercle

côte d'Abraham

rue Saint-Augustin

rue d'Youville

Hôtel Palace
Royal

Le Café du
Clocher Penché

rue Ste-
Madeleine

avenue Honoré-Mercier

Porte
Kent

Battuto

Phil Smoked
Meat

rue Narcisse
Belleau

rue Lavigueur

rue Tourelle

Courtyard
Marriott
Québec

rue Christophe Colomb E

rue Sainte Claire

rue Saint-Olivier

Le Hobbit
Bistro

**QUÉBEC
CONVENTION
CENTER**

rue Arago E

rue Deligny

rue Richelieu

rue d'Aiguillon

rue St-Gabriel

rue St-Joachim

Hilton
Québec

rue Sutherland

rue St-Jean

Le Billig

Buvette Scott

rue Scott

Hôtel Delta
Québec

rue Joly de-
Lotbinière

Le Parlementaire

**PARLIAMENT
BUILDINGS**

rue Philippe-Dorval

SAINT-JEAN-BAPTISTE

rue Lockwell

boulevard René-Lévesque Est

rue Bon-Pasteur

rue de la Chevrotière

**OUTSIDE
THE OLD CITY**

Grande Allée Est

Chez Victor

Château Bonne Entente

av. Turnbull

Parc de
l'Amérique
Française

rue de l'Amérique Française

rue St-Amable

rue Berthelot

pl. Georges-V Est

Hôtel Château
Laurier

rue Maisonneuve

av. de la Tour

rue Claire-Fontaine

Cours du
Général-de-
Montcalm

Ciel!
Hôtel Loews
Le Concorde

Le Café
Krieghoff

avenue de Salaberry

Grande Allée Est

avenue Laurier

Plains of
Abraham

avenue Ontario

Bistro B

avenue Cartier

rue de Bernières

avenue Georges VI

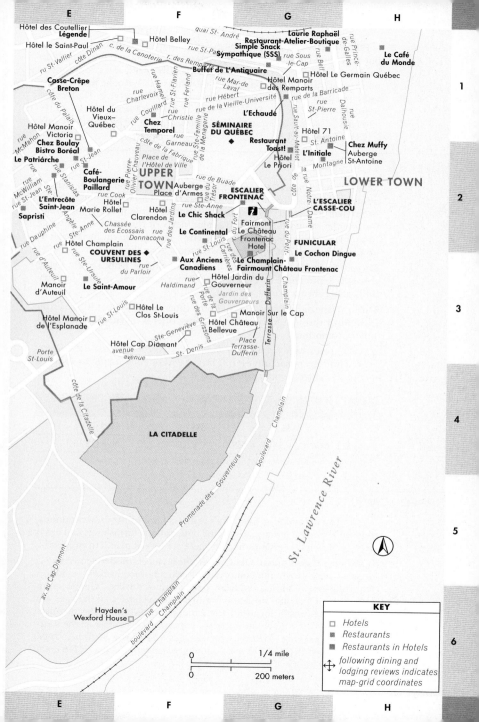

$ DELI 🍴 **Phil Smoked Meat.** There are plenty of smoked meat places in Québec, but Phil Smoked Meat manages to stand out. Frequented by lunching locals and families seeking a budget-friendly meal, the restaurant is on a quiet street behind a cluster of offices in St-Roch. **Known for:** tasty smoked meat sandwiches; quick, friendly service. [$] *Average main: C$12* ✉ *275 rue St-Vallier Est, St-Roch, Outside the Old City* ☎ *418/523–4545* 🌐 *www.philsmokedmeat.com* 💳 *No credit cards* 🕒 *Closed Sun.* ✣ *A2.*

WHERE TO STAY

More than 35 hotels are located in Old Québec, and there's also an abundance of family-run bed-and-breakfasts. Landmark hotels are as prominent as the city's most historic sights, while modern high-rises outside the ramparts have spectacular views of the Old City. Another option is to immerse yourself in the city's historic charm by staying in an old-fashioned inn, where no two rooms are alike.

Be sure to make a reservation if you visit during peak season (May through September) or during the Winter Carnival, in late January and early February.

During especially busy times, hotel rates usually rise 30%. From November through April, many lodgings offer weekend discounts and other promotions.

Hotel reviews have been shortened. For full information, visit Fodors.com. Use the coordinate (✣ B2) at the end of each listing to locate a site on the corresponding map.

	WHAT IT COSTS IN CANADIAN DOLLARS			
	$	**$$**	**$$$**	**$$$$**
Hotels	under C$160	C$160–C$200	C$201–C$250	over C$250

Hotel prices are the lowest cost of a standard double room in high season.

UPPER TOWN

Upper Town, inside the Old City's walls, is famous for its accommodations in historic buildings, decorated with antique furnishings and heavy fabrics. Few have restaurants, but there are lots of places to eat nearby.

$$$ HOTEL 🏨 **Auberge Place d'Armes.** Old Québec charm meets modern convenience at this Upper Town inn, comprised of two adjoined historic buildings, featuring exposed brick and beams, with homey duvets, "Québec country" furnishings, and modern comforts like oversize soaking tubs and Wi-Fi. **Pros:** central location; romantic; good restaurant on premises, Chez Jules. **Cons:** no elevator means working off breakfast on the stairs; no on-site parking. [$] *Rooms from: C$235* ✉ *24 rue St-Anne, Upper Town* ☎ *418/694–9485* 🌐 *www.aubergeplacedarmes.com* 💳 *No credit cards* 🛏 *21 rooms* 🍽 *Breakfast* ✣ *F2.*

$$ HOTEL **Courtyard Marriott Québec.** This former bank building exudes a quiet elegance, with stained-glass windows, two fireplaces, and a tiny wood-lined corner bar in the lobby. **Pros:** the French food from Que Sera Sera restaurant's open kitchen; thoughtful facilities like coffeemakers and baby cribs; laundry machines are a bonus. **Cons:** a bit starchy. [$] *Rooms from: C$199* ✉ *850 pl. d'Youville, Upper Town* ☎ *418/694–4004, 866/694–4004* 🌐 *www.marriott-quebec.com* 🛏 *111 rooms* 🍴 *No meals* ✥ *D3.*

$$$$ HOTEL FAMILY Fodor's Choice ★ **Fairmont Le Château Frontenac Hotel.** In this landmark building, perked up with some sleek and well-integrated modern touches, the public rooms—from the cozy and elegant Bar 1608 to the 700-seat ballroom reminiscent of the Hall of Mirrors at Versailles—are all opulent; guest rooms are just as elegantly furnished, like minichâteaux, with gold and green touches. **Pros:** historic aura and top attraction; great river views; restaurants offer a true gastronomical experience. **Cons:** it gets busy in the public spaces; some rooms are small for the price. [$] *Rooms from: C$259* ✉ *1 rue des Carrières, Upper Town* ☎ *418/692–3861, 800/441–1414* 🌐 *www.fairmont.com/frontenac* 🛏 *618 rooms, 30 suites* 🍴 *No meals* ✥ *G3.*

$$ HOTEL **Hilton Québec.** Just next to Parliament Hill, the Hilton's chic and contemporary rooms have views of Vieux-Québec or the Laurentian mountains to the north. **Pros:** direct access to the convention center; amazing executive lounge; great city views. **Cons:** blocky exterior; conventioneers. [$] *Rooms from: C$199* ✉ *1100 boul. René-Lévesque Est, Upper Town* ☎ *418/647–2411, 800/447–2411 in Canada* 🌐 *www.hiltonquebec.com* 🛏 *571 rooms* 🍴 *No meals* ✥ *D3.*

$$ B&B/INN **Hôtel Cap Diamant.** An eclectic collection of vintage furniture and ecclesiastical accents—stained glass from a church, a confessional door, an angel or two—complement the decorative marble fireplaces, stone walls, and hardwood floors at this hotel, which is made up of two adjacent 1826 houses. **Pros:** baggage lift; a four-season veranda overlooks the garden; well-located and quiet. **Cons:** stairs to third-floor rooms are a bit steep. [$] *Rooms from: C$190* ✉ *39 av. Ste-Geneviève, Upper Town* ☎ *418/694–0313, 888/694–0313* 🌐 *www.hotelcapdiamant.com* 🛏 *12 rooms* 🍴 *Breakfast* ✥ *F3.*

$$ HOTEL **Hôtel Champlain.** Tucked away on a quiet street in Old Québec, with small but well-equipped rooms and a good breakfast buffet, the Champlain is a good fit for those after attentive service, boutique charm, and a central location. **Pros:** close to main attractions; on-site parking—rare in this part of town; good value. **Cons:** small bathrooms; no in-room coffee pots. [$] *Rooms from: C$179* ✉ *115 rue Ste-Anne, Upper Town* ☎ *418/694–0106* 🌐 *www.champlainhotel.com* 💳 *No credit cards* 🛏 *47 rooms, 5 suites* 🍴 *Breakfast* ✥ *E3.*

$$ HOTEL **Hôtel Château Bellevue.** Behind the Château Frontenac, facing a pleasant park, this 1898 hotel occupies four heritage houses with the same green roofing, and offers modern rooms in a good location, often with views of the St. Lawrence River. **Pros:** packages include attractions; good continental breakfast; views of the river. **Cons:** small rooms lack style. [$] *Rooms from: C$199* ✉ *16 rue de la Porte, Upper Town* ☎ *418/692–2573, 800/463–2617* 🌐 *www.hotelchateaubellevue.com* 🛏 *48 rooms, 1 suite* 🍴 *Breakfast* ✥ *F3.*

$$ Hôtel Clarendon. Built in 1870, this is the oldest operating hotel in
HOTEL   Québec City; half of its rooms have excellent views over Old Québec,
and the others overlook a courtyard. Pros: the piano in the lounge
attracts merrymakers; interesting historic features. Cons: brassy acoustics on the reception level. $\boxed{\$}$ *Rooms from: C$164* ✉ *57 rue Ste-Anne,
Upper Town* ☎ *418/692–2480, 888/554–6001* ⊕ *www.hotelclarendon.
com* ⤳ *143 rooms* ꙳ *No meals* ✛ *F2.*

$ Hôtel du Vieux-Québec. Nicely situated at the end of rue St-Jean this
HOTEL   friendly spot has rooms spread over three floors, including a suite with
Fodor'sChoice   a king bed and huge flat-screen television, and a "superior room" with
★   two queen beds and an exposed brick wall. Pros: lively location; breakfast delivered to your door with a weather report; good restaurant.
Cons: student guests can mean noise. $\boxed{\$}$ *Rooms from: C$159* ✉ *1190
rue St-Jean, Upper Town* ☎ *418/692–1850, 800/361–7787* ⊕ *www.hvq.
com* ⤳ *45 rooms* ꙳ *Breakfast* ✛ *E1.*

$ Hôtel Jardin du Gouverneur. Behind the Château Frontenac, within a
B&B/INN   cream-color stone house with blue-trimmed windows, the inexpensive,
unpretentious Jardin du Gouverneur has rooms with light wood furnishings, new bedding, and climate control. Pros: sweet staff; central
location; stone walls and old fireplaces in some rooms. Cons: steep
stairs from the third to the fourth floor; tight lobby; some rooms are
tiny. $\boxed{\$}$ *Rooms from: C$139* ✉ *16 rue Mont-Carmel, Upper Town*
☎ *418/692–1704, 877/692–1704* ⤳ *17 rooms* ꙳ *Breakfast* ✛ *F3.*

$$ Hôtel Le Clos St-Louis. Winding staircases, period antiques, and crystal
HOTEL   chandeliers add to the Victorian elegance of this central inn, made up of
two updated 1845-era houses Pros: four-poster and sleigh beds; cheery
breakfast room; bar and massotherapy on premises. Cons: Victorian ruffles
not for everyone; no elevator; guests must remove footwear upon entry.
$\boxed{\$}$ *Rooms from: C$199* ✉ *69 rue St-Louis, Upper Town* ☎ *418/694–1311,
800/461–1311* ⊕ *www.clossaintlouis.com* ⤳ *18 rooms* ꙳ *Breakfast* ✛ *F3.*

$ Hôtel Manoir de l'Esplanade. The four 1845 stone houses at the corner of
HOTEL   rues d'Auteuil and St-Louis conceal one of the city's good deals: a charming hotel with well-appointed rooms that include a continental breakfast
with fruit, cheese, and yogurt. Pros: fireplaces and dormer windows add
to charm; elevator is a luxury in this part of town; all rooms have full
private bathrooms. Cons: central location means some nighttime noise.
$\boxed{\$}$ *Rooms from: C$155* ✉ *83 rue d'Auteuil, Upper Town* ☎ *418/694–
0834* ⊕ *www.manoiresplanade.ca* ⤳ *36 rooms* ꙳ *Breakfast* ✛ *E3.*

$ Hôtel Manoir des Remparts. With its homey furnishings, basic, cheery
HOTEL   rooms and reasonable rates, this serviceable central hotel set in two
historical houses above the city walls and with views of lower town,
attracts budget-conscious travelers who can't bring themselves to stay
in a hostel. Pros: good alternative to antiques-filled B&Bs; affordable
option; rooftop terrace with river views. Cons: some rooms share bathrooms and a TV; no elevator. $\boxed{\$}$ *Rooms from: C$110* ✉ *3½ rue des
Remparts, Upper Town* ☎ *418/692–2056* ⊕ *www.manoirdesremparts.
com* ⤳ *34 rooms, 24 with bath* ꙳ *Breakfast* ✛ *G1.*

$$$ Hôtel Manoir Victoria. Understated and demure, this recently reno-
HOTEL   vated European-style hotel, with a discreet entrance on Côte du Palais,
includes elegantly simple rooms with hardwood furnishings and white

bedding, a library, one of the city's top restaurants, and an in-house spa. **Pros:** room service from Chez Boulay; heated bathroom floors; indoor parking is a luxury for winter guests. **Cons:** lobby can get busy with restaurant or convention crowds; pool no good for laps. [$] *Rooms from: C$215* ✉ *44 Côte du Palais, Upper Town* ☎ *418/692–1030, 800/463–6283* 🌐 *www.manoir-victoria.com* 🛏 *156 rooms* 🍴 *No meals* ✥ *E1.*

$ B&B/INN 🏨 **Hôtel Marie Rollet.** Located on a charming street corner at the heart of Vieux-Québec, this intimate inn built in 1876 by the Ursuline Order has quaint decor and antiques and sometimes small but warm rooms. **Pros:** central location; rooftop terrace with garden view; private bathroom in every room. **Cons:** no elevator; steep stairs; heavy outer and inner doors. [$] *Rooms from: C$129* ✉ *81 rue Ste-Anne, Upper Town* ☎ *418/694–9271, 800/275–0338* 🌐 *www.hotelmarierollet.com* 🛏 *11 rooms* 🍴 *No meals* ✥ *F2.*

$$ HOTEL 🏨 **L'Hôtel du Capitole.** This turn-of-the-20th-century gem just outside the St-Jean Gate combines a quirky hotel with a fully restored 1920s cabaret-style dinner theater, plus a respected Italian restaurant. **Pros:** theatrical style and vibe; rooftop garden with views; bar is a hub for after-theater drinks. **Cons:** theater-hotel complex not very peaceful; tubs in some bedrooms not for everyone. [$] *Rooms from: C$195* ✉ *972 rue St-Jean, Upper Town* ☎ *418/694–4040, 800/363–4040* 🌐 *www.lecapitole.com* 🛏 *39 rooms, 1 suite* 🍴 *No meals* ✥ *D2.*

$$ HOTEL 🏨 **Manoir d'Auteuil.** Art deco and art nouveau combine in this hotel, where an ornately sculpted iron banister wraps up through four floors, leading to guest rooms with varying styles and features including the Edith Piaf Suite, named for the French singer who used to frequent the hotel. **Pros:** direct view of the Parliament building; close to the convention center; deco charm. **Cons:** midweek business clientele takes over lobby; no elevator; not all rooms are created equal. [$] *Rooms from: C$179* ✉ *49 rue d'Auteuil, Upper Town* ☎ *418/694–1173, 866/662–6647* 🌐 *www.manoirdauteuil.com* 🛏 *27 rooms* 🍴 *Breakfast* ✥ *E3.*

$ HOTEL 🏨 **Manoir Sur le Cap.** From the wooden sign by the door, to the decorative fireplaces, and the views of Governors' Park, the Château Frontenac, and the St. Lawrence River, this elegant 19th-century inn is special. **Pros:** great views; a two-level deluxe suite in an old stable; charming location. **Cons:** no elevator; no breakfast; some bathrooms have only showers and no tubs. [$] *Rooms from: C$145* ✉ *9 av. Ste-Geneviève, Upper Town* ☎ *418/694–1987, 866/694–1987* 🌐 *www.manoir-sur-le-cap.com* 🛏 *14 rooms* 🍴 *No meals* ✥ *F3.*

10

LOWER TOWN

Many visitors insist on staying near the water, among the quays, warehouses, and cobblestone squares—as well as many boutique hotels, inspired eateries, and impressive entertainment venues.

$$$$ HOTEL Fodor's Choice ★ 🏨 **Auberge St-Antoine.** This charming hotel incorporates the historic stone walls of a 19th-century warehouse along with artifacts dating to the 1600s, many of which were found during an expansion and are now in glass displays in the public areas and guest rooms. **Pros:** unique architectural accents and exhibits; some rooms have fireplaces

North America's first ice hotel, rebuilt each winter, is only 15 minutes from Québec City by car, and worth a tour even if you don't spend the night.

and terraces; excellent restaurant. **Cons:** low vacancy means guests must plan well in advance. [$] *Rooms from: C$349* ✉ *8 rue St-Antoine, Lower Town* ☎ *418/692–2211, 888/692–2211* 🌐 *www.saint-antoine.com* 🛏 *95 rooms* 🍴 *No meals* ✣ *G2.*

$ B&B/INN **Hayden's Wexford House.** The attentive hosts make budget travelers and young couples feel right at home at this charming B&B, comfortably removed from the torrent of tourists but only a scenic 15-minute walk from all the Lower Town sites. **Pros:** big breakfast; quiet location near the river with ample street parking; discounted balloon rides available to guests. **Cons:** no TVs or telephones; books up fast in the summer months. [$] *Rooms from: C$140* ✉ *450 rue Champlain, Lower Town* ☎ *418/524–0524* 🌐 *www.haydenwexfordhouse.com* 💳 *No credit cards* 🛏 *3 rooms* 🍴 *Breakfast* ✣ *F6.*

$ HOTEL **Hôtel Belley.** Above the popular Belley Tavern, and conveniently located just next to the Old Harbor area and the Antiques district, this modest hotel features simple rooms, with exposed brick walls and beamed ceilings. **Pros:** modest and cheerful; close to antiques district; lively tavern downstairs. **Cons:** rooms are a bit sparse; no elevator. [$] *Rooms from: C$115* ✉ *249 rue St-Paul, Lower Town* ☎ *418/692–1694, 888/692–1694* 🌐 *www.hotelbelley.com* 🛏 *8 rooms* 🍴 *No meals* ✣ *F1.*

$$$ HOTEL Fodor's Choice ★ **Hôtel des Coutellier.** Charming details like buttery croissants delivered to the room each morning, exposed brick walls, and lush linens make this boutique hotel a popular roosting spot for lovebirds. **Pros:** elevator, a rarity in this part of town; breakfast delivered each morning. **Cons:** small bathrooms; in-room temperature controls aren't intuitive; a bit of a climb to Upper Town attractions. [$] *Rooms from: C$205* ✉ *253 rue St. Paul,*

Lower Town ☎ *418/692–9696, 888/523–9696* ⊕ *www.hoteldescoutellier.com* 🗀 *No credit cards* 🗝 *21 rooms, 3 suites* ⦿| *Breakfast* ✛ *F1.*

$$$$
HOTEL
Fodor'sChoice
★

🛏 **Hôtel Le Germain Québec.** Sophistication and attention to every detail prevails in the modern rooms of this chic boutique hotel—from the custom-designed swing-out night tables to the white goose-down duvets and custom umbrellas. **Pros:** impressive design; higher floors have views of the St. Lawrence River or the Old City; pets welcome. **Cons:** minimal interior is not for everyone. Ⓢ *Rooms from: C$295* ✉ *126 rue St-Pierre, Lower Town* ☎ *418/692–2224, 888/833–5253* ⊕ *www.legermainhotels.com/en/quebec* 🗝 *60 rooms* ⦿| *Breakfast* ✛ *G1.*

$$
HOTEL

🛏 **Hôtel Le Priori.** Housed in a 300-year-old building with stone and brick walls, this boutique hotel has a rigorously modern decor, with custom leather beds, stainless steel sinks, slate floors, and three-head shower jets. **Pros:** both hot and cold food at the buffet breakfast; modern but warm rooms; solid restaurant connected to the hotel. **Cons:** high-occupancy rates mean that you'll need to reserve some time ahead. Ⓢ *Rooms from: C$199* ✉ *15 rue Sault-au-Matelot, Lower Town* ☎ *418/692–3992, 800/351–3992* ⊕ *www.hotellepriori.com* 🗝 *28 rooms* ⦿| *Breakfast* ✛ *G2.*

$$
HOTEL

🛏 **Hôtel Le St-Paul.** Perched at the edge of the antiques district, this basic four-story hotel inside what was once a 19th-century office building, is near art galleries and the train station, and features a good restaurant and wine bar on the ground floor. **Pros:** charming vintage details; modern bathrooms; excellent value. **Cons:** lobby is modest; not all rooms are renovated; some rooms get ambient street noise. Ⓢ *Rooms from: C$209* ✉ *229 rue St-Paul, Lower Town* ☎ *418/694–4414, 888/794–4414* ⊕ *www.lesaintpaul.qc.ca* 🗝 *23 rooms, 4 suites* ⦿| *Breakfast* ✛ *F1.*

$$$$
HOTEL

🛏 **Hôtel 71.** Guest rooms at this luxury hotel, inside the city's first National Bank of Canada office, have 12-foot-high ceilings, excellent amenities, and stunning views of Old Québec. **Pros:** decadent and modern; luxurious packages; excellent Italian restaurant on-site. **Cons:** chic interiors not kid-friendly; valet service is steep. Ⓢ *Rooms from: C$299* ✉ *71 rue St-Pierre, Lower Town* ☎ *418/692–1171, 888/692–1171* ⊕ *www.hotel71.ca* 🗝 *69 rooms* ⦿| *Breakfast* ✛ *G2.*

10

OUTSIDE THE OLD CITY

Booking a room outside the walled city puts you in a mixed area of student housing, convention hotels, and chains, although there are still numerous inns, hotels, and B&Bs to choose from here. Many of the options are within easy proximity to the Plains of Abraham, Hôtel du Parlement, and museums like the Musée des Beaux-Arts du Québec.

$$
HOTEL

🛏 **Château Bonne Entente.** Sitting on 11 acres of gardens, le Bonne Entente is a self-contained resort about 25 minutes from downtown, a stylish boutique hotel within the main property, excellent amenities, a variety of dining options, and a pool you might just never want to leave. **Pros:** country-club feel; chic, relaxing atmosphere; free shuttle to Old Québec and downtown. **Cons:** a bit out of the way, with little to see in its neighborhood. Ⓢ *Rooms from: C$199* ✉ *3400 chemin Ste-Foy, Ste-Foy, Outside the Old City* ☎ *418/653–5221, 800/463–4390* ⊕ *www.chateaubonneentente.com* 🗝 *165 rooms* ⦿| *No meals* ✛ *A4.*

$$ **Hôtel Château Laurier.** Brown leather sofas and wrought-iron chan-
HOTEL deliers fill the spacious lobby of this former private house. **Pros:** some
rooms for budget travelers; Saint-Hubert BBQ serves great rôtisserie
chicken and a great breakfast; convenient to Grande-Allée. **Cons:**
some ambient noise; hotel a bit of a maze. $ *Rooms from: C$199*
✉ *1220 pl. George V Ouest, Outside the Old City* ☎ *418/522–8108,
877/522–8108* ⊕ *www.hotelchateaulaurier.com* ⌖ *289 rooms* �‖ *No
meals* ✛ *D5.*

$$$ **Hôtel Delta Québec.** Opposite the Parliament buildings, this recently
HOTEL renovated hotel with large, functional rooms is an excellent and styl-
ish option for business and design-minded travelers. **Pros:** kid-friendly
environment; some rooms are adapted for people with limited mobil-
ity; four-season outdoor pool. **Cons:** building is uninspiring; attracts
convention groups; drab lobby. $ *Rooms from: C$229* ✉ *690 boul.
René-Lévesque Est, Montcalm, Outside the Old City* ☎ *418/647–1717,
800/268–1133* ⊕ *www.marriott.com/hotels/travel/yqbdr-delta-hotels-
quebec* ⌖ *377 rooms* �‖ *No meals* ✛ *C4.*

$$ **Hôtel Loews Le Concorde.** Built in 1974, this 29-story concrete high-rise
HOTEL with an excellent location on Grande Allée offers larger-than-average
rooms Keurig coffeemakers, huge windows, and good views of Battle-
fields Park and the St. Lawrence River. **Pros:** central location; revolving
rooftop restaurant; heated pool has great views. **Cons:** high-traffic hotel;
pool is open only in summer; some rooms have outdated fabrics and
decor. $ *Rooms from: C$185* ✉ *1225 cours du Général-de Montcalm,
Montcalm* ☎ *418/647–2222, 800/463–5256* ⊕ *www.loewshotels.com*
⌖ *425 rooms* �‖ *No meals* ✛ *C5.*

$$ **Hôtel-Musée Premières Nations.** A warm welcome, spacious rooms
HOTEL outfitted with real pelts, and river views await at this luxury rural
FAMILY hotel, restaurant, and museum complex in Wendake, a 15-minute
drive north of the city. **Pros:** luxury rural escape; spa features Nordic pools, heated sidewalks, a fire pit, and yurt; excellent restaurant.
Cons: rustic-meets-contemporary style might not appeal to animal
lovers; uneven service. $ *Rooms from: C$179* ✉ *5 pl. de la Rencontre,
Wendake* ☎ *418/847–2222* ⊕ *www.tourismewendake.ca/hotel* ▭ *No
credit cards* ⌖ *55 rooms* ✛ *C1.*

$ **Hôtel Palace Royal.** A soaring indoor atrium with balconies overlook-
HOTEL ing a tropical garden, swimming pool, and hot tub lends a sense of
drama to this family-friendly hotel. **Pros:** eclectic design; rooms have
views of the Old City or the atrium; good packages. **Cons:** With the
pool, atrium can feel a bit hot and humid. $ *Rooms from: C$159* ✉ *775
av. Honoré-Mercier, Outside the Old City* ☎ *418/694–2000, 800/567–
5276* ⊕ *www.hotelsjaro.com/palaceroyal/index-en.aspx* ⌖ *234 rooms*
�‖ *No meals* ✛ *D2.*

$ **Hôtel Royal William.** Like its namesake, the first Canadian steamship
HOTEL to cross the Atlantic (in 1833), the Royal William embodies the spirit
of technology and innovation. **Pros:** friendly staff; convenient location
in a hip area. **Cons:** the public areas are uninspired; business travelers
aren't usually big minglers. $ *Rooms from: C$150* ✉ *360 boul. Charest
Est, St-Roch, Outside the Old City* ☎ *418/521–4488, 888/541–0405*
⊕ *www.royalwilliam.com* ⌖ *36 rooms, 8 suites* �‖ *Breakfast* ✛ *A2.*

$$$ HOTEL **Ice Hotel** (*Hôtel de Glace*). The first of its kind in North America, this hotel, open from the first week in January to the end of March at Village Vacances Valcartier, is built entirely from ice and snow each year. **Pros:** unique experience; spectacular engineering feat and design; festive ambience. **Cons:** thick snow and ice walls make for very silent rooms, which can be eerie; limited availability; about 20 minutes from downtown Québec City. [$] *Rooms from: C$219* ✉ *Village Vacances Valcartier, 1860 boul. Valcartier, about 20 minutes from downtown Québec City, Outside the Old City* ☎ *418/623–2888, 877/505–0423* 🌐 *www.hoteldeglace-canada.com* 🛏 *44 rooms* 🍴 *No meals* ✥ *D1.*

$ HOTEL **Hotel Pur.** Travelers with a preference for minimal and modern design will appreciate this slick boutique hotel with its light-filled rooms, great views, and location in an interesting neighborhood. **Pros:** clean, modern design; great dining room doubles as a bar late evenings; in bustling St-Roch district. **Cons:** minimal design doesn't work for everyone. [$] *Rooms from: C$139* ✉ *395 rue de la Couronne, St-Roch, Outside the Old City* ☎ *418/647–2611* 🌐 *www.hotelpur.com* 🛏 *242 rooms* 🍴 *No meals* ✥ *A1.*

NIGHTLIFE AND PERFORMING ARTS

Québec City has a good variety of cultural institutions for a town of its size, from its renowned symphony orchestra to several small theater companies. To sample its nightlife, you'll probably find yourself heading to the clubs and cafés of rue St-Jean, avenue Cartier, and Grande-Allée, and to a lesser extent Lower Town.

Billetech. Tickets for most shows in town are sold through this company. There are outlets around town. ✉ *Centre Vidéotron, Parc de l'Expocité, 250 boul. Wilfrid-Hamel, Limoilou* ☎ *418/643–8131* 🌐 *www.billetech.com.*

NIGHTLIFE

In winter, nightlife activity grows livelier as the week nears its end, beginning on Wednesday. As warmer temperatures set in, the café-terrace crowd emerges, and bars are active just about every night. Most bars and clubs stay open until 3 am.

UPPER TOWN

BARS AND LOUNGES

Bar Les Voûtes Napoléon. The brick walls and wine cellar–like atmosphere help make Les Voûtes a popular place to listen to Quebecois music. Much of the beer here's from local microbreweries. ✉ *680 rue Grande-Allée Est, Upper Town* ☎ *418/640–9388* 🌐 *www.voutesdenapoleon.com.*

Bar 1608. One of the city's most romantic spots is the Château Frontenac's bar, which boasts one of the most interesting cocktail lists in town. You can also have some wine, a bit of charcuterie and cheese, and relax while looking at the St. Lawrence River or the two fireplaces. ✉ *1 rue des Carrières, Upper Town* ☎ *418/266–3906.*

L'Atelier. Doubling up as a restaurant that notably serves all kinds of tartares, L'Atelier is a hot spot of Québec City mixology, as the haunt of Patrice Plante, aka Monsieur Cocktail, whose knack for creative and delicious cocktails have garnered national attention. ✉ *624 rue Grande-Allée Est, Upper Town* ☎ *418/522–2225.*

La Ninkasi. Just outside the walls, La Ninkasi has an art-exhibition space, plasma-screen TVs often tuned to hockey, a stage for local bands or improv shows, and several gaming tables. Sample from an expansive collection of local brews and find out what's going on in the area's thriving art scene. ✉ *811 rue St-Jean, Upper Town* ☎ *418/529–8538* ⊕ *www.ninkasi.ca.*

Le Cosmos. This trendy restaurant and club is on the ground floor under Chez Maurice. Simple eats, a slick decor and lively conversations are all part of the mix. There are now three other locations in greater Québec City, each with their own signature style. ✉ *575 rue Grande-Allée Est, Upper Town* ☎ *418/640–0606* ⊕ *www.lecosmos.com.*

Le Pub Saint-Alexandre. This popular English-style pub offers dozens of single-malt scotch and more than 200 kinds of beer, 30 of which are on tap, and many of which are exclusive imports. ✉ *1087 rue St-Jean, Upper Town* ☎ *418/694–0015* ⊕ *www.pubstalexandre.com.*

L'Inox. A popular Upper Town brewpub, L'Inox serves beers that have been brewed on-site, like Trouble-Fête and Coulée-Douce, as well as a rotating list of limited edition brews. Inside are billiard tables and excellent European-style hot dogs (featuring long, tasty sausages served on a baguette); outside there's a summer terrace. ✉ *655 rue Grande-Allée Est, Upper Town* ☎ *418/692–2877* ⊕ *www.brasserieinox.com.*

Maurice. This is a three-storied bar complex named after the former premier of Québec, Maurice Duplessis. The crowd is young, and the atmosphere is racy and provocative. ✉ *575 rue Grande-Allée Est, 2nd fl., Upper Town* ☎ *418/647–2000* ⊕ *www.mauricenightclub.com.*

FOLK, JAZZ, AND BLUES

Bar Le Sacrilège. Across the street from Église St-Jean-Baptiste, this place bears its name well, with a couple of church pews and religious icons. Le Sacrilège has local microbrews like Boréale and Trou du Diable in bottles and on tap, and the special changes daily. It also has the best terrace in the city, an enclosed garden that's constantly full in summer. Live music or DJs play on a regular basis. ✉ *447 rue St-Jean, Upper Town* ☎ *418/649–1985* ⊕ *http://lesacrilege.com/.*

Bar Ste-Angèle. This cozy hipster hideaway features live jazz some nights, a variety of delicious cocktails, and a vintage Hollywood theme. There are drink specials on Tuesday. ✉ *26 rue Ste-Angèle, Upper Town* ☎ *418/692–2171.*

OUTSIDE THE OLD CITY

BARS AND LOUNGES

Korrigane Brasserie Artisanale. A popular after-work spot with the locals, this brewery crafts high-quality beer and tapas-inspired pub fare. A friendly vibe and ample seating make Korrigane the ideal spot for a *cinq à sept* or a low-key night out. In addition to the house brews, there's a good selection of other local options. ✉ *380 rue Dorchester, St-Roch* ☎ *418/614–0932* ⊕ *www.korrigane.ca.*

The rue du Trésor in Upper Town is an alleyway lined with local artists selling paintings and sketches.

Les Salons d'Edgar. Set on the southern edge of the St-Roch neighborhood, this bar and eatery attracts a crowd of friendly regulars, mostly in their thirties and forties, but also students from the Université Laval visual arts pavilion, across the street. You can listen to an eclectic selection of music while chatting the night away or having simple, tasty food with a beer or glass of wine from the inexpensive list. ⊠ *263 rue St-Vallier Est, St-Roch* ☎ *418/523–7811* ⊕ *www.lessalonsdedgar.com* ☽ *Closed July and Aug.*

PERFORMING ARTS

Art is everywhere in Québec City—from theater and chic galleries to accordion street performers and statue mimes in the parks. From September through May, a steady stream of concerts, plays, and performances is presented in theaters and halls. In summer, many indoor theaters close, and outdoor shows of all kinds abound, most of them free.

ARTS CENTERS

Fodor'sChoice
★

Grand Théâtre de Québec. Québec City's main theater has two stages for symphonic concerts, opera, plays, and touring companies of all sorts. The Grand Théâtre also presents a dance series with Canadian and international companies. Inside, a three-wall mural by the Québec sculptor Jordi Bonet depicts Death, Life, and Liberty. Bonet wrote "La Liberté" on one wall to bring attention to the Québécois struggle for freedom and cultural distinction. ⊠ *269 boul. René-Lévesque Est, Upper Town* ☎ *418/643–8131* ⊕ *www.grandtheatre.qc.ca.*

MUSIC

Centre Vidéotron. This state-of-the-art arena opened in the fall of 2015, with the hope of attracting a National Hockey League franchise. For now, the hockey is from a junior league, but there are world-class concerts and popular acts playing here regularly. ⊠ *Parc de l'Expocité, 250 boul. Wilfrid-Hamel, Limoilou* ☎ *855/790–1245* ⊕ *www.lecentrevideotron.ca.*

Fodor's Choice **Orchestre Symphonique de Québec** (*Québec Symphony Orchestra*).
★ Canada's oldest symphony orchestra, directed by the dynamic French conductor Fabien Gabel, performs mainly at Louis-Fréchette Hall in the Grand Théâtre de Québec. ⊠ *269 boul. René-Lévesque Est, Upper Town* ☎ *418/643–8486* ⊕ *www.osq.org.*

Théâtre Petit-Champlain. The charming and intimate Théâtre Petit-Champlain is a fine spot to hear contemporary Francophone music during the year and take in a play in summer. ⊠ *68 rue du Petit-Champlain, Lower Town* ☎ *418/692–2631* ⊕ *www.theatrepetitchamplain.com.*

THEATER

Most theater productions are in French. In summer, open-air concerts are presented at place d'Youville (just outside St-Jean Gate) and on the Plains of Abraham. *The theaters listed below schedule shows from September to May.*

Carrefour international de théâtre de Québec. This international theatrical festival takes over several spaces in late May and early June: the Salle Albert-Rousseau, the Grand Théâtre de Québec, the Théâtre Périscope (near avenue Cartier), and Complexe Méduse. There are usually at least one or two productions in English or with English subtitles, and an outdoor show that takes over different parts of the downtown area. ⊠ *Québec City* ☎ *418/692–3131* ⊕ *www.carrefourtheatre.qc.ca.*

Coopérative Méduse. This multidisciplinary arts center, built in a row of historic houses mixed with new structures, is a hub for local artists and presents edgy installations and live shows, including a modern dance series. ⊠ *541 rue de St-Vallier Est, St-Roch* ☎ *418/640–9218* ⊕ *www.meduse.org.*

École de Cirque. For three weeks every May, students of this circus school and others take to the trapeze to promote their art form through the Circus Days festival. Throughout the year, students and teachers put on various shows, training camps, and workshops, including a Christmas Cabaret, in the former church that now houses their school. ⊠ *750 av. 2e, Limoilou* ☎ *418/525–0101* ⊕ *www.ecoledecirque.com.*

Théâtre Capitole. This cabaret-style theater schedules pop music and musical comedy shows. It also specializes in revival pieces by singers like Elvis or Johnny Cash, or whole genres, like disco. ⊠ *972 rue St-Jean, Upper Town* ☎ *418/694–4444* ⊕ *www.lecapitole.com.*

Théâtre Périscope. This multipurpose theater hosts about a dozen different productions a year, staged by several different theater companies. New creations and experimental productions are always a strong part of the mix. ⊠ *2 rue Crémazie Est, Montcalm* ☎ *418/529–2183* ⊕ *www.theatreperiscope.qc.ca.*

QUÉBEC SUMMER FESTIVAL

Festival d'Été International de Québec (*Québec City Summer Festival*). An annual highlight in the first half of July is this exuberant Summer Festival, 11 days of rock, folk, hip-hop, and world music. It's a great event for hearing unfamiliar performers and expanding your musical horizons. The main concerts take place each evening on three outdoor stages in or near the Old City, including one holding up to 80,000 people on the Plains of Abraham. A pass (C$95) admits you to all events throughout the festival, and single-night passes, for around C$30, may be available for some nights. Some concerts at indoor theaters cost extra, but free music and activities, such as family concerts and street performers during the day, are also plentiful. At night rue St-Jean near the city gate turns into a free street theater, with drummers, dancers, and skits. Book a room several months in advance if you plan to attend. ⊠ *Québec City* ☎ *418/523–4540, 888/992-5200* ⊕ *www. infofestival.com.*

SPORTS AND THE OUTDOORS

Scenic rivers and nearby mountains (no more than 30 minutes away by car) make Québec City a great place for exploring the outdoors.

Québec City Tourist Information. Contact the tourist board for information about sports and fitness activities around the city. ⊠ *399 rue St-Joseph Est., St-Roch* ☎ *418/641–6654, 877/783–1608* ⊕ *www. quebecregion.com.*

BIKING

There are over 100 km (60 miles) of fairly flat, well-maintained bike paths on Québec City's side of the St. Lawrence River and a similar amount on the south shore. Detailed route maps are available through tourism offices. The best and most scenic of the bike paths are the one that follows the old railway bed in Lévis, accessible near the Québec-Lévis ferry terminal, and the one that follows the Saint-Lawrence River on the north shore, all the way to Montmorency Falls. Many parts of the regional network are now part of the province-wide Route Verte, a government-funded, 4,000-km-long (2,500-mile-long) circuit of long-distance bicycle paths and road routes.

Corridor des Cheminots. Ambitious cyclists can embark on the 22-km-long (14-mile-long) trail that runs from Québec City near Old Québec to the town of Shannon. It's a slow uphill on the way out—with the reward of an easier ride back. ⊠ *Québec City.*

Côte-de-Beaupré. Paths along the beginning of the Beaupré coast, at the confluence of the St. Charles and St. Lawrence rivers, are especially scenic. They begin northeast of the city, at rue de la Vérendrye and boulevard Montmorency or rue Abraham-Martin and Pont Samson (Samson Bridge), and continue 10 km (6 miles) along the coast to Montmorency Falls. ⊠ *Québec City.*

10

Mont-Ste-Anne. The site of the 1998 world mountain-biking championship and races for the annual World Cup has around 150 km (93 miles) of mountain-bike trails and an extreme-mountain-biking park. ⊠ *Québec City* ☎ *800/463–1568* ⊕ *www.mont-sainte-anne.com* ✉ *C$15 trails only; C$43 unlimited access to ski lift and trails.*

DOG SLEDDING

For centuries, dog sledding has been a part of the Canadian winter experience. Outfitters around Québec City generally offer excursions from January through March.

FAMILY   **Aventures Nord-Bec Stoneham.** This outfitter will teach you how to mush in the forest. A half-day expedition, which includes initiation, dog sledding, a guided tour of kennels, and a snack, costs C$120 per person. Overnight camping trips, snowshoeing, and ice fishing are also available. In summer, this location offers fishing, mountain biking and kennel tours. Transportation between Stoneham (a 30-minute drive from the Old City) and your hotel costs extra. ⊠ *4 chemin des Anémones, Stoneham* ☎ *418/848–3732* ⊕ *www.traineaux-chiens.com.*

GOLF

The Québec City region has 18 golf courses, and most are open to the public. Reservations are essential in summer.

Club de Golf Cap-Rouge. Established in 1959, this is one of the closest courses to the city center, just 25 minutes by car from Vieux-Québec in a pleasant suburban area. Its 18-hole course is set up with variations for women, men, and advanced players. You're close to the St. Lawrence River, so be careful that the wind doesn't play tricks on you. ⊠ *4600 rue St-Felix, Cap-Rouge* ☎ *418/653–9381* ⊕ *www.golfcap-rouge.qc.ca* ✉ *Nonmembers: C$35–C$95 for 18 holes. Members: C$32–C$77 for 18 holes* ⚲ *18 holes, 6756 yards, par 72* ⚐ *Facilities: driving range, putting green, golf carts, rental clubs, pro shop, lessons, restaurant.*

Club de Golf de Mont Tourbillon. The cooler air of the Laurentian mountains is quite welcome on a hot summer day, as you play golf and enjoy views of the rolling hillside and Lac Beauport. Mont Tourbillon features three courses and the brand-new, modern clubhouse offers a bistro with a pleasant terrace. It's 25 minutes from the city by car via Route 73 North (take the Lac Beauport exit). In winter, golfing yields the way to tubing, fun slides. ⊠ *55 montée du Golf, Lac-Beauport* ☎ *418/849–4418* ⊕ *www.monttourbillon.com* ✉ *C$55 weekends, C$40 weekdays* ⚲ *Blue Course: 18 holes, 6090 yards, par 70; White Course: 18 holes, 5590 yards, par 70; Red Course: 18 holes, 4625 yards, par 70* ⚐ *Facilities: driving range, putting green, golf carts, rental clubs, lessons, restaurant, bar.*

Le Saint-Ferréol. Located within sight of the Mont-Sainte-Anne ski slopes, this club has one of the best and best-priced courses in the region—it's been fine-tuned by pro Denis Gagné. The course is a half-hour drive northeast of Québec City, and features a large driving range for practice. ⊠ *1700 boul. les Neiges, St-Ferréol-les-Neiges* ☎ *418/827–3778*

⊕ *www.golfstferreol.com* ✉ *C$24 for 9 holes, C$48 for 18 holes* 🏌 *18 holes, 6445 yards, par 72* ☞ *Facilities: Driving range, golf carts, rental clubs, pro shop, lessons, restaurant, bar.*

ICE-SKATING

Ice-skating in Québec City is a popular pastime for locals and visitors alike. In addition to rinks in town, Village Vacances Valcartier (see Snow Slides), just outside Québec City, offers skating trails with lighting and sound systems.

Place d'Youville. This well-known outdoor rink, just outside St-Jean Gate, is open daily October through the end of March, from noon to 10 pm. Skate rental is C$8, and skating itself is free. A locker will run you C$1. ✉ *Québec City* ☎ *418/641–6256.*

Plains of Abraham. The sports field at the western end of Battlefields park features a large skating rink. ✉ *Montcalm* ✉ *Free. Skate rental C$8 for 2 hrs.*

RAFTING

Just outside the city, the Jacques-Cartier River (to the west) and Riviére Malbaie (to the east) both make for an easy white-water rafting day trip. Village Vacances Valcartier (see Snow Slides) also runs three-hour rafting excursions on the river from May through September.

Excursions Jacques-Cartier. This outfitter runs rafting trips on the Jacques-Cartier River, about 48 km (30 miles) northwest of Québec City, from May through October. Tours originate from Tewkesbury, a half-hour drive from Québec City. A half-day trip ranges from C$55 per person on weekdays to C$77 on weekends, wet suits included. Horseback riding is also available. ✉ *860 av. Jacques-Cartier Nord, Stoneham-et-Tewkesbury* ☎ *418/848–7238* ⊕ *www.excursionsj-cartier.com.*

SKIING

Skiing is very popular here, whether it's downhill on one of the mountains surrounding the city or cross-country in an urban park. A dynamic landscape, top-notch ski resorts, and lots of fresh powder have helped make this a major training area for some of Canada's top athletes.

⇨ *For more cross-country and downhill skiing options near Québec City, see the Side Trips from Québec City chapter.*

Québec City Tourism. General information about ski centers in Québec is available from Québec City Tourism. ✉ *Québec City* ☎ *877/783–1608, 418/641–6290* ⊕ *www.quebecregion.com.*

CROSS-COUNTRY

Regroupement des Stations de Ski de Fond. Thirty-seven cross-country ski centers in the Québec area have 2,000 km (1,240 miles) of groomed trails and heated shelters between them; contact this group for more information. Many also offer snowshoeing trails. ✉ *Québec City* ⊕ *www.skidefondraquette.com.*

SKI CENTERS

Les Sentiers du Moulin. This center is 19 km (12 miles) north of the city and has more than 20 marked trails covering 48 km (28 miles), overall, with 28 km (17 miles) multitrack. ⊠ *99 chemin du Moulin, Lac-Beauport* ☎ *418/849–9652.*

Parc des Champs-de-Bataille (*Battlefields Park*). You can reach this park from Place Montcalm. It has more than 10 km (6 miles) of scenic, marked, cross-country skiing trails. Skis and snowshoes can be rented at the Musée des Plaines. ⊠ *835 av. Wilfrid-Laurier, Montcalm.*

DOWNHILL

Multiple downhill ski resorts are nearby, and some are barely 30 minutes away from downtown Québec City. Most have night skiing. ⇨ *For information on Le Massif and Mont-Ste-Anne, see the Côte-de-Beaupré section in Chapter 11, Side Trips from Québec City.*

Le Relais. There are 28 trails and a vertical drop of 734 feet at this relatively small, family-friendly ski center, where you can buy lift tickets by the hour. Le Relais is about 20 minutes from downtown Québec City. ⊠ *1084 boul. du Lac, Lac-Beauport* ☎ *418/849–1851* ⊕ *www.skirelais.com.*

Station Touristique Stoneham. Stoneham is 20 minutes north of Old Québec. The hill has a vertical drop of 1,380 feet, with a number of long, easy slopes and some more challenging runs. It has 42 downhill runs and seven lifts, plus three terrain parks and one super-half-pipe. ⊠ *1420 av. du Hibou, Stoneham* ☎ *418/848–2411, 800/463–6888* ⊕ *www.ski-stoneham.com.*

SNOW SLIDES

The snow slide from Dufferin Terrace is easily one of the most exciting winter activities in Québec.

FAMILY **Glissades de la Terrasse.** A wooden toboggan takes you down a 270-foot-high snow slide that's adjacent to the Château Frontenac. Three rides cost C$10. ⊠ *Québec City* ☎ *418/829–9898.*

FAMILY **Village Vacances Valcartier.** Hop on an inner tube or carpet and shoot down one of more than 35 snow slides here. Or join 6 to 12 others for a snow-raft ride on one of three groomed trails. You can also take a dizzying ride on the Tornado, a giant inner tube that seats eight and spins down the slopes. Rafting and sliding cost C$35 per day for those taller than 52 inches, C$27 for those between 39 and 52 inches, and free for those under 39 inches. Trails open daily at 10 am; closing times vary. ⊠ *1860 boul. Valcartier, St-Gabriel-de-Valcartier* ☎ *418/844–2200, 888/384–5524* ⊕ *www.valcartier.com.*

SNOWMOBILING

Québec is the birthplace of the snowmobile, and with 32,000 km (19,840 miles) of trails, it's one of the best places in the world for the sport. Two major trails, the 2,000-km (1,250-mile) Trans-Québec Snowmobile Trail and the 1,300-km (806-mile) Fur Traders Tour, run just north of Québec City. Trail maps are available at tourist offices.

DID YOU KNOW?

If you visit Québec City during the Carnaval de Québec you'll have the opportunity to tour Bonhomme's Ice Palace.

SM Sport. Snowmobile rentals with this company begin at C$45 per hour, or C$118 per day, plus tax and the cost of gas. They also provide various packages for multiday excursions around the region. These folks will pick up from several downtown hotels for an additional price, starting at C$20 per person. ⊠ *11337 boul. Valcartier, Loretteville* ☎ *418/842–2703* ⊕ *www.smsport.ca.*

WATER PARKS

FAMILY **Village Vacances Valcartier.** The largest water park in Canada has a wave pool, a 1-km (½-mile) tropical-river adventure called the Amazon, more than 35 waterslides, and a 100-foot accelerating slide on which bathers reach a speed of up to 80 kph (50 mph). The interior Bora Parc, featuring 14 slides, a river and a wave pool, is open year-round. Admission is C$42 a day for those at least 52 inches tall, C$35 for those between 39 and 52 inches, and free for those under 39 inches. The park also offers a flurry of winter slides and activities, a hotel and rafting excursions. ⊠ *1860 boul. Valcartier, St-Gabriel-de-Valcartier* ☎ *418/844–2200, 888/384–5524* ⊕ *www.valcartier.com.*

WINTER CARNIVAL

For three weekends in January and February, Québec City throws one of the biggest winter parties in the world. Each year, an Ice Palace is built as the center of the festivities, which include dog sled races, two parades, and events on several city streets. Ice bars are plentiful on the Grande Allée, and the streets fill with families and visitors singing songs and blowing into trumpets.

FAMILY
Fodor's Choice
★
Carnaval de Québec. A flurry of activity, mainly on the Plains of Abraham but also on several of the city's main drags, surrounds Carnaval de Québec, which occurs over three weekends every January and February. Snow and ice sculpture contests, dog sled relays, and canoe races on the icy St. Lawrence River chase away winter doldrums. Visitors brave the cold to get a glimpse of Bonhomme, the friendly Carnival Master, and tour his Ice Palace, which is rebuilt each year. Caribou, a strong mixture of red wine, hard liquor, and maple syrup, is a popular libation during the festivities. ⊠ *Québec City* ⊕ *www.carnaval.qc.ca.*

SHOPPING

On the fashionable streets of Vieux-Québec, shopping has a European tinge. The boutiques and specialty shops clustered along narrow streets such as rue du Petit-Champlain and rues de Buade and St-Jean are especially traditional.

Stores are generally open Monday–Wednesday 9:30–5:30, Thursday and Friday until 9, Saturday until 5, and Sunday noon–5. In summer most shops have later evening hours.

UPPER TOWN

ART GALLERIES

Galerie Art Inuit Brousseau et Brousseau. Inuit art is the specialty of this large, well-known gallery. The gallery director, Jean-Francois Brousseau, selects works by artists represented by the North Canadian Inuit cooperatives, and the gallery receives much praise for improving life in the Canadian Arctic. ⊠ *35 rue St-Louis, Upper Town* ☎ *418/694–1828* ⊕ *www.artinuitbrousseau.ca.*

Galerie Michel Guimont. Located in the Old Port area, this is probably the most sought-after gallery for contemporary art in Québec City, with solid exhibits of paintings, drawings, and prints from emerging and well-established artists. ⊠ *273 rue St-Paul, Lower Town* ☎ *418/692–1188* ⊕ *galeriemichelguimont.com.*

CLOTHING

Bedo. Head to this popular chain for trendy, well-priced items to round out your work wardrobe. Bedo also has great sales racks to sort through at the end of seasons. ⊠ *1161 rue St-Jean, Upper Town* ☎ *418/692–0761* ⊕ *www.bedo.ca.*

CRAFTS

Les Trois Colombes. Handmade items, including native and Inuit carvings, furs, ceramics, and clothing made from handwoven fabric, are available at this interesting shop. ⊠ *46 rue St-Louis, Upper Town* ☎ *418/694–1114.*

DEPARTMENT STORES

La Maison Simons. This growing Canadian chain store started here in Québec City in the 19th century, and is still owned by its founding family. The store carries designer clothing, linens, and other household items. Two other locations at Place Sainte-Foy and Galeries de la Capitale shopping centers. ⊠ *20 côte de la Fabrique, Upper Town* ☎ *418/692–3630* ⊕ *www.simons.ca.*

FOOD

Les Délices de l'Érable. Find a sweet souvenir at this maple syrup shop, which has everything from maple cookies to muffins and serves some of the best gelato in town. An exhibit space upstairs explains the process behind maple syrup and showcases artifacts from this Québec tradition. ⊠ *1044 rue St-Jean, Upper Town* ☎ *418/692–3245* ⊕ *www.mapledelights.com.*

GIFTS

Point d'Exclamation! Handcrafted fashion, bags, jewelry, hair accessories, paper, notebooks, cards, essential oils and artwork by dozens of Quebecois artisans fill Diane Bergeron's shop. ⊠ *762 rue St-Jean, Upper Town* ☎ *418/525–8053.*

JEWELRY

Zimmermann. Exclusive handmade jewelry can be found at this Upper Town shop, a city landmark. ⊠ *46 côte de la Fabrique, Upper Town* ☎ *418/692–2672* ⊕ *www.zimmermann-quebec.com.*

10

LOWER TOWN

ANTIQUES

French-Canadian, Victorian, and art deco furniture, clocks, silverware, and porcelain are some of the rare collectibles found here, mainly on quaint and historic Saint-Paul street. Authentic Québec pine furniture, characterized by simple forms and lines, is rare—and pricey.

Antiquités Bolduc. The largest antiques store on rue St-Paul sells furniture, household items, old paintings, and knickknacks from the 19th and 20th centuries. ⊠ *89 rue St-Paul, Lower Town* ☎ *418/694–9558* ⊕ *www.lesantiquitesbolduc.com.*

Gérard Bourguet Antiquaire. You're not likely to find any bargains here, but this shop has a very good selection of authentic 18th- and 19th-century Québec pine furniture. ⊠ *97 rue St-Paul, Lower Town* ☎ *418/694–0896.*

L'Héritage Antiquité. This is probably the best place in the antiques district to find good Quebecois furniture, clocks, oil lamps, porcelain, and ceramics. It's a very welcoming store as well. ⊠ *109 rue St-Paul, Lower Town* ☎ *418/692–1681.*

ART GALLERIES

Lacerte Art Contemporain. Head to this well-established gallery in an old car-repair garage for contemporary art and sculpture. ⊠ *1 côte Dinan, Lower Town* ☎ *418/692–1586* ⊕ *www.galerielacerte.com* ☺ *Closed Mon. and Tues.*

CLOTHING

Le Blanc Mouton. Locally designed creations for women, including accessories and jewelry, fill this family-run boutique in Quartier Petit-Champlain. ⊠ *51 Sous le Fort, Lower Town* ☎ *418/692–2880.*

m0851. This chic boutique offers distinctive, elegant, and well-designed leather goods, from coats and jackets to sleek computer bags. ⊠ *66, boul. Champlain, Lower Town* ☎ *418/614–0851* ⊕ *www.m0851.com.*

SHOPPING MALLS

Fodor's Choice ★ **Quartier Petit-Champlain.** A pedestrian mall in Lower Town, surrounded by rues Champlain and du Marché-Champlain, Quartier Petit-Champlain has some 50 boutiques, local businesses, and restaurants. This popular district is the best area for Québec wood sculptures, weavings, ceramics, and jewelry. ⊠ *Lower Town* ☎ *418/692–2613* ⊕ *www. quartierpetitchamplain.com.*

OUTSIDE THE OLD CITY

CLOTHING

Aliksir. This small boutique is packed with essential oils and natural beauty products of all kinds, from skin care to dental care products, mostly organic and largely produced just outside of Québec City. ⊠ *89 rue Saint-Joseph Est, St-Roch* ☎ *418/977–3715* ⊕ *aliksir.com.*

Boutique Flirt. This brightly colored boutique carries some underwear for men as well as its main specialty, women's lingerie (including many pieces in hard-to-find sizes). They carry Aubade, Freya, Parah, Simone Perèle, Prima Donna, Marie Jo, and Empreinte, among others. ⊠ *525* *rue St-Joseph Est, St-Roch, Outside the Old City* ☎ *418/529–5221* ⊕ *www.lingerieflirt.com.*

DEPARTMENT STORES

Large department stores can be found in the malls of suburban Ste-Foy.

La Baie. Part of the historic Hudson's Bay Company chain, La Baie carries clothing for the entire family, as well as household wares and cosmetics. ✉ *Pl. Laurier, Ste-Foy* ☎ *418/627–5959.*

FOOD

Camellia Sinensis Maison de Thé. This modern and elegant space stocks 150 different teas from China, Japan, Africa, and beyond, most of them imported by the owners themselves. You can sign up for a number of tea-tasting sessions and workshops, or just sip some tea on premises ✉ *624 rue St-Joseph Est, St-Roch, Outside the Old City* ☎ *418/525– 0247* ⊕ *www.camellia-sinensis.com.*

La Boîte à Pain. Baker Patrick Nisot offers a selection of baguettes, multigrain breads (pumpernickel, rye), special flavors (olive, tomato and pesto, Sicilian), and dessert breads. Even something as common as a date square has a special and delicious twist to it. Sandwiches and salads are also available for lunch. No credit cards are accepted. Two more locations are available in Sainte-Foy and in the quaint Limoilou neighborhood. ✉ *289 rue St-Joseph Est, St-Roch, Outside the Old City* ☎ *418/647–3666* ⊕ *http://boiteapain.com.*

FURS

J.B. Laliberté. In business since 1867, the well-established Laliberté carries men's and women's fashions, furs and accessories. ✉ *595 rue St-Joseph Est, St-Roch, Outside the Old City* ☎ *418/525–4841.*

GIFTS

Zone. Design-oriented, whimsical yet practical objects abound in this popular store, which features tons of interesting gadgets, tools, and accessories for the home and office. From the latest cooking implement to lovely decorative objects and fancy clocks, there's something for just about everyone. ✉ *999 av. Cartier, Montcalm* ☎ *418/522–7373.*

SHOPPING MALLS

FAMILY **Galeries de la Capitale.** Thirty-five restaurants, some 280 shops, an IMAX theater, and an adjacent indoor amusement park make this recently and extensively renovated mall ideal for a whole day of family retail therapy. ✉ *5401 boul. des Galeries, Lebourgneuf, Outside the Old City* ☎ *418/627–5800* ⊕ *www.galeriesdelacapitale.com.*

Laurier Québec. There are more than 300 stores in Québec City's busiest mall, with everything from fashion and electronics to children's toys and books. Easily accessible by bus or (from some downtown hotels) shuttle, it's next door to Place de la Cité and Place Sainte-Foy. Together, the three malls form the largest stretch of shopping in the city. ✉ *2700 boul. Laurier, Ste-Foy* ☎ *418/651–5000* ⊕ *laurierquebec.com.*

10

SPAS

Sky Spa. Set on the 17th floor of a modern tower in the bustling Sainte-Foy district, near the city's main shopping centers, the spa features a terrace that is open all year, thermal care programs and a full set of spa care packages. Massages start at C$60, with a full treatment package offered for C$210. There's also a bistro, and lots of spots to enjoy the view. ✉ *2828 boul. Laurier, 17th fl., Ste-Foy* ☎ *866/656–9111* ⊕ *sky-spa.ca/quebec.*

Sibéria Spa. A 20-minute drive from Vieux-Québec, Siberia Spa offers thermal and cold baths, a eucalyptus steam room, a relaxing yurt, an elegant café set inside a former chapel,and a quiet pavilion where you can sit by a fire and look out to the Jacques Cartier River. Admission is C$42 (C$29, evenings) for use of the spa, with massages and packages running from C$80 to C$254. It's normally adults only, but families are welcome on Sunday mornings, between 9 am and noon, and on regular hours during the holidays and spring break. ✉ *339 boul. du Lac, Lac-Beauport* ☎ *418/841–1325* ⊕ *www.siberiastationspa.com.*

TOYS/GAMES

FAMILY **Benjo.** Whimsy runs wild at Benjo. This store features games and toys, kids' clothes, a large café with thrones for little princes and princesses, an ample bookstore filled with French storybooks (and some English), and even an electric train you can ride around the store. ✉ *550 boul. Charest Est, St-Roch, Outside the Old City* ☎ *418/640–0001* ⊕ *www.benjo.ca.*

EXCURSIONS

Huron-Wendat Village. A 25-minute drive outside city limits takes you into another world, that of the Huron-Wendat Nation, one group of Canada's First Nations peoples. The Huron-Wendat are famous for their handcrafted clothing, decorations, and hunting tools, which are on display at the village. A "traditional site" offers a fascinating traditional village exhibition, complete with longhouse, dances, and storytelling. Visitors can take guided tours and discover some stunning crafts in the huge gift shop. Traditional meals are served in an on-site restaurant. The spectacular Kabir Kouba waterfall, carved into a deep and steep gorge, is definitely worth a stop as well. ✉ *575 rue Stanislas-Kosca, Wendake* ☎ *418/842–4308* ⊕ *www.huron-wendat.qc.ca* 🎫 *Guided tour C$13.*

SIDE TRIPS FROM QUÉBEC CITY

WELCOME TO
SIDE TRIPS FROM QUÉBEC CITY

TOP REASONS TO GO

★ **Ski at Le Massif:** This three-peak ski resort has the largest vertical drop in Eastern Canada, at more than 2,500 feet.

★ **Whale-watch in Tadoussac:** About 220 km (137 miles) east of Québec City, you can see small white beluga whales—an endangered species—year-round in the Saguenay River.

★ **Farm-hop on Île d'Orléans:** The "Garden of Québec" is covered with farmland and bed-and-breakfasts, and makes for the perfect day or overnight trip from Québec City.

★ **Take the footbridge across Montmorency Falls:** These waterfalls on the Côte-de-Beaupré are double the height of Niagara Falls. The bridge and stairs, which go over and around them, make for a spectacular stroll.

★ **See Basilique Ste-Anne-de-Beaupré:** More than a million people a year make pilgrimages to this church, named after the patron saint of Québec.

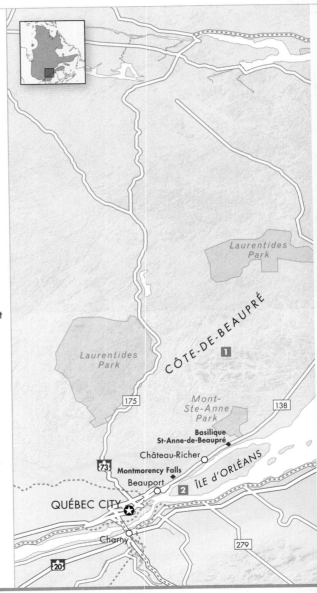

Saguenay

Route Verte Bike Route 🚲

Saguenay *River*

Sacré-Coeur

Petit-Saguenay

Tadoussac

Saguenay–St. Lawrence Marine Park

170

C H A R L E V O I X

3

Sagard

St-Siméon

La Malbaie

381

St-Joseph-de-la-Rive

St. Lawrence River

132

Saint-Pascal

Baie-Saint-Paul

◆ Le Massif

La Pocatière

Route Verte Bike Route 🚲

20

204

Montmagny

283

MAINE

281

UNITED STATES

0   20 mi

0   20 km

Île d'Orléans and the Côte-de-Beaupré are about 25 km (15 miles) east of Québec City.

The Charlevoix region is about 110 km (70 miles) northeast of Québec City, so consider spending the night.

1 **Côte-de-Beaupré.** Driving along this coast offers views of Île d'Orléans, as well as Montmorency Falls and the famous pilgrimage site, Ste-Anne-de-Beaupré.

2 **Île d'Orléans.** This island is called the "Garden of Québec" for all the produce, flowers, and prepared goods that stock restaurants and homes throughout the province. Spend the day here farm-hopping and sampling everything from ice wine to foie gras as you go.

3 **Charlevoix.** People refer to Charlevoix as the "Switzerland of Québec" due to its terrain of mountains, valleys, streams, and waterfalls. Charlevoix's charming villages line the shore of the St. Lawrence River for about 200 km (125 miles).

Updated by
Rémy Charest

Experience a deeper understanding of this region's history and culture by venturing outside the city. In addition to the beauty of Montmorency Falls and Côte-de-Beaupré, get acquainted with rural life and the region's French heritage on the charming Île d'Orléans. There's also much to see and do in the Charlevoix area—a diverse landscape of mountains and rolling valleys with stunning views of the St. Lawrence River. Baie-St-Paul is a hub for art and food lovers, and Tadoussac is known for its rustic excursions, such as whale-watching and fjord tours.

Montmorency Falls is an excellent first stop on any adventure outside the city. From there, you can cruise up Québec's Côte-de-Beaupré and eventually make your way to Ste-Anne-de-Beaupré, where there's an immense neo-Roman basilica. Or take the bridge to Île d'Orléans, where you can pick fresh berries, sample ice cider, fermented from frozen apples, and shop for antiques. A leisurely drive around the island can be done in a day.

Charlevoix, a couple of hours from Québec City, takes more planning and probably an overnight stay, but is well worth the drive. There are plenty of gorgeous villages and picnic spots along the way. Artists of all disciplines draw inspiration from this region, which is steeped in natural beauty and Algonquin history. Approaching Tadoussac, at the eastern edge of Charlevoix, the St. Lawrence River begins to seem like the open sea—it's more than 20 km (12 miles) wide at this point. Slicing into the land is the dramatic Saguenay Fjord, one of the largest fjords in the world.

WHEN TO GO
Côte-de-Beaupré, Île d'Orléans, and Charlevoix are spectacular in the fall, when you can leaf-peep and go apple picking. Summer means roadside stands featuring fresh-from-the-farm produce on Île d'Orléans

or Côte-de-Beaupré. Artists and art lovers flock to Baie-St-Paul in Charlevoix for festivals and gallery openings. It's also the perfect time to see beluga whales in Tadoussac. In winter, in all regions, there are plenty of cold-weather activities, including cross-country skiing, snowshoeing, and ice fishing. The area's best downhill skiing can be found in Charlevoix, but if you don't want to tackle driving on mountain roads, consider taking a shuttle. Spring has its own magic, when the snow melts and the maple syrup starts to flow.

GETTING HERE AND AROUND
The best, and in some cases the only way to explore these regions is by car, and this makes it easy to spend as much or as little time as desired in any given area. Start by heading northeast out of Québec City on Route 440 (Autoroute Dufferin–Montmorency) and then Route 138 (Boulevard Ste-Anne).

Another way to explore the exceptional beauty of the region is to hop aboard Le Train du Massif Charlevoix, a train that runs mid-June through mid-October along the shoreline from Parc de la Chute-Montmorency station to Baie-St.-Paul or La Malbaie, with several excursion options. ⇨ *For further details, see under Baie-St.-Paul and La Malbaie.*

Train Information Le Train de Charlevoix. 🕾 *418/240–4124, 844/737–3282* ⊕ *www.traindecharlevoix.com.*

Québec continues to expand its Route Verte (Green Route), a 5,000-km (3,100-mile) network of bike trails in the southern part of the province.
⇨ *For more information on getting here and around, refer to Travel Smart.*

RESTAURANTS
Some of the restaurants on the Côte-de-Beaupré and Île d'Orléans are open only during high season, May to October, so check ahead. But visitors who do arrive in season won't be disappointed. Fast-food or chain outlets are essentially absent from the island, and your best—and most widely available—option is to sample some of the regional cuisine on offer. And while fine dining is the order of the day on Île d'Orléans, those traveling on a budget won't go hungry, as there are some good pubs and family-style restaurants with fairly reasonable prices.

In Charlevoix, the same rules apply—call ahead if you're visiting from June to September or during the Christmas holidays. During summer, Charlevoix is a food lover's haven, with fresh berries and cheeses sold roadside and plenty of bistros in the towns. Pick up a map (available at most hotels and restaurants) of *La Route des Saveurs*, a route through the region dotted with restaurants and farms, and taste your way to Tadoussac.

HOTELS
Reservations at hotels are highly recommended, although off-season it's possible to book a room the same day. B&Bs are the most common lodging options on Île d'Orléans, although there is a handful of inns and one motel. Côte-de-Beaupré, on the other hand, not only has plenty of inns and B&Bs, but several hotels and motels as well.

Given its status as one of Québec's premier summer vacation destinations, the Charlevoix region has lots to offer travelers on almost any budget. Nevertheless, it's wise to book ahead in high season, especially if you're looking for one of the less expensive rooms here, which tend to fill up pretty quickly during the summer months.

Hotel reviews have been shortened. For full information, visit Fodors.com.

WHAT IT COSTS IN CANADIAN DOLLARS				
	$	$$	$$$	$$$$
Restaurants	under C$12	C$12–C$20	C$21–C$30	over C$30
Hotels	under C$160	C$160–C$200	C$201–C$250	over C$250

Restaurant prices are the average cost of a main course at dinner or, if dinner is not served, at lunch. Hotel prices are the lowest cost of a standard double room in high season.

VISITOR INFORMATION

Association Touristique Régionale de Charlevoix. ⊠ *495 boul. de Comporté, C.P. 275, La Malbaie* ☎ *418/665–4454, 800/667–2276* ⊕ *www.tourisme-charlevoix.com.*

Centre d'Interpretation de la Côte-de-Beaupré (*Beaupré Coast Interpretation Center*). ⊠ *7976 av. Royale, C.P. 40, Château-Richer* ☎ *418/824–3677, 877/824–3677* ⊕ *www.histoire-cotedebeaupre.org.*

CÔTE-DE-BEAUPRÉ

As legend has it, when explorer Jacques Cartier first caught sight of the north shore of the St. Lawrence River in 1535, he exclaimed, "*Quel beau pré!*" ("What a lovely meadow!"), because the area was the first inviting piece of land he had spotted since leaving France. Today the Côte-de-Beaupré (Beaupré Coast), first settled by French farmers, stretches 40 km (25 miles) east from Québec City to the famous pilgrimage site of Ste-Anne-de-Beaupré. Historic Route 360, or avenue Royale, winds its way from Beauport to St-Joachim, east of Ste-Anne-de-Beaupré. The impressive Chute Montmorency (Montmorency Falls) lie between Québec City and Ste-Anne-de-Beaupré.

GETTING HERE AND AROUND

Route 440 (Autoroute Dufferin–Montmorency) heads northeast from Québec City along the Côte-de-Beaupré. It's approximately 9.5 km (6 miles) to the exit for the Chutes Montmorency and about 35 km (21 miles) to Ste-Anne-de-Beaupré.

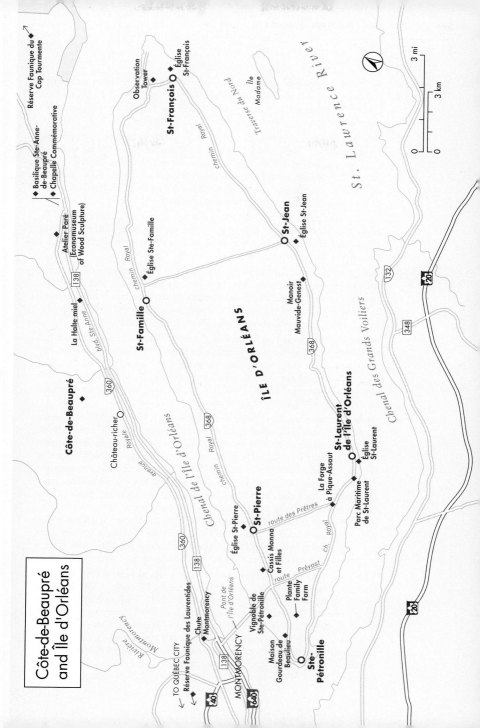

Côte-de-Beaupré and Île d'Orléans

St. Lawrence River

Réserve Faunique du Cap Tourmente

Basilique Ste-Anne-de-Beaupré

Chapelle Commémorative

Observation Tower

Église St-François

St-François

Île Madame

Traverse du Nord

chemin Royal

Atelier Paré (Economuseum of Wood Sculpture)

La Halte miel

blvd. Ste-Anne

138

chemin Ste-Anne

Église Ste-Famille

chemin Royal

St-Famille

Église St-Jean

St-Jean

Côte-de-Beaupré

360

Manoir Mauvide-Genest

ÎLE D'ORLÉANS

368

Château-richer

Royale

avenue

Chenal de l'Île d'Orléans

368

chemin Royal

St-Laurent de l'Île d'Orléans

Église St-Laurent

La Forge à Pique-Assaut

Parc Maritime de St-Laurent

Chenal des Grands Voiliers

132

20

348

Église St-Pierre

St-Pierre

route des Prêtres

360

Cassis Monna et Filles

route Prévost

ch. Royal

138

Vignoble de Ste-Pétronille

Plante Family Farm

Pont de l'Île d'Orléans

Chute Montmorency

Réserve Faunique des Laurentides

Maison Gourdeau de Beaulieu

Ste-Pétronille

20

Rivière Montmorency

TO QUÉBEC CITY

138

MONTMORENCY

40

640

N

3 mi

3 km

EXPLORING

TOP ATTRACTIONS

Fodor's Choice
★

Basilique Ste-Anne-de-Beaupré. Named for Québec's patron saint (the mother of the Virgin Mary), this small town is on Route 138, east of Québec City. It attracts more than a million pilgrims each year who come to visit the region's most famous religious site.

The French brought their devotion to St. Anne (also the patron saint of shipwrecked sailors) when they sailed across the Atlantic to New France. According to local legend, St. Anne was responsible for saving voyagers from shipwrecks in the harsh waters of the St. Lawrence. In 1650, Breton sailors caught in a storm vowed to erect a chapel in honor of this patron saint at the exact spot where they landed.

The present neo-Roman basilica, constructed in 1923, is the fifth to be built on the site where the sailors first touched ground. The original 17th-century wood chapel was built too close to the St. Lawrence and was swept away by river flooding.

The gigantic structure is in the shape of a Latin cross and has two imposing granite steeples. The interior has 22 chapels and 18 altars, as well as rounded arches and numerous ornaments in the Romanesque style. The 214 stained-glass windows, completed in 1949, are by Frenchmen Auguste Labouret and Pierre Chaudière.

Tributes to St. Anne can be seen in the shrine's mosaics, murals, altars, and ceilings. A bas-relief at the entrance depicts St. Anne welcoming her pilgrims, and ceiling mosaics represent her life. Numerous crutches and braces posted on the back pillars have been left by those who have felt the saint's healing powers. ⊠ *10018 av. Royale, Ste-Anne-de-Beaupré* ☎ *418/827–3781* ⊕ *www.ssadb.qc.ca* ⬟ *C$2.*

Fodor's Choice
★

Chute Montmorency. The river cascading over a cliff into the St. Lawrence is one of the most beautiful sights in the province—and at 27 stories high, the falls are almost double the height of Niagara's. The Montmorency River was named for Charles de Montmorency, viceroy of New France in the 1620s and explorer Samuel de Champlain's immediate commander. A cable car runs to the top of the falls in **Parc de la Chute-Montmorency** (Montmorency Falls Park) from late April to late October. During very cold weather the falls' heavy spray freezes and forms a giant loaf-shape ice cone known to the Quebecois as the Pain de Sucre (Sugarloaf); this phenomenon attracts sledders and sliders from Québec City. Summer activities include three via ferrata trails built onto the cliff, as well as a zip line that shoots across the canyon, in front of the falls.

The park also has a history. The British general James Wolfe, on his way to conquer New France, camped here in 1759. In 1780 Sir Frederick Haldimand, then the governor of Canada, built a summer home atop the cliff. The structure burned down in 1993, however, and what stands today, Manoir Montmorency, is a re-creation. Offering a stunning view of the falls and river below, it's open year-round, with a restaurant and terrace open in summertime. ⊠ *2490 av. Royale, Beauport* ☎ *418/663–3330* ⊕ *www.sepaq.com* ⬟ *Free. Cable car from C$10 one-way or C$14 round-trip; parking C$10 ($7 Nov.–Apr.).*

WORTH NOTING

Atelier Paré (Economuseum of Wood Sculpture). Two centuries of wood sculpture tradition are showcased at this "economuseum," a combination workshop and store. Visitors can watch artisans at work, tour an outdoor museum, see a 13-minute video presentation (in English and French), and learn about key characters in Québec's history and culture through the Legend Theatre Workshop. ⊠ *9269 av. Royale, Ste-Anne-de-Beaupré* ☎ *418/827–3992* ⊕ *www.atelierpare.com* ▣ *Free; guided tour C$4.*

Chapelle Commémorative (*Memorial Chapel*). Across from Basilique Ste-Anne-de-Beaupré, this chapel was designed by Claude Bailiff and built in 1878. It was constructed on the transept of a church built in 1676, and Bailiff made use of the old stones and foundation. Among the remnants is a white-and-gold-trimmed pulpit designed by François Baillargé in 1807 and adorned with a sculpture depicting Moses and the Ten Commandments.

Scala Santa, a smaller chapel next to this one, resembles a wedding cake. On bended knees, pilgrims climb its replica of the Holy Stairs, representing the steps Jesus climbed to meet Pontius Pilate. ⊠ *10018 av. Royale, Ste-Anne-de-Beaupré* ☎ *418/827–3781* ⊕ *www.sanctuaire-sainteanne.org.*

FAMILY **La Halte Miel.** Things are buzzing at this workshop and store devoted to bees and honey. An exhibit explains every aspect of honey production, and you can taste honey and honey ice creams, chocolates, and snacks made by bees that have fed on different kinds of flowers, including clover and blueberry. It's a 10-minute drive east of Montmorency Falls. ⊠ *8862 boul. Ste-Anne, Château-Richer* ☎ *418/824–4411* ⊕ *www. naturoney.com/en/honey-place* ▣ *Free.*

OFF THE
BEATEN
PATH

Réserve Faunique des Laurentides. The wildlife reserve, incorporating the Parc national de la Jacques-Cartier, is approximately 60 km (37 miles) north of Québec City via Highway 73, which leads to the Saguenay region. It has great hiking trails and camping spots, and good lakes for fishing (phone ahead 48 hours to reserve a time). ☎ *418/528–6868, 418/890–6527 fishing reservations* ⊕ *www.sepaq.com/rf/lau.*

FAMILY **Réserve Faunique du Cap Tourmente** (*Cap Tourmente Wildlife Reserve*). Recognized as a Wetland of International Significance, this nature reserve protects a vital habitat for migrating greater snow geese, and sees more than a million fly through every October and May, with tens of thousands of birds present every day. The park harbors hundreds of other kinds of birds and mammals, and more than 700 plant species. This enclave also has 18 km (11 miles) of hiking trails; naturalists give guided tours. It's on the north shore of the St. Lawrence River, about 8 km (5 miles) east of Ste-Anne-de-Beaupré. ⊠ *570 chemin du Cap Tourmente, St-Joachim* ☎ *418/827–4591* ⊕ *ec.gc.ca* ▣ *C$6.*

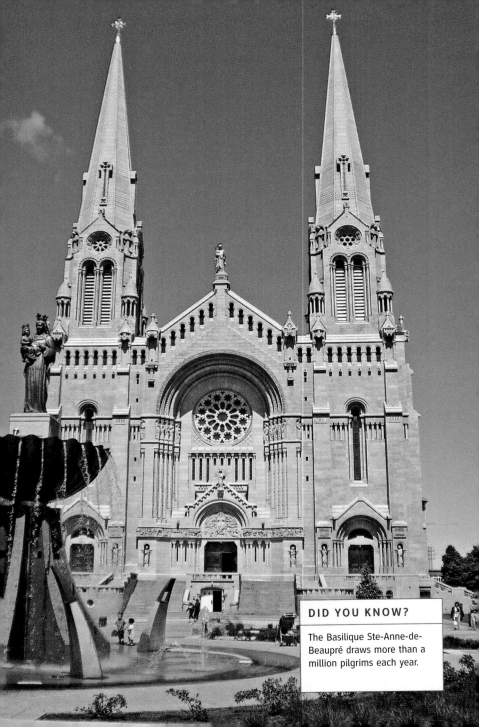

DID YOU KNOW?

The Basilique Ste-Anne-de-Beaupré draws more than a million pilgrims each year.

WHERE TO EAT

$$$$ 🍴 **Auberge Baker.** The best of old and new blend at this restaurant in
CANADIAN an 1840 French-Canadian farmhouse, built by the owners' ancestors, which lies east of Château-Richer toward Ste-Anne-de-Beaupré. Antiques and old-fashioned woodstoves decorate the dining rooms, where you can sample traditional Québec dishes, from *tourtière* (meat pie) and pork hocks to maple-sugar pie. [$] *Average main: C$35* ✉ *8790 av. Royale, Château-Richer* ☎ *418/824–4478, 866/824–4478* 🌐 *www.aubergebaker.com.*

SPORTS AND THE OUTDOORS

Le Massif. This three-peak ski resort has Canada's longest vertical drop east of the Rockies—2,526 feet. Owned by Daniel Gauthier, a cofounder of Cirque du Soleil, the resort has two multiservice chalets at the top and bottom. Six lifts and one gondola service the 53 trails, which are divided into runs for different levels; the longest run is 4.8 km (3 miles). There's also a section of expert glades. Nonskiers can go snowshoeing at the top of the mountain, and there is also an exciting, 7½-km (4¾-mile) sled trail. Equipment can be rented on-site, and the resort offers daycare for younger children and shuttles from Québec City, Beaupré, Baie-St-Paul, and the Montréal area. ✉ *1350 rue Principale, Petite-Rivière-St-François* ☎ *418/632–5876, 877/536–2774* 🌐 *www.lemassif.com.*

Mont-Ste-Anne. Part of the World Cup downhill circuit, Mont-Ste-Anne is one of the largest resorts in eastern Canada, with a vertical drop of 2,050 feet, 71 downhill trails, two half-pipes for snowboarders, a terrain park, and 13 lifts, including a gondola. The mountain stays active even after the sun goes down, with 19 lighted downhill trails. Cross-country skiing is also a draw here, with 21 trails totaling 224 km (139 miles). When the weather warms, mountain biking becomes the sport of choice. Enthusiasts can choose from 150 km (93 miles) of mountain-bike trails and 14 downhill runs (and a gondola up to the top). Three bike runs are designated "extreme zones." ✉ *2000 boul. du Beau-Pré, Beaupré* ☎ *418/827–4561, 888/827–4579* 🌐 *www.mont-sainte-anne.com.*

SHOPPING

SPAS

Spa des neiges. An *inukshuk* (Inuit stone marker) greets you at the entrance to this spa, set in elegant wood buildings right by the St. Lawrence River. Just the view, looking toward Île d'Orléans, is enough to relax anyone, but you can also enjoy the thermal baths (starting at C$35) or get one of many treatments, including massages, body wraps, mani-pedis, exfoliation, and light therapy. ✉ *9480 boul. Ste-Anne, Ste-Anne-de-Beaupré* ☎ *418/702–0631* 🌐 *www.spadesneiges.com.*

ÎLE D'ORLÉANS

Fodor's Choice
★

The Algonquins called it Minigo, the "Bewitched Place," and over the years the island's tranquil rural beauty has inspired poets and painters. Île d'Orléans is only 15 minutes by car from downtown Québec City, but a visit here is one of the best ways to get a feel for traditional life in rural Québec. Centuries-old homes and some of the oldest churches in the region dot the road that rings the island.

Île d'Orléans is at its best in summer, when the fields burst with strawberries and raspberries, and, later, lush orchard trees bend under the weight of apples, plums, or pears. Roadside stands sell woven articles, maple syrup, baked goods, jams, fruits, and vegetables. You can also pick your own produce at about two-dozen farms. During apple-picking season, weekends get remarkably busy. The island, immortalized by one of its most famous residents, the poet and songwriter Félix Leclerc (1914–88), is still fertile ground for artists and artisans.

The island was discovered at about the same time as the future site of Québec City, in 1535. Explorer Jacques Cartier noticed an abundance of vines and called it the Island of Bacchus, after the Greek god of wine. (Today, a couple of vineyards are working hard to earn back that moniker, with increasing success.) In 1536, Cartier renamed the island in honor of the duke of Orléans, son of the French king François I. Its fertile soil and abundant fishing made it so attractive to settlers that in the 17th century there were more people living here than in Québec City.

About 8 km (5 miles) wide and 35 km (22 miles) long, Île d'Orléans is made up of six small villages that have sought over the years to retain their identities. The bridge to the mainland was built in 1935, and in 1970 the island was declared a historic area to protect it from most sorts of development.

GETTING HERE AND AROUND

To get to Île d'Orléans, take Route 440 (Autoroute Dufferin–Montmorency) northeast. After a drive of about 10 km (6 miles) take the bridge (Pont de l'Île d'Orléans) to the island. The main road, chemin Royal (Route 368), circles the island, extending 67 km (42 miles) through the island's six villages; the route turns into chemin du Bout de l'Île as it loops around the western tip of the island.

VISITOR INFORMATION

Contact **Bureau touristique de l'île d'Orléans** (*Tourist Information Center Île d'Orléans*). ✉ 490 Côte du Pont, St-Pierre-de-l'Île-d'Orléans ☎ 418/828–9411, 866/941–9411.

STE-PÉTRONILLE

11

17 km (10½ miles) northeast of Québec City.

The lovely village of Ste-Pétronille, the first to be settled on Île d'Orléans, is west of the bridge to the island. Founded in 1648, the community was chosen in 1759 by British general James Wolfe for his headquarters. With 40,000 soldiers and a hundred ships, the English bombarded French-occupied Québec City and the surrounding shorelines.

In the late 19th century, the English population of Québec developed Ste-Pétronille into a resort village. This area is considered to be the island's most beautiful, not only because of its spectacular views of Montmorency Falls and Québec City but also for its Regency-style English villas and exquisitely tended gardens.

WORD OF MOUTH

"In the summer I just love Île d'Orléans, the island on the St. Lawrence, with its galleries, farms, and cideries ... If you wanted to go much farther afield, go east to Baie St. Paul (hometown to the founder of Cirque de Soleil) an hour or so. It's a beautiful little town full of great galleries and restaurants and has fantastic Le Massif skiing next door during the winter." —MsLizzy

GETTING HERE AND AROUND
Once across the bridge from the mainland, the Côte du Pont leads to Route 368. Turn right on chemin Royal and drive 4 km (2½ miles) to Ste-Pétronille.

EXPLORING
Maison Gourdeau de Beaulieu. The island's first home was built in 1648 for Jacques Gourdeau de Beaulieu, who was the first seigneur (a landholder who distributed lots to tenant farmers) of Ste-Pétronille. Remodeled over the years, this white house with blue shutters now incorporates both French and Québec styles. Its thick walls and dormer windows are characteristic of Breton architecture, but its sloping, bell-shape roof, designed to protect buildings from large amounts of snow, is typical Québec style. The house is not open to the public. ✉ *137 chemin du Bout de l'Île.*

Plante Family Farm. Pick apples and strawberries (in season) or buy fresh fruits, vegetables, and apple cider at this family farm. In March/April, enjoy maple-sugar treats from the roadside shack. ✉ *20 chemin du Bout de l'Île* ☎ *418/828–9603.*

Vignoble de Ste-Pétronille. Since they bought it in 2003, Louis Denault and Nathalie Lane have turned this vineyard into one of the best wine producers in Québec. Most of the wine is produced from a hybrid variety called vandal-cliche, which was bred by a Laval University biologist to thrive in the area's climate, along with a growing proportion of vidal. The results are a range of fresh, crisp white wines (still and bubbly), as well as ice wine. The winery has also started producing small amounts of riesling, and does some tasty reds. In the summer, Panache Mobile, a food cart managed by Panache, one of

Montmorency Falls along the Côte-de-Beaupré might not be as wide, but it's nearly twice as tall as Niagara Falls.

Québec City's best restaurants, serves delicious lunches on a terrace with a stunning view of the St. Lawrence River and Montmorency Falls. ✉ *1A chemin du Bout de l'Île* ☎ *418/828–9554* ⊕ *www.vignobleorleans.com* ✉ *Guided tour C$6.*

WHERE TO STAY

$$
B&B/INN
🛏 **Auberge La Goéliche.** This English-style country manor (rebuilt in 1996–97 following a fire) is steps away from the St. Lawrence River, and the small but elegant rooms, decorated with antiques, all have river views. **Pros:** spectacular location; notably pleasant staff. **Cons:** riverfront but no access to the water; some rooms have only very small TVs. 💲 *Rooms from: C$188* ✉ *22 chemin du Quai* ☎ *418/828–2248, 888/511–2248* ⊕ *www.goeliche.ca* 🛏 *16 rooms, 3 suites* 🍴 *Breakfast.*

SHOPPING
FOOD
Chocolaterie de l'Île d'Orléans. Belgian chocolate is combined with local ingredients to produce the handmade confections here: with a maple butter filling, for example, or *framboisette,* made from raspberries. In summer try the 24 different kinds of ice creams and sherbets, or bring home some chocolate-infused jams. They've also opened a smaller counter in the presbytery of Saint-François, at the other end of the island. ✉ *150 chemin du Bout de l'Île* ☎ *418/828–2250* ⊕ *www.chocolaterieorleans.com.*

ST-LAURENT DE L'ÎLE D'ORLÉANS

9 km (5½ miles) east of Ste-Pétronille.

Founded in 1679, St-Laurent is one of the island's maritime villages. Until as late as 1935, residents used boats as their main means of transportation. St-Laurent has a rich history in farming and fishing. Work is underway to help bring back to the island some of the species of fish that were once abundant here.

WORD OF MOUTH

"Ile d'Orleans is a must and you need a car to appreciate it. Combine it with a trip to Montmorency Falls. Both are very close to Québec City ..." —QuebecFan

GETTING HERE AND AROUND

Continue along chemin Royal from Ste-Pétronille, looping around the western end of the island and driving east along the southern shore.

EXPLORING

Église St-Laurent. The tall, inspiring church that stands next to the village marina on chemin Royal was built in 1860 on the site of an 18th-century church that had to be torn down. One of the church's procession chapels is a miniature stone reproduction of the original. ✉ *1532 chemin Royal, St-Laurent* ☎ *418/828–2551* 🎫 *Free.*

La Forge à Pique-Assaut. This working forge belongs to the talented local artisan Guy Bel, who has done ironwork restoration for Québec City. He was born in Lyon, France, and studied there at the École des Beaux-Arts. You can watch him and his team at work; his stylish candlesticks, chandeliers, fireplace tools, and other ironwork are for sale. ✉ *2200 chemin Royal, St-Laurent* ☎ *418/828–9300* 🌐 *www.forge-pique-assaut.com.*

Parc Maritime de St-Laurent. This former boatyard includes the Chalouperie Godbout (Godbout Longboat), which holds a collection of tools used by specialist craftsmen during the golden era of boat-building. You can picnic here and watch fishermen at work, trapping eels in tall nets at low tide. ✉ *120 chemin de la Chalouperie, St-Laurent* ☎ *418/828–9672* 🌐 *www.parcmaritime.ca* 🎫 *C$5.*

WHERE TO EAT AND STAY

$$$ CAFÉ 🍴 **Moulin de St-Laurent.** You can dine inside amid old stone walls or outside on the patios at the foot of a tiny, peaceful waterfall at this restaurant, which was converted from an early-18th-century stone mill. Scrumptious snacks, such as quiche and salads, are available on the terrace, and evening dishes include local pork tenderloin and venison stew. **Known for:** cozy atmosphere; hearty dishes; pleasant patio. [$] *Average main: C$24* ✉ *754 chemin Royal, St-Laurent* ☎ *418/829–3888, 888/629–3888* 🌐 *www.moulinstlaurent.qc.ca* 🕒 *Restaurant closed mid-Oct.–May.*

ST-JEAN

12 km (7 miles) northeast of St-Laurent.

The village of St-Jean used to be occupied by river pilots and navigators. At sea most of the time, the sailors didn't need the large homes and plots of land that the farmers did. Often richer than farmers, they displayed their affluence by building their houses with bricks brought back from Scotland as ballast. Most of St-Jean's small, homogeneous row houses were built between 1840 and 1860.

GETTING HERE AND AROUND

From St-Laurent, continue northeast along chemin Royal.

EXPLORING

Église St-Jean. At the eastern end of the village sits a massive granite structure built in 1749, with large red doors and a towering steeple. The church resembles a ship; it's big and round and appears to be sitting right on the river. Paintings of the patron saints of seamen line the interior walls. The church's cemetery is also intriguing, especially if you can read French. Back in the 1700s, piloting the St. Lawrence was a dangerous profession; the cemetery tombstones recall the many lives lost in these harsh waters. ✉ *2001 chemin Royal* ☎ *418/828–2551* 🎟 *Free.*

Manoir Mauvide-Genest. St-Jean's beautiful Normandy-style manor was built in 1734 for Jean Mauvide, the surgeon to Louis XV, and his wife, Marie-Anne Genest. The most notable thing about this house, which still has its original thick walls, ceiling beams, and fireplaces, is the degree to which it has held up over the years. The house serves as an interpretation center of New France's seigneurial regime, with 18th-century furniture, a historic vegetable garden, a multimedia presentation, and tours with guides dressed in 18th-century costumes. ✉ *1451 chemin Royal* ☎ *418/829–2630* 🌐 *www.manoirmauvidegenest.com* 🎟 *C$6, C$9 with guided tour.*

WHERE TO EAT

$ 🍴 **La Boulange.** This excellent, friendly bakery is located in the village
BAKERY of St-Jean's historic rectory, across the street from the church and a promenade along the river. In addition to delicious fresh croissants, pastries, and breads, La Boulange also offers pizzas and other light lunches that you can enjoy on the large covered porch in the summer. **Known for:** great pastries; light lunches; covered patio. [$] *Average main: C$12* ✉ *2001 chemin Royal* ☎ *418/829–3162* 🌐 *laboulange.ca* 💳 *No credit cards* 🕓 *No dinner. Closed Jan.–Mar.; Mon.–Wed. May, June, Sept., and Oct.; Mon.–Thurs. Nov., Dec., and Apr.*

ST-FRANÇOIS

12 km (7 miles) northeast of St-Jean.

Sprawling open fields separate 17th-century farmhouses in St-François, the island's least-toured and most rustic village. At the eastern tip of the island, this community was settled mainly by farmers. St-François is the perfect place to visit one of the island's *cabanes à sucre* (maple-sugaring shacks), found along chemin Royal. Stop at a hut for a tasting tour; sap is gathered from the maple groves and boiled until it's reduced to syrup (it takes 40 gallons of sap to produce one gallon of syrup). Boiled a little more and poured over snow, it becomes a delicious toffee. Maple-syrup season is from mid-March through April.

GETTING HERE AND AROUND

From St-Jean, continue northeast along chemin Royal.

EXPLORING

Église St-François. Built in 1734, St-François is one of eight extant churches in Québec dating from the French regime. At the time the English seized Québec City in 1759, General James Wolfe knew St-François to be a strategic point along the St. Lawrence. Consequently, he stationed British troops here and used the church as a military hospital. In 1988 a car crash set the church on fire, and most of the interior treasures were lost. A separate children's cemetery stands as a silent witness to the difficult life of early residents. ✉ *341 chemin Royal* ☎ *418/828–2551* 🎟 *Free.*

Observation Tower. This 60-foot-high wooden tower within a picnic area is well sited for viewing the majestic St. Lawrence and the many small islands in the estuary. In spring and fall, wild Canada geese can be seen here. The area is about 2 km (1 mile) north of Eglise St-François on chemin Royal. ✉ *St-François.*

STE-FAMILLE

14 km (9 miles) west of St-François.

The village of Ste-Famille, founded in 1661, has exquisite scenery, including abundant apple orchards and strawberry fields with views of Côte-de-Beaupré and Mont-Ste-Anne in the distance. But it also has historic charm, with the area's highest concentration of stone houses dating from the French regime.

GETTING HERE AND AROUND

From St-François, chemin Royal cuts north across the eastern tip of the island and continues west along the northern shore.

EXPLORING

Église Ste-Famille. This impressive church, constructed in 1749, is the only one in Québec to have three bell towers at its front. The ceiling was redone in the mid-19th century with elaborate designs in wood and gold. The church also holds a famous painting, *L'Enfant Jésus Voyant la Croix* (Baby Jesus Looking at the Cross); it was done in 1670 by Frère Luc (Brother Luc), who had been sent from France to decorate churches in the area. ✉ *3915 chemin Royal* ☎ *418/828–2656* 🎟 *Free.*

WHERE TO EAT

$$ CANADIAN 🍴 **Microbrasserie de l'île d'Orléans.** This is one of the most interesting microbreweries in the Québec City region, producing a colorful range of beers named after historical characters from Île d'Orléans. You can taste them all at the adjoining Pub Le Mitan, along with standard pub fare including burgers, pizzas, and fries. **Known for:** great beer; pub fare; river view. [$] *Average main: C$15* ✉ *3885 chemin Royal* ☎ *418/203–0588* 🌐 *www.microorleans.com* 💳 *No credit cards* 🕒 *Closed Mon.–Thurs. mid-Oct.–May.*

ST-PIERRE

14 km (9 miles) southwest of Ste-Famille.

Established in 1679, this town is set on a plateau that has the island's most fertile land and has long been the center of traditional farming industries. The best products grown here are potatoes, asparagus, and corn. The Espace Félix-Leclerc—an exhibit by day and a *boîte à chansons* (combination coffeehouse and bar with live performances) by night—works to honor the late singer and songwriter, who made St-Pierre his home. The bridge back to the mainland and Route 440 is just west on chemin Royal.

GETTING HERE AND AROUND

From Ste-Famille, continue southwest along chemin Royal. After visiting St-Pierre, the same road will take you back to the bridge to return to the mainland.

EXPLORING

Cassis Monna et filles. This family farm has won international awards for its crème de cassis, a liqueur made from black currants. In its vast and attractive tasting room and shop, you can taste free samples of the strong, sweet cassis or black currant wines; the tour explains how they are made. In summer you can sample foods made with cassis at La Monnaguette, the house bistro featuring a terrace overlooking the river. ✉ *726 chemin Royal, St-Pierre-de-l'Île-d'Orléans* ☎ *418/828–1057* ⊕ *www.cassismonna.com* ✉ *Free; guided tour C$5.*

Église St-Pierre. The oldest church on the island dates from 1717. It's no longer used for worship, but it was restored during the 1960s and is open to visitors. Many original components are still intact, such as benches with compartments below where hot bricks and stones were placed to keep people warm in winter. Félix Leclerc, the first Quebecois singer-songwriter to make a mark in Europe, is buried in the cemetery nearby. ✉ *1249 chemin Royal, St-Pierre-de-l'Île-d'Orléans* ☎ *418/828–9824* ✉ *Free.*

CHARLEVOIX

Bordered by the Laurentian Mountains to the north, the Saguenay River to the east, and the St. Lawrence River to the south, the Charlevoix region is famous for awe-inspiring vistas and kaleidoscopes of color that change throughout the day. The region also has rich historical significance for both French Canadians and English Canadians.

Jacques Cartier is believed to have explored the area in 1535. More certain is a visit 73 years later by Samuel de Champlain.

New France's first historian, the Jesuit priest François-Xavier de Charlevoix (pronounced shar-le- *vwah*), is the region's namesake. The area's first nonindigenous inhabitants arrived as early as the mid-1600s. Among other things, they developed a small shipbuilding industry that eventually specialized in sturdy schooners called *goélettes,* which were used to haul everything from logs to lobsters up and down the coast in the days before rail and paved roads. In the 19th century, as steamships plied the St. Lawrence, Charlevoix became a popular summer destination for well-to-do English Canadians and British colonial administrators from Montréal and Québec City. Since then, tourism—and hospitality—has become Charlevoix's trademark.

The region has attracted and inspired generations of painters, poets, writers, and musicians from across Québec and Canada, and became a UNESCO World Biosphere Reserve in 1989. In summer, hiking, fishing, picnicking, sightseeing, and whale-watching are the area's main attractions. Winter activities include downhill and cross-country skiing, snowmobiling, ice fishing, dog sledding, and snowshoeing. Charlevoix's many great local food products and restaurants are also a big draw for tourists.

GETTING HERE AND AROUND

To get to Charlevoix from Québec City, take Route 440 (Autoroute Dufferin–Montmorency) northeast and then continue on Route 138 past Côte-de-Beaupré. From there you'll be able to branch out for destinations such as Petite-Rivière-St-François or Baie-St-Paul.

BAIE-ST-PAUL

120 km (72 miles) northeast of Québec City.

Baie-St-Paul, one of the oldest towns in the province, is popular with craftspeople, artists, and foodies. With its centuries-old mansard-roof houses, the village is on the banks of a winding river, on a wide plain encircled by high hills—the crater of a large meteor that crashed to earth 350 million years ago. Boutiques and a handful of commercial galleries line the historic narrow streets in the town center; most have original artwork and crafts for sale. In addition, each August more than a dozen artists from across Canada take part in the "Symposium of Modern Art."

GETTING HERE AND AROUND

By road, Baie-St-Paul is approximately 95 km (59 miles) northeast of Québec City via Route 440 and Route 138. Le Massif de Charlevoix train runs day trips from the Chutes Montmorency station mid-June–early July Thursday through Sunday, then Wednesday through Sunday until mid-October. Departing at 9:10 am and including breakfast en route, it arrives in Baie-St-Paul at 11:45 am; the return journey, including dinner, leaves at 3 pm and arrives back at Chutes Montmorency station at 4:45 pm. The fare is C$229 round-trip, plus C$60 for a guaranteed river-side seat.

EXPLORING

FAMILY **Maison d'affinage Maurice Dufour.** The Dufour family produces some of the best cheese in the region, made from the milk of the herds of sheep and cows that can be seen grazing around the property in the summer. A modern and elegant tasting room allows visitors to discover the various cheeses and find out more about production, and taste the fresh and fun wines that they make from local vines. They've even started distilling vodka and spirits from whey, a fun way to produce something delicious from cheese-making by-products. A restaurant called Les Faux Bergers, featuring lots of wood-fired dishes, is also on the premises. ⊠ *1339 boul. Mgr de Laval* ☎ *418/435–5692* ⊕ *www.fromagefin.com.*

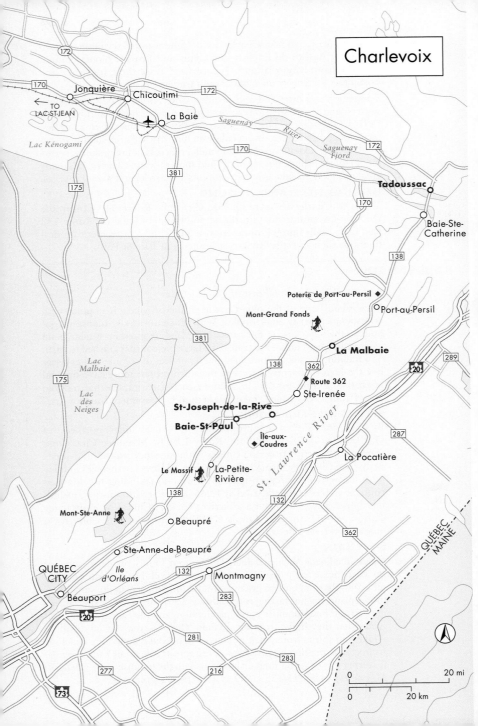

Charlevoix

172
170
Jonquière
TO
LAC-ST-JEAN
Chicoutimi
172
La Baie
Saguenay
River
Lac Kénogami
170
Saguenay
Fjord
172
381
175
Tadoussac
170
Baie-Ste-
Catherine
138
Poterie de Port-au-Persil ◆
Mont-Grand Fonds
○ Port-au-Persil
381
La Malbaie
138
362
Route 362 ◆
Lac
Malbaie
Ste-Irenée
175
Lac
des
Neiges
St-Joseph-de-la-Rive
Baie-St-Paul
289
20
287
Île-aux-
Coudres ◆
St. Lawrence River
La Pocatière
Le Massif
La-Petite-
Rivière
138
132
Mont-Ste-Anne
132
362
○ Beaupré
QUÉBEC
MAINE
QUÉBEC
CITY
Ile
d'Orléans
Ste-Anne-de-Beaupré
132
Montmagny
Beauport
283
20
281
283
277
216
73

0   20 mi

0   20 km

Maison René Richard. Many of Québec's greatest landscape artists, including Jean-Paul Lemieux and Clarence Gagnon, have depicted the area, and a selection of these works is on show here (some are also for sale). The gallery was Gagnon's former studio and also the home of painter René Richard for the last 43 years of his life. Guided tours of the studio are available for groups. ✉ *58 rue St-Jean-Baptiste* ☎ *418/435–5571* 🎫 *Free; call for group tour rates.*

Musée d'Art Contemporain de Baie-St-Paul. This museum highlights modern and contemporary art created by Charlevoix artists from 1920 to 1970. It also has a robust collection from the province in general, with works from Georges D. Pepper, Kathleen Daly, René Richard, the Bolduc sisters, and others. For more than 30 years, the museum has been organizing a yearly modern art symposium, held in late July and early August. ✉ *23 rue Ambroise-Fafard* ☎ *418/435–3681* 🌐 *www.macbsp.com* 🎫 *C$10.*

WHERE TO STAY

$$ B&B/INN

🏨 **Auberge à l'Ancrage.** A restored 1920s redbrick home with antiques, a maritime theme, a wraparound porch, and a back garden that sits at the edge of the Gouffre River, Auberge à l'Ancrage is run by a charming couple who offer delicious, multicourse breakfasts and eagerly share information about activities and attractions in the area. **Pros:** quiet and privacy; only a few minutes' walk from downtown; riverside yard. **Cons:** rooms are on the smaller side. [$] *Rooms from: C$169* ✉ *29 rue Ste-Anne* ☎ *418/240–3264* 🌐 *www.aubergeancrage.com* 🛏 *4 rooms* 🍴 *Breakfast.*

$$ HOTEL Fodor's Choice ★

🏨 **Hotel Le Germain Charlevoix.** This stylish and modern hotel, owned by one of the best boutique hotel groups in Canada, consists of five distinct pavilions housing three eateries and rooms in various styles, including lofts and dormitories, all with contemporary finishes and elegant design. **Pros:** location on public square with train station; in-room espresso makers; excellent food and design. **Cons:** layout with multiple pavilions is a bit complicated. [$] *Rooms from: C$175* ✉ *50 rue de la Ferme* ☎ *418/240–4100, 877/536–2774* 🌐 *www.legermainhotels.com/en/charlevoix* 💳 *No credit cards* 🛏 *152 rooms* 🍴 *No meals.*

EN ROUTE

Route 362. From Baie-St-Paul, instead of the faster Route 138 to La Malbaie, drivers can choose the open, scenic coastal drive on Route 362. This section of road has memorable views of charming villages and rolling hills—green, white, or ablaze with fiery hues, depending on the season—meeting the broad expanse of the "sea," as the locals like to call the St. Lawrence estuary. ✉ *Baie-St-Paul.*

ST-JOSEPH-DE-LA-RIVE

20 km (12½ miles) northeast of Baie-St-Paul.

A secondary road descends sharply into St-Joseph-de-la-Rive, with its line of old houses hugging the mountain base on a narrow shore route. Enjoyed for its warm microclimate, the town features peaceful inns and inviting restaurants. Drive through and see the traces of early town life and the beginning of local industry: an old firehouse and a hydroelectric building that houses a generator dating back to 1928.

GETTING HERE AND AROUND

From Baie-St-Paul, drive northeast on rue Leclerc (Route 362).

EXPLORING

Île-aux-Coudres. A free, government-run ferry from the wharf in St-Joseph-de-la-Rive takes you on the 15-minute trip to the island where Jacques Cartier's men gathered *coudres* (hazelnuts) in 1535. Since then, the island has produced many a *goélette* (a type of sailing ship), and the families of former captains now run several small inns. You can bike around the island and see windmills and water mills, or stop at the stores selling paintings and crafts, such as traditional hand-woven household linens. ✉ *St-Joseph-de-la-Rive* ☎ *877/787–7483 ferry schedules.*

Musée Maritime de Charlevoix (*Maritime Museum*). This museum, housed in an old shipyard, commemorates the days of the St. Lawrence goélettes , the feisty little wooden freighters that were the chief means of transporting goods along the north shore of the St. Lawrence River well into the 1960s. Very large families lived in cramped conditions aboard the boats, some of which are part of the exhibits. To modern eyes, it doesn't look like a comfortable existence, but the folklore of the goélettes, celebrated in poetry, paintings, and song, is part of the region's strong cultural identity. ✉ *305 rue de l'Église* ☎ *418/635–1131* 🌐 *www.museemaritime.com/en/* 🎟 *C$7.*

WHERE TO STAY

$ HOTEL 🏨 **Hôtel Cap-aux-Pierres.** New ownership invested in a substantial renovation of the Cap-aux-Pierres, and the rooms now have a modern and stylish decor and many have river views. **Pros:** indoor and outdoor pools; beautiful environment; good food. [$] *Rooms from: C$150* ✉ *444 chemin la Baleine, Île-aux-Coudres* ☎ *888/554–6003, 418/438–2711* 🌐 *www.hotelcapauxpierres.com* 🕓 *Closed mid-Oct.–Apr.* 🛏 *98 rooms* 🍴 *Breakfast; Some meals.*

SHOPPING

BOOKS

Papeterie Saint-Gilles. This paper factory produces handcrafted stationery using a 17th-century process. There's also a small museum, which explains through photographs and demonstrations how paper is manufactured the old-fashioned way. Slivers of wood and flower petals are pressed into the paper sheets, which are as thick as the covers of a paperback book. The finished products—made into writing paper, greeting cards, and one-page poems or quotations—make beautiful, if pricey, gifts. Visitors can wander through the museum for free, and guided tours can be arranged for groups. ✉ *354 rue F.A. Savard* ☎ *418/635–2430, 866/635–2430* 🌐 *www.papeteriesaint-gilles.com.*

Baie-St-Paul is a charming small town popular with writers and artists. Each August it hosts a modern art show.

LA MALBAIE

35 km (22 miles) northeast of St-Joseph-de-la-Rive.

La Malbaie, one of the province's most elegant and historically interesting resort towns, was known as Murray Bay when wealthy Anglophones summered here. The area became popular with American and Canadian politicians in the late 1800s, when Ottawa Liberals and Washington Republicans partied decorously all summer with members of the Québec bourgeoisie. William Howard Taft built the "summer White House," the first of three summer residences, in 1894, when he was the American civil governor of the Philippines. He became the 27th president of the United States in 1908.

Many Taft-era homes now serve as handsome inns, offering old-fashioned coddling with such extras as breakfast in bed, whirlpool baths, and free shuttles to the ski areas in winter. Many serve lunch and dinner to nonresidents, so you can tour the area going from one great French or Quebecois meal to the next.

GETTING HERE AND AROUND

Even if you don't want to visit St-Joseph-de-la-Rive, Route 362 between Baie-St-Paul and La Malbaie is much more scenic and well worth the extra half hour it adds to the trip from Québec City. Le Train de Charlevoix offers a day trip to La Malbaie Thursday through Sunday from mid-June to early July and Wednesday through Sunday until mid-October. It departs Chute Montmorency station at 9:10 am, with a stop en route at Baie-St-Paul; the round-trip takes 11 hours including time to get off and explore, and the fare, including breakfast and a four-course dinner, is C$369 (plus C$60 for a guaranteed river-side seat).

A hiker takes in the view of an ancient glacial valley.

EXPLORING

Casino de Charlevoix. The casino is one of four gaming halls in Québec (the others are in Montréal, Gatineau, and Mont-Tremblant) owned and operated by Loto-Québec. Charlevoix's, the smallest of the lot, still draws around 800,000 visitors a year—some of whom stay at the Fairmont Le Manoir Richelieu, which is connected to the casino by a tunnel. Largely renovated in 2016, it offers 21 gaming tables and more than 800 slot machines. The minimum gambling age is 18, and a photo ID is required to enter the casino. ✉ *183 rue Richelieu, Pointe-au-Pic* ☎ *418/665–5300, 800/665–2274* ⊕ *www.casino-de-charlevoix.com.*

Musée de Charlevoix. The museum traces the region's history through a major permanent exhibit. Folk art, paintings, and artifacts help reveal the past, starting with the French, then the Scottish settlers, and the area's evolution into a vacation spot and artists' haven. Temporary exhibits change every season. ✉ *10 chemin du Havre* ☎ *418/665–4411* ⊕ *www.museedecharlevoix.qc.ca* 🎫 *C$7.*

FAMILY **Parc national des Hautes-Gorges-de-la-Rivière-Malbaie.** A 40-minute drive from La Malbaie will bring you to a stunning stretch of the Malbaie river, surrounded by impressive, steep slopes and rocky peaks. There are plenty of beautiful views to take in—whether it's from a kayak on the river or while hiking a network of trails—and lots of fresh air, in this central part of the Charlevoix Biosphere Preserve. ✉ *25 boul. Notre-Dame* ☎ *418/439–1227* ⊕ *www.sepaq.com/pq/hgo* 🎫 *Park access, daily: C$9. Camping from C$31 per night.*

OFF THE BEATEN PATH

Poterie de Port-au-Persil. Visiting potters, many from France, study Canadian ceramic techniques at this pottery studio, about 25 km (15½ miles) east of La Malbaie. Classes for amateurs are available from late June through August (by the hour or longer, starting at C$12). Half of the bright yellow barn housing the studio is a store, with ceramics and other crafts made by Québec artists. ✉ *1001 rue St-Laurent (Rte. 138), St-Siméon* ☎ *418/638–2349* 🌐 *www.poteriedeportaupersil.com.*

WHERE TO EAT AND STAY

$ BAKERY FAMILY

🍴 **Pains d'exclamation.** This lively cafe and bakery offers a wide variety of classic and unique pastries and breads (hello, preserved-lemon bread!), sandwiches and quick breakfast and lunch options. It's a favorite with locals, who either eat-in or take out after a quick chat with the friendly staff. **Known for:** great pastries; patio dining; quick, delicious lunches. [$] *Average main: 10* ✉ *398 rue Saint-Étienne, Pointe-au-Pic* ☎ *418/665–4000* 🌐 *www.painsdexclamation.com* 🕒 *Closed Sun. and Mon.*

$ B&B/INN

🏨 **Auberge des Peupliers.** About half the guest rooms at this hilltop inn overlook the St. Lawrence River, and the country-style accommodations are spread among three buildings, including a farmhouse more than two centuries old. **Pros:** lounge with fireplace and bar perfect for relaxing; excellent service. **Cons:** need to drive to downtown La Malbaie. [$] *Rooms from: C$149* ✉ *381 rue St-Raphaël* ☎ *418/665–4423, 888/282–3743* 🌐 *www.aubergedespeupliers.com* 🛏 *22 rooms* 🍽 *Breakfast.*

$$$ RESORT FAMILY

🏨 **Fairmont Le Manoir Richelieu.** Linked to the Casino de Charlevoix by tunnel, this castlelike building and its sweeping grounds come with stunning views and some great sports and leisure facilities. **Pros:** good for families, with kids' club, kids' menu, and babysitting; scenic location; variety of dining options on-site. **Cons:** some rooms could use updating. [$] *Rooms from: C$229* ✉ *181 rue Richelieu, Pointe-au-Pic* ☎ *418/665–3703, 800/463–2613* 🌐 *www.fairmont.com* 🛏 *422 rooms* 🍽 *Breakfast.*

PERFORMING ARTS

Domaine Forget. This music and dance academy has a 604-seat hall in Ste-Irenée, 15 km (9 miles) south of La Malbaie. Musicians from around the world, many of whom teach or study at the school, perform during its International Festival. The festival, which runs from mid-June to late August, includes Sunday brunches with music, a buffet, and a view of the St. Lawrence. Some weekend concerts are also held in the fall and spring. ✉ *5 rang St-Antoine, St-Irénée* ☎ *418/452–3535, 888/336–7438* 🌐 *www.domaineforget.com.*

SPORTS AND THE OUTDOORS

GOLF

Club de Golf Fairmont Le Manoir Richelieu. Be warned: if you play this course, you'll have to work hard to focus on the game and not the gorgeous scenery overlooking the St. Lawrence River. Originally established in 1925 and recently restored and expanded, this is a links-style course with three 9-hole courses that offers quite a bit of challenge, thanks to the design (the fairways are relatively wide but feature a

In Tadoussac from May to October, you can see whales living in the Saguenay River.

number of strategically placed bunkers, trees, and mounds) and to the course's hilltop undulations. ✉ *181 rue Richelieu, Pointe-au-Pic* ☎ *418/665–2526, 800/665–8082* ⊕ *www.fairmont.com/richelieu-charlevoix/golf* ✉ *C$45–C$119 for all courses* ⚑ *St-Laurent Course: 9 holes, 3178 yards, par 36; Richelieu Course: 9 holes, 3148 yards, par 36; Tadoussac Course: 9 holes, 2918 yards, par 35* ☞ *Facilities: driving range, putting green, golf carts, rental clubs, restaurant, bar.*

SKIING

Mont-Grand Fonds. This winter-sports center 12 km (7 miles) north of La Malbaie has 20 downhill slopes (including four recently opened glades in an area called The Lynx), an 1,105-foot vertical drop, and three lifts. It also has 184 km (113 miles) of cross-country trails. Two trails meet International Ski Federation standards, and the ski center occasionally hosts major competitions. You can also go dogsledding, sleigh riding, ice-skating, and tobogganing here. ✉ *1000 chemin des Loisirs* ☎ *418/665–0095, 877/665–0095* ⊕ *www.montgrandfonds.com* ✉ *Full day tickets: C$46.*

TADOUSSAC

71 km (44 miles) north of La Malbaie.

Most people come to Tadoussac for the whale-watching excursions and cruises along the magnificent Saguenay Fjord. Beluga whales, highly recognizable because of their all-white color, small size, and high-pitch call, live here year-round and breed in the lower portion of the Saguenay in summer. The many marine species that live at the confluence of the fjord and the seaway attract other whales, too, such as pilots, finbacks, and humpbacks.

Sadly, the beluga is endangered; the whales, together with 35 other species of mammals and birds and 21 species of fish, are threatened by pollution in the St. Lawrence River. This has spurred a C$100 million project (funded by the federal and provincial governments) aimed at removing or capping sediment in the most polluted areas, stopping industrial and residential emissions into the river, and restoring natural habitat. There's still much work to be done, but greater attention is being given to this unique ecosystem, now a National Marine Conservation Area.

The short drive here from La Malbaie leads past lovely villages and views along the St. Lawrence. Jacques Cartier made a stop at this point in 1535, and from 1600 to the mid-19th century it was an important meeting site for fur traders. As the Saguenay River flows south from Lac St-Jean, it has a dual character: between Alma and Chicoutimi, the once rapidly flowing river has been harnessed for hydroelectric power; in its lower section, it becomes wider and deeper and flows by steep mountains and cliffs en route to the St. Lawrence.

GETTING HERE AND AROUND
From La Malbaie, drive northeast on Route 138. You must take a free 10-minute ferry ride from Baie-Ste-Catherine to get to Tadoussac. The ferries leave every 20 minutes, from 4 am to midnight, then every half hour until 4 am. For more information on ferry schedules, call *418/643–2019.*

VISITOR INFORMATION
Contact Tourist Information Center Tadoussac. ⊠ *197 rue des Pionniers* ☎ *418/235–4744, 866/235–4744.*

EXPLORING
Centre d'Interprétation des Mammifères Marins. You can learn more about the whales and their habitat at this interpretation center run by a locally based research team. They're only too glad to answer questions. In addition, explanatory videos and exhibits (including a collection of whale skeletons) serve as a good introduction to the mighty but endangered cetaceans. ⊠ *108 rue de la Cale-Sèche* ☎ *418/235–4701* ⊕ *baleinesendirect.org* ⊠ *C$12.*

Parc Marin du Saguenay–St-Laurent. The 800-square-km (309-square-mile) marine park, at the confluence of the Saguenay and St. Lawrence rivers, has been created to protect this marine area's three fragile ecosystems. ⊠ *Park office, 182 rue de l'Église* ☎ *418/235–4703, 888/773–8888* ⊕ *parcmarin.qc.ca.*

WHERE TO STAY

$ HOTEL FAMILY 🏨 **Hôtel Tadoussac.** A stunning natural environment and the 1942 Victorian-style building make this an equally great choice for an active or romantic stay. **Pros:** views over the bay; summer kids' club with day care; spa; ongoing sustainability program; restaurants suit different tastes and budgets. **Cons:** no air-conditioning in rooms. [$] *Rooms from: C$149* ✉ *165 rue du Bord de l'Eau* ☎ *418/235–4421, 800/561–0718* 🌐 *www.hoteltadoussac.com* 🕒 *Closed Nov.–early May* 🛏 *149 rooms* 🍴 *Breakfast.*

SPORTS AND THE OUTDOORS

WHALE-WATCHING

The best months for seeing whales are August and September, although some operators extend the season at either end if whales are around. Fjord tours are also available.

Croisières AML. This outfitter offers two- and three-hour whale-watching cruises starting at C$69.95. The tours, in Zodiacs or larger boats, depart from Tadoussac pier. Tours of the Saguenay Fjord are available, and you can also take a day-long excursion on a chartered bus from Québec City, including a three-hour whale-watching cruise. ✉ *Tadoussac* ☎ *418/692–1159, 800/463–1292* 🌐 *www.croisieresaml.com.*

UNDERSTANDING MONTRÉAL AND QUÉBEC CITY

FRENCH VOCABULARY

FRENCH VOCABULARY

One of the trickiest French sounds to pronounce is the nasal final *n* sound (whether or not the n is actually the last letter of the word). You should try to pronounce it as a sort of nasal grunt—as in "huh." The vowel tha precedes the *n* will govern the vowel sound of the word, and in this list we precede the final *n* with an *h* to remind you to be nasal.

Another problem sound is the ubiquitous but untransliterable *eu*, as in *bleu* (blue) or *deux* (two), and the very similar sound in *je* (I), *ce* (this), and *de* (of). The closest equivalent might be the vowel sound in "put," but rounded. The famous rolled *r* is a glottal sound. Consonants at the ends of words are usually silent; when the following word begins with a vowel, however, the two are run together by sounding the consonant. There are two forms of "you" in French: *vous* (formal and plural) and *tu* (a singular, personal form). When addressing an adult you don't know, *vous* is always best.

ENGLISH	PRONUNCIATION	FRENCH

BASICS

ENGLISH	PRONUNCIATION	FRENCH
Yes/no	wee/nohn	Oui/non
Please	seel voo play	S'il vous plaît
Thank you	mair- **see**	Merci
You're welcome	deh ree- **ehn**	De rien
Excuse me, sorry	pahr- **don**	Pardon
Good morning/ afternoon	bohn- **zhoor**	Bonjour
Good evening	bohn- **swahr**	Bonsoir
Good-bye	o ruh- **vwahr**	Au revoir
Mr. (Sir)	muh- **syuh**	Monsieur
Mrs. (Ma'am)	ma- **dam**	Madame
Miss	mad-mwa- **zel**	Mademoiselle
Pleased to meet you	ohn-shahn- **tay**	Enchanté(e)
How are you?	kuh-mahn- tahl-ay **voo**	Comment allez-vous?
Very well, thanks	tray bee-ehn, mair- **see**	Très bien, merci
And you?	ay voo?	Et vous?

NUMBERS

ENGLISH	PRONUNCIATION	FRENCH
one	uhn	un
two	deuh	deux
three	twah	trois
four	**kaht**-ruh	quatre

ENGLISH	PRONUNCIATION	FRENCH
five	sank	cinq
six	seess	six
seven	set	sept
eight	wheat	huit
nine	nuf	neuf
ten	deess	dix
eleven	ohnz	onze
twelve	dooz	douze
thirteen	trehz	treize
fourteen	kah-torz	quatorze
fifteen	kanz	quinze
sixteen	sez	seize
seventeen	deez- **set**	dix-sept
eighteen	deez- **wheat**	dix-huit
nineteen	deez- **nuf**	dix-neuf
twenty	vehn	vingt
twenty-one	vehnt-ay- **uhn**	vingt-et-un
thirty	trahnt	trente
forty	ka- **rahnt**	quarante
fifty	sang- **kahnt**	cinquante
sixty	swa- **sahnt**	soixante
seventy	swa-sahnt- **deess**	soixante-dix
eighty	kaht-ruh- **vehn**	quatre-vingts
ninety	kaht-ruh-vehn- **deess**	quatre-vingt-dix
one hundred	sahn	cent
one thousand	meel	mille

COLORS

black	nwahr	noir
blue	bleuh	bleu
brown	bruhn/mar- **rohn**	brun/marron
green	vair	vert
orange	o- **rahnj**	orange
pink	rose	rose

ENGLISH	PRONUNCIATION	FRENCH
red	rouge	rouge
violet	vee-o- **let**	violette
white	blahnk	blanc
yellow	zhone	jaune

DAYS OF THE WEEK

Sunday	dee- **mahnsh**	dimanche
Monday	luhn- **dee**	lundi
Tuesday	mahr- **dee**	mardi
Wednesday	mair-kruh- **dee**	mercredi
Thursday	zhuh- **dee**	jeudi
Friday	vawn-druh- **dee**	vendredi
Saturday	sahm- **dee**	samedi

MONTHS

January	zhahn-vee- **ay**	janvier
February	feh-vree- **ay**	février
March	marce	mars
April	a- **vreel**	avril
May	meh	mai
June	zhwehn	juin
July	zhwee- **ay**	juillet
August	ah- **oo**	août
September	sep- **tahm**-bruh	septembre
October	awk- **to**-bruh	octobre
November	no- **vahm**-bruh	novembre
December	day- **sahm**-bruh	décembre

USEFUL PHRASES

Do you speak English?	par-lay **voo ahn**-glay	Parlez-vous anglais?
I don't speak . . .	zhuh nuh parl pah	Je ne parle pas . . .
French	frahn- **say**	français
I don't understand.	zhuh nuh kohm- **prahn** pah	Je ne comprends pas.
I understand.	zhuh kohm- **prahn**	Je comprends.

ENGLISH	PRONUNCIATION	FRENCH
I don't know.	zhuh nuh say **pah**	Je ne sais pas.
I'm American/British.	a-may-ree- **kehn** / ahn- **glay**	Je suis américain/ anglais.
What's your name?	ko-mahn voo za-pell-ay- **voo**	Comment vous appelez-vous?
My name is . . .	zhuh ma- **pell** . . .	Je m'appelle . . .
What time is it?	kel air eh- **teel**	Quelle heure est-il?
How?	ko- **mahn**	Comment?
When?	kahn	Quand?
Yesterday	yair	Hier
Today	o-zhoor- **dwee**	Aujourd'hui
Tomorrow	duh- **mehn**	Demain
Tonight	suh **swahr**	Ce soir
What?	kwah	Quoi?
What is it?	kess-kuh- **say**	Qu'est-ce que c'est?
Why?	**poor**-kwa	Pourquoi?
Who?	kee	Qui?
Where is . . .	oo ay	Où est . . .
the train station?	la gar	la gare?
the subway station?	la sta- **syon** duh may- **tro**	la station de métro?
the bus stop?	la- **ray** duh **booss**	l'arrêt de bus?
the post office?	la post	la poste?
the bank?	la bahnk	la banque?
the . . . hotel?	lo- **tel**	l'hôtel . . .?
the store?	luh ma-ga- **zehn**	le magasin?
the cashier?	la **kess**	la caisse?
the . . . museum?	luh mew- **zay**	le musée . . .?
the hospital?	lo-pee- **tahl**	l'hôpital?
the elevator?	la-sahn- **seuhr**	l'ascenseur?
the telephone?	luh tay-lay- **phone**	le téléphone?
Where are the restrooms?	oo sohn lay twah- **let**	Où sont les toilettes?
(men/women)	(**oh**-mm/ **fah**-mm)	(hommes/femmes)

ENGLISH	PRONUNCIATION	FRENCH
Here/there	ee- **see** /la	Ici/là
Left/right	a goash/a draht	A gauche/à droite
Straight ahead	too drwah	Tout droit
Is it near/far?	say pray/lwehn	C'est près/loin?
I'd like . . .	zhuh voo- **dray**	Je voudrais . . .
a room	ewn **shahm**-bruh	une chambre
the key	la clay	la clé
a newspaper	uhn zhoor- **nahl**	un journal
a stamp	uhn **tam**-bruh	un timbre
I'd like to buy . . .	zhuh voo- **dray** **ahsh**-tay	Je voudrais acheter . . .
cigarettes	day see-ga- **ret**	des cigarettes
matches	days a-loo- **met**	des allumettes
soap	dew sah- **vohn**	du savon
city map	uhn plahn de **veel**	un plan de ville
road map	ewn cart roo-tee- **air**	une carte routière
magazine	ewn reh- **vu**	une revue
envelopes	dayz ahn-veh- **lope**	des enveloppes
writing paper	dew pa-pee- **ay** a **let**-ruh	du papier à lettres
postcard	ewn cart pos- **tal**	une carte postale
How much is it?	say comb-bee- **ehn**	C'est combien?
A little/a lot	uhn peuh/bo- **koo**	Un peu/beaucoup
More/less	plu/mwehn	Plus/moins
Enough/too (much)	a-say/tro	Assez/trop
I am ill/sick.	zhuh swee ma- **lahd**	Je suis malade.
Call a . . .	a-play uhn	Appelez un . . .
doctor	dohk- **tehr**	Docteur
Help!	o suh- **koor**	Au secours!
Stop!	a-reh- **tay**	Arrêtez!
Fire!	o fuh	Au feu!
Caution!/Look out!	a-tahn-see- **ohn**	Attention!

ENGLISH	PRONUNCIATION	FRENCH
DINING OUT		
A bottle of . . .	ewn boo- **tay** duh	une bouteille de . . .
A cup of . . .	ewn tass duh	une tasse de . . .
A glass of . . .	uhn vair duh	un verre de . . .
Bill/check	la-dee-see- **ohn**	l'addition
Bread	dew pan	du pain
Breakfast	luh puh- **tee** day-zhuh- **nay**	le petit-déjeuner
Butter	dew burr	du beurre
Cheers!	ah vo-truh sahn- **tay**	A votre santé!
Cocktail/aperitif	uhn ah-pay-ree- **teef**	un apéritif
Dinner	luh dee- **nay**	le dîner
Dish of the day	luh plah dew **zhoor**	le plat du jour
Enjoy!	bohn a-pay- **tee**	Bon appétit!
Fixed-price menu	luh may- **new**	le menu
Fork	ewn four- **shet**	une fourchette
I am diabetic.	zhuh swee dee-ah- bay- **teek**	Je suis diabétique.
I am vegetarian.	zhuh swee vay-zhay-ta-ree- **en**	Je suis végétarien(ne).
I cannot eat . . .	zhuh nuh **puh** pah mahn- **jay** deh	Je ne peux pas manger de . . .
I'd like to order.	zhuh voo- **dray** ko-mahn- **day**	Je voudrais commander.
Is service/the tip included?	ess kuh luh sair- **veess** ay comb- **pree**	Est-ce que le service est compris?
It's good/bad.	say bohn/mo- **vay**	C'est bon/mauvais.
It's hot/cold.	Say sho/frwah	C'est chaud/froid.
Knife	uhn koo- **toe**	un couteau
Lunch	luh day-zhuh- **nay**	le déjeuner
Menu	la cart	la carte
Napkin	ewn sair-vee- **et**	une serviette
Pepper	dew **pwah**-vruh	du poivre
Plate	ewn a-see- **et**	une assiette
Please give me . . .	doe-nay- **mwah**	Donnez-moi . . .

ENGLISH	PRONUNCIATION	FRENCH
Salt	dew sell	du sel
Spoon	ewn kwee-air	une cuillère
Sugar	dew **sook**-ruh	du sucre
Waiter!/Waitress!	muh- **syuh** / mad-mwa- **zel**	Monsieur!/ Mademoiselle!
Wine list	la cart day vehn	la carte des vins

MENU GUIDE

FRENCH	ENGLISH

PETIT DÉJEUNER (BREAKFAST)

Confiture	Jam
Miel	Honey
Oeuf à la coque	Boiled egg
Oeufs sur le plat	Fried eggs
Oeufs brouillés	Scrambled eggs
Tartine	Bread with butter

POISSONS/FRUITS DE MER (FISH/SEAFOOD)

Anchois	Anchovies
Bar	Bass
Brandade de morue	Creamed salt cod
Brochet	Pike
Cabillaud/Morue	Fresh cod
Calmar	Squid
Coquilles St-Jacques	Scallops
Crevettes	Shrimp
Daurade	Sea bream
Ecrevisses	Prawns/Crayfish
Harengs	Herring
Homard	Lobster
Huîtres	Oysters
Langoustine	Prawn/Lobster
Lotte	Monkfish
Moules	Mussels

FRENCH	ENGLISH
Palourdes	Clams
Saumon	Salmon
Thon	Tuna
Truite	Trout

VIANDE (MEAT)

Agneau	Lamb
Boeuf	Beef
Boudin	Sausage
Boulettes de viande	Meatballs
Brochettes	Kebabs
Cassoulet	Casserole of white beans, meat
Cervelle	Brains
Chateaubriand	Double fillet steak
Choucroute garnie	Sausages with sauerkraut
Côtelettes	Chops
Côte/Côte de boeuf	Rib/T-bone steak
Cuisses de grenouilles	Frogs' legs
Entrecôte	Rib or rib-eye steak
Épaule	Shoulder
Escalope	Cutlet
Foie	Liver
Gigot	Leg
Porc	Pork
Ris de veau	Veal sweetbreads
Rognons	Kidneys
Saucisses	Sausages
Selle	Saddle
Tournedos	Tenderloin of T-bone steak
Veau	Veal

METHODS OF PREPARATION

A point	Medium
A l'étouffée	Stewed
Au four	Baked

FRENCH	ENGLISH
Ballotine	Boned, stuffed, and rolled
Bien cuit	Well-done
Bleu	Very rare
Frit	Fried
Grillé	Grilled
Rôti	Roast
Saignant	Rare

VOLAILLES/GIBIER (POULTRY/GAME)

Blanc de volaille	Chicken breast
Canard/Caneton	Duck/Duckling
Cerf/Chevreuil	Venison (red/roe)
Coq au vin	Chicken stewed in red wine
Dinde/Dindonneau	Turkey/Young turkey
Faisan	Pheasant
Lapin/Lièvre	Rabbit/Wild hare
Oie	Goose
Pintade/Pintadeau	Guinea fowl/Young guinea fowl
Poulet/Poussin	Chicken/Spring chicken

LÉGUMES (VEGETABLES)

Artichaut	Artichoke
Asperge	Asparagus
Aubergine	Eggplant
Carottes	Carrots
Champignons	Mushrooms
Chou-fleur	Cauliflower
Chou (rouge)	Cabbage (red)
Laitue	Lettuce
Oignons	Onions
Petits pois	Peas
Pomme de terre	Potato
Tomates	Tomatoes

TRAVEL SMART
MONTRÉAL AND
QUEBÉC CITY

GETTING HERE AND AROUND

▌ AIR TRAVEL

Flying time (gate-to-gate) to Montréal is about 1½ hours from New York, 2½ hours from Chicago, 4 hours from Dallas, and 6 hours from Los Angeles. Flying time to Québec City is about 2 hours from New York, 3 hours from Chicago, 5 hours from Dallas, and 7 hours from Los Angeles.

Trudeau Airport offers self-serve check-in and boarding passes at electronic kiosks throughout the airport. Make sure you arrive at the airport two hours before your flight's scheduled departure.

Security measures at Canadian airports are similar to those in the United States.

Airport Security Issues Transportation Security Administration. ⊕ www.tsa.gov.

AIRPORTS

For service to Montréal, Montréal–Pierre Elliott Trudeau International Airport, also known by its previous name, Dorval International Airport, is 20 km (12.5 miles) west of the city. Québec City's Jean Lesage International Airport is about 13 km (9 miles) northwest of Downtown. Both airports handle domestic and international flights.

Airport Information Aéroports de Montréal. ✉ 800 pl. Leigh-Capreol, Suite 1000, Dorval ☎ 514/394-7200 ⊕ www.admtl.com. **Jean Lesage International Airport** (YQB). ☎ 418/640-3300, 877/769-2700 ⊕ www.aeroportdequebec.com. **Montréal–Pierre Elliott Trudeau International Airport** (YUL). ☎ 800/465-1213, 514/394-7377 ⊕ www.admtl.com.

GROUND TRANSPORTATION

In Montréal, a taxi from Trudeau International to Downtown costs C$40. All taxi companies must charge the same rate for travel between the airport and Downtown.

The least expensive way to get from Trudeau International Airport into the city is to take the 747 Express Bus, operated by Société de transport de Montréal. Shuttles leave from Montréal Central Bus Station, which is connected to Berri–UQAM métro station. They run approximately every 15 minutes all day long, except during the rush hours of 4 pm to 6 pm, when they leave every 10 minutes. The cost is C$10 one-way, payable in coins only (no bills). Also available from automated dispensers in the airport are C$10 day bus passes, which not only buy you a ticket for the airport shuttle but also unlimited travel on the entire Montréal bus and métro system for a 24-hour period.

In Québec City, taxis are available immediately outside the airport exit near the baggage-claim area. A ride into the city costs a flat rate of C$34.25. Taxi Coop de Québec is the largest taxi company in the city. Private limo service is expensive, starting at C$65 for the ride from the airport into the city. Try Groupe Limousine A-1.

Montréal Contact Société de transport de Montréal. ☎ 514/786-4636 ⊕ www.stm.info.

Québec City Contact Groupe Limousine A-1. ☎ 418/523-5059, 866/523-5059 ⊕ www.limousinequebec.com. **Taxi Coop de Québec.** ☎ 418/525-5191 ⊕ www.taxicoop-quebec.com.

FLIGHTS

All the major U.S. airlines, including American, Delta, and United, serve Montréal and Québec City.

Regularly scheduled flights from the United States to Montréal and Québec City as well as flights within Canada are available on Air Canada and the regional airlines associated with it, including Air Canada Express (reservations are made through Air Canada). Porter Airlines also has connecting service to Montréal and Québec City from select U.S. cities, via Toronto's Billy Bishop Airport.

Airline Contacts Air Canada. ☎ *888/247–2262* ⊕ *www.aircanada.com.* **American Airlines.** ☎ *800/433–7300* ⊕ *www.aa.com.* **Delta Airlines.** ☎ *800/221–1212 for U.S. reservations, 800/241–4141 for international reservations* ⊕ *www.delta.com.* **Porter Airlines.** ☎ *888/619–8622* ⊕ *www.flyporter.com.*

▌ BIKE TRAVEL

Québec continues to expand its Route Verte (Green Route), a network of bike trails covering the southern half of the province, which will eventually link with trails in New England and New York. More than 90% of the marked trails are already open, and when the project is completed, there will be 5,000 km (more than 3,100 miles) of bikeways. For information and a map, head to Vélo Québec's website.

Contact Vélo Québec. ☎ *514/521–8356, 800/567–8356* ⊕ *www.velo.qc.ca.*

▌ BOAT AND FERRY TRAVEL

The Québec–Lévis ferry, which crosses the St. Lawrence River, gives you a magnificent panorama of Old Québec on its trips to and from Lévis. Although the crossing takes only 15 minutes, the waiting time can increase the trip to an hour. The cost is C$3.35. The first ferry from Québec City leaves weekdays at 6:20 am from the pier at rue Dalhousie, opposite Place Royale. Crossings run every 20 minutes during weekday rush hours, from 6:20 am to 9 am and 3 pm to 6 pm. At other times it runs every 30 minutes until 2:20 am. On weekends and holidays, the ferry leaves every 30 minutes from 6:30 am to 2:20 am. Schedules can change, so be sure to check the ferry website or call ahead.

Boat and Ferry Information Québec–Lévis ferry. ☎ *877/787–7483* ⊕ *www.traversiers.com.*

▌ BUS TRAVEL

Several private bus lines serve the province. Orléans Express is probably the most convenient, as it offers regular service between Montréal and Québec City and its buses are clean and comfortable. The trip takes three hours. Limocar, another bus line, serves the Eastern Townships. Greyhound Lines offers interprovincial service and is timely and comfortable, if not exactly plush. Megabus offers somewhat more luxurious service to the province of Ontario and the city of Buffalo. Smoking isn't permitted on any buses.

Bus terminals in Montréal and Québec City are usually efficient operations, with service all week and plenty of agents on hand to handle ticket sales. In villages and some small towns the bus station is simply a counter in a local convenience store, gas station, or snack bar. Getting information on schedules beyond the local ones is sometimes difficult in these places. In rural Québec it's a good idea to bring along a French–English dictionary, although most merchants and clerks can handle a simple ticket sale in English.

On a daily basis, buses from Montréal to Québec City depart 17 times per day between 6 am and 11 pm. A one-way ticket booked at least a week in advance starts at C$25. All intercity bus lines servicing Montréal arrive at and depart from the city's Downtown bus terminal, the Gare d'Autocars de Montréal, which is conveniently located next to the Berri-UQÀM métro station. The staff has schedule and fare information for all bus companies at the station.

Many bus companies offer discounts if you book in advance, usually either 7 or 14 days ahead. Discounts are also often available for kids (children ages 15 and under can travel for free on most bus lines if tickets are booked three days in advance).

In major bus terminals, most bus lines accept at least some of the major credit cards. Some smaller lines require cash or take only Visa or MasterCard. All accept traveler's checks in U.S. or Canadian currency with suitable identification, but it's advisable to exchange foreign currency (including U.S. currency) at a bank or exchange office. Be prepared to use cash to buy a ticket in really small towns.

Most bus lines don't accept reservations for specific seats. You should plan on picking up your tickets at least 45 minutes before the bus's scheduled departure time.

Bus Information Gare d'autocars de Montréal. ⊠ *1717 rue Berri, Montréal* 🖼 *514/842–2281* ⊕ *www.gamtl.com.* **Gare du Palais Bus Station.** ⊠ *320 rue Abraham-Martin, Québec City* 🖼 *418/525–3000.* **Greyhound Lines.** 🖼 *800/231–2222, 800/661–8747 in Canada* ⊕ *www.greyhound. com.* **Limocar.** 🖼 *866/692–8899* ⊕ *limocar. ca.* **Orléans Express.** 🖼 *888/999–3977, 514/395–4000* ⊕ *www.orleansexpress.com.*

▮ CAR TRAVEL

Montréal is accessible from the rest of Canada via the Trans-Canada Highway, which crosses the southern part of the island as Autoroute 20, with Autoroute 720 leading into Downtown. Autoroute 40 parallels Route 20 to the north; exits to Downtown include St-Laurent and St-Denis. From New York, take I–87 north until it becomes Autoroute 15 at the Canadian border; continue for another 47 km (29 miles) to the outskirts of Montréal. You can also follow U.S. I–89 north until it becomes the two-lane Route 133, which eventually joins Autoroute 10, an east–west highway that leads west across the Champlain Bridge and into Downtown. From I–91 through Massachusetts via New Hampshire and Vermont, you can take Route 55 to Autoroute 10. Again, turn west to reach Montréal.

At the border you must clear Canadian Customs, so be prepared with your passport and car registration. On holidays

and during the peak summer season, expect to wait a half hour or more at the major crossings. Border wait times can be checked on the Transport Québec website. ▮TIP➔ **At the border you must clear Canadian Customs, so be prepared with your passport and car registration. On holidays and during the peak summer season, expect to wait a half hour or more at the major crossings. Border wait times can be checked on the Transport Québec website.**

Montréal and Québec City are linked by Autoroute 20 on the south shore of the St. Lawrence River and by Autoroute 40 on the north shore. On both highways, the ride between the two cities is about 240 km (149 miles) and takes about three hours. U.S. I–87 in New York, U.S. I–89 in Vermont, and U.S. I–91 in New Hampshire connect with Route 20, as does Highway 401 from Toronto.

Driving northeast from Montréal on Route 20, follow signs for Pont Pierre-Laporte (Pierre Laporte Bridge) as you approach Québec City. After you've crossed the bridge, turn right onto boulevard Laurier (Route 175), which becomes the Grande Allée.

The speed limit is posted in kilometers; on highways the limit is 100 kph (about 62 mph), and the use of radar-detection devices is prohibited.

In Québec the road signs are in French, but the important ones have pictograms. Signs with a red circle and a slash indicate that something, such as a left or right turn, is prohibited. Those with a green circle show what's permitted. Parking signs display a green-circled "P" with either the number of hours you can park or a clock showing the hours parking is permitted. It's not unusual to have two or three road signs all together to indicate several different restrictions. Keep in mind the following terms: *centre-ville* (Downtown), *arrêt* (stop), *détenteurs de permis* (permit holders only), *gauche* (left), *droit* (right), *ouest* (west), and *est* (east).

Drivers must carry vehicle registration and proof of insurance coverage, which is compulsory in Canada. Québec drivers are covered by the Québec government no-fault insurance plan. Drivers from outside Québec can obtain a Canadian Non-Resident Inter-Provincial Motor Vehicle Liability Insurance Card, available from any U.S. insurance company. The card is accepted as evidence of financial responsibility in Canada, but you're not required to have one. The minimum liability in Québec is C$50,000. If you are driving a car that isn't registered in your name, carry a letter from the owner that authorizes your use of the vehicle.

GASOLINE
Gasoline is always sold in liters; 3.8 liters make a gallon. As of this writing, gas prices in Québec fluctuate considerably, ranging from C$1 to C$1.30 per liter (this works out to about $3 to $4 per gallon U.S.). Fuel comes in several grades, denoted as *regulière, supérieure,* and *prémium.*

PARKING
Expect on-street parking in Montréal to be hard to find; your best bet is to leave the car at your hotel garage and take public transportation or a cab. If you must drive, ask your concierge to recommend a garage near your destination. Be extra careful where you park if it snows, to avoid getting towed. Parking in Québec City is much less stressful, although it's also advisable to leave the car at the hotel and walk—especially if you're heading to Vieux-Québec.

ROAD CONDITIONS
In Montréal and Québec City the jumble of bicycle riders, delivery vehicles, taxis, and municipal buses can be chaotic. In the countryside at night, roads are lighted at exit points from major highways but are otherwise dark. Roads in the province aren't very good, especially during the spring pothole season—be prepared for some spine-jolting bumps and potholes, and check tire pressure once in a while.

In winter, Montréal streets are kept mostly clear of snow and ice, but outside the city the situation can deteriorate. Locals are notorious for exceeding the speed limit, so keep an eye on your mirrors. For up-to-date reports on road conditions throughout the province, go to Transport Québec's website.

Contact Transport Québec.
⊕ *www.quebec511.info.*

ROADSIDE EMERGENCIES
Dial 911 in an emergency. Contact CAA, the Canadian Automobile Association, in the event of a flat tire, dead battery, empty gas tank, or other car-related mishap. Automobile Association of America membership includes CAA service.

Emergency Services CAA. ☎ 800/222–4357, 514/861–1313 ⊕ *www.caaquebec.com.*

Insurance Information Insurance Bureau of Canada. ☎ 514/288–4321, 866/422–4331 in Québec ⊕ *www.ibc.ca.* **Société de l'assurance automobile du Québec.** ☎ 800/361–7620, 514/873–7620, 418/643–7620 ⊕ *www.saaq.gouv.qc.ca.*

RULES OF THE ROAD
By law, you're required to wear seat belts even in the backseat. Infant seats also are required. Radar-detection devices are illegal in Québec; just having one in your car is illegal. Speed limits, given in kilometers, are usually within the 90 kph–100 kph (50 mph–60 mph) range outside the cities.

Right turns on a red light are allowed in most of the province, the island of Montréal being the notable exception, where they're prohibited. Driving with a blood-alcohol content of 0.08% or higher is illegal and can earn you a stiff fine and jail time. Headlights are compulsory in inclement weather. Drivers aren't permitted to use handheld cell phones. The laws here are similar to the rest of North America; to consult Québec's Highway Code go to the Société de l'assurance automobile du Québec's website.

Contacts **Ministère des Transports du Québec.** ☎ 888/355–0511 ⊕ www.mtq.gouv. qc.ca. **Société de l'assurance automobile du Québec.** ☎ 800/361–7620, 514/873–7620, 418/643–7620 ⊕ www.saaq.gouv.qc.ca.

CAR RENTAL

Rates in Montréal run from about C$30 to C$60 a day for an economy car with air-conditioning and unlimited kilometers. If you prefer a manual-transmission car, check whether the rental agency of your choice offers stick shifts; many agencies in Canada don't.

You must be at least 21 years old to rent a car in Québec, and some car-rental agencies don't rent to drivers under 25. Most rental companies don't allow you to drive on gravel roads. Child seats are compulsory for children ages five and under.

Rentals at the airports near Québec City and Montréal are usually more expensive than neighborhood rentals.

Major Rental Agencies Alamo. ☎ 888/233-8749 ⊕ www.alamo.com. **Avis.** ☎ 800/331–1084 ⊕ www.avis.com. **Budget.** ☎ 800/268–8900 from Canada, 800/218–7792 from U.S. ⊕ www.budget.com. **Hertz.** ☎ 800/654–3001 ⊕ www.hertz.com. **National Car Rental.** ☎ 877/222–9058 ⊕ www.nationalcar.com.

▮ TRAIN TRAVEL

Amtrak offers its daily Adirondak service from New York City's Penn Station to Montréal, although the train sometimes arrives too late to make any connecting trains that evening. Connections are available, often the next day, to Canadian rail line VIA Rail's Canadian routes. The ride takes up to 11 hours, and one-way tickets start at C$69.

VIA Rail trains run from Montréal to Québec City in three hours, arriving at the 19th-century Gare du Palais in Lower Town. Trains on the Montréal—Québec City route run five times daily on weekdays, three times daily on weekends, with a stop in Ste-Foy. Tickets can be purchased in advance at VIA Rail offices, at the station prior to departure, through a travel agent, or online. VIA's supersaver (escape) fare ranges from C$38 to C$65, and is usually nonrefundable. If you're lucky you can sometimes find Web-only fares for as little as C$33. Keep in mind such discounted fares are usually nonrefundable as well.

Business class tickets start at C$109 each way and include early boarding, seat selection, and a three-course meal with wine.

To save money, look into rail passes. But be aware that if you don't plan to cover many miles, you may come out ahead by buying individual tickets. VIA Rail offers a BizPack Pass (for travel between two predetermined cities in either economy or business class). Senior citizens (60 and older), children (11 and under), and students are often entitled to discounts.

The Massif de Charlevoix train system takes you from Québec City to Baie-St-Paul and stops in between, priced at C$74 round-trip. From Baie St-Paul, one can go on to La Malbaie, Charlevoix for C$45 round-trip. If you get an early start, both can be done in a one-day excursion. The small villages and the natural beauty along the route are impressive.

Information Amtrak. ☎ 800/872–7245 ⊕ www.amtrak.com. **Le Massif de Charlevoix.** ☎ 418/240–4124 ⊕ www.reseaucharlevoix.com. **VIA Rail Canada.** ☎ 888/842–7245 from U.S., 514/989–2626 Montréal ⊕ www.viarail.ca.

ESSENTIALS

■ ACCOMMODATIONS

In Montréal and Québec City you have a choice of luxury hotels, moderately priced modern properties, and small older hotels with fewer conveniences but sometimes more charm. Options in small towns and in the country include large, full-service resorts; small, privately owned hotels; roadside motels; and bed-and-breakfasts. Even outside the cities it's a good idea to make reservations before you plan to pull into town.

Expect accommodations to cost more in summer than in the colder months (except for places such as ski resorts, where winter is high season). When making reservations, ask about special deals and packages. Big-city hotels that cater to business travelers often offer weekend packages, and many city hotels offer rooms at up to 50% off in winter. If you're planning to visit Montréal or Québec City or a resort area in high season, book well in advance. Also be aware of any special events or festivals that may coincide with your visit and fill every room for miles around. For resorts and lodges, remember that winter ski season is a period of high demand, and plan accordingly.

⇨ *For more information on apartment rentals, student housing options, and B&Bs, see the Lodging Alternatives box in Chapter 8.*

APARTMENT AND HOUSE RENTALS

The *Gazette* (⊕ *www.montrealgazette. com*), Montréal's English-language daily, has a wide selection of rental listings.

BED-AND-BREAKFASTS

B&Bs, which are also known as *gîtes* in Québec, can be found in both the country and the cities. For assistance in booking these, be sure to check out B&B websites (⊕ *www.gitesetaubergesdupassant. com* and ⊕ *www.bedandbreakfast.com*

are good resources for B&Bs throughout the province). Room quality varies from house to house as well, so ask to see a few rooms before making a choice.

The nonprofit organization Association de l'Agrotourisme et du Tourisme Gourmand du Québec has extensive listings of B&Bs, both urban and rural, as well as farms that take paying guests.

Reservation Services Association de l'Agrotourisme et du Tourisme Gourmand du Québec. ☎ *514/252–3138* ⊕ *www. terroiretsaveurs.com.* **BB Canada.** ⊕ *www. bbcanada.com.* **Bed and Breakfast Québec.** ⊕ *www.bedbreakfastsquebec.com.* **Bed & Breakfast.com.** ☎ *512/322–2710, 800/462– 2632* ⊕ *www.bedandbreakfast.com.*

HOTELS

Canada doesn't have a national rating system for hotels, but Québec's tourism ministry rates the province's hotels and bed-and-breakfasts; the stars are more a reflection of the number of facilities and amenities than of the hotel's performance. Hotels are rated zero to three stars (B&Bs, zero to four suns), with zero stars or suns representing minimal comfort and few services and three stars or four suns being the very best. All hotels listed have private baths unless otherwise noted.

■ COMMUNICATIONS

LANGUAGE

Although Canada as a whole has two official languages—English and French—the province of Québec has only one. French is the language you hear most often on the streets here; it's also the language of government, businesses, and schools. Only in Montréal, the Gatineau (the area around Hull), and the Eastern Townships is English more widely spoken. Most French Canadians speak English as well, but learning a few phrases before you go is useful. Canadian

French has many distinctive words and expressions, and it's as different from the language of France as North American English is from British English.

PHONES

CALLING WITHIN CANADA

As you'd expect, pay phones are scarce these days. Phone numbers appear just as they do in the United States, with a three-digit area code followed by a seven-digit number. The area codes for Montréal are 514 and 438; in Québec City, it's 418.

CALLING OUTSIDE CANADA

The country code for the United States is 1.

▮ CUSTOMS AND DUTIES

U.S. Customs and Immigration has preclearance services at **Pierre Elliott Trudeau International Airport,** which serves Montréal. This allows U.S.-bound air passengers to depart their airplane directly on arrival at their U.S. destination without further inspection and delays.

American visitors may bring in, duty-free, for personal consumption, 200 cigarettes; 50 cigars; 7 ounces of tobacco; and 1 bottle (1.5 liters or 40 imperial ounces) of wine or liquor respectively or up to 8.5 liters of beer or ale. Any alcohol and tobacco products in excess of these amounts are subject to duty, provincial fees, and taxes. You can also bring in gifts for friends or family duty-free, as long as each gift does not exceed C\$60 in value.

Cats and dogs must have a certificate issued by a licensed veterinarian that clearly identifies the animal and vouches that it has been vaccinated against rabies during the preceding 36 months. Certificates aren't necessary for Seeing Eye dogs. Plant material must be declared and inspected. There may be restrictions on some live plants, bulbs, and seeds. You may bring food for your own use, as long as the quantity is consistent with the duration of your visit and restrictions or prohibitions on some fruits and vegetables are observed.

Canada's firearms laws are significantly stricter than those in much of the United States. All handguns and semiautomatic and fully automatic weapons are prohibited and cannot be brought into the country. Sporting rifles and shotguns may be imported provided they are to be used for sporting, hunting, or competing while in Canada. All firearms must be declared to Canada Customs at the first point of entry. Failure to declare firearms will result in their seizure, and criminal charges may be made. Regulations require visitors to have a confirmed Firearms Declaration to bring any guns into Canada; a fee of C\$25 applies, valid for 60 days but good for one year if renewed before it expires. For more information, contact the Canadian Firearms Centre.

Information in Montréal and Québec City Canada Border Services Agency. ✉ 2265 boul. St-Laurent, Ottawa ☎ 800/461–9999 in Canada ⊕ www.cbsa-asfc.gc.ca. **Canadian Firearms Centre.** ☎ 800/731–4000 ⊕ www. rcmp-grc.gc.ca/cfp-pcaf/index-eng.htm.

U.S. Information U.S. Customs and Border Protection. ⊕ www.cbp.gov.

▮ EMERGENCIES

All embassies are in Ottawa. The U.S. consulate in Montréal is open weekdays 8:30–noon; additionally it's open Wednesday 2–3:30 pm. The U.S. Consulate maintains a list of medical specialists in the Montréal area.

In Montréal, the main English-language hospital is the Montréal General Hospital (McGill University Health Centre). Many pharmacies in Montréal stay open until midnight, including Jean Coutu and Pharmaprix stores. Some are open around the clock, including the Pharmaprix on chemin de la Côte-des-Neiges.

In Québec City, the Centre Hospitalier Universitaire de Québec is the city's largest institution and incorporates the teaching hospitals Pavillon CHUL in

Ste-Foy and Pavillon Hôtel-Dieu, the main hospital in Vieux-Québec. Most outlets of the big pharmacy chains in the region (including Jean Coutu, Brunet and Uniprix) are open every day and offer free delivery.

Foreign Embassies and Consulates
U.S. Consulate General. ⊠ *1155 rue St-Alexandre, Montréal* ☎ *514/398–9695* ⊕ *ca. usembassy.gov/embassy-consulates/montreal.* **U.S. Consulate General.** ⊠ *2 pl. Terrasse Dufferin, Québec City* ☎ *418/692–2095* ⊕ *ca. usembassy.gov/embassy-consulates/quebec.* **U.S. Embassy.** ⊠ *490 Sussex Dr., Ottawa* ☎ *613/688–5335* ⊕ *ca.usembassy.gov.*

Hospitals Centre Hospitalier Universitaire de Québec, Pavillon CHUL. ⊠ *2705 boul. Laurier, Ste-Foy* ☎ *418/525–4444, 418/654–2114 emergencies* ⊕ *www.chuq.qc.ca.* **Centre Hospitalier Universitaire de Québec, Pavillon Hôtel-Dieu.** ⊠ *11 côte du Palais, Upper Town* ☎ *418/525–4444, 418/691–5042 emergencies* ⊕ *www.chuq.qc.ca/fr/le_chuq/ nos_etablissements/hdq.* **Montréal General Hospital (McGill University Health Centre).** ⊠ *1650 av. Cedar, Downtown* ☎ *514/934–1934* ⊕ *muhc.ca/mgh* Ⓜ *Guy-Concordia.*

Pharmacies Pharmaprix. ☎ *800/746–7737* ⊕ *www1.pharmaprix.ca/en/home.* **Pharmaprix.** ⊠ *1500 rue Ste-Catherine Ouest, Downtown* ☎ *514/933–4744* ⊕ *www1. pharmaprix.ca* Ⓜ *Guy-Concordia* ⊠ *901 rue Ste-Catherine Est, The Village* ☎ *514/842–4915* ⊕ *www1.pharmaprix.ca* Ⓜ *Berri-UQAM* ⊠ *5038 Sherbrooke Ouest, Notre-Dame-de-Grace* ☎ *514/484–3531* ⊕ *www1.pharmaprix. ca* Ⓜ *Vendôme* ⊠ *5122 chemin de la Côte-des-Neiges, Côte-des-Neiges* ☎ *514/738–8464* ⊕ *www1.pharmaprix.ca* Ⓜ *Côte-des-Neiges.*

▌ FOOD AND DRINK

French-Canadian fast food follows the same concept as American fast food, though barbecue chicken is also popular. Local chains to watch for include St-Hubert, which serves rotisserie chicken; Chez Cora, which specializes in breakfasts; and La Belle Province, Lafleur, and

Valentine, all of which serve hamburgers, hot dogs, and fries. For a vegetarian option, try the excellent Montréal chain Resto Végo.

MEALS AND MEALTIMES
Unless otherwise noted, the restaurants listed *in this guide* are open daily for lunch and dinner.

PAYING
Major credit cards are widely accepted in both Montréal and Québec City.

For guidelines on tipping, see Tipping below.

WINES, BEER, AND SPIRITS
Some of the best local microbreweries include Unibroue (Fin du Monde, U Blonde, U Rousse), Brasseurs du Nord (Boréale), and McAuslan (Griffon, St. Ambroise). The local hard cider P.O.M. is also excellent. Caribou, a traditional concoction made from red wine, vodka (or some other liquor), spices, and, usually, maple syrup, is available at many winter events and festivals throughout the province, such as Québec City's winter carnival. Small bars may also offer the drink in season.

The province's liquor purveyor, SAQ, stocks a wide choice of wines (with a heavy emphasis on those from France) and is also the only place you can buy hard liquor; most SAQ stores are open regular business hours. Supermarkets and convenience stores carry lower-end wines at notably higher prices but they can sell wine and beer until 11 pm all week (long after SAQ stores have closed). The minimum legal age for alcohol consumption is 18.

▌ HOLIDAYS

Canadian national holidays are as follows: New Year's Day (January 1), Good Friday (late March or early April), Easter Monday (the Monday following Good Friday), Victoria Day (called Fête des Patriotes in Québec; late May), Canada Day (July 1), Labor Day (early

September), Thanksgiving (mid-October), Remembrance Day (November 11), Christmas, and Boxing Day (December 26). St. Jean Baptiste Day (June 24) is a provincial holiday.

▌ MONEY

Throughout this book, prices are given in Canadian dollars, which at this writing are worth roughly 80¢ to the American dollar. The price of a cup of coffee ranges from C$1 to C$2.50 or more, depending on how upscale or downscale the place is; beer costs C$3 to C$7 in a bar; a smoked-meat sandwich costs about C$8 to C$10; and museum admission can cost anywhere from nothing to C$20.

Prices throughout this guide are given for adults. Substantially reduced fees are almost always available for children, students, and senior citizens.

ATMS AND BANKS

Your own bank will probably charge a fee for using ATMs abroad; the foreign bank you use may also charge a fee. Nevertheless, you'll usually get a better rate of exchange at an ATM than you will at a currency-exchange office or even when changing money in a bank. And extracting funds as you need them is a safer option than carrying around a large amount of cash.

ATMs are available in most bank, trust-company, and credit-union branches across the province, as well as in most convenience stores, malls, and self-serve gas stations.

CREDIT CARDS

It's a good idea to inform your credit-card company before you travel, especially if you're going abroad and don't travel internationally very often. Otherwise, the credit-card company might put a hold on your card owing to unusual activity—not a good thing halfway through your trip. Record all your credit-card numbers—as well as the phone numbers to call if your

cards are lost or stolen—in a safe place, so you're prepared should something go wrong. Both MasterCard and Visa have general numbers you can call (collect if you're abroad) if your card is lost, but you're better off calling the number of your issuing bank, since MasterCard and Visa usually just transfer you to your bank; your bank's number is usually printed on your card.

Reporting Lost Cards American Express. ☎ 800/528-4800 in U.S., 800/668-2639 in Canada ⊕ www.americanexpress.com. **Diners Club.** ☎ 800/234-6377 in U.S., 800/363-3333 in Canada ⊕ www.dinersclub.com. **Master-Card.** ☎ 800/627-8372 in U.S., 800/307-7309 in Canada ⊕ www.mastercard.com. **Visa.** ☎ 800/847-2911 in U.S. and Canada ⊕ www.visa.com.

CURRENCY AND EXCHANGE

U.S. dollars are accepted in much of Canada, especially in communities near the border. Traveler's checks (some are available in Canadian dollars) and major U.S. credit cards are accepted in most areas.

The units of currency in Canada are the Canadian dollar (C$) and the cent, in almost the same denominations as U.S. currency ($5, $10, $20, 5¢, 10¢, 25¢, etc.). The $1 and $2 bill are no longer used in Canada; they have been replaced by $1 and $2 coins (known as "loonies," because of the loon that appears on the coin, and "toonies," respectively).

At this writing, the exchange rate is US$1 to C78¢.

Bank cards are widely accepted in Québec and throughout Canada. There are many branches of Québec's financial cooperative, La Caisse populaire Desjardins (a "Caisse Pop" as it's locally referred to), as well as bank machines (ATMs), throughout the region.

Currency Conversion Google. ⊕ www.google.com. **Oanda.com.** ⊕ www.oanda.com. **XE.com.** ⊕ www.xe.com.

PACKING

If you're visiting Montréal anytime between November and May be sure to bring some warm clothes, or be prepared to purchase some while you're here. Come winter Montréal gets cold—very cold—with temperatures almost always dipping below the freezing mark from December until late March. A good winter coat, scarf, hat (locally called a "tuque"), gloves, and warm winter boots are pretty much a necessity in Québec if you want to be comfortable going outside in the winter months. In summer, however, temperatures regularly rise above 86°F (30°C) and Downtown Montréal in particular can get very humid, so bring a few pairs of shorts, sandals, and warm weather clothes. While it seems unbelievable, tales abound here of hapless tourists arriving at the airport in June with their skis and snowshoes in tow, wondering where all the snow is. Also, while a large Anglophone community resides in Montréal and many of its immediate surroundings, the official language here is French, and all road signs are in this language, so having a good French/English dictionary with you is always helpful.

PASSPORTS AND VISAS

All travelers will need a passport or other accepted secure documents to enter or reenter the United States. Naturalized U.S. residents should carry their naturalization certificate. Permanent residents who aren't citizens should carry their "green card." U.S. residents entering Canada from a third country must have a valid passport, naturalization certificate, or "green card."

TAXES

A goods and services tax (GST or TPS in Québec) of 5% applies on virtually every transaction in Canada except for the purchase of basic groceries. In addition to imposing the GST, Québec levies

a provincial sales tax of 9.975% on most goods and services as well.

Departing passengers in Montréal pay a C$25, plus GST, airport-improvement fee that's included in the cost of an airline ticket.

Information Canada Customs and Revenue **Agency.** ✉ Summerside Tax Centre, 275 Pope Rd., Suite 104, Summerside ☎ 800/668–4748 in Canada, 902/432–5608 ⊕ www.ccra-adrc. gc.ca.

TIME

Montréal and Québec City are both in the Eastern Standard Time zone. Los Angeles is three hours behind local time and Chicago is one hour behind.

TIPPING

Tips and service charges aren't usually added to a bill in Canada. In general, tip 15% of the total bill. This goes for waiters and waitresses, barbers and hairdressers, and taxi drivers. Porters and doormen should get about C$2 a bag. For maid service, leave at least C$2 per person a day (C$3 to C$5 in luxury hotels).

TOURS

DAY TOURS AND GUIDES
In Montréal, from May through October, Bateau-Mouche runs four harbor excursions and an evening supper cruise daily. The boats are reminiscent of the ones that cruise the canals of the Netherlands—wide-beamed and low-slung, with a glassed-in passenger deck. Boats leave from the Jacques Cartier Pier at the foot of Place Jacques-Cartier in the Vieux-Port.

Gray Line has nine different types of tours of Montréal from June through October and one tour for the rest of the year. There are also day trips to Mont Tremblant and Québec City. The company offers pickup service at the major hotels and at Info-Touriste (*1001 sq. Dorchester*).

In Québec City, Autocar Dupont/Old Québec Tours runs bus tours of the city, departing across the square from the Hôtel Château Laurier (*1230 pl. Georges V*); you can buy tickets at most major hotels. The company runs guided tours in a minibus as well as tours of Côte-de-Beaupré and Île d'Orléans, and whale-watching excursions to Charlevoix. Tours run year-round and cost C$36–C$135. Call for a reservation and the company will pick you up at your hotel.

Croisières AML has day and evening cruises, some of which include dinner, on the St. Lawrence River aboard the MV *Louis-Jolliet*. The 1½- to 4-hour cruises run from May through mid-October and start at C$35 plus tax.

Contacts Bateau-Mouche. ☎ 514/849–9952, 800/361–9952 ⊕ www.bateaumouche.ca. **Croisières AML.** ✉ 10 rue Dalhousie, Lower Town ☎ 866/856–6668 ⊕ www.croisieresaml. com. **Fitz and Follwell Co.** ✉ 115 av. du Mont-Royal Ouest, The Plateau ☎ 514/840–0739 ⊕ www.fitzandfollwell.co. **Gray Line.** ☎ 800/472–9546 ⊕ www.grayline.com. **Old Québec Tours.** ☎ 418/664–0460, 800/267–8687 ⊕ www.oldquebectours.com.

▌ VISITOR INFORMATION

In Montréal, Centre Info-Touriste, on Square Dorchester, has extensive tourist information on Montréal and the rest of the province of Québec, as well as a currency-exchange service and Internet café. It's open June 21 through August, daily 9–7; September through October, daily 9–6; November through March, daily 9–5; and April through June 20, daily 9–6. The Vieux-Montréal branch is open May from 10 to 6, June through September from 9 to 7, and October from 10 to 6.

Tourisme-Montréal, the city tourist office, doesn't operate an information service for the public, but its website has a wealth of well-organized information.

In Québec City, the Québec City Region Tourism and Convention Bureau's visitor information center in Montcalm is open June 21–to August 31, daily 9–7; September through October, daily 9–6; and November 1–June 20, daily 9–5. A mobile information service operates between mid-June and September 7 (look for the mopeds marked with a big question mark).

The Québec government tourism department, Tourisme Québec, has a center open September–June 20, daily 9–5; and June 21–August 31, daily 8:30–7. Tourisme Québec can provide information on specific towns' tourist bureaus.

In the Laurentians, the major tourist office is the Association Touristique des Laurentides, just off Route des Laurentides 15 Nord at Exit 51 in Les Portes des Nord service center. The office is open mid-June–September, daily 8:30–7; October–mid-June, daily 9–5. Mont-Tremblant, Piedmont/St-Sauveur, Ste-Adèle, St-Adolphe-d'Howard, Ste-Agathe-des-Monts, St-Eustache, St-Jovite, and Val-David have regional tourist offices that are open year-round. Seasonal tourist offices (open mid-June–early September) are in Ferme Neuve, Grenville, Labelle, Lac-du-Cerf, Lachute, Nominique, Notre-Dame-du-Laus, Oka, St-Jérôme, Ste-Marguerite-Estérel, and St-Sauveur.

In the Eastern Townships, year-round regional provincial tourist offices are in Bromont, Coaticook, Granby, Lac-Mégantic, Magog-Orford, Sherbrooke, and Sutton. Seasonal tourist offices (open June–early September) are in Birchton, Cowansville, Danville, Dudswell, Dunham, Eastman, Frelighsburg, Lac-Brome (Foster), Lambton, Masonville, Pike River, Ulverton, and Waterloo. The schedules of seasonal bureaus are irregular, so it's a good idea to contact the Association Touristique des Cantons de l'Est before visiting. This association also provides lodging information.

At the Beaupré Coast Interpretation Center, in a former convent, guides in costume explain displays on the history of the region. Admission is C$6. The center is open daily from 9 to 5 from June 24 to Labor Day. The rest of the year, call to find out their opening hours. For information about Canadian national parks in Québec, contact Parks Canada. Contact Sépaq for information about camping and lodgings in Québec province's network of 22 "Parcs Nationaux" and 15 game reserves (*réserves fauniques*). For information on camping in the province's private trailer parks and campgrounds, request the free publication "Québec Camping," from Tourisme Québec.

Association de l'Agrotourisme et du Tourisme Gourmand du Québec (also known as Terroirs et Saveurs), the Québec farm-vacation association, can provide lists of guest farms in the province.

Contacts Association Touristique des Cantons de l'Est. ✉ *20 rue Don Bosco Sud, Sherbrooke* ☎ *819/820–2020 administration, 800/355–5755* ⊕ *www.cantonsdelest.com.* **Association Touristique des Laurentides.** ✉ *La Porte-du-Nord rest area, Autoroute des Laurentides, Exit 51* ☎ *450/224–7007, 800/561–6673* ⊕ *www.laurentides.com.* **Association Touristique Régionale de Charlevoix.** ✉ *495 boul. de Comporté, C.P. 275, La Malbaie* ☎ *418/665–4454, 800/667–2276* ⊕ *www.tourisme-charlevoix. com.* **Canadian Tourism Commission.** ☎ *604/638–8300* ⊕ *www.travelcanada. ca.* **Centre d'Interpretation de la Côte-de-Beaupré** (*Beaupré Coast Interpretation Center*). ✉ *7976 av. Royale, C.P. 40, Château-Richer* ☎ *418/824–3677, 877/824–3677* ⊕ *www.histoire-cotedebeaupre.org.* **Centre Info-Touriste.** ✉ *1255 rue Peel, suite 100, Downtown* ☎ *514/873–2015, 877/266–5687* ⊕ *www.bonjourquebec.com* Ⓜ *Peel*

or Bonaventure ✉ *174 rue Notre-Dame Est, at pl. Jacques-Cartier, Old Montréal* ☎ *514/873–2015* Ⓜ *Champ-de-Mars.* **Parks Canada.** ☎ *819/420–9486, 888/773–8888* ⊕ *www.pc.gc.ca.* **Québec City Tourist Information.** ✉ *12 rue Sainte-Anne, Upper Town* ☎ *418/641–6290, 877/266–5687* ⊕ *www. quebecregion.com.* **Sépaq.** ☎ *800/665–6527* ⊕ *www.sepaq.com.* **Terroir & Saveurs.** ☎ *514/252–3138* ⊕ *www.terroiretsaveurs. com.* **Tourisme-Montréal.** ☎ *877/266–5687* ⊕ *www.tourisme-montreal.org.* **Tourisme Québec.** ✉ *1001 rue du Sq. Dorchester, No. 100, C.P. 979, Downtown* ☎ *877/266–5687, 514/873–2015* ⊕ *www.bonjourquebec.com* ✉ *12 rue Ste-Anne, Place-d'Armes, Upper Town* ☎ *877/266–5687* ⊕ *www.bonjourquebec.com.*

INDEX

PHOTO CREDITS

ABOUT OUR WRITERS

Chris Barry is a native Montrealer and freelance journalist who has contributed to scores of publications over the years and has been writing for the *Fodor's Montréal and Québec City* guide since 2002. He's currently finishing a book documenting his years as a professional rock-and-roll musician in the 1970s, '80s, and '90s. Chris updated the Montréal Nightlife, Performing Arts, and Sports and the Outdoors chapters of this book.

Rémy Charest is a Québec City–based writer and translator. He has been writing about wine and food since 1997 for *Le Devoir, Coup de Pouce, EnRoute, Wine Access, Châtelaine, Palate Press,* and the Quebecor/Sun Media chain of newspapers. Time permitting, he posts on two wine blogs (⊕ *www.winecase.ca* in English, and ⊕ *www.achacunsabouteille. wordpress.com* in French) as well as two food blogs (⊕ *www.foodcase.ca* in English, and ⊕ *www.achacunsafour- chette.wordpress.com* in French). He updated the Québec City and Side Trips from Québec City chapters.

Joanne Latimer doesn't expect any sympathy, since she's tasked with grading the linens at boutique hotels. As a freelance writer and Canadian National Magazine Award winner, her work appears in *Maclean's,* the *New York Times,* the *Montreal Gazette,*and the *Ottawa Citizen.* Her blog, ⊕ *www.sinussister.com,* is a comedy sensation, with endorsement from comics Rob Corddry, Colin Quinn, Jimmy Carr, Russell Howard, and Alonzo Bodden. Joanne is based in Montréal and updated the Where to Stay chapter.

Born and raised in Montréal, **Marie-Eve Vallieres** knows the city like the back of her hand, despite that it is constantly evolving. Marie-Eve has written for *AFAR Magazine,* Expedia Canada, and Viator, and she has been interviewed regularly on CBC Radio One. Her blog is called To Europe And Beyond (⊕ *http://toeuropeandbeyond. com*). Marie-Eve updated the Where to Eat chapter for this edition.

Elizabeth Warkentin is a freelance writer who was born and raised in Montreal and is enjoying getting reacquainted with her native city after a 20-year absence. She is an avid photographer and freelance journalist and has contributed to a variety of publications including, BBC Travel, the *Boston Globe,* the *Toronto Star,* and the *Vancouver Sun.* She updated the Experience, Exploring, Shopping, and Side Trips from Montréal chapters for this edition.

Montréal métro

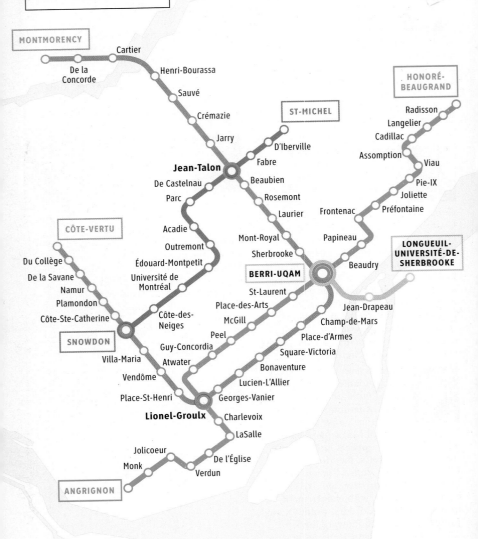

MONTMORENCY
Cartier
De la Concorde
Henri-Bourassa
Sauvé
Crémazie
Jarry
D'Iberville
Fabre
Jean-Talon
De Castelnau
Beaubien
Parc
Rosemont
Laurier
Acadie
Mont-Royal
Outremont
Sherbrooke
Édouard-Montpetit
Université de Montréal
BERRI-UQAM
St-Laurent
Place-des-Arts
McGill
Peel
Guy-Concordia
Atwater
Vendôme
Place-St-Henri
Lionel-Groulx
Charlevoix
LaSalle
Jolicoeur
Monk
De l'Église
Verdun
ANGRIGNON

CÔTE-VERTU
Du Collège
De la Savane
Namur
Plamondon
Côte-Ste-Catherine
SNOWDON
Villa-Maria
Côte-des-Neiges

ST-MICHEL

HONORÉ-BEAUGRAND
Radisson
Langelier
Cadillac
Assomption
Viau
Pie-IX
Joliette
Frontenac
Préfontaine
Papineau
Beaudry
LONGUEUIL-UNIVERSITÉ-DE-SHERBROOKE
Jean-Drapeau
Champ-de-Mars
Place-d'Armes
Square-Victoria
Bonaventure
Lucien-L'Allier
Georges-Vanier